D1765083

The Matter of History

New insights into the microbiome, epigenetics, and cognition are radically challenging our very idea of what it means to be "human," while an explosion of neo-materialist thinking in the humanities has fostered a renewed appreciation of the formative powers of a dynamic material environment. *The Matter of History* brings these scientific and humanistic ideas together to develop a bold new postanthropocentric understanding of the past, one that reveals how powerful organisms and things help to create humans in all their dimensions, biological, social, and cultural. Timothy J. LeCain combines cutting-edge theory and detailed empirical analysis to explain the extraordinary late nineteenth-century convergence between the United States and Japan at the pivotal moment when both were emerging as global superpowers. Illustrating the power of a deeply material, social, and cultural history, *The Matter of History* argues that three powerful things – cattle, silkworms, and copper – helped to drive these previously diverse nations toward a global "great convergence."

Timothy J. LeCain is the author of the prize-winning book *Mass Destruction*. He was a Senior Fellow at the Rachel Carson Center in Munich, Germany, and a Fellow at the Center for Advanced Study in Oslo, Norway. He is Associate Professor of History at Montana State University in Bozeman, Montana.

Studies in Environment and History

Editors

J. R. McNeill, *Georgetown University*
Edmund P. Russell, *University of Kansas*

Editors Emeritus

Alfred W. Crosby, *University of Texas at Austin*
Donald Worster, *University of Kansas*

Other Books in the Series

Andy Bruno, *The Nature of Soviet Power: An Arctic Environmental History*

Erik Loomis, *Empire of Timber: Labor Unions and the Pacific Northwest Forests*

Ling Zhang *The River, the Plain, and the State: An Environmental Drama in Northern Song China, 1048-1128*

Abraham H. Gibson *Feral Animals in the American South: An Evolutionary History*

Peter Thorsheim *Waste into Weapons: Recycling in Britain during the Second World War*

Micah S. Muscolino *The Ecology of War in China: Henan Province, the Yellow River, and Beyond, 1938–1950*

David A. Bello *Across Forest, Steppe, and Mountain: Environment, Identity, and Empire in Qing China's Borderlands*

Kieko Matteson *Forests in Revolutionary France: Conservation, Community, and Conflict, 1669–1848*

George Colpitts *Pemmican Empire: Food, Trade, and the Last Bison Hunts in the North American Plains, 1780–1882*

John L. Brooke *Climate Change and the Course of Global History: A Rough Journey*

Emmanuel Kreike *Environmental Infrastructure in African History: Examining the Myth of Natural Resource Management*

Kenneth F. Kiple *The Caribbean Slave: A Biological History*

Alfred W. Crosby *Ecological Imperialism: The Biological Expansion of Europe, 900–1900, second edition*

Arthur F. McEvoy *The Fisherman's Problem: Ecology and Law in the California Fisheries, 1850–1980*

Robert Harms *Games against Nature: An Eco-Cultural History of the Nunu of Equatorial Africa*

Warren Dean *Brazil and the Struggle for Rubber: A Study in Environmental History*

Samuel P. Hays *Beauty, Health, and Permanence: Environmental Politics in the United States, 1955–1985*

Donald Worster *The Ends of the Earth: Perspectives on Modern Environmental History*

Michael Williams *Americans and Their Forests: A Historical Geography*

Timothy Silver *A New Face on the Countryside: Indians, Colonists, and Slaves in the South Atlantic Forests, 1500–1800*

Theodore Steinberg *Nature Incorporated: Industrialization and the Waters of New England*

J. R. McNeill *The Mountains of the Mediterranean World: An Environmental History*

Elinor G. K. Melville *A Plague of Sheep: Environmental Consequences of the Conquest of Mexico*

Richard H. Grove *Green Imperialism: Colonial Expansion, Tropical Island Edens and the Origins of Environmentalism, 1600–1860*

Mark Elvin and Tsui'jung Liu *Sediments of Time: Environment and Society in Chinese History*

Robert B. Marks *Tigers, Rice, Silk, and Silt: Environment and Economy in Late Imperial South China*

Thomas Dunlap *Nature and the English Diaspora*

Andrew Isenberg *The Destruction of the Bison: An Environmental History*

Edmund Russell *War and Nature: Fighting Humans and Insects with Chemicals from World War I to Silent Spring*

Judith Shapiro *Mao's War against Nature: Politics and the Environment in Revolutionary China*

Adam Rome *The Bulldozer in the Countryside: Suburban Sprawl and the Rise of American Environmentalism*

Nancy J. Jacobs *Environment, Power, and Injustice: A South African History*

Matthew D. Evenden *Fish versus Power: An Environmental History of the Fraser River*

Myrna I. Santiago *The Ecology of Oil: Environment, Labor, and the Mexican Revolution, 1900–1938*

Frank Uekoetter *The Green and the Brown: A History of Conservation in Nazi Germany*

James L. A. Webb, Jr. *Humanity's Burden: A Global History of Malaria*

Richard W. Judd *The Untilled Garden: Natural History and the Spirit of Conservation in America, 1740–1840*

Edmund Russell *Evolutionary History: Uniting History and Biology to Understand Life on Earth*

Alan Mikhail *Nature and Empire in Ottoman Egypt: An Environmental History*

Sam White *Climate of Rebellion in the Early Modern Ottoman Empire*

Gregory T. Cushman *Guano and the Opening of the Pacific World: A Global Ecological History*

Donald Worster *Nature's Economy: A History of Ecological Ideas, second edition*

The Matter of History

How Things Create the Past

TIMOTHY J. LECAIN

Montana State University

CAMBRIDGE
UNIVERSITY PRESS

CAMBRIDGE
UNIVERSITY PRESS

University Printing House, Cambridge CB2 8BS, United Kingdom

One Liberty Plaza, 20th Floor, New York, NY 10006, USA

477 Williamstown Road, Port Melbourne, VIC 3207, Australia

4843/24, 2nd Floor, Ansari Road, Daryaganj, Delhi – 110002, India

79 Anson Road, #06–04/06, Singapore 079906

Cambridge University Press is part of the University of Cambridge.

It furthers the University's mission by disseminating knowledge in the pursuit of education, learning, and research at the highest international levels of excellence.

www.cambridge.org
Information on this title: www.cambridge.org/9781107134171
DOI: 10.1017/9781316460252

First published 2017

Printed in the United States of America by Sheridan Books, Inc.

A catalogue record for this publication is available from the British Library.

ISBN 978-1-107-13417-1 Hardback
ISBN 978-1-107-59270-4 Paperback

For
Douglas Shaw LeCain
&
Frances Murchie LeCain

Contents

Illustrations

Acknowledgments

In Prague, just a short stroll from where the Charles Bridge so famously spans the Vltava River, there is a wonderful little restaurant named for the poet Rainer Maria Rilke, who was born and spent his youth in the city. I found myself there one evening a few years back, having spent the previous several days at a workshop dedicated to a theme that is also central to this book: "Object Matters." Afterward, I stayed on a few days to explore the city's Old Town, whose winding medieval streets were especially charming and free of tourist hordes in the frosty mid-December air. That evening at the Restaurant Rilke, alone at my table aside from a flickering candlestick grown companionably plump with years of dripping wax, I began to idly page through some of the books stacked nearby, all of them by or about the mystical Bohemian poet. In one, a small brown leather-bound chapbook titled *Recital*, I stumbled across a line that has stuck with me since: "... ich bin in der Arbeit wie der Kern in der frucht" – I am in the work as the seed is in the fruit.

At the time I was in the midst of writing this book, and Rilke's words reminded me that, even when I might appear most alone, I am always surrounded by the nourishing influences of countless other scholars, friends, and family – and, yes, creative objects, creatures, machines, buildings, and things like plump candles – that spark and sustain my thoughts and actions. At one level this book might be read as another argument against the still-persistent romantic-modernist celebration of the individual human creator and inventor, and if I am going to deny the great Thomas Edison his status as the inventor of the light bulb – as I do in Chapter 6 – then I can hardly claim any great powers of creation or insight for myself. In other words, here I have the somewhat daunting pleasure of writing an acknowledgment to a book whose essential argument suggests that even my best efforts will inevitably fall badly short. How does the seed of an apple recognize the fruit that engulfs it – much less the tree on which it depends and suspends?

Still, many of my dependencies will be readily obvious. The work of Bruno Latour, arguably the most important philosopher of our time, has nurtured a tree of ideas so novel and robust as to support the fruit of countless others, myself included. I have also taken much inspiration from the work of scholars in many fields outside my own: the anthropologists Philippe Descola and Tim Ingold; the archaeologists Bjørnar Olsen, Ian Hodder, and Nicole Boivin; the political ecologist Jane Bennett; the philosopher Graham Harman; the feminist theorists Donna Haraway and Elizabeth Grosz; the linguistic and cognitive theorists Benjamin Bergen, Andy Clark, and George Lakoff; and the biologists Andreas Wagner, Lynn Margulis, and Kevin Laland. Among my own tribe of historians, the list would be much longer, and I hope my broader debts are fully evident in the text and footnotes. But to mention just a few whose imprints have been the most indelible: Richard White, Donald Worster, Dipesh Chakrabarty, Edmund Russell, David Noble, Timothy Mitchell, Langdon Winner, Thomas Andrews, Linda Nash, Mark Fiege, William Cronon, John McNeill, Nancy Langston, Julia Adeney Thomas, and Brett Walker all stand out.

Brett Walker, my friend and colleague of many years, first proposed that we collaborate on a comparative study of the environmental history of Ashio and Anaconda almost a decade ago. Our research was subsequently funded by a three-year collaborative grant from the National Science Foundation's Division of Social and Economic Sciences (Award No. 0646644), where the program director Frederick Kronz provided invaluable support and assistance. That grant permitted us to employ two talented graduate research assistants, Robert Gardner and Connie Staudohar, and their diligent work provided much of the detailed historical evidence used in this book, as well as in several other books and articles that have previously emerged out of that project. While *The Matter of History* goes well beyond the initial aims of the NSF grant to develop a much-broader argument for a neo-materialist theory and method, the empirically driven comparison between Ashio and Anaconda is still very much at its heart. I ultimately ended up writing these comparative chapters, but many of the overarching ideas are as much Brett's as mine, and he provided essential feedback and suggestions on Chapters 5 and 6, where the Japanese story figures most centrally. His arguments on the independent agency of nonhuman organisms and things and the human bodily engagement with the material world also play an important role throughout the book.

Equally critical to the gestation and creation of this book, particularly to its neo-materialist ideas, was a wonderful year spent at the Rachel Carson Center for Environment and Society in Munich, Germany. Christof Mauch and Helmuth Trischler, the directors of the center, have created an extraordinary scholarly institution that has in the course of just a few years succeeded in making Germany one of the leading centers for environmental history and humanities in the world. My year at the RCC provided me with that most precious of scholarly commodities: the time to read broadly, to chase down intriguing intellectual leads, and to nurture new ideas. Fittingly, it was at this center, named in honor of a great American environmental scientist and author, that this book evolved from being a comparative environmental study to encompass a much more ambitious argument for a new environmental or materialist understanding of humans and their histories. I was aided in this evolution not only by the smoothly functioning support and good humor of the RCC staff – thanks especially to Claudia Reusch, Andrea Cooke, Katie Ritson, and Arielle Helmick – but also by the conviviality and intellectual inspiration of the many other RCC fellows whose stays coincided with mine. My warm thanks to Dan Philippon, Bron Taylor, Paul Josephson, Fiona Cameron, Edmund Russell, Clapperton Mavhunga, Claudia Leal, Shawn Van Ausdal, and Eagle Glassheim, among others, for all the stimulating conversations, during both our regular Thursday seminars and our decidedly more irregular seminars over beers and wurst at Munich's many charming locales. Indeed, I would be a very poor neo-materialist if I did not also express my heartfelt thanks to the city of Munich itself, a place whose tree-lined boulevards, vibrant sidewalk culture, and peaceful parks surely conspire to encourage creative thinking. The material power of great cities to create and shape our ideas is, I think, an underappreciated and understudied topic. Finally, our year in Germany would not have been nearly so pleasant and productive but for the kind assistance and friendship of our landlords, Heide and Heinrich Quenzel, and our wonderful neighbors, Lisette and Andre Talkenberg, and Andre's son Patrick Hartmann, who not only tolerated the American family upstairs with the boisterous young children but befriended them all. They are part of the fruit that nurtured this book, too.

Many of the ideas in *The Matter of History* have been refined and sharpened in discussions with other scholars at invited workshops around the world. The members of the interdisciplinary workshops "Ruin Memories" (Falmouth, England) and "Object Matters" (Prague and Vardø, Norway), and most recently "After Discourse" (Oslo), all organized by the Norwegian archaeologist Bjørnar Olsen, have been a wonderful source of insights and ideas. As I was making the final copy edits and proofing the galleys for this book, I was also fortunate to be spending six months as part of Bjørnar's "After Discourse" team at the Center for Advanced Study in Oslo, where the unparalleled support of the staff helped me speed the book to production. First, thanks, of course, to Bjørnar for inviting me to participate in these fascinating projects and for his always perceptive and valuable comments, and also to the other participants, including Caitlin Desilvey, Marek Tamm, Þóra Pétursdóttir, Hein Bjerck, Mats Burström, Saphinaz-Amal Naguib, Elin Andreassen, Svetlana Vinogradova, Kerstin Smeds, Stein Farstadvoll, Ingar Figenschau, and Torgeir Bangstad, among others. Thanks also to the marvelous social anthropologist Luděk Brož of the Prague Academy of Science of the Czech Republic for his invitation to present my work on the creative intelligence of animals to the Ernest Gellner Seminar, which generated many useful comments.

I have found similarly helpful colleagues during my participation at two workshops on the Environmental Post-Humanities, funded by the Swedish Riksbankens Jubileumsfond and organized by the superb scholar of social and technological change Martin Hultman of Linköping University. In addition to Martin himself, my thanks go especially to Owain Jones, Jonathan Metzger, Bjørn Wallsten, and Kristina Lindström, as well as to the dedicated defenders of the fragile beauty of Gotland, Sweden, who shared their extraordinary island home with us in May of 2016.

Frank Uekötter and Corey Ross kindly invited me to join their workshop on "Making Resources Speak" sponsored by the Institute of Advanced Studies at the University of Birmingham, where I was able to try out some of my ideas for a postanthropocentric approach to history. Thanks to Frank for marking my "coming out" as an animal historian and also for the sharp insights of Stefanie Gänger, Hugh Gorman, Sebastian Haumann, Simon Jackson, Hamza Meddeb, and Uwe Lübken.

The members of the "World of Copper" project, sponsored by the British Leverhulme Trust, shared their deep knowledge of the transformative global effects of the red metal at a fascinating workshop in Santiago, Chile. Many thanks to the project leaders Chris Evans and Olivia Saunders of the University of South Wales for including me and good-humoredly pondering my then still-nascent ideas about the "power of copper."

It is hard to imagine that any workshop could accord better with the questions raised in this book than "Manufacturing Landscapes: Nature and Technology in Environmental History," organized by Helmuth Trischler, Mingfang Xia, and Donald Worster, and cosponsored by Renmin University (Beijing) and the Rachel Carson Center (Munich). This book benefited greatly from the insights and critiques offered by the three organizers, as well as Shen Hou, Agnes Kneitz, Thomas Zeller, Craig Colten, Maurits Ertsen, and Edmund Russell, among others. I also owe the opening discussion of the silk sellers at Beijing's Panjiayuan market in Chapter 5 to this workshop.

The ideas on human niche construction discussed throughout the book, though especially in Chapter 3, were in significant part the product of a workshop on the topic organized by Maurits Ertsen, Edmund Russell, and Christof Mauch, again sponsored by the Rachel Carson Center. My thanks especially to Maurits for first introducing me to this powerful evolutionary approach that accords in many ways with neo-materialist thinking, as well as to the other participants, including Laura Martin, Gregory Cushman, Erle Ellis, Ove Eriksson, David Bello, and Michael Just.

Stefan Berger (Rhur University-Bochum) and Peter Alexander (University of Johannesburg) organized an excellent workshop on "Digging for Treasure: Mining in Global Perspective" held at the Rhur Museum and Zollverein coal mine (now a UNESCO World Heritage site) in Essen, Germany. Both the participants and Stefan Siemer's brilliant exhibit on coal at the Ruhr Museum helped shape my thinking about the material power of minerals.

My discussion of phosphate and phosphorous in Chapter 7 was greatly influenced by my participation in the workshop "Global TraPs" in El-Jadida, Morocco, that was sponsored by Eidgenössische Technische Hochschule in Zürich. My thanks to Roland Scholz for his generous invitation to join his global team and to the employees of Office Chérifien des Phosphates for giving us a rare opportunity to see their massive dredge line at the Khouribga phosphate mine up close and in operation.

Closer to home, I want to thank Thomas Lekan and Robert Emmett for the chance to refine some of my thinking on a new humanism at the workshop "After Nature: Politics and Practice in Dipesh Chakrabarty's Four Theses of Climate History" sponsored by the University of South Carolina and the Rachel Carson Center. Thanks especially to Dipesh Chakrabarty himself for his critique of my own somewhat abstract critique of modernity, reminding me that, whatever its limits, many around the globe still seek to share in its material benefits. The members of the WEST Network, a consortium of faculty and graduate students interested in environmental history from several western universities, provided feedback on my then still-crystalizing critique of the Anthropocene concept. Thanks especially to Jeremy Vetter, Mark Fiege, Cindy Ott, Ruth Alexander, Paul Sutter, and David Quammen. Finally, while it might at first seem far removed from the topics in this book, my participation in the Aspen Institute's Wye Faculty Seminar in Queenstown, Maryland, provided a wealth of ideas and inspirations – ironically, many of them classically "humanist" – that I am still working through today. The cameo appearances of both Plato and Vaclav Havel in this book are a direct product of the provocative readings and questions provided by our seminar leader, David Townsend.

Montana State University generously provided me with a sabbatical year (2010–11) during which I first began to formulate some of the ideas discussed here, as well as a subsequent Faculty Excellence Grant (2015) that gave me much-needed time to complete the resulting manuscript. Thanks specifically to Nic Rae, the Dean of the College of Letters and Science, who has long supported my work. Several of my colleagues in other departments at MSU generously took the time to read and comment on those parts of the manuscript where I wade into technical subjects outside my own field: thanks to Matt Lavin (Department of Plant Sciences and Plant Pathology), Jack Fisher (Department of Sociology and Anthropology), and Philip Eaton (Department of Physics) for keeping me from drowning in deep waters. My own colleagues in the Department of History and Philosophy have been preternaturally generous in giving me the time and support needed for this book. My thanks especially to Brett Walker, David Cherry, and Susan Cohen, who served as department chairs during the planning and writing of the book. Thanks also to Amanda Hendrix-Komoto for pointing me toward some key works in feminist theory, Catherine Dunlop for her early and enthusiastic support of my ideas, and Margaret Greene for her assistance in interpreting my silk wall hanging from Beijing. A word of special gratitude to Michael Reidy, both for his sharp insights into the history of science and for doing so much to make the department and university a congenial professional and intellectual home. The superb office staff of the department was also an inexhaustible source of support: Katie Yaw, Cassandra Balent, and Kori Robbins have been brilliant in too many ways to list. Finally, I first tried out many of these ideas during graduate seminars on environmental history and in one-on-one discussions with the department's many talented graduate students. Thanks especially to Robert Gardner, Jerry Jessee, Daniel Zizzamia, Kelsey Matson, Kerri Clement, Reed Knappe, Alexander Aston, Jeffrey Bartos, Jennifer Dunn, Bradley Snow, Cheryl Hendry, Clinton Colgrove, Gary Sims, Patrick Collier, Will Wright, LaTrelle Scherffius, Laurel Angell, and Yu Hirano for their insights and for letting me know when I just wasn't making any sense.

Several colleagues read and commented on all or parts of earlier drafts of this book. Mark Fiege, who I am delighted to now count as a departmental colleague at Montana State University, kindly read the entire manuscript, even though he was right in the midst of uprooting and moving to Montana at the time. Moreover, Mark has been an inexhaustible source of useful ideas and suggestions since the early days of this project, and I am deeply in his debt. As already noted, Brett Walker provided essential feedback on the two chapters dealing most centrally with the Ashio story, helping me to better understand and utilize the Japanese sources. Bjørnar Olsen drew on his immense knowledge of the theoretical literature to provide highly detailed comments that greatly improved Chapters 2 and 3. Lisa Onaga read my chapter on silkworms and helped me to better understand the complex nature of silkworm breeding and hybridization. Thanks to Ian Miller for his reading of the chapter on copper and also for allowing me to draw on parts of his work-in-progress on the electrification of Tokyo. Though she is of course a bit more than just a colleague, my wife Cherí was one of my first and most perceptive readers, subjecting the entire book to her exacting standards of clarity and her eagle-eyed ability to spot errors and less-than-felicitous phrasings. Finally, my thanks to the anonymous reviewers for Cambridge University Press who offered many useful suggestions that improved the final product.

At Cambridge University Press, thanks first to John McNeill and Edmund Russell, the coeditors of the series Studies in Environment and History, for their enthusiastic responses to my early proposal to write a book bringing environmental history into dialogue with the new materialism. John has long argued for and demonstrated the importance of material factors in his own work, providing a scholarly model I have tried to emulate. I have been greatly influenced by Ed's ideas for many years, and his concepts of coevolutionary history and the technology of animals are central to this book. It is difficult for me to imagine two editors whose work I admire more and whose series could provide a more suitable home for *The Matter of History*. Many thanks as well to the Senior Editor in history at Cambridge, Deborah Gershenowitz, for her vital support and assistance, and to Kristina Deusch (Editorial Assistant), Allan Alphonse (Project Manager), and Matt Sweeney (Content Manager) for their help in shepherding this book through the production process.

Lisa Sederis generously shared her research and ideas on the troublingly transcendent concept of the noösphere discussed in Chapter 7. Mark Stoll provided much-needed advice on the history of Christian theological ideas about nature and the environment. At the Grant-Kohrs Ranch National Historic Site in Montana, Chance Reynolds treated me to a brilliant tour of the Conrad Kohrs home and ranch, greatly deepening my sense of the place and its material dynamic. Chance also took time out of his busy schedule to chase down several leads, including the history of the mounted longhorns in the Kohrs home. Kyle Tusler generously shared his research on the brutal Montana winter of 1886–87 discussed in Chapter 4. Bruce Whittenberg, Jennifer Bottomly-O'Looney, and Kendra Newhall at the Montana Historical Society tracked down the history of Charlie Russell's "Waiting for a Chinook" and helped me gain permission to reprint it here. Equally helpful was Hiromi Myo of Hakodate City Central Library in Japan whose efforts made it possible to publish Kakizaki Hakyō's dynamic painting of the Ainu chief Ikotoi sporting a silk robe.

Though they will never read it, thanks are nonetheless due to the many nonhuman organisms and things whose intelligence, creativity, and always-surprising powers have so profoundly shaped human history. Thanks go especially to the Texas Longhorns, mulberry silkworms, and copper metal that are the true stars of this book and that have most certainly taught me to think in new ways.

A few sections of the book have been published in different forms, and I am grateful to several editors for their permission to reuse this material. Parts of Chapter 4 appear in "Copper and Longhorns: Material and Human Power in Montana's Smelter Smoke War, 1860–1910," in John McNeill and George Vrtis, eds., *Mining North American, 1522–2012: An Environmental History* (Berkeley: University of California Press, forthcoming 2017). Some of my discussion of the spatial powers of copper in Chapter 6 was first published in "The Persistence of Things: Copper and the Evolution of Space in Modernist America and Japan," a special issue on the theme of "Rohstoffräume/Sites of Resource Extraction," in *Jahrbuch für Wirtschaftsgeschichte* (*Yearbook for Economic History*), 57 (2016): 169–86. My thanks to the editors of De Gruyter Oldenbourg in Berlin, as well as to the special issue editors Nora Thorade and Sebastian Haumann, who invited me to contribute and provided valuable feedback on early drafts of the article. Finally, parts of my critique of the Anthropocene term and concept first appeared as, "Against the Anthropocene: A Neo-materialist Perspective," *History, Culture, and Modernity* 3 (2015): 1–28. Thanks to Corey Ross for asking me to contribute to the journal's special issue on neo-materialism.

My final and most heartfelt thanks go as always to my family. When I was a boy, my mother gave me leave to explore wherever my wide-ranging interests led, asking only that I always read, whether it be comic books or finer fair. I did so voraciously and with enduring consequences. To the degree I have become something of a scientific storyteller, I credit my father, who, on our many family camp outs under the Montana Big Sky, would take us away from the fire to see the stars and relate the mysteries of astronomy and relativity. He is our family Carl Sagan. Even by the measure of delayed adulthood that has become more common today, I still required an embarrassingly long time to grow up. But I hope there is at least some reason to believe that all those years of "exploration" eventually paid off. Their patient support was inexhaustible, as was that of my four brothers – a number sadly now reduced to three.

One of the harder realities of life is that there are far too many worthwhile things to do than the brief time allotted permits. I have always tried to prioritize what is most precious, and for more than a decade now this has unquestionably been my wife Cherí and our children Carina and Daniel. I fear there were still too many times when this book kept me from a sledding excursion or a science fair project, or too many moments of absent distraction, even when I was physically there. But if practice was imperfect, please know that there was never any question that you have and always will be the best justification for my imperfect existence. Whether my many absences are ultimately justified by the results, I leave for you to judge. I can only say that I have tried my best to write a book that you might consider worthy of the time together lost. I hope you do.

Fellow Travelers

The Nonhuman Things That Make Us Human

For some years now I've had a growing sense that we are on the cusp of big changes in history and the humanities – an intellectual sense, of course, but also something that you might call a gut feeling. But I had not expected that new research on our guts would actually give those changes a push forward. Back in 2007, the National Institutes of Health (NIH) began a major five-year Human Microbiome Project that provided $153 million in funds to scores of scientists and institutions in a coordinated effort to identify and describe the microorganisms that live on and in the human body, many of them in our digestive tracts. Five years later, the early research results were in and papers began to appear in top scientific journals. One was *Nature*, which featured the topic on its June 14, 2012, cover with the intriguing headline "Fellow Travelers."[1] In the subsequent flurry of press attention to all the many surprising new insights into this human "microbiome," one idea especially captured the public imagination: nearly 90 percent of the cells in your body are not yours at all but belong instead to a genetically diverse population of trillions of bacteria, viruses, and other microbes, a majority of them inside your gut, but others living on your skin, in your mouth, and even in your lungs.[2] "We are," the director of the NIH concluded, "more microbial than human."[3]

---

[1] *Nature* 486 (June 24, 2014): cover.
[2] Julia Adeney Thomas, "History and Biology in the Anthropocene: Problems of Scale, Problems of Value," *American Historical Review* 119 (2014): 1587–607, here 1593 and fn. 20. A good popular account of the significance of the microbiome is Michael Pollan, "Some of My Best Friends Are Germs," *New York Times Magazine*, May 15, 2013.
[3] Peter Andrey Smith, "Can the Bacteria in Your Gut Explain Your Mood?" *New York Times*, June 23, 2015.

It later became apparent that this 90 percent figure, though still widely cited to this day, was almost certainly inaccurate.[4] Arriving at definitive numbers on these counts is hardly the most pressing of research topics for microbiologists today, so it is perhaps no surprise that the estimates of both the number of microbes in a typical microbiome and the number of cells in a typical human body range by orders of magnitude: from 30 to 400 trillion microbes and from 5 to 724 trillion human cells. Depending on which estimates you favor, researchers suggest that our microbes might be roughly as numerous as our body cells, or, on the other extreme, they might outnumber human cells by as much as a *hundred* to one.[5] Part of the confusion stems from whether viruses are included in the microbiome count rather than just bacteria. In a 2013 report by the American Academy of Microbiology, the authors suggested a reasonable estimate is that an average human body has about three times more *bacterial* cells than human ones. But viruses may outnumber bacteria by as much as five to one, so counting them would push the ratio of nonhuman microorganisms up much higher. Whatever the exact numbers may turn out to be, we should also keep in mind that those tiny bacteria are typically about a tenth the size of an average human cell and viruses (simple little packages of DNA which are unable to replicate on their own) are even tinier, so the microbiome of an average adult only weighs about 1.1 kilograms (2.5 pounds). By mass, our human cells definitely dominate. These caveats aside, the human microbiome is clearly immense and immensely diverse: most likely more than 100 trillion cells from over a thousand different species.[6] Humans have about 23,000 unique genes. Our community of microbes has more than two million.

These "fellow travelers" are also doing far more than just hitching a comfortable ride. As one microbiologist notes, "The most important thing is that much of what makes us human – many of [the] important aspects of health and the predisposition to disease and recovery – depends on metabolic activity of these microbes."[7] Some researchers even argue that we need to rethink our conventional concept of the unitary individual

---

[4] Judah L. Rosner, "Ten Times More Microbial Cells than Body Cells in Humans?" *Microbe Magazine*, February 2014.

[5] Peter Andrey Smith, "Is Your Body Mostly Microbes? Actually, We Have No Idea," *Boston Globe*, September 14, 2014.

[6] Ann Reid and Shannon Greene, *Human Microbiome: A Report from the American Academy of Microbiology* (Washington, DC: American Academy of Microbiology, 2013): 6.

[7] Quoted in Smith, "Is Your Body Mostly Microbes?"

human, suggesting that the human organism might be better thought of as analogous to a coral reef, an "assemblage of life-forms living together."[8] Some of these microbes play a pivotal role in sustaining human life, particularly in our digestive system where they help to break down foods that would otherwise be indigestible and to synthesize many of the chemical compounds essential to human metabolism. Even more striking, recent collaborations between microbiologists and neuropsychologists have created a growing body of evidence that these tiny fellow travelers may exert a powerful influence over our brains by producing so-called psychobiotics, hormones, and other chemicals that can affect whether we feel optimistic or pessimistic, bold or timid, energetic or lethargic.[9] The microbiome typically manufactures some 95 percent of our body's supply of serotonin, a neurochemical that powerfully influences our brains – hence the utility of the widely used anti-depressant drugs known as serotonin reuptake inhibitors. Some researchers suggest that we have a sort of second brain in our guts that is as much microbial as human.[10] One of the pioneers of these psychobiotic studies has even found compelling evidence (albeit in nonhumans) that "if you transfer the microbiota from one animal to another, you can transfer behavior."[11]

Now it is hardly big news that various chemicals can change the way the human brain works, and hence our personalities and behaviors – a sizable number of us deliberately and regularly consume substances that do just that. What is really intriguing about these microbiochemical factories in our guts is that these are not external chemicals, like alcohol or caffeine, that we can choose to ingest or not. Rather, these psychoactive chemicals are the products of billions of nonhuman organisms that began colonizing our guts on the day we were born entirely for their own purposes. By the time you are an adult, almost three pounds of your

[8] Quoted in Thomas, "History and Biology in the Anthropocene," 1594.
[9] Timothy G. Dinan, Catherine Stanton, and John F. Cryan, "Psychobiotics: A Novel Class of Psychotropics," *Biological Psychiatry* 74 (2013): 720–26.
[10] Siri Carpenter, "That Gut Feeling," *American Psychological Association* 43, no. 8 (September 2012): 50.
[11] Quoted in Smith, "Can the Bacteria in Your Gut Explain Your Mood?" A seminal early paper was Mark Lyte, Jeffrey J. Varcoe, and Michael T. Bailey, "Anxiogenic Effect of Subclinical Bacterial Infection in Mice in the Absence of Over Immune Activation," *Physiology and Behavior* 65 (1998): 63–8. See also Elaine Y. Hsiao et al., "Microbiota Modulate Behavioral and Physiological Abnormalities Associated with Neurodevelopmental Disorders," *Cell* 155 (2013): 1451–63, and Javier A. Bravo et al., "Ingestion of *Lactobacillus* Strain Regulates Emotional Behavior and Central GABA Receptor Expression in a Mouse via the Vagus Nerve," *Proceedings of the National Academy of Sciences* 108 (2011): 16050–5.

body is not "you" at all, but this mass of bacteria, and our relationship seems more commensal than domesticated. These bacterial fellow travelers can also evolve much more rapidly than can their less genetically nimble human hosts. As one researcher puts it: "The bacteria in our guts are continually reading the environment and responding [in ways that] help our bodies respond to changes in our environment."[12] Given all this new evidence, it seems fair to say that there is within each of us a biologically creative population of organisms that not only help to keep us alive – or, at times, threaten to harm or kill us – but also play a significant role in making us who we are. We are always a "we," even when we are alone.

As a historian, and a neo-materialist environmental historian at that, I was immediately intrigued by what these new scientific insights might mean for our understanding of history and the broader humanities. But a good measure of caution is warranted. The science of the microbiome is in its infancy. Much of the work on psychobiotics has been done with mice or other nonhuman animals, and the same is the case with other recent studies suggesting the microbiome might play a role in human problems like autism and depression.[13] I might identify as "mammal,"[14] but I know better than to think that all my furry endothermic cousins share every aspect of my biochemical metabolism. At this early point it might be a bit premature to apply these insights to our study of the past, except perhaps, as some historians have suggested, in collaboration with microbiologists using historical evidence to study the topic.[15] Still, if these early results are confirmed and extended, eventually the microbiome could easily fit in with the recent spate of historical studies examining the influence of alcohol, caffeine, DES, and other chemical and environmental factors on past humans. The potential questions are endlessly fascinating. How might the shift in affluent societies in the nineteenth century to the regular consumption of unprecedented amounts of beef and sugar have influenced gut microbiomes and human moods and actions? Likewise, it is well known that the aggressive use of broad-spectrum antibiotics in the post-war period was akin to carpet-bombing our microbiomes. How might this

---

[12] Quoted in Pollan, "Some of My Best Friends Are Germs."

[13] Carpenter, "That Gut Feeling," 50, and Sara Reardon, "Bacterium Can Reverse Autism-like Behaviour in Mice," *Nature News* (December 5, 2013).

[14] Randy Laist, "Why I Identify as Mammal," *New York Times*, October 24, 2015.

[15] "Introduction: History Meets Biology – AHR Roundtable," *American Historical Review* (2014): 1492–9, here 1496.

have influenced the way people felt, thought, and acted during this period of history?[16]

But even if the day of "microbiomic history" is perhaps not yet quite upon us, I begin with this brief discussion of the new science of the microbiome because it offers such a (literally) visceral example of a much-broader point: we live in a time when our basic understanding of what it means to be "human" is radically changing. Insights from across the spectrum of both the sciences and the humanities are telling us that the human body, mind, and culture are even more deeply embedded in our biological and material environments than we could have previously imagined. Let me quickly highlight here a few more examples that I will deal with in more detail later in the book:

- **Epigenetics:** When I was in college in the 1980s, I was taught that, other than mutations caused by radiation or other relatively rare and random mutagenic factors, the genome preserved in my DNA is impervious to most environmental influences during my lifetime. There was no greater sin in evolutionary biology than Lamarckianism: no matter how accomplished I become at Ping-Pong, I was not supposed to be able to pass on my hard-won skills to my offspring. But now epigenetic theory tells us that environmental factors (if perhaps not rigorous Ping-Pong training) can actually turn parts of our genetic code off and on in ways that affect the physiology and behaviors of living organisms in "real time." Commenting on a recent study that suggested the distinct behaviors of ants in different castes could be changed through epigenetically mediated environmental factors, one geneticist observed that we are now beginning to understand "how the environment gets under the skin to affect gene expression, and consequently, neural activity and behavior."[17] More controversially, a growing body of evidence suggests that at least some of these epigenetic changes might in a limited sense be heritable over several generations – a sort of "inheritance of acquired traits" that had once been thought entirely impossible.

[16] See, for example, Martin J. Blaser, *Missing Microbes: How the Overuse of Antibiotics Is Fueling Our Modern Plagues* (New York: Henry Holt, 2014).
[17] Quoted in Elizabeth Pennisis, "Bipolar Drug Turns Foraging Ants into Scouts," *Science Magazine*, December 31, 2015. The original article is Daniel F. Simola et al., "Epigenetic (Re)programming of Caste-Specific Behavior in the Ant *Camponotus floridanus*," *Science* 351 (January 2016).

- **The Extended Evolutionary Synthesis:** Some evolutionary biologists are now calling for an "extended evolutionary synthesis" that would expand beyond a "gene-centric" understanding of evolution to better recognize the way in which highly plastic organisms develop in response to an environment they themselves alter, what they refer to as niches. Living things do not simply evolve to fit into preexisting environments, they argue, but co-construct and coevolve with their environments. Along with this concept of niche construction, the extended evolutionary synthesis stresses the plasticity of organismal development that allows, for example, the color of butterflies or the shape of leaves on a tree to change depending on environmental factors – not just over the course of generations of evolution, but during the developmental lifetime of a single organism.[18]
- **The Extended or Embodied Mind:** On the cognitive front, many thinkers have now clearly abandoned the old Cartesian idea of a disembodied, abstract mind to argue for what they call an "embodied" or "extended" mind. How we think, they suggest, emerges in significant part from our bodily and sensory engagement with *things* in our environment. The prominent cognitive theorist Andy Clark argues that there is an "unexpected intimacy of brain, body and world," suggesting that the mind itself "is best understood as the activity of an essentially *situated* brain: a brain at home in its proper bodily, cultural and environmental niche."[19] Another researcher in the new field of haptics – the science of human touch – also stresses how our senses embed our mind in the material world: "Haptic intelligence is human intelligence."[20]
- **Cognitive Linguistics:** In a forceful challenge to the once-popular postmodern emphasis on the power of discourse to construct reality, some cognitive linguists now argue that language and language-based thought must be understood in material terms, as they emerge from the way our brains have evolved to efficiently engage the environment through our sensory systems. "We use our primate perception and

---

[18] Kevin Laland et al., "Does Evolutionary History Need a Rethink? Yes, Urgently," *Nature* 514 (2014): 161–4, quote on 162.
[19] Andy Clark, "Where Brain, Body, and World Collide," in *Material Agency: Toward a Non-Anthropocentric Approach*, ed. Carl Knappett and Lambros Malafouris (New York: Spring, 2008), 1–18, quote on 1, emphasis in original.
[20] Adam Gopnik, "Feel Me: What the New Science of Touch Says about Ourselves," *The New Yorker* (May 16, 2016): 56–66, quote on 65.

action systems," the cognitive linguist Benjamin Bergen writes, "not only when we're actually perceiving or acting but also when we're understanding language about perceiving and acting."[21]

While diverse in their disciplines, methods, and theories, all of these insights seem to point squarely toward the same basic realization: humans do not just manipulate a clearly separate and distinct material environment that exists beyond the bounds of our genes, bodies, brains, and minds. Rather, this material environment is the very stuff out of which the changing and evolving amalgam that we call human emerges. Our human fellow travelers include not just the bacteria in our guts, but countless other material things, both biotic and abiotic, that have in very concrete and specific ways helped to create who we are in all dimensions: biological, social, and cultural. Echoing the realizations sparked by our new understanding of the microbiome, the cognitive linguist George Lakoff captures the broader significance of our historic moment: "As a society," Lakoff concludes, "we have to rethink what it fundamentally means to be human."[22]

If our understanding of what it means to be human is now undergoing such fundamental revisions, it seems evident that our idea of what we call the humanities must change as well. Indeed, these changes have already begun in some humanist disciplines, and part of the purpose of this book is to round some of these new insights up into a coherent new synthesis. My hope is that the result will be of interest to many humanists, social scientists, and other scholars, although my focus is particularly on the practical utility of this new materialism for my own discipline of history. In recent years historians have made great progress in writing a more embodied, biological, and environmental history of the past, and they have sometimes anticipated the ideas noted above. Despite this progress, a great deal remains to be done. As a more materialist and less anthropocentric understanding of the human animal begins to move toward center stage, historians should also take a leading role in both interrogating and guiding its development. Even though the research supporting a materialist understanding of humans and their histories offers powerful evidence *against* any simplistic reductionism or essentialism, history suggests there will inevitably be those who will try to misuse powerful and

[21] Benjamin K. Bergen, *Louder Than Words: The New Science of How the Mind Makes Meaning* (New York: Basic Books, 2012), 253.
[22] Quoted in Bergen, *Louder Than Words*, x.

even liberating new ideas to justify their own repressive ends. All the more reason that historians need to incorporate these new ideas into their work and provide compelling stories about the past that offer much-needed insights into the profound moral, ethical, and philosophical questions that they raise. The drumbeat of recent news reporting the imminent demise of the humanities notwithstanding, in a time of such radical change the humanistic disciplines are more essential than ever. Relatively few scientists have the inclination, time, or training to explore the broader social and cultural consequences of their insights. Yet it is equally true that humanists cannot hope to play a leading role in shaping these new ideas if they are intent only on defending an older humanism that, for all its many strengths, often reflected ideas about the human place in the world that compelling evidence now suggests were deeply mistaken. Many of these earlier mistakes derived from what was once seemed to be an entirely reasonable assumption that humans and their extraordinary cultures, cities, and technologies were largely or entirely distinct from the material world around them. Humans no longer came *from* nature, it was believed, but had instead left nature behind to henceforth shape the material world to their own end. Yet today convincing new evidence is telling us that humans are both far more embedded in material things than we had previously realized and that these things with which we are entangled are far more dynamic and creative than we had once understood. If these propositions are true, as I will argue, then we humanists need to create a less anthropocentric history of our species, one in which what we had once understood as solely "our" intelligence, creativity, culture, power, technologies, and cities are understood as emerging in significant part from a broader world of intelligent and creative animals, plants, metals, and other material things that have made us. In this book I want to explore some of the many ways in which humans are the products of an infinitely generative partnership with the things that surround us – a partnership that can be both wonderfully creative and horrifically destructive.

A few years back while my family and I were living in Munich, Germany, we became good friends with our downstairs neighbors, a couple who grew up in the then–East German city of Leipzig but had moved to Bavaria after reunification. They spoke little English (Russian having been the proper second language to learn in the old Soviet bloc), but this gave my wife and me an opportunity to improve our German during weekend *kaffeeklatsche* that became our habit. The husband had a son who would also occasionally join us, a thoughtful young man who had just finished a year in the German army. Knowing that I was working on this book, one morning he asked me what it was about. I tried to compress the book to what I thought was its essence. It was, I said, an argument for how we can understand humans and their histories as natural – that we are what I was just then starting to call "natural-born humans." I was a bit annoyed that, instead of finding this idea intriguing or challenging, he responded, "But, of course, it's obvious that humans are natural!" Since humans come from nature, he argued, then everything that humans did must also be natural. Trying to explain that my meaning was a bit more complicated, I countered, "But don't most people think that things like technology or culture are basically unnatural – that they're entirely human inventions?" If they did, he responded, they were wrong. "Human brains evolved from nature," he said, "so the human way of thinking is natural too."

I started to respond, but the conversation at the table was already shifting to the more immediately engaging topic of the relative merits of different Bavarian sausages. Since then, though, I have been surprised by how frequently I encounter this same basic idea: since humans are natural, everything they do must be natural. Surely, I realized, this said something important about the meaning of "nature" today, at least in those mostly Western-influenced corners of the globe I know best. Earlier generations of thinkers found all sorts of seemingly good reasons to believe that humans were unnatural or at least clearly separate from nature: various religious faiths that viewed humans as divine creations; the manifest uniqueness of powerful human technologies; and the see-mingly obvious superiority of humans over all other animals on the planet, who had been either domesticated, confined to vestigial remnants of "wilderness," or wiped out altogether. In 1991 the sociologist of science Bruno Latour had felt such a pressing need to explain that "we have never been modern" – by which he meant, at least in part, that humans had never really left nature – he published a whole book on the subject.[23] Yet now, a mere quarter of a century later, seemingly the opposite view has become common if not dominant: it seems we are no longer "modernists," we are all "naturalists" – even if most of us still prefer to keep our clothes on in public.

---

[23] Bruno Latour, *We Have Never Been Modern*, trans. Catherine Porter (Cambridge, MA: Harvard University Press, 1993).

This constitutes progress of a sort. Better a simplistic naturalism than an overly dichotomist modernism. But still, the ease with which so many people had apparently decided that humans were, after all, entirely natural left me feeling suspicious. Could the grounds have really shifted that quickly? Hopefully it was not just self-servingly, but I eventually concluded my suspicions were justified and that this apparent shift to naturalism was often little more than a clever ontological sleight of hand. It offers a simple explanation of how humans came to be and why they do things differently from other animals on the planet, effectively forestalling the need for much further thought on the matter. The supposedly natural explanation is that humans evolved from earlier life forms on the planet, and as my young German friend suggested, evolution eventually gave rise to the human brain and the mind's seemingly infinite capacity for creative ideas. Now this sounds very rational and scientific, and so it is for the most part. But notice the slippery trick at the very end: nature, which up until that point had been solidly in the material realm, effortlessly jumps into the realm of abstract ideas. The brain remains material, but the abstract mind apparently has no limits. Here humans can imagine all sorts of things that do not exist in the material world around them: unicorns and flying pigs, warp drives and transporters, world peace and universal social justice, and on and on. Yet in this shift to abstracted idealism, naturalism abandons the material world and starts to seem again like the antithesis of matter. In fact, it would only take a light shove to push it right back over into the realm of supernatural creators or the divine spark of the mind, topics I will return to in the next chapter. So maybe the new naturalism is not so far from the old modernism after all: the human mind, whether it came from god or nature, still rises above materiality and even its own material matrix to become the ultimate creative force. Nature may have created humans, but oddly, once the job was done, it appears to have transferred all the *real* creativity to big-brained humans.

For the idea that we are natural-born humans to be worth anything, then, it became clear to me that it had to offer some explanation for how even the seemingly most cerebral and abstract human traits – phenomena like intelligence and creativity – are the products of bodies, brains, and minds that extend out into and constantly intermingle with the environment around us. The goal of this book is to offer just such an explanation, though obviously this modest volume can at best be only a step in that direction. But now, several years of writing and thinking later, if I had a chance to explain the topic of this book to my German friend, I would say: It is about how humans are deeply embedded in and the product of a dynamic and creative material environment; that everything from the most basic nonliving elements, like phosphorous and copper, all the way up to our fellow complex organisms, like cows and silkworms, have helped to create humans and their thoughts, ideas, culture, and history. Well-known historical events – such as the era of American open-range cattle ranching, the rise of the modern Japanese silkworm industry, and the advent of global copper mining and electrification – should be understood as creations of the material world as a whole, not just of humans and their creative thinking. Matter, I wish to argue, plays an essential role in making both humans and human history.

The Western humanist project long took it as largely self-evident that humans were fundamentally different from, and separate from, all the other organisms and things on the planet. While there were many competing ideas and approaches, an earlier "sacred history" had justified this divide on the grounds that humans alone carried the spark of a divine soul. Later humanists abandoned overtly religious explanations, yet the divide endured in the guise of a human intellect and culture that served equally well in lifting them out of the base material world. As the influential British historian and philosopher R. G. Collingwood argued in the late 1940s, the proper subject of history was the human being as a thinking cultural creature largely of its own creation. "So far as man's conduct is determined by what may be called his animal nature, his impulses and appetites," Collingwood argued, "it is non-historical."[24] History was the study of a largely abstract and immaterial human mind that certainly acted on and might be influenced by the natural environment but was itself neither natural nor really material. History properly construed, Collingwood wrote, is "only concerned with those events which are the outward expression of thoughts."[25] Not surprisingly, Collingwood's abstracted anthropocentrism was also deeply androcentric, dismissing the significance of the domestic sphere where "men" go merely to satisfy their animal appetites: to "eat and sleep and make love." Accepting the modernist assumption that women were somehow closer to "nature" and hence creatures more of body and emotion than of mind and intellect, Collingwood suggests that cooking, reproduction, and other solidly material domestic work – traditionally gendered as female – had no real

[24] R. G. Collingwood, *The Idea of History* (Mansfield Center, CT: Martino, [1946] 2014), 216.
[25] Ibid., 217.

history.[26] In a closely related manner, Collingwood also dismisses the idea that other nonhuman creatures might be a part of history. While he admitted that other animals could possess some degree of self-conscious rationality, none was capable of the level of cognitive transcendence evinced by men – and here one suspects the use of the male pronoun was not in the least inclusive.[27] In all this, Collingwood argues that true history only began when men left their natural animal selves and the constraints of the material world behind to become thinking creatures who created cultures and societies. Thus history and the broader idea of humanism are erected on a seemingly solid foundation of human and largely male exceptionalism. Men conjured the course of history out of their inventive minds, shaping a largely static, passive, and female material world in their image. Humans shape matter, matter does not shape us.[28]

Obviously not all historians followed Collingwood's lead. Many long embraced a sort of rough-and-ready empiricism that often included some nod toward the influence of the material environment and even our "animal natures." (Though, until recently, only rarely the influence of "nature's animals.") Historians of women and gender would soon reveal the centrality of both of these topics to the historical enterprise. Some historians also made material things like technologies into powerful historical determinants, often to the dismay of a later generation of historians of technology who emphasized instead the ways in which human culture shaped technology. There are many other examples, and I discuss the problematic divide between culture and matter at length in the next two chapters. Nonetheless, I would argue that the *essence* of Collingwood's idea of history – that human thought, culture, and society are largely or entirely distinct from the material world and thus the only proper subject of historical study – often still prevails, albeit more as an unexamined axiom than as a reasoned position. It offers a good example of what Daniel Lord Smail has evocatively referred to as "ghost theories" and "sacred history" that quietly shape contemporary thinking but are rarely consciously acknowledged. Since Collingwood assumed that human bodily "impulses and appetites" were largely fixed and enduring – outside of the realm of history, just like the rest of the nonhuman material world and

---

[26] For an excellent account of the profession's broader dismissal of women's history, see Bonnie G. Smith, *The Gender of History: Men, Women, and Historical Practice* (Cambridge, MA: Harvard University Press, 1998).

[27] Collingwood, *The Idea of History*, 227.

[28] I derive these insights into Collingwood in part from Dipesh Chakrabarty, "The Climate of History: Four Theses," *Critical Inquiry* 35 (Winter 2009): 197–222, especially 201–3.

even the human body itself – he could safely talk about an abstract, almost-immaterial human "mind" as the essential driver of history, rather akin to Hegel's *Geist*. A ghost theory indeed!

Yet what might Collingwood have said if confronted with the contemporary scientific realization that we are in some sense "more microbial than human"? If our brains are influenced by trillions of microbial "animals" that have colonized our guts, it seems a stretch to argue that we should ignore our "animal natures" in favor of studying a disembodied abstract realm of human "thought." To be fair, Collingwood might well have had a perfectly reasonable response: Whether influenced by gut bacteria or alcohol or caffeine, the human *brain* is not the same thing as the human *mind*. To be sure, the mind resides in our brains, perhaps in our guts as well, but the brain might still be understood as clearly distinct from the abstract and symbolic realm of the mind where novel ideas, cultures, and societies are created and nurtured. At first glance this seems a valid response, and it highlights the weaknesses of both the potential use of microbiome theory for history and the current attempts to fold the psychotropic effects of alcohol and other drugs into our understanding of the past. Even assuming we could make the case that an individual's or a society's gut bacteria or fondness for caffeine provided the confidence and energy to think and act in new ways, this would not tell us much about where new ideas came from or how humans marshaled the material and social power necessary to put them into action. Further, such biologically based explanations are also often only useful when discussing large groups of people acting on large time scales. As fascinating as the Olympian "big history" overviews of such historians like David Christian and William McNeill, or the historians of the Annales school before them, may be, these can never be more than a rough frame for the more fine-grained historical studies of individuals or small groups acting in specific places and times that clearly also deserve our attention.[29] Indeed, in its embrace of such grand scales, there can at times be an odd *lack* of materiality in the deep history approach, as it substitutes broad phenomena like aggregate energy use for the smaller scale lived phenomena of individual embodied human beings trying to warm their frosty fingers by tossing a few extra lumps of coal on the fire.

A renewed attention to a much-broader materialist understanding of the past can offer a more fine-grained way of analyzing both individuals and the

---

[29] David Christian and William H. McNeill, *Maps of Time: An Introduction to Big History* (Berkeley: University of California Press, 2005).

briefer time spans where the historian's skill in mastering detail is most apparent and needed. Materiality resides at all scales of human history, not just the macro. Further, historians need not use cutting-edge biological theories like the psychobiotic effects of the microbiome in order to incorporate a more materialist understanding of the past. As the historians John Brooke and Clark Larsen note in a recent article, the tremendous physical and intellectual plasticity of the human body and brain can be shaped by environmental forces through a wide array of material pathways.[30] Consider that many cultural, social, and economic factors are in reality intimately connected with very concrete material things and processes that persist in time and space – what could be more concrete than concrete buildings and dams? More often than not, it is not so much the case that abstract human minds interact with abstract sociocultural phenomena but rather that embodied human beings interact with material organisms and things that have lives, histories, and trajectories of their own.

Some will understandably fear that this return to materiality would be a capitulation to a reductionist scientific view, an attempt to reduce the marvelous complexity of the human experience to nothing more than a means of biological self-perpetuation. But this is a misunderstanding of both recent scientific and neo-materialist thought. While there may still be plenty of reductionists to be found among scientists of all stripes, much of the most interesting work of the past few decades has pointed toward the opposite realization, an understanding of the material world as creative, dynamic, and emergent. Consider, for example, the work of the philosopher Stuart Kauffman, who titled his 2016 critique of reductive scientism *Humanity in a Creative Universe*.[31] While Kauffman takes some scientists to task for their continuing embrace of reductivism, he also notes the irony that it is science itself that has done more than any other field to reveal the surprising creativity of matter which defies easy reduction to any deterministic set of laws. Even after 13.7 billion years of existence, Kauffman observes, the universe has not even come close to working through the multitude of ways in which basic organic molecules can be arranged. "We co-create with one another and with nature," he observes, "but by the very creativity of the Universe and us in it, we cannot know

---

[30] John L. Brooke and Clark Spencer Larsen, "The Nurture of Nature: Genetics, Epigenetics, and Environment in Human Biohistory," *American Historical Review* 119 (2014): 1500–13, here 1510.

[31] Stuart Kauffman, *Humanity in a Creative Universe* (Oxford, UK: Oxford University Press, 2016).

what we will co-create."[32] In a somewhat similar way, I argue for a neo-materialist stance, not because I think critical humanist questions can now be answered by science but because I suspect they cannot be answered effectively so long as we hold to an anthropocentric idea of the human as unique and distinct from the material world. A neo-materialist humanism is not against humanism per se but rather for a richer and more inclusive humanism that might emerge from escaping the often-overwhelming pull of anthropocentrism. In this book I will deal with a number of themes that lie at the heart of the human experience and the humanist enterprise, including questions of beauty, creativity, intelligence, and mortality. To engage these humanistic subjects without engaging their material dimensions is, I argue, to bleed much of the flesh and blood – or metal and concrete – life from them.

In recent years historians have made great progress in bringing biological insights into history. In their introduction to a roundtable on "History Meets Biology" in the *American History Review*, the authors rightly note, "It is no longer possible to think of history as the story of humanity, or of ecology only as the story of nonhuman organisms and their interactions with one another and with habitats and climates."[33] But while embracing the biological and embodied nature of human history is an important step in the right direction, to focus solely on biology risks neglecting the many ways in which human history emerges from their engagement with both the biotic and abiotic world. Biocentrism is in some sense an adjunct to anthropocentrism. Nonliving things do not coevolve with humans like bacteria, cattle, and silkworms do, but nor are they merely passive raw materials which humans bend to their will. As I will argue in the chapters to come, the extraordinary material powers of elemental atoms like copper and carbon can shape humans as much as humans shape them – indeed, the two cannot be logically separated. Microbiomes, epigenetics, and neuroscience promise much, but if we are to move beyond idealism, historians must also bring all manner of non-living things with them. The result will be a new type of history and humanism, one in which we recognize that history, culture, and creativity arise from the things around us. In this model, humans are not an exception to the material world so much as an expression of it.

---

[32] Stuart Kauffman, "Why Science Needs to Break the Spell of Reductive Materialism," *Aeon* (May 20, 2016).
[33] *American Historical Review*, "History Meets Biology," 1492.

A few words of definition and explanation about the pages to come. I use both the term "new materialism" and the closely related "neo-materialism." But by the former I generally mean to reference that body of recent work that constitutes a diverse but still coherent set of ideas by scholars who self-identify under that rubric. Oddly, though, this new materialism has often proven to be surprisingly immaterial in its execution, frequently preferring to discuss human ideas about matter more than material organisms and things themselves. With the term "neo-materialism," then, I wish to point toward a much-broader body of ideas associated with scholars working in many disciplines who are concretely engaging with things in-and-of themselves, and thus more effectively avoiding the powerful pull of anthropocentrism that seems to constantly drag many back into its orbit. Ultimately, I draw on all of these intellectual threads to develop my own neo-materialist theory in the book, which, while very much a product of these ideas, is I believe distinct in two principal ways: first, for its focus on the way human thought and culture are intimately embedded in their bodies and the material environment; and, second, for its emphasis on the creative powers and independent nature of that material environment. To the degree that humans are indeed somewhat unique creatures, I argue that it is in significant part because a creative material world has made us so.

When I refer to the material world or things, I mean everything beyond the bounds of our own bodies, things both living and dead, natural and human-made. Since these things are constantly interacting, I also include all the organic and inorganic processes that drive the planet, from the rock cycle to the carbon cycle. At times I refer to other living organisms, including highly intelligent ones, as things. At least in terms of their material effects on others, our fellow human beings might also be included as things, though I do not pursue that here. Regardless, my intent is not to lower other organisms, nonhuman or human, down to the level of base matter or mere objects, but rather to raise things up several notches in our esteem, to suggest the essential role, both creative and destructive, of nonliving things in making living things, including ourselves. As my opening discussion of our microbiomes suggests, drawing the line at the boundaries of our own bodies is less than ideal. I argue that each of us is fundamentally an amalgam of material things as well. Yet the idea of a contained unitary human self roughly contiguous with our bodies can still be helpful when considering how we interact with other things. For the sake of clarity, it is useful at times to maintain a more traditional understanding of the individual bounded human being. However, the reader should understand that, when I refer to humans, I do not intend to suggest any hard categorical divide between the human and nonhuman – quite the opposite.

I also try to keep my use of the words "nature" and "natural" to a minimum, though I have found it impossible to dispense with them entirely, and I've even somewhat ironically proposed the term "natural-born humans." One of the points of a neo-materialist approach to history is that we should largely abandon the conventional distinctions between the natural and the human-made on the grounds that we need to more clearly recognize how supposedly unnatural human technologies, buildings, and artifacts always marshal and guide the flows of natural materials and processes. What we often think of as entirely human-made things and cultures emerge from and with this material world of nature, not in distinction to it. Still, the term "natural" can be useful in conveying that a particular thing is, or was, relatively free from being entangled with human history – an empirical rather than ontological distinction. Likewise, it is impossible to dispense with the word when discussing the vast majority of past and present humans who did and still do take these distinctions for granted. Rather than adopt the annoying practice of constantly putting the words in quotation marks, I ask the reader to understand that when I say nature or natural, or refer to natural-born humans, I never intend to suspend my deeper claim that humans themselves are thoroughly and entirely natural.

Another sticky word is "culture." One goal of the book is to challenge the commonly understood meaning of culture as those aspects of human existence that are distinct from our material existence – that material things might have cultural meanings but solely because people have put them there. One still-popular definition of culture is ideas about the world and how to do things that can be passed on to others through supposedly abstract means like teaching or writing. However, this view often misleadingly suggests that humans have ideas or culture first and then apply these to the material world by shaping it to their desires and giving objects symbolic meanings. Things themselves typically play no significant role in creating meanings and are largely interchangeable.[34] Likewise, culture is often contrasted with biology in terms of nurture-versus-nature debates: the idea of eating squid is cultural and a product of nurture, whereas

---

[34] Nicole Boivin makes this point: Nicole Boivin, *Material Cultures, Material Minds: The Impact of Things on Human Thought, Society, and Evolution* (New York: Cambridge University Press, 2008), 46–7.

whether humans can digest squid is a matter of nature. As I will discuss, this sounds perilously like Collingwood's distinction between human history and natural history and the assertion that true history involves the human mind, which is to say abstract ideas and culture. Today some of the most interesting work in anthropology challenges this abstracted idea of culture, suggesting that human ideas emerge from and with the material world around us. As the anthropologist Nicole Boivin writes, "In many cases, ideas and cultural understandings do not precede, but rather are helped into becoming, by the material world and human engagement with it."[35] In this I also second Daniel Lord Smail's attempt to develop a "deep cultural history," one that folds the material, biological, and embodied into the cultural rather than seeing them as distinct or even opposed.[36]

As to the style of the book, I hope to have found a felicitous spot somewhere between an academic and popular tome and tone. I try to avoid excessive neologisms and jargon, whether of the humanistic or scientific variety. Still, some of the concepts here are by their very nature difficult, and once explained I occasionally indulge in a few specialized terms. I have long taught my students that the first person is a lazy way of writing anything other than their memoirs. But I have found it useful to draw on my own experiences to illustrate arguments that might otherwise seem overly abstracted and difficult, and to avoid the first person seemed both awkward and ineffective. Some may find these narratives self-indulgent, though I hope they will not see them as entirely lacking in utility. If we humanists are to provide the useful cultural and political insights that the deliberately constrained methodologies of science often cannot, it seems reasonable that we should use all the narrative tools available to us, including the judicious use of autobiography. On the other extreme, some readers may find my at times lengthy scientific discussions of animals, minerals, and vegetables overly detailed and inade-quately historical. But to take other things seriously it is essential to use the best available scientific insights, holding in mind, of course, that these are always subject to revision, depending on new evidence and arguments, as is the case with all forms of knowledge. Moreover, a central plea of the book is that to shepherd a more decent future into existence we must better understand both the creative wonders and destructive dangers of the nonhuman world that makes us. The scientific study of material things

[35] Boivin, *Material Cultures, Material Minds*, 47.
[36] Daniel Lord Smail, *On Deep History and the Brain* (Berkeley: University of California Press, 2007), 156.

is a manner of humanism, because humans emerge from things and are themselves material beings.

Being that it seems intellectually hypocritical to me to make a theoretical argument for greater materialism without engaging with real material things, this book is an amalgam of theoretical discussions and empirical case studies. I could have picked all sorts of things and organisms to illustrate my arguments, literally a whole world of them. But most of my concrete examples derive from the global environmental history of mining, especially in the United States and Japan but with briefer excursions to South Africa and Morocco. This focus on mining and its environmental effects is in part a consequence of my previous research on the topic. It is the historical subject I know best. As an inherently global and international topic, mining history also gives me a reasonable point of entry for analyzing Japanese mining, though, as I detail in the acknowledgements, I have also depended on the kindness of both strangers and friends for their expertise in Japanese history. Much the same can be said for my forays into various scientific fields, including thermodynamics, organic chemistry, material science, and evolutionary biology, among others.

As to organization, the next two chapters focus on the more theoretical and methodological aspects of my story, while the subsequent four offer concrete illustrations of the theory and method in action. These historical case studies are grounded in a great deal of empirical historical and scientific evidence, yet they also push forward the overarching concepts of the book by putting material flesh on theoretical bones. In Chapter 2, "We Never Left Eden," I argue that the roots of the modern neglect of the material world run deep, all the way back to some strands of western Christian thought that emphasized the centrality of a divinely immaterial soul and mind. Later secularized into what I term a "Soul 2.0," in the first half of the twentieth century these idealist theories became all the more compelling in the face of the crude biological racism and environmental determinism that bred so much horror. Yet if the resulting desire to draw a bright line between human biology and culture was understandable and frequently valuable, it also constrained our ability to perceive and under-stand the material nature of embodied humans deeply embedded in their environment. In Chapter 3, "Natural-Born Humans," I draw on scholar-ship from many humanistic and scientific disciplines to develop a more materially grounded theory of the past, one that takes the importance of both the biotic and abiotic world seriously. I summarize this neo-materialist theory with four basic concepts:

1. *"The Material Environment,"* which rejects any essential categorical distinction between the natural and anthropogenic;
2. *"Thing-Power,"* which stresses the creative dynamism of both biotic and abiotic matter, particularly in their interactions with humans;
3. *"The Matter of Culture,"* which eliminates the conventional distinctions between the material and ideal to emphasize how things help to create humans in all their dimensions, both biological and cultural; and,
4. *"The End of Anthropocentrism,"* which argues that historians and other humanists should therefore develop a much less anthropocentric approach to understanding both their human and nonhuman subjects.

The next three chapters put this neo-materialist theory into action with a comparative historical study of two very similar large-scale copper mining operations that occurred in two very different nations and cultures: The Anaconda mine in the United States and the Ashio mine in Japan. My overriding question here is simple: What happened when the same toxic pollutants like sulfur and arsenic were released into such different places? But rather than just tell a conventionally anthropocentric story, I answer this question through a close study of the human relationships with three powerful material things: cows, silkworms, and copper. Chapter 4, "The Longhorn," takes these extraordinary mammals as its protagonists, arguing that their fierce intelligence and independence were a critical source of the human power associated with the American open-range cattle industry. Chapter 5, "The Silkworm," applies a similar approach to the Japanese sericulture industry, suggesting that the creative biological nature of the silkworms themselves was essential to the rapid growth of the Japanese economy and new ways of thinking in the second half of the nineteenth century. However, in Chapter 6, "The Copper Atom," I explain how both the American culture created by Longhorns and the Japanese culture created by silkworms ultimately proved to be no match for the juggernaut of human power and culture enabled by the metal copper. Pollution from industrial copper mining destroyed the subtle human-animal bonds that had once made Ashio and Anaconda so culturally distinct. Differences increasingly gave way to what several leading scholars of Japan have recently termed the "great convergence," as both Japan and the United States used their copper deposits to become strikingly similar modern nations with electrically lit cities and mighty battleships strung with sinews of copper wire. Put simply, American "Longhorn people" and Japanese "silkworm people" increasingly came to resemble something much more like "copper people." Explicit in this is a central contention of the book: that the things we interact with are an inescapable part of who we are. So I conclude in Chapter 7, "The Matter of Humans," that the humanistic disciplines should develop and explore a much less anthropocentric understanding of the rather humble place our species occupies on a powerful and not infrequently dangerous planet. The contemporary advocates of the Anthropocene notwithstanding, I argue that the earth is not in our hands – we are in its.

This book is not necessarily meant as a manifesto. Those who know me will confirm that I am a mild-mannered sort, certainly no bomb-throwing revolutionary. Still, I recognize that my argument may at times be a bit overly strident and one-sided. It will seem self-serving to claim that I have intentionally left out some of the many possible caveats and complexities in the name of brevity and clarity, but I do think this is true in many cases, though I am sure that I have unintentionally missed others. In any event, the book is meant not to be definitive or exhaustive, but exploratory and suggestive. Given the scope of the matter at hand, how could it be anything else? I offer some guidelines for a neo-materialist approach to history, but I hope these will be starting points for others to explore, ideally by subjecting them to the exacting empirical demands of studying real material things and their complex historical interactions with humans. I am no fan of theory for theory's sake, so the value of these neo-materialist ideas will depend on their ability to elicit interesting new historical questions, studies, and insights.

Finally, while such a rich topic as neo-materialism certainly warrants a longer and more detailed treatment than I provide here, I felt a certain sense of urgency to finish the book. Without being overly alarmist, I do fear that if we continue to imagine that a clear line separates humans from the many powerful things around them, we will continue to overestimate human power and underestimate the power of materials like coal, oil, and countless other things to both create and trap us in behaviors we often did not intend yet find exceedingly difficult to escape. In an era of reckless global environmental change and species extinction, I fear we are also losing many of the material conditions and evolutionary creations that have historically proved most central to making us human. To date, researchers have identified a mere 1 percent of the planet's rich diversity of species, each one a marvel of millions of years of biological creativity, and any one of which might someday prove of transformative importance.

The dangers of leaving the stable conditions of the Holocene are a risk not only to our physical survival, but also to our cultural and in some broad sense perhaps even our spiritual survival. To change our material environment is to change ourselves, and no merely abstract ideas, beliefs, and memories will ever recapture what we once were or what we might once have become. If ever the moment was right to embrace the hard material reality that surrounds us and in some sense *is* us, it surely is now. It has, in any event, already embraced us.

2

We Never Left Eden

The Religious and Secular Marginalization of Matter

In what surely must belong on any list of the great ironic twists in human history, modern industrialized gold mining is now threatening to destroy the Garden of Eden – or at least something close to it. The Cradle of Humankind, one of the better candidates for something like a genetic human Garden of Eden, is less than an hour's drive from Johannesburg, South Africa. The road north and west out of the sprawling modern metropolis skirts the South Western Townships area, better known as Soweto. Before his decades-long imprisonment, Nelson Mandela lived here in a modest four-room brick house that is now an eclectic museum. Soweto was also once a cradle, the center of the long struggle waged by Mandela and his allies in the African National Congress to end South Africa's apartheid regime. Their success is evident today in the stylish new homes that cluster in scattered clumps, testaments to the new wealth enjoyed by a small but growing segment of South Africa's majority black population. Yet much of Soweto still lives in tin-roofed shacks like those found in the many other sprawling shantytowns around the city. Shockingly, millions who lack even indoor plumbing or basic electricity live next to what were once the biggest and richest gold deposits to be found anywhere on this planet.

Though close in miles, the Cradle of Humankind might at first feel impossibly distant in time from the modern urban world of Johannesburg. Here beneath the dry rolling highveld of brown grass and scattered trees lies a vast maze of subterranean caves that were carved by the slow dissolution of a limestone deposit created 2.6 billion years ago, a time when the waves of an ancient sea washed over a thriving coral reef. Fossils of blue-green algae, among the oldest forms of life on Earth, can still be found in the rock that remains. The caves were already unimaginably old when another and far more complex future fossil arrived. Some two million years ago – recent by geological time scales – a small, lightly built animal that walked upright on two legs lived in South Africa. Resembling a cross between a chimpanzee and a modern human, these were the hominin species called *Australopithecus africanus*. (In modern nomenclature, the hominin group includes humans and their very closely related genetic relatives, like *Australopithecus*, but not their more distant hominid relatives that arose after the evolutionary divergence between humans and chimpanzees about six million years ago.)[1] Most paleoanthropologists agree that *A. africanus* was a distant ancestor to a lineage of other species that eventually led to the genus of *Homo*, the hominin group that includes extinct species like *Homo erectus* and *Homo neanderthalensis* as well as humans, *Homo sapiens*. Just a mere 100,000 years ago there were at least six human species on the earth, just as today there are numerous species of apes or bears. But of all these earlier *Homo* species, *Homo sapiens* are the only ones to have survived to the present.[2] There is an ongoing scientific debate about whether the South African *Australopithecus africanus* or the very similar East African *Australopithecus afarensis*, or even some other species, was the more immediate predecessor to the *Homo* lineage. But regardless of how further evidence eventually settles the issue, there is little question that the *A. africanus* who lived in what is now South Africa were close early relatives of humans.[3] While these animals were erect and bipedal like humans, their brains were about the size of a grapefruit and their jaws and lips protruded forward, giving their faces the sloping profile characteristic of contemporary chimps. About 1.3 meters tall, *A. africanus* lived in a harshly competitive subtropical environment dominated by other now-extinct animals like the saber-toothed cat *Dinofelis* that hunted them.

This relatively small brain size (about a third the size of modern humans) perhaps played some role in dooming one specific *Australopithecus*

---

[1] Erin Wayman, "What's in a Name? Hominid versus Hominin," *Smithsonian*, November 16, 2011.

[2] Yuval Noah Harari, *Sapiens: A Brief History of Mankind* (New York: Vintage, 2011), 5–9.

[3] For an accessible exploration of the case for the South African origins, see Kate Wong, "First of Our Kind," *Scientific American: What Makes Us Human* 22, no. 1 (Winter 2013): 12–21. For a rather sharp critique, see Paige Williams, "Digging for Glory: Fossils and Hype in South Africa," *The New Yorker* (June 27, 2016).

africanus individual, though her odd manner of death would also grant her a sort of scientific immortality. Roughly two million years ago, what appears to have been a female (but might also have been a small male or juvenile) had the misfortune to fall through the roof of one of those subterranean caves. Paleontologists would later nickname her Mrs. Ples. Perhaps Mrs. Ples was foraging in the area for food when the ground beneath her suddenly gave way, or perhaps she was fleeing a predator or other danger and stumbled into an open hole. Regardless, if she did survive the fall down into the dark cave, her fate was likely sealed. Paleoanthropologists speculate that she would have been utterly paralyzed by fear, her brain too small to formulate any realistic means of rescuing herself. Indeed, unless they had a flashlight or other source of light, a comparatively big-brained modern human might do little better. Even if

FIGURE 2.1 At the South African "Cradle of Humankind," a plaque memorializes the *Australopithecus africanus* nicknamed "Mrs. Ples," a distant evolutionary ancestor of modern humans whose nearly complete fossilized skull was discovered in Sterkfontein cave in 1947. Photograph by author.

another way out of the cave was within reach, few would probably have the courage to leave the comforting light streaming down from the hole above to blindly explore the dark unknown reaches.

There is no way to know whether Mrs. Ples was killed in the fall or died slowly from thirst or hunger. Regardless, over the centuries to come, her skeleton was gradually covered in rock and debris and mineralized into a stone-encased fossil. There the bones sat for more than two million years until some not-so-distant descendants of Mrs. Ples found a reason they considered compelling enough to enter and begin excavating the cave: gold. The discovery of gold in 1884 in the Witwatersrand Basin around Johannesburg sparked one of the biggest global mining rushes in history. Eventually, more than half of the current stock of gold in the world, a breathtaking 45,000 *tons*, came from these South African rocks.[4] Gold mining in turn created a huge new demand for lime to process and purify the gold ore, which could be found in abundance in the limestone caves north of Johannesburg. In 1896, a miner named Guglielmo Martinaglia blasted his way down into Sterkfontein (Afrikaans for "strong spring") cave and began removing the limestone rock, paying little heed to whatever ancient fossils he encountered. Luckily, a representative of the South African Geological Survey explored the cave soon after it was opened, and he convinced Martinaglia to set aside a remarkable geological area where a large underground lake and massive stalactites and stalagmites were found. Still, for another three decades the value of the cave as a treasure trove of hominin fossils remained largely unrecognized, in part because early fossils discovered in China had convinced many scientists that East Asia was the most likely birthplace of humankind. However, inspired by the 1925 discovery of what appeared to be a hominin skull not too far to the west, a Scottish-born South African doctor named Robert Broom began searching the Sterkfontein limestone deposits for similar fossils. In 1947 his search paid off when he discovered the almost complete skull of Mrs. Ples using the crude but effective technique of blasting through the limestone with dynamite.[5]

In 2000, UNESCO designated Sterkfontein Cave and others in the area a World Heritage Site, granting it the none-too-modest name of the Cradle of Humankind. But as the former president of the postapartheid South Africa, Thabo Mbeki, notes, the name is perhaps not too much of

---

[4] Brett Hilton-Barber and Lee R. Berger, *The Official Field Guide to the Cradle of Humankind* (Cape Town, South Africa: Struik, 2002), 46.

[5] Ibid., 58–62.

a stretch.[6] Paleontologists have discovered more than a third of the globe's early hominin remains at Sterkfontein and other caves in the area. The skull of Mrs. Ples was critical to establishing *Australopithecus africanus* as a close relative of humans, thus helping to confirm Darwin's speculation that humans had evolved in Africa. Subsequent hominin species in the area, most likely *Homo habilis* and *Homo erectus* (or perhaps the closely related species *Homo rudolfensis* and *Homo egaster*), were also among the first of our early *Homo* ancestors to control fire and make stone tools. As mentioned before, given all the fossil evidence from Sterkfontein and other caves in the area, some paleoanthropologists have forwarded the controversial claim that the early ancestors of anatomically modern humans, *Homo sapiens*, might have first evolved in this region.[7] South Africa, then, would be a sort of species Garden of Eden. "If there is a possibility that Johannesburg was once the Garden of Eden," the South African writer Rian Malan notes in discussing the cave, "then our ancestors would have lived there 150,000 to 200,000 years ago."[8] Before leading a group of tourists from all around the world down into the depths of Sterkfontein, a guide tells them: "Welcome home."

Many paleoanthropologists still believe that *Homo sapiens* probably first evolved somewhere in East Africa, not South Africa, and the debate continues. But even if anatomically modern humans did not first emerge at Sterkfontein, the caves do offer some of the best fossil evidence of our even earlier human ancestors. More importantly for my purposes here, as I headed down into the cool maze of limestone passages, and later while examining the specimens of stone tools in the small but rich museum at the site, I realized the guide's good-humored "welcome home" could also be taken to have a broader meaning. He meant to suggest that the distant *Homo sapiens* who would evolve from Mrs. Ples or her relatives had long ago moved out of Africa and spread to the four corners of the world. But if we think of Sterkfontein as a sort of real world Garden of Eden, the guide's greeting might also be understood as meaning: Welcome back to the place where humans first left Eden to become the only unnatural creatures on the planet. Thousands of stone tools have been discovered at Sterkfontein and other caves in the complex, including hand axes, points, and many microliths. The neighboring cave Swartkrans also has what could be the oldest yet discovered evidence of hominin use of fire, the Promethean tool said to be stolen from the heavenly gods in early Western myths.

[6] Ibid., 5.   [7] Ibid., 19.
[8] David Smith, "Visit to the Cradle of Humankind," *The Guardian* (January 15, 2010).

Widespread evidence of human use of fire in European sites only dates to about 300,000 to 400,000 years ago.[9] However, animal bones found in one corner of Swartkrans had been heated up to 500 degrees centigrade in what may have been a deliberately constructed fireplace as early as 1 to 1.5 million years ago.[10] Regardless, it seems clear that Sterkfontein was one of the first places on the planet where the ancestors of modern humans began to use the technological skills that would eventually become one of the defining traits of *Homo sapiens*. But did these new technological abilities also mark the moment when hominins became unnatural? Particularly in Western thought, making and using tools has long been thought to offer one of the clearest markers of the moment when our ancestors parted ways with other natural animals and instead became unnatural creatures who manipulated (literally, formed with our hands) nature but were no longer part of it. So if Sterkfontein was the real human Garden of Eden, was it also the place where we left Eden behind?

MAKING HUMANS UNNATURAL

Today the idea that humans or even very early human ancestors were the first to make and use tools appears hopelessly anthropocentric, the product of an almost willful human desire to ignore the abundant proof that many other animals use tools. As the primatologist and student of animal intelligence Frans de Waal notes, many animals living today are tool users, including crows who have been witnessed actually manufacturing simple tools.[11] Some animals like apes not only use tools in the spur of the moment, but deliberately gather multiple tools with the conscious plan to use them later. "They carry tools over long distances to places where they use them," de Waal notes, "sometimes up to five different sticks and twigs to raid a bee nest or probe for underground ants. In the lab, they fabricate tools in anticipation of future use."[12] Given such contemporary evidence, it seems likely that many different animals probably used tools

---

[9] Rachael Moeller Gorman, "Cooking Up Bigger Brains," *Scientific American: What Makes Us Human* 22, no. 1 (Winter 2013): 36–7.

[10] C. K. Brain, *The Hunters or the Hunted? An Introduction to African Cave Taphonomy* (Chicago: University of Chicago Press, 1981), 376, and Brain, "Structure and Stratigraphy of the Swartkans Cave in Light of New Excavations," in *Swartkrans: A Cave's Chronicle of Early Man*, ed. C. K. Brain (Pretoria, South Africa: Transvaal Museum, 1983).

[11] Frans de Waal, *Are We Smart Enough to Know How Smart Animals Are?* (New York: Norton, 2016), 89–95.

[12] Frans de Waal, "Who Apes Whom?" *New York Times*, September 15, 2015.

of some sort well before the emergence of the *Homo* lineage. Likewise, there is growing evidence that *Australopithecus africanus* may have used tools as long as 3.2 million years ago.[13] If so, even Mrs. Ples herself might have used simple tools. Still, if tool use is a widespread and perhaps even relatively common trait of the animal kingdom, it is obvious that no other animal has developed this trait to a level anywhere close to that of humans. I will discuss contemporary explanations for what anthropologists now term the advent of "modern human behavior" in more detail in the next chapter. However, earlier humans must have long remarked on and sought to explain why they were so different than other animals.

In Hebraic and Christian-influenced thought, one possible explanation was captured in the enduringly popular biblical story of Adam and Eve in the Garden of Eden. In this story (which is also mentioned in a different form in the Koran) the Garden of Eden was a fertile paradise of luxuriant trees and meadows. Today the model for the idea of Eden is often thought to be the fertile region between the Tigris and Euphrates Rivers in Mesopotamia (now mostly in Iraq), a place where "every tree that is pleasant to the sight and good for food" could be found.[14] However, when Eve could not resist eating a tempting fruit (often represented as a red apple) from the forbidden tree of knowledge, God banished the first couple from Eden. Having previously lived in harmony with a beneficent natural world, Adam and Eve and their offspring would henceforth have to develop and use technologies to control and subdue a hostile world. Many have remarked that the story of Adam and Eve might well have been an outgrowth of the technological and cultural shifts that marked the "Neolithic Revolution" in Mesopotamia some 12,000 years ago, the era when Eurasian humans gradually began to abandon their ancient nomadic hunter-gatherer ways to take up farming and settle in permanent villages. As one archaeologist puts it: "The transition in lifeways caused by the Neolithic Revolution resulted in deep-seated cultural shock [that was] retained in the oral history of the populations of the Near East."[15] As these Neolithic villagers became increasingly "civilized," a term that has its roots in the Latin word "civis," meaning a citizen who lived in a city or town, the memory of an earlier nomadic way of life lingered even as

[13] Matthew M. Skinner et al., "Human-like Hand Use in *Australopithecus africanus*," *Science* 347 (2015): 395–9.

[14] See, for example, Carl G. Rasmussen, *The Zondervan Atlas of the Bible* (Grand Rapids, MI: Zondervan, 2010): 82–3.

[15] Alan H. Simmons, *The Neolithic Revolution in the Near East: Transforming the Human Landscape* (Tucson: University of Arizona Press, 2011), ix.

they increasingly saw themselves and their settlements as superior to this more "natural" world they had left behind. By definition, civilized people lived in cities built by human hands. Uncivilized brutes and animals lived in nature.

The story of the expulsion of Adam and Eve from the Garden of Eden also offered a clear explanation for why humans were different from all other animals on the planet: because a supernatural god created the first humans in his own image and had endowed them with an immortal and immaterial soul. As the historian of technology David Noble argues in his penetrating study *The Religion of Technology*, some influential Western thinkers believed that this spark of the divine also gave humans the power to recreate their lost Eden through technology.[16] Far from seeing technology as antithetical to religion, these church fathers believed it was the path to transcendence. The thirteenth-century Franciscan monk and technological visionary Roger Bacon argued that Adam (he says little about Eve) had shared in God's omniscient knowledge of the universe, including the knowledge of all conceivable science and technology. When they lived in a paradise, where nature provided everything they desired, Adam had no need to smelt copper or build water wheels, but Bacon believed that he knew full well how to do so. After the fall and expulsion into a less beneficent nature that was now separate from him, Adam lost this innate technological know-how just when he needed it most. Yet Bacon argued that the enduring spark of a supernatural soul would, in time, allow humans to recapture their earlier god-like knowledge and power of creativity. Human progress in science and technology was thus divinely ordained and even seen as a means of returning to a lost Eden. Tellingly, once they left the Garden of Eden, Adam and Eve did not become simple hunter-gatherers, but instead immediately began inventing and using all sorts of technologies. Like the early agriculturalists who had abandoned their hunter-gatherer ways, the children of Adam and Eve could grow crops, weave clothes, and build mud-brick houses and cities. In time, they would create steam engines and nuclear reactors. Importantly for my purposes here, though, all of these came not from the human engagement with a powerfully creative natural world but rather from the *super*natural creative spirit given them by God. Humans and their technologies were by definition unnatural.

---

[16] David Noble, *The Religion of Technology: The Divinity of Man and the Spirit of Invention* (New York: Penguin, 1997). See also Carolyn Merchant, *Reinventing Eden: The Fate of Nature in Western Culture* (New York: Routledge, 2003).

There were many other consequences of this supernatural view of the human mind and its divinely inventive powers – women, for example, were seen as derivative of men and thus less capable, particularly in terms of technology. Apparently little of God's spark of creativity passed over to Eve with that rib bone. In a somewhat similar manner, all nonhuman animals were understood to have been created separately and without a soul or spirit. Certainly animals could not think or create tools. As the scholar of Medieval history Lynn White argued in an influential 1967 article, "The Historical Roots of Our Ecologic Crisis," this Judeo-Christian tradition contrasted sharply with previously dominant animistic understandings of the human place in the world which understood human power as intimately linked to a vibrant natural world filled with other intelligent beings. White argued that this sharp cleaving of humans from nature in Judeo-Christian thought thus justified the Western exploitation of the environment and brutal treatment of other animals, which were understood to be categorically distinct from the humans for whom the world was made. "Especially in its Western form," White asserted, "Christianity is the most anthropocentric religion the world has seen."[17] Critics of White's thesis countered that the Judeo-Christian tradition also offered an ethic of stewardship of nature, and there is at least some reason to believe that the hubristic drive to dominate nature is tempered by a strain of theology that suggests the faithful should act with humble caution in the face of God's awesome creation. Ultimately, the Judeo-Christian tradition, mixed with strains of thought from ancient Greece and other sources, has constituted a complex and often even contradictory set of ideas. There is no one coherent "Christian tradition."[18] Nonetheless, it seems evident that at least some Judeo-Christian thought both stemmed from and reinforced a growing human belief that they were divinely special creatures, distinct from both nature and other animals.

---

[17] Lynn White, "The Historical Roots of Our Ecological Crisis," *Science* 155 (1967): 1203–7, quote on 1205.
[18] My thanks to Mark Stoll for his guidance on this complex topic. Good overviews are offered in H. Paul Santmire, *The Travail of Nature: The Ambitious Ecological Promise of Christian Theology* (Minneapolis, MN: Fortress Press, 1985), and Clarence Glacken, *Traces on the Rhodian Shore: Nature and Culture in Western Thought from Ancient Times to the End of the Eighteenth Century* (Berkeley: University of California Press, 1976). On the role of Protestant Christian theology in fostering the modern conservation movement, see especially Mark Stoll, *Protestantism, Capitalism, and Nature in America* (Albuquerque: University of New Mexico Press, 1997), and Stoll, *Inherit the Holy Mountain: Religion and the Rise of American Environmentalism* (Oxford, UK: Oxford University Press, 2015).

Over the centuries, Noble argues, these ideas became further cemented into the Western consciousness, often stripped of their overtly religious elements so they could be re-presented as more rational and even secular views. In lieu of a divine soul, Renaissance and Enlightenment thinkers instead argued that the individual human mind or intellect held the spark of divinity – what we might call a "Soul 2.0." In perhaps the most famous assertion of Western idealist belief, the French philosopher René Descartes concluded that the human intellect, like a soul, was essentially separate from the body and nature. Since the mind was neither natural nor embodied, Descartes reasoned, its functions were entirely liberated from the world around it.[19] Assuming that no other creatures on the planet could think as humans did, Descartes also concluded that all other animals were really just machines or living automatons, further deepening the earlier Judeo-Christian dismissal of any fundamental ties between humans and animals. Even the universe itself could best be understood by the measure of human technologies: perhaps the world and all of its surroundings were akin to an immense mechanical clock?[20]

All this is, of course, a simplification of a much more complex story. In his 1781 work *Critique of Pure Reason*, Immanuel Kant fundamentally altered the landscape of Western philosophy by arguing that the true nature of things could never be comprehended by a merely finite human mind. Things did exist in and of themselves, Kant argued, even if we humans can only imperfectly apprehend them. (Though Kant maintained the essential Cartesian anthropocentrism in his unexamined assumption that humans alone possess minds that are capable of bringing the properties of other things to light.)[21] Despite its emphasis on an immortal immaterial soul, Christian theology also understood the body as an essential vessel for achieving salvation.[22] The material embodiment of God in

---

[19] Steven Pinker, *The Blank Slate: The Modern Denial of Human Nature* (New York: Penguin, 2003), 9–10. For a contrary view of the importance of the body and emotion in cognition, see Antonio Damasio, *Descartes' Error: Emotion, Reason, and the Human Brain* (New York: Penguin, 2005).

[20] Ian Bogost notes the long human tendency to imagine that the universe operates like whatever the preeminent technology of the era happens to be. Today it is computers. See Ian Bogost, "The Cathedral of Computation," *The Atlantic* (March 19, 2016).

[21] Graham Harman, *Immaterialism: Objects and Social Theory* (Cambridge, UK: Polity, 2016), 27. A recent extended critique of the enduring anthropocentrism of Kantian philosophy is Dipesh Chakrabarty, "Humanities in the Anthropocene: The Crisis of and Enduring Kantian Fable," *New Literary History* 47 (2016): 377–97.

[22] See, for example, Sally M. Promey, ed., *Sensational Religion: Sensory Cultures in Material Practice* (New Haven, CT: Yale University Press, 2014).

Christ and his subsequent death are also obviously central to the faith, and some strains of the religion put tremendous weight on the spiritual power of physical relics like pieces of the true cross and the bones and bodies of saints. As I will discuss in the next chapter, there is also a long lineage of more materially rooted views of the human mind, from the Greek Epicureans to Dewey's pragmatism to the current concepts of extended cognition. Nonetheless, it is difficult to deny that there is a pronounced predilection in Western thought to understand the essence of humanity as stemming from an immaterial soul or mind. This is especially evident in comparison to many other non-Western ways of understanding the human place in the world such as animism. This faith in a Soul 2.0 also endured into the modern era, even among many who might not have thought of themselves as especially religious. As David Noble points out, technological endeavors from the development of nuclear weapons to the space race and the advent of genetic engineering have all been infused with either an overtly Christian spirit of transcendence or a secularized version of it. Stanley Kubrick's 1968 epic film *2001: A Space Odyssey* beautifully captured the way a transcendent religious spirit could be seamlessly grafted onto the modern space age of science and technology. In the famous opening scene, two bands of ape-men fight over a water hole in Africa during the day and huddle in fear during the night as hungry cat-like predators hunt them. Then a mysterious black monolith appears in their midst and somehow passes the spark of technological know-how to one of the ape-men. During the next battle over the water hole, the thus blessed ape-man has the dawning realization that he can use an animal bone as a club, and he beats the leader of the competing band to death and claims the water hole. When he throws the bone into the air in triumphant exaltation, the slow-motion image of its turning form suddenly cuts to that of a modern spaceship gracefully floating in orbit around the earth. Kubrick's message was hardly subtle: Whether it came from a supernatural god or a quasi-supernatural alien monolith, the spark of technological creativity has taken the human species out of the base natural world of this earth and lifted them up into the realm of the gods – literally into the heavens, thanks to the miracle of space travel.

As the enduring popularity of Kubrick's film suggests, at some level many today continue to believe that humans and their technologies are both fundamentally unnatural and a means of transcending the mere material world. The psychologist Steven Pinker notes that most Americans still believe in a literal immortal soul that can exist apart from the body and can easily enough be associated with an abstract understanding of the mind. In this view, Pinker argues that the human mind "is an immaterial substance; it has powers possessed by no purely physical structure, and can continue to exist when the body dies."[23] As the philosopher Gilbert Ryle observed some years ago, this is the "ghost in the machine" concept of consciousness in which the mind is clearly separated from both the body and the environment. Bodies are understood to be part of the material world that may be subject to scientific investigation, he writes, "but minds are not in space, nor are their operations subject to mechanical laws."[24]

The idea that the mind is a disembodied immaterial entity is also central to the modern hope that humans may soon achieve technological immortality. Ever since the advent of digital computers in the 1940s, some scientists have argued that the human brain and mind are literally or metaphorically akin to computers – yet another example of the way we tend to think through the material technologies and conditions of our time. In 1958, the mathematician John Neumann argued in his short book *The Computer and the Brain* that the human brain is "*prima facie* digital." Since then it has become common to speak of the brain and mind as analogous to a computer, a machine that "processes" and "stores" information through algorithms and software. However, as the psychologist Robert Epstein observes, while digital computers may be able to imitate some elements of human intelligence, this does not mean that the brain literally operates like a computer any more than a hawk literally flies like a jet airplane. The visual memory of a face, for example, is not "processed" into digital data that are literally "stored" in a specific set of neurons like a computer would store such information on a hard drive. Rather, our memory of a face, or anything else, emerges from a far more complex and still little-understood process that involves many parts of our brains, whose evolution has emerged from our bodily engagement with the material world through our senses and emotions. Humans "do not make sense of the world by performing computations on mental representations of it," Epstein argues, but rather through "a *direct interaction* between organisms and their world." Put succinctly: "We are organisms, not computers."[25]

---

[23] Pinker, *Blank Slate*, 1.   [24] Quoted in Pinker, *The Blank Slate*, 9.
[25] Robert Epstein, "The Empty Brain," *Aeon* (May 18, 2016). A similar point is made in Anthony Chemero, *Radical Embodied Cognitive Science* (Boston, MA: MIT Press, 2011).

I will return to the importance of such "embodied" or "extended" concepts of cognition in the next chapter, as these new theories provide a powerful rebuttal to the conventional humanistic emphasis on the role of abstract discourse, ideas, and information as a driving force in history. The supposed antagonism between postmodern and scientific thinking notwithstanding, in recent decades such abstracted ideas of human cognition have often dominated in the sciences every bit as much as they have in the humanistic disciplines. Consider, for example, the neuroscientist Kenneth Hayworth who argues that by precisely mapping all of the neural connections in the brain – what are called connectomes – it will eventually be possible to upload an individual human consciousness to a computer. Hayworth confidently predicts that, in less than a century, this kind of "mind uploading" of a biological brain to a silicon-based computer will be as routine as laser eye surgery is today. Linked to a robotic body, these silicon brains would seem to promise digital immortality – a Soul 2.0 indeed.[26] To be sure, many of Hayworth's colleagues dismiss his more outrageous predictions. But if his faith in technological transcendence is extreme, it is hardly rare among many contemporary scientists and engineers, much less among the general population. The so-called transhumanism movement, for example, foresees the development of an artificial intelligence that will far surpass the meager abilities of conventionally embodied humans. Some look forward with optimism to this so-called singularity as an opportunity for the human species to transcend their material bodies and achieve a sort of digital immortality. Others, like the philosopher Nick Bostrom, warn that if humans do not take steps now to control such "superintelligence" it could evolve so rapidly as to present a dangerous threat to the survival of the species. Bostrom's fears of an impending "doomsday invention" are taken seriously by at least some, attracting the attention of technological literati like Bill Gates and Elon Musk.[27] Yet even as he warns that such superintelligence may pose an existential threat greater than any humans have previously faced, Bostrom refuses to suggest that humans should stop developing artificial intelligence. "It would be tragic if machine intelligence were never developed to its full capacity," he argues. "I think this is ultimately the key, or the portal, we have to pass through to realize the full dimensions of

---

[26] Evan R. Goldstein, "The Strange Neuroscience of Immortality," *The Chronicle of Higher Education* (July 16, 2012).

[27] Nick Bostrom, *Superintelligence: Paths, Dangers, Strategies* (Oxford, UK: Oxford University Press, 2014).

humanity's long-term potential." Indeed, Bostrom has personally bet on
the possibility of technological immortality: immediately after he dies
a cryonics company will freeze his brain in the hopes that he can later be
resurrected, most likely in some cybernetic form.[28]

The influences of the idealist transcendentalism of Bacon and
Descartes, as well as the Judeo-Christian faith in an immortal soul, are
obvious here. Hayworth and Bostrom believe that whatever it is that
defines their essence as unique individual human beings clearly resides
solely or primarily in an abstract mind. Whether the mere material con-
tainer is made of protein or silicon makes little difference – the mind can
literally become *dis*embodied without undergoing any significant change.
What is striking in these technological forms of transcendence is their
almost willful rejection of the physical world of brains, bodies, and
material things. Rather than understanding the material world as
a creative force that is inextricable from an embodied human existence
and identity, mere matter is understood as an obstacle to the full realization of some imagined future human potential. In a telling echo of
Collingwood's theory of history discussed in Chapter 1, the advocates of
technological transcendence assume that the essence of humans are their
immaterial minds, not their "animal natures." Yet would our future
silicon selves also have a circuit that would capture the psychobiotic
capabilities of the trillions of constantly changing and evolving bacteria
that make up the "brain" in our guts? Would it make allowances for the
way environmental factors can literally reprogram our epigenetic code
and which genes are expressed in our constantly changing bodies? Would
it be able to think through the senses of touch, sight, and all the many
other ways the brain extends itself into the world around it? Perhaps
transhumanists have anticipated all these issues and imagine that their
computer minds might be embedded in a living body so sophisticated it
could replicate the trillions of connections between our brains, bodies, and
the environment – after all, if they can recreate a mind, surely they can
recreate a mere body. Regardless, there can be little doubt that these
ideas reflect a modernist spirit in which the material world is associated
with the base, mean, and passive, while the mind alone is the realm of
ideas, culture, and all other truly elevating abstractions. The archaeologist
Nicole Boivin provides a perceptive summary of the dynamic: in the
long competition between idealists and materialists, she writes, "It is

[28] Raffi Khatchadourian, "The Doomsday Invention," *The New Yorker* (November 23,
2015).

inevitably the mind and its apparent objectivity that have been favoured, and with it a view of humans as apart from nature, categorically different from other animals, and defined, inevitably and irrefutably, by a capacity for symbolism, language, and the creation of a unique, cultural order."[29]

During the so-called science wars of the 1990s, the supposed realist materialism of science was often placed in opposition to postmodern idealism. Yet from a neo-materialist perspective, scientists and humanists have not infrequently worshiped at the very same altar: that of a disembodied mind and intellect that is largely abstract in its essence, whether it emerges from processing "information" or linguistic "discourse." Likewise, both retain elements of the early modern notion of the lone transcendent genius as the architect of human progress and destiny. The German romantic-era composer Ludwig van Beethoven caught the spirit of the similarity nearly two centuries ago when he confidently asserted that "only art and science can raise men to the level of gods."[30] Having devoted much of their lives to ideas, perhaps it is no surprise that intellectuals like scientists and humanists have both been prone to embrace idealism. Precisely because careful scientific study largely eliminated the need for any supernatural explanation for human existence, many concluded that the human intellect was the true driving force of history. Today more than a few of us essentially worship human intelligence, making scientists and inventors like Albert Einstein, Thomas Edison, and even far-less significant businessmen like Steven Jobs, into modern-day saints whose brilliance promises ever more novel ways in which we can transcend this mortal coil.

Yet if the modern age has most often favored its great scientists and engineers as exemplars of the Promethean mind unbound, the actual work of these intellects often remained solidly grounded in the investigation and manipulation of the real material world. Whatever the rarified realms of abstraction they might have reached, the goal was typically to better understand the world around them, even if only to more effectively manipulate it. Yet for those scholars whose subject of study was in essence themselves, the earthly bonds of a material gravity were sometimes more easily shaken off altogether.

---

[29] Nicole Boivin, *Material Cultures, Material Minds: The Impact of Things on Human Thought, Society, and Evolution* (Cambridge, UK: Cambridge University Press, 2008), 15.

[30] Quoted in Jan Swafford, *Beethoven: Anguish and Triumph* (New York: Houghton Mifflin Harcourt, 2014), 78.

MARGINALIZING MATTER

As I have already suggested, humans have long tended to be rather unabashedly anthropocentric. Yet perhaps none more so than those who go to the eponymic extreme of calling themselves humanists. A few, like the environmental historian John McNeill, have had the good grace to apologize for our "arrogantly species-centric" manners. But as McNeill goes on to note, such arrogance might be excused among historians given that their "subject is mainly (not exclusively) the human career."[31] Indeed, the sheer transformative power of that human career over the past few millennia might at first seem to offer ample justification for a good measure of self-obsession. What other species has made such immense changes to the world and themselves in such a brief time?

However, this penchant for anthropocentrism hangs upon what may be a flawed premise: that humans and their cultures are best understood as unnatural creatures who live in but are not fundamentally part of the material world. For if the contrary were true – if humans remained embedded in and derived much of their power, intelligence, and creativity from the natural world – then would it not be evident that a goodly portion of what we term "human" really emerges from the material world around us? I will make that argument in earnest in the next chapter. But before then, it will be useful to understand why so many humanists, though certainly not all, have tended to minimize the importance of the material world in pursuing their various subjects of study or, in a few extreme cases, even dismissed it altogether. As I suggested in the previous section, the historical roots for this neglect of the material might at least in part stem from the Western tendency toward idealism, whether in its religious or secular forms. Yet in the twentieth century the story became even more complicated. For many humanist scholars at mid-century, the denial of matter stemmed at least in part from an entirely noble desire to protect the essential dignity of humankind and the lives of individual humans from the very real threats of racism and fascism and a crude environmental determinism.

During the early decades of the twentieth century, the geographer Ellsworth Huntington became the leading advocate of a strong environmental determinism that focused primarily on what he termed "climatic energy." The more temperate areas of the globe, Ellsworth argued, were

---

[31] J. R. McNeill, "Observations on the Nature and Culture of Environmental History," *History and Theory* 42 (December 2003): 6.

most conducive to vigorous human health and intellectual stimulation, whereas extremely hot or cold regions farther to the south or north tended to impede the development of advanced civilization. European and northeastern American climates (where Ellsworth, a professor at Yale University, not coincidentally lived) thus dominated the globe, he argued, because their vibrant climates had created a uniquely vigorous and inventive people. While Huntington himself was not as crudely racist as some of his contemporaries and the later European fascists (contrary to the Nazis, for example, Ellsworth suggested that the Jews "are probably the greatest of all races"), climate-based environmental determinism could easily enough be turned toward justifying European imperialism and a biologically rooted racial determinism.[32]

Such was the case with the work of the American conservationist Madison Grant, whose widely read and admired 1916 book *The Passing of the Great Race, or the Racial Basis of European History*, embraced an unapologetic biological racism. The so-called Nordic peoples, he argued, had evolved in northern environments, where the challenging climate eliminated "defectives" and favored humans who were "naturally" civilized, noble, and generous. The material environment, Grant suggested, determined material biology, and biology in turn determined culture. By comparison, the darker hued peoples who had evolved in "Alpine" and "Mediterranean" environments were not just *culturally* inferior – rather, their cultural inferiority stemmed from a deeper genetically determined biological inferiority which could not be rapidly changed. Adolf Hitler was an admirer and called Grant's book "my Bible," though he preferred the term "Aryan" to "Nordic." So was Theodore Roosevelt, who further wed the proto-environmentalism of the conservationist movement to a nasty strain of racist environmental and biological determinism.[33] Meanwhile prominent industrialists like John D. Rockefeller and Andrew Carnegie embraced social Darwinism, which argued that helping the less well-off merely interfered with the salutary forces of natural selection. Francis Galton went even further to insist that states should give nature a hand by doing the selection themselves through eugenicist policies.[34]

---

[32] See especially, Ellsworth Huntington, *Civilization and Climate* (New Haven: Yale University Press, 1915); and Martin W. Lewis, "Environmental Determinism, Ellsworth Huntington, and the Decline of Geography," *GeoCurrents*, February 10, 2011.

[33] Jedediah Purdy, "Environmentalism's Racist History," *The New Yorker* (August 13, 2015).

[34] Pinker, *The Blank Slate*, 16.

Given the wide currency of such ideas and their role in creating the hydra-headed evil of eugenics, global apartheid, anti-immigrant nativism, colonial oppression, and ultimately the horrors of World War II and the Holocaust, many scholars were understandably tempted to entirely separate the realm of human culture from any links with human biology and the material environment whatsoever. In part because of his alarm over the growing anti-Semitism and nationalism in his home country of Germany, the anthropologist Franz Boas mounted an ultimately effective attack on all such material determinisms – indeed, Grant considered Boas an intellectual enemy and tried to have him fired from his teaching job at Columbia. Eager to develop a more egalitarian anthropology that would challenge the crude racism of their day, Boas and his followers helped to create the new disciplines of cultural anthropology and cultural geography where human behaviors and societies were understood as self-generated products of abstract human thinking that were largely divorced from either environmental or biological factors. Environments and material things were studied as the *reflections* of human culture, not as its creators.[35] Tellingly, Boas took some inspiration for his more immaterial idea of culture from the idealism of the Anglo-Irish philosopher George Berkeley, who argued that ideas make reality rather than material things. (You may recall that Samuel Johnson famously and vigorously rejected Berkeley's idealism by proclaiming, "I refute it thus!" and kicking a heavy rock.) Boas was thus in some sense an early proponent of what would later be termed social constructivism, though he clearly framed his views in contrast to the threat of genetic (or hereditary) determinism more than any broader rejection of the importance of biology. "I claim that, unless the contrary can be proved," he wrote, "we must assume that all complex activities are socially determined, not hereditary."[36]

Boas himself, however, did not go so far as to reject the possibility there might be traits of human nature and culture that were rooted in biology and essentially universal to the species. However, not all of his followers were as measured. As the psychologist Steven Pinker observes, in the postwar period some anthropologists seemed to suggest that *every* aspect of human existence was solely the result of cultural influences – human biology, whether of brain or body, as well as the influences of the material environment and other organisms, all became secondary if not entirely irrelevant.[37] In such a view there was little space to consider how culture

---

[35] Lewis, "Environmental Determinism."   [36] Quoted in Pinker, *Blank Slate*, 22.
[37] Pinker, *Blank Slate*, 23.

might emerge from an embodied human interaction with a creative environment. Instead, technology, language, and art were all understood primarily as the manifestations of symbolic thinking: tools for manipulating matter, not as the products of matter. The material world might constrain what human cultures could do in a practical sense, but matter – dead or alive – would increasingly become a relatively minor player in its actual creation.[38] As the anthropologist Michael Jackson has observed, this idea of culture not only separated humans from their own materiality but also from the broader world of nature: culture was defined as "the emergent properties of mind and language that separated humans from animals."[39] To be sure, important elements of materialist thinking endured – the influential anthropologist Leslie White, for example, argued that a society's technological ability to harness energy played a central role in shaping their social and cultural systems.[40] In the 1970s Marvin Harris's cultural materialism and Julian Steward's cultural ecology emphasized the functionalist value of culture, arguing it was primarily a means for adapting to the demands of the material environment. Yet the more materialist ideas of White, Harris, Steward, and others would decline in influence as postmodernist theories became increasingly dominant.

Regardless, if the motives for a highly abstracted idea of culture had often been noble, the later refusal to recognize almost any material biological basis for humans and their cultures eventually reached dangerous extremes that at times threatened to preclude rational discussion. As Pinker notes, by the post–World War II period, to suggest that human biology might play any role whatsoever in human culture was seen by many scholars "to endorse racism, sexism, war, greed, genocide, nihilism, reactionary politics, and neglect of children and the disadvantaged."[41] With the benefit of hindsight, it seems apparent that such extreme reactions were based on a confusing conflation of genetics, environment, and biology. In reality, the seeming environmental determinism of Grant, Hitler, and other racists had always been a form of

[38] Philippe Descola, *The Ecology of Others* (Chicago: Prickly Paradigm, 2013), 35.
[39] Michael Jackson, *Lifeworlds: Essays in Existential Anthropology* (Chicago: University of Chicago Press, 2012), 53.
[40] Leslie White, *The Science of Culture.*
[41] Pinker, *Blank Slate*, viii. Azar Gat notes the continuing reluctance of historians to recognize any biological explanation for why humans tend to develop fiercely held nationalistic or ethnic identities: Azar Gat, *Nations: The Long History and Deep Roots of Political Ethnicity and Nationalism* (Cambridge, UK: Cambridge University Press, 2012), 27–8.

genetic determinism. The environment mattered to them only on the macroscale where various human groups supposedly evolved over many millennia to become genetically distinct "species." Indeed, the whole point was to *deny* the possibility that the environment might influence humans on the much shorter time scales of lived human existence. An "Alpine" or "Mediterranean" people might in theory evolve to be more like the good "Nordic" folk if they moved to the supposedly more invigorating northern climes, but Grant and his supporters assumed that, absent the aggressive state-sponsored eugenics programs they advocated, the transformation would take tens of thousands of years of slow Darwinian natural selection. Even by the standards of the knowledge of the time, this crude understanding of environment and genetics was pseudoscientific nonsense. Likewise, note that there was no room to consider the ways in which different material environments might shape biological, social, and cultural patterns in the short term – the "human niche construction" that I will discuss in the next chapter. The advocates of a genetically focused environmentalism would, for example, have been entirely uninterested in considering the effects that chronic family stress, environmental toxins, insufficient nutrition, and lack of cognitive stimulation might have on brain development in children. Yet as one recent scientific study suggests, such environmental factors may play a key role in explaining why children from impoverished families have measurably less development of the cerebral cortex, an area of the brain which is critical to higher cognitive functions like language and reading.[42] Racists like Grant and Hitler wanted nothing to do with a "real-time" theory of environmental causation because it would suggest, as do many more recent scientific studies, that observed differences among individuals and groups are in significant part the results of material inequities of wealth and opportunity, *not* genetic heritage.

Indeed, as the geographer Martin Lewis argues, in their entirely justifiable desire to reject any element of genetic, biologically grounded environmental determinism, geographers also marginalized far more interesting human geographers who revealed the many non-genetic ways

---

[42] The effects of socioeconomic status on the brain are discussed in D. A. Hackman and M. J. Farah, "Socioeconomic Status and the Developing brain," *Trends in Cognitive Science* 13 (2009): 65–73. Genetic factors play a role in these differences; however, recent efforts to eliminate this variable highlight the importance of environmental factors. See Kimberly G. Noble et al., "Family Income, Parental Education, and Brain Structure in Children and Adolescents," *Nature Neuroscience* 18 (2015): 773–8, and Michael Balter, "Poverty May Affect the Growth of Children's Brains," *Science* (April 6, 2015).

in which the landscape shapes human thought and culture. For example, Ellen Church Semple, who would eventually become the first female president of Association of American Geographers, offered a more nuanced understanding of the many ways in which geography might influence the development of human culture and history in ways that clearly overwhelmed any possible racial or genetic influence.[43] In a 1901 article she attacked the claim of Anglo-Saxon racial superiority by drawing on the extensive fieldwork she had done in the isolated woodlands of eastern Kentucky, an area largely populated by the descendants of British colonists. If Anglo-Saxon heredity was the key to advanced civilization, why, Semple asked, was this region largely stagnant and economically undeveloped? The answer, she argued, lay with neither the virtues nor vices of a biological race but rather with the rugged topography and primitive transportation infrastructure in the area, which led to economic, social, and cultural isolation.[44] In this and her later works, Semple pioneered a line of geographic thought that in some ways anticipates the modern return to a more materialist and environmental understanding of the human animal. In her 1911 book *Influences of Geographic Environment*, she insisted that humans and their cultures could not be understood apart from their immersion in their material environment:

Man is a product of the earth's surface. This means not merely that he is a child of the earth, dust of her dust; but the earth has mothered him, fed him, set him tasks, directed his thoughts, confronted him with difficulties that have strengthened his body and sharpened his wits, given him his problems of navigation or irrigation, and at the same time whispered hints for their solution. She has entered into his bone and tissue, into his mind and soul ... Man can no more be scientifically studied apart from the ground which he tills, or the lands over which he travels, or the seas over which he trades, than polar bear or desert cactus can be understood apart from its habitat.[45]

But despite Semple's vigorous rejection of both racial and environmental determinism, later generations of geographers often lumped her work together with the less nuanced or overtly racist work of Huntington and

---

[43] Martin W. Lewis, "Ellen Churchill Semple and Paths Not Taken," *GeoCurrents*, February 11, 2011.

[44] Ellen Church Semple, "The Anglo-Saxons of the Kentucky Mountains: A Study in Anthrogeography," *Journal of Geography*, June 1901.

[45] Ellen Churchill Semple, *Influences of Geographic Environment on the Basis of Ratzel's System of Anthropo-Geography* (New York: Henry Holt, 1911), 1–2.

Grant. Her efforts to understand how a creative earth enters into the bones, tissues, minds, and souls of humans were largely forgotten.

Historians, for their part, were somewhat less central in developing an immaterial understanding of culture than were anthropologists. Nonetheless, the anthropological emphasis on culture as largely a product of abstract thought was not a bad fit for the profession's methodological and theoretical proclivities. As Daniel Lord Smail perceptively observes, historians had long staked out their professional territorial claims on the largely immaterial grounds of what he terms "sacred history."[46] In their recent argument for a more materially rooted "deep history," Smail and his colleagues argue that historians helped to separate culture and matter by adopting written documents, rather than artifacts or things, as their primary means of investigation. Historians left the tens of thousands of years of human "prehistory" to their colleagues in archaeology and paleoanthropology, who became increasingly adept at using scientific methods to analyze the material evidence of the past. As a result, archaeologists were, at least before the postmodern turn, better positioned to understand humans as fundamentally material creatures, while the historians' dependence on written records tended to foster a more abstract and immaterial view of humans and their history.[47]

Even self-avowedly materialist approaches to history could be oddly immaterial. Most famously, Marx and Engels turned Hegel's *Geist*-haunted idealism on its head to argue that social infrastructure was the product of a dialectical interchange with material substructures. One of the great insights of this dialectical materialism was that human identities emerge from the way they interact with the material means of subsistence available at any point in time, including both raw materials and technologies. As humans change the tools and materials they work with, they also fundamentally change themselves.[48] In this, Marx and Engels anticipated some of the key insights of recent neo-materialist thinking, which also emphasize the many ways in which humans emerge from their bodily engagement with things and environments. Nonetheless, the Marxist theoretical conception of the material world often reflected rather than

[46] Daniel Lord Smail, *Deep History and the Brain* (Berkeley: University of California Press, 2008), 3–9.
[47] Andrew Shryock, Daniel Lord Smail, and Timothy K. Earle, eds., *Deep History: The Architecture of Past and Present* (Berkeley, CA: University of California Press, 2011).
[48] Langdon Winner, "Technologies as Forms of Life," in David M. Kaplan, ed., *Readings in the Philosophy of Technology* (Oxford, UK: Rowman and Littlefield, 2004), 103–13, here 110.

challenged modernist idealism, as it still kept humans and their cultures squarely at the center of a narrative of triumphant progress and mastery over nature.[49] Echoing Noble's observations on the modern "religion of technology," Patrick Joyce and Tony Bennett observe, "Nineteenth-century materialism, and many subsequent versions (extending into the present) simply inverted the Christian division by now finding reality in the laws and hence order of the earthly and illusion in the heavens."[50] Even the materialist side of the Marxist dialectic is, as numerous commentators have noted, strangely immaterial and heavily dependent on idealist and largely anthropocentric assumptions.[51] As the archaeologist Bjørnar Olsen notes, Marxist theory recognized the central importance of productive forces like technologies and other material things in generating unsustainable contradictions within societies – the so-called social relations of production. Nonetheless, Olsen observes that in practice Marxist analyses often ignored the broader importance of all manner of other material things, treating societies and cultures "as collectives of humans held together by social relations and social forces – in short, by *people without things.*"[52] In the 1970s the Italian neo-Marxist theorist Sebastiano Timpanaro leveled a devastating critique against the essential immaterialism of traditional Marxist thought and attempted to reintegrate biological and physical materialism into the theory.[53] More recently, ecologically grounded thinkers have also incorporated a more dynamic understanding of the material world – topics I will return to in the next chapter. Nonetheless, for much of the past century, Marxist materialism suffered badly from its lack of a sufficiently robust understanding of the vibrant creative nature and ecology of material things, resulting in a tendency to focus on social relations and to view commodities, machines, and the forces of production as solely human-made phenomena.

---

[49] The essential modernist idealism of classical Marxist dialectical materialism has been noted by many scholars. Some recent examples from a neo-materialist perspective include Patrick Joyce and Tony Bennett, "Material Powers: Introduction," and John Frow, "Matter and Materialism: A Brief Pre-History of the Present," in *Material Powers: Cultural Studies, History, and the Material Turn*, ed. Tony Bennett and Patrick Joyce (London: Routledge, 2010), 29, 33.

[50] Joyce and Bennett, "Material Powers: Introduction," 1.

[51] See especially Frow, "Matter and Materialism," 29, 33.

[52] Bjørnar Olsen, *In Defense of Things: Archaeology and the Ontology of Objects* (Lanham, MD: AltaMira, 2010), 5.

[53] Sebastiano Timpanaro, *On Materialism* (London: Verso, [1970] 1980).

   Another prominent vein of materialist historical thinking was opened
up during the postwar period by Marc Bloch, Lucien Febvre, Fernand
Braudel, and others within the Annales School, particularly with their
argument that in the *longue durée* material forces of geography and
climate shape the broad outlines of human history.[54] As H. R. Trevor-
Roper put it in a 1972 overview, one of the school's defining features was
"the conviction that history is at least partly determined by forces which
are external to man and yet not entirely neuter or independent of him, nor,
for that matter, of each other: forces which are partly physical, visible,
unchanging, or at least viscous and slow to change, like geography and
climate."[55] Swept along by his careful study of the material conditions of
life and land in the Mediterranean during the sixteenth century, Braudel
writes that he came to "ask myself finally whether the Mediterranean did
not possess … its own history and destiny, a powerful vitality of its
own."[56] But while often praised, the Annalists attracted relatively few
imitators, particularly outside of France, perhaps in part because some
historians remained uncomfortable with even their very measured materialism while memories of the crude environmental and genetic determinism
of the past were still relatively fresh.[57] Nonetheless, the school's emphasis
on the importance of geography, climate, and other environmental forces
in shaping history had a significant influence on the development of
environmental history in the 1980s. For all its innovative strengths,
though, from a neo-materialist perspective the materialism of the
Annales school was, like Marxist materialism, a rather limited one.
Braudel and others tended to see the environment as a powerful but
largely static historical influence. Rather than being a dynamic source of
human creativity, knowledge, and culture over the short term, the material environment influenced history in ways that could be perceived only
over the slow passage of the *longue durée*. Like the contemporary "deep
history" it is more akin to, this was a materialism that was most useful at
the macroscale, while the shorter time spans that interest many historians

---

[54] The seminal text in this regard is Fernand Braudel, *La Méditerranée et le
monde méditerranéen a l'époque de Philippe II* (Paris: SEVPEN, 1949).

[55] H. R. Trevor-Roper, "Fernand Braudel, the Annales, and the Mediterranean,"
The Journal of Modern History 44 (1972): 468–79, quote on 470–1.

[56] Quoted in Trevor-Roper, "Fernand Braudel," 473–4.

[57] McNeill, "Observations on the Nature and Culture of Environmental History," 12. See
also John Robert McNeill, José Augusto Pádua, and Mahesh Rangarajan, *Environmental
History: As If Nature Existed* (Oxford, UK: Oxford University Press, 2010), 5.

were often reduced to mere epiphenomena, "the crests of foam that the tides of history carry on their strong backs."[58]

Yet if relatively few historians adhered to any formal materialist theory, as a practical matter many embraced a significant degree of materialism, recognizing the readily obvious point that changes in the material basis of a society influence historical developments. However, starting in the 1980s even this modest ad hoc materialism was challenged by the growing dominance of a more abstracted and anthropocentric approach to understanding the past. This so-called cultural turn was rooted in an earlier "linguistic turn" that sparked a shift toward a renewed idealism during the second half of the twentieth century that was only abetted by the postwar distrust of materialism and dominance of cultural anthropology. The roots of the linguistic turn can in part be traced back to the influential turn-of-the-century Swiss linguist Ferdinand de Saussure, who had argued that any sign, symbol, or word has two distinct parts: the "signifier," which was the physical material thing (such as a red octagonal shape or the written or spoken word "dog"), and the "signified," by which he meant the concept or thing that was expressed (such as the command to stop or a domesticated wolf). Saussure observed that the appearance or material nature of the signifier or symbol was entirely arbitrary. What really mattered was the culturally determined relationship of a signifier to other signifiers or signs in an entirely abstract system of symbols. All linguistic meaning emerged from these symbolic relationships. As the archaeologist Nicole Boivin explains, "An individual word such as 'girl' derives its meaning from its relationship to other words in the system, such as 'boy' and 'woman.'"[59] The meaning of a sign does not derive from any material properties of the sign (the signifier), and nor does it really stem from the material nature of the thing itself (the signified). The real creature that we call a "dog" might just as well be called a "girl." But more importantly, the *meaning* of words and other signs and symbols is created by their relationship to each other, Saussure argued, not by their ongoing reference to actual material things. Systems of symbols, including language, then, were abstract creations of the human mind, wholly idealist in nature. Unlike some later poststructuralists, Saussure still recognized that a society would by convention link words or other symbols to real things like a "dog." The thing being signified still mattered – all was not yet discourse for Saussure. Nonetheless, once in the realm of language he insisted the meaning associated with the word "dog" no longer came from

[58] Quoted in Trevor-Roper, "Fernand Braudel," 475.   [59] Boivin, *Material Cultures*, 32

an embodied physical experience of a real dog but rather from the internal linguistic relationship of the word "dog" to other words, like "cat," "tail," "bark," "fur," and so on.

This idealist concept of the origins of symbols and language makes a certain amount of sense – obviously whether I call the animal with whiskers and a long tail who likes to sleep on my office chair a "cat" or "neko" or "Katze" is largely arbitrary. Likewise, it seems reasonable to say that the meaning of words in a language emerge at least in part from their relationship to other words, particularly with our human tendency to understand a thing or concept in terms of binary oppositions: life-death, day-night, man-woman, and of course, nature-culture. Indeed, this more materially based formulation – what could be more material than whether an organism is dead or alive? – played an influential role in the more structurally oriented work of the anthropologist Claude Lévi-Strauss and other scholars who still believed that there must be a material foundation for language and culture in the structural nature of human bodies, brains, and things.[60] However, problems subsequently arose when *post*structuralist theorists took inspiration from linguistic theory to argue that even this circumscribed structural materialism was an error. Challenging the overconfident positivism and realism of the modernist scientific spirit that claimed to have access to a straightforward "real world," these scholars argued there was *nothing* outside of language and discourse, or at least nothing that could be accessed other than through language and discourse.[61] In the second half of the twentieth century, poststructuralists like the French philosopher Jacques Derrida developed a technique of literary analysis termed deconstruction, in essence suggesting that all human thought was fundamentally a creation of abstract systems of symbols. As Derrida famously wrote, "There is nothing outside the text." In its most radical form, deconstruction insisted that since this infinite play of symbolic differences created all meaning, and there was

---

[60] Lévi-Strauss and other structuralists were more directly influenced by the Russian-American linguist Roman Jakobson, who in turn had taken inspiration from Saussure. See Olsen, *In Defense of Things*, 41.

[61] The work of the philosopher Ludwig Wittgenstein was also often used to justify an idealist understanding of the world, as Wittgenstein, like Saussure, did reject the idea that there was a simple correlation between words and material things in the world. However, as Susan Hekman notes, Wittgenstein never went to the extreme of arguing that language was constitutive or determinative of reality. See Susan Hekman, "Constructing the Ballast: An Ontology for Feminism," in *Material Feminisms*, ed. Stacy Alaimo and Susan Hekman (Bloomington: Indiana University Press, 2008): 85–118, here 98.

no way to access reality save through language-based thought, language itself must therefore construct or determine reality. *Context* was in some sense meaningless, Derrida argued, because the world itself also acted like a text. As Bjørnar Olsen notes, Derrida and other poststructuralists did not thereby mean to suggest there was no real world beyond the text: "Rather, it opposes the idea of a strict divide between the world (or reality) on one side and the textual representation of it on the other."[62] Matter should have, at least in theory, still mattered a great deal, as things became a part of the way humans understand and think about the world around them. However, in practice many poststructuralist scholars put far more effort into analyzing the abstract and textual than in trying to discern the real world that was also supposed to be contiguous with that text. Indeed, poststructuralism largely eliminated the possibility of seriously engaging with the world of nonhuman things through its tendency to treat the scientific enterprise itself as a text that scholars could freely deconstruct while largely ignoring the material aspects and results of scientific research. Oddly, while poststructuralists often suggested scientific methods of discerning reality were shaped by discourse and thus no more accurate or true than any other discursive process, they often seemed to assume that their own methods of deconstruction were somehow more capable of accurately revealing what they saw as the more fundamental social realities that supposedly shaped scientific discourse. As the feminist theorists Stacy Alaimo and Susan Hekman note, in rightly rejecting the overconfident modernist faith that reality was easily accessible, some postmodern thinkers embraced an equally problematic and anthropocentric view in which "what we call real is a product of language and has its reality only in language."[63]

Such idealist linguistic approaches were perhaps not unreasonable when discussing the analysis of a literary text, which is, after all, almost entirely a product of language. Likewise, language is obviously one of the most powerful tools humans possess, and it deeply shapes the way we think about and interact with the world. However, today this abstract postmodern approach increasingly appears to have been based on a fundamental misunderstanding of how language and meaning emerge

---

[62] Olsen, *In Defense of Things*, 45.

[63] Stacy Alaimo and Susan Hekman, "Introduction: Emerging Models of Materiality in Feminist Theory," in *Material Feminisms*, ed. Stacy Alaimo and Susan Hekman (Bloomington: Indiana University Press, 2008), 1–2, quote on 2; and, Boivin, *Material Cultures*, 32.

in the human brain. The cognitive linguist Benjamin Bergen, for example, draws on evidence from brain imaging techniques to argue that, when we think or speak with a language, the process constantly engages parts of the brain having to do with sight, touch, sound, and other aspects of our embodied interaction with the real material world. In other words, when I speak or think with the word "cat" my brain draws on its ability to make sense of the environment where I have interacted with real cats through brain-body circuits devoted to touch, sound, smell, and so on. Our embodied sensory experience of the world thus plays a central role in creating meaning that language then manipulates to understand the real world. Contrary to Saussure's theory, this is not just an abstract process of manipulating symbolic relationships, but rather a process in which the meaning of symbols also emerges from a body, brain, and mind that is constantly interacting with material things. Even more surprisingly, these brain-body circuits kick into action even when we think about the seemingly most abstracted of concepts – freedom, truth, or justice, for example – a process that suggests even our most immaterial of ideas remain deeply rooted in our embodied interactions with the world around us.[64] We may feel or perhaps even taste "freedom" as much as we think about it in an abstract way.

At the time when postmodern theories were popular, though, these insights into the cognitive roots of language – which I will discuss in more detail in the next chapter – were still decades in the future. Absent such scientific checks, this emphasis on a highly abstracted concept of language and the related tendency to reject science as a useful guide to the material properties of the real world tended to undermine the initial poststructuralist impetus to *transcend* the boundaries between ideas and matter. Instead, much postmodern analysis developed a one-sided focus on ideas, texts, discourse, and an abstracted concept of culture, while largely ignoring or minimizing the importance of the nonhuman world of things. Moreover, the poststructural and postmodern "linguistic turn" began to move beyond departments of literature to influence historians and other humanists as part of a broader "cultural turn." Some scholars began to argue that all sorts of human phenomena were actually "texts" that thus could be freely read and deconstructed through an analytical lens that was unapologetically social and anthropocentric.[65] Even disciplines like

---

[64] Benjamin K. Bergen, *Louder Than Words: The New Science of How the Mind Makes Meaning* (New York: Basic Books, 2012).

[65] Boivin, *Material Cultures*, 13.

archaeology that had maintained a significant grounding in materialist thinking and methodologies began to embrace postmodern theories. A new generation of postmodernists criticized earlier archaeological theories like the processual school, a science-based and positivist approach that had viewed human-made material things primarily in terms of their functional use to humans in interacting with and adapting to environments. Archaeologists of the processual school believed they could use scientific techniques to arrive at an objectively accurate interpretation of past cultures and societies. By contrast, postprocessual theory stressed not the functional use of things nor their physical material qualities but rather their active role in creating societies, a role somewhat analogous to the way postmodern literary theorists argued that language created minds, ideas, and hence reality. The previous processual thinkers did not exclude the symbolic meaning of things or "material culture," which they regarded as important for marking and expressing social differences in a culture which could subsequently be read by the archaeologist.[66] But the postprocessualists, by contrast, saw material things acting as a sort of language out of which social and cultural practices emerged, thus attempting to avoid and transcend the processual opposition between the material and the cultural.[67] Somewhat in keeping with later neo-materialist thought, the postprocessualists insisted on the active role of material things in creating meaning. Crucially, though, they often saw things primarily as signs and symbols, not as real material things with functional physical properties that humans adapted to and worked with. Things were important, but they were important primarily for their symbolic and quasi-linguistic role in making human meaning, not as things in themselves. As the influential British archaeologist Christopher Tilley argued, the goal of postprocessual archaeology was the "pursuit of sign systems."[68]

Anthropology, which as I noted earlier had also often drawn a clear line between the cultural and the material, also embraced the linguistic turn and constructivist perspectives in the work of scholars like Claude Lévi-Strauss, Émile Durkheim, Mary Douglas, and Marshall Sahlins. Lévi-

[66] See, for example, Lewis R. Binford, "Archaeology as Anthropology," *American Antiquity* 28 (1962): 217–25.
[67] See Ian Hodder, *Reading the Past: Current Approaches to Interpretation in Archaeology* (Cambridge, UK: Cambridge University Press, 1986), and Matthew Johnson, *Archaeological Theory: An Introduction* (Blackwell, 1999), especially ch. 7 "Postprocessual and Interpretive Archaeologies."
[68] Boivin, *Material Cultures*, 11.

Strauss pioneered linguistically based theories that challenged more
functional explanations for much social phenomena. Animals, he
famously observed in 1962, were primarily of interest not because of
their own inherent behaviors or ecological roles, but because they were
bonnes à penser – "good to think with."[69] Likewise, kin networks and
myths, Lévi-Strauss argued, were best understood as symbolic systems
akin to language. But unlike some of his colleagues, Lévi-Strauss stopped
short of arguing that kin networks were entirely social constructs, as he
continued to believe they were ultimately a product of brain structures
that he suspected were universal to all human beings – a form of structur-
alism that poststructuralists would later question.[70] In the United States,
Clifford Geertz argued that such a "symbolic anthropology" showed
"that man is an animal suspended in webs of significance he himself has
spun," and that the analysis of these cultural webs was "not an experimental science in search of law, but an interpretive one in search of
meaning." Just as Derrida analyzed or deconstructed systems of symbolic
meaning, so, too, should anthropologists emphasize the interpretive
deconstruction of cultural meaning.[71] Geertz called for what he termed
the "thick" analysis of things and their many human connections, but
mostly only as texts whose meanings were to be "read" or deciphered by
the anthropologists.[72] Things were thick with meaning, it seems, but their
independent existence and influence outside of human ideas about them
was often painfully thin. Even as late as 1996, the anthropologists Mary
Douglas and Baron Isherwood continued to argue that the practical
chemical, physical, or biological nature of things was largely irrelevant,
or perhaps simply unknowable. Echoing Lévi-Strauss's words from 1962,
they exhorted: "Forget that commodities are good for eating; forget their
usefulness, and try instead the idea that commodities are good for
thinking."[73]

   In the social sciences, some scholars also began to argue that all
advanced human cognition and ideas were really the product of
language – that we think not with reference to the actual things around
us but rather through the words we assign to those things. However, social
scientists also often put great emphasis on the ability of the environment

[69] Lévi-Strauss, *La pensée sauvage*.   [70] Boivin, *Material Cultures*, 43.
[71] Quoted in Boivin, *Material Cultures*, 12.
[72] Clifford Geertz, *The Interpretation of Cultures: Selected Essays by Clifford Geertz*
(New York: Basic Books, 1973), 5–6.
[73] Quoted in Boivin, *Material Cultures*, 44.

to shape humans and their cultures. Also responding at least in part to the racist and genetic determinism of the first half of the century, discussed earlier, some social scientists went to the other extreme to argue that almost nothing about humans had a biological basis, whether that was the biology associated with genetics, the brain, or the body. Often the critical differences between these were not well articulated, but the tendency was to put the overwhelming causal weight on environmental rather than biological factors. The Harvard psychologist Steven Pinker refers to this as the "blank slate" theory of human nature, which he argues endured well into the twenty-first century. "A long and growing list of concepts that would seem natural to the human way of thinking (emotions, kinship, the sexes, illness, nature, the world)," Pinker observed in 2003, "are now said to be have been 'invented' or 'socially constructed.'"[74] More importantly, from a neo-materialist perspective, even though the advocates of the "blank slate" argued that the environment (nurture) created humans rather than genes (nature), their concept of the environment was largely an abstracted one, which emphasized the ways social and cultural *ideas or practices* impinged on a malleable brain. Most scholars were often far less interested in the real material properties and dynamics of the environment as a physical place of buildings, cars, cattle, trees, concrete, plastic, and countless other things with which humans actually interacted through their embodied minds and senses.[75]

The influence of postmodernist ideas varied widely between and within the disciplines devoted to studying humans, and they never went unchallenged, even where they took deepest root. An early and incisive critic was the anthropologist Michael Jackson, who observed that the turn to idealism "etherealized" both the human body and culture, transforming humans into creatures solely of mind and thought while entirely ignoring their biological engagement with the world as embodied sensory creatures. Likewise, Jackson recognized the problematic historical lineage of the cultural turn (at least as it was often actually practiced), noting that since the Enlightenment onward an idealist view of humans had repeatedly and mistakenly placed culture in opposition to the material and

---

[74] Pinker, *Blank Slate*, 6.

[75] Oddly, even as he effectively dismantles the blank slate argument of the extreme advocates of the nurture argument, Pinker has little to say about how that brain interacts with an active material world. In this, his view remains as squarely anthropocentric as that of the advocates of nurture.

biological and divided humans from all other animals.[76] In some fields, increasingly heated disagreements over postmodernism proved permanently divisive. In the 1970s anthropologists who embraced an evolutionary or ecological approach had already begun parting ways with their more culturally oriented colleagues, and the postmodern cultural turn only deepened the divisions. The cultural materialists, like Marvin Harris and Julian Steward, who saw culture as being ecologically adaptive and amenable to analysis through positivist scientific methods, had little in common with those who viewed culture as largely independent of practical material concerns and who dismissed scientific insights as social constructs.[77] Some anthropologists also attempted to blend the cultural with a more material and scientific approach, as with hybrid disciplines like cultural ecology or ecological anthropology, though these did little to bridge the deeper divide.[78] While the division was not solely driven by the debate over cultural versus material approaches, today cultural and physical anthropology are almost entirely distinct fields.[79] A similar divorce occurred in the discipline of geography, which had long taken its professional identity as the field that studied the *interactions* between the social and the material landscape – both culture and matter were required. However, as some geographers gravitated toward one or the other poles of cultural or materialist positions, the field increasingly split between "human" and "physical" geographers, with the former embracing a more humanistic (and at times postmodern) approach and the latter emphasizing the material aspects of the landscape amenable to analysis with more scientific methodologies.[80]

Traditionally more inclined to write empirically driven narratives than to engage theory, historians played an important if somewhat less central role in the early theoretical developments of postmodernism.[81] Among the first and most influential was the historian Hayden White, who in the early 1970s began to apply the tools of postmodern literary criticism to historical texts, arguing that historical narratives and sources share much in

---

[76] Michael Jackson, *Things as They Are: New Directions in Phenomenological Anthropology* (Bloomington: Indiana University Press, 1996); Boivin, *Material Cultures*, 16.

[77] Descola, *The Ecology of Others*, 12.   [78] Boivin, *Material Cultures*, 17.

[79] Descola, *The Ecology of Others*, 1–2, 19–20.

[80] The geographer Sarah Whatmore makes this point in her Latourian-inflected attempt to bring the cultural and material back together. See Sarah Whatmore, *Hybrid Geographies: Natures, Cultures, Spaces* (London: Sage, 2002), 2–3.

[81] Geoff Eley, *A Crooked Line: From Cultural History to the History of Society* (Ann Arbor: University of Michigan Press, 2005), 125.

common with literary narratives and were thus open to subjective interpretation by the reader.[82] Many other historians were subsequently influenced by elements of postmodernism, even if they may not have explicitly
identified themselves with any specific theoretical "turn." As the historian
Geoff Eley argues, the cultural turn ultimately created a "huge tectonic
shift" in historical thought that influenced nearly every field of study in the
discipline.[83] During the 1980s the previously dominant approach associated with social history – which had strong roots in Marxist dialectical
materialism, class analysis, and blue-collar history – was increasingly
challenged on theoretical and methodological grounds by new "cultural"
approaches. The cultural turn had the good effect of pushing historians to
examine how their own methods of knowledge production had been and
continued to be influenced by culturally rooted assumptions that reflected
wider dynamics of power and control in society. Nowhere was the shift
more powerfully and usefully felt than in the emergence of gender history,
which revealed the broad significance of ideas about sex and sexuality
within every field of history.[84] While earlier social historians had
succeeded in bringing more women into history, the new generation of
cultural historians now sought to interrogate deeper questions about the
ways thinking and knowledge production had for so long concentrated
power in the hands of men.[85] As the feminist scholars Stacy Alaimo and
Susan Hekman note, this postmodern feminist approach "exposed the
pernicious logic that casts women as subordinated, inferior, a mirror of
the same, or all but invisible." In what would eventually prove to also be
a signal contribution to neo-materialist theory, feminist scholars demonstrated how the male-female dichotomy underwrote other problematic
modernist dichotomies: culture-nature, mind-body, rational-emotional,
and many others.[86]

The cultural turn had a similarly salutary effect in broadening the
analysis of key social history topics like race. Whereas earlier social
historians had largely accepted the validity of race as an analytical category, the postmodern cultural historians effectively revealed the ways in
which social forces constructed ideas of race to legitimize the power of one
group over another. The turn also influenced the new work associated

[82] See especially *Metahistory: The Historical Imagination in Nineteenth-Century Europe* (Baltimore, MD: Johns Hopkins University Press, 1973).

[83] Eley, *A Crooked Line*, xii.

[84] See especially Joan Scott, "Gender: A Useful Category of Historical Analysis," *The American Historical Review* 91 (1986): 1053–75.

[85] Eley, *A Crooked Line*, 126–7.   [86] Alaimo and Hekman, "Introduction," 1–2.

with postcolonialism, as with Edward Said's trenchant critique of imperial discourses that permeated and justified global inequities of power.[87] Because it suggested that every aspect of human thought and action was implicated in weighty matters of individual, social, and national power, the cultural turn also suggested that subjects of study that might previously have been dismissed as marginal or trivial were now worthy of historical attention. Topics proliferated accordingly: fashion, shopping, travel, toys, hobbies, museums, occultism, emotions, and many others, all found their theoretically grounded chroniclers.[88]

Whether addressing gender, race, or other topics, the cultural turn in history reflected a deep debt to the work of the French philosopher Michel Foucault, a scholar who emphasized the ways in which ideas and knowledge production shaped history. In a series of influential works, Foucault suggested that the task of the historian should be to deconstruct claims of social or scientific "fact" created through "discourse" to reveal how these actually served as means of buttressing unjust regimes of power. Social power, Foucault argued, was largely based on this discursive process – the use of ideas, words, and symbols – more than on the institutional marshaling of material forces by states or other organizations. To be sure, the physical bodily power of humans – what Foucault termed "biopower" – was critical to maintaining any state, yet discursive means were key to the successful management and control of this biopower. Foucault's theory emphasized the constructed and contingent nature of human history, largely rejecting any materialist determinism. As he observed in 1981, this discursive, culturally rooted approach revealed that:

things weren't as necessary as all that; it wasn't as a matter of course that mad people came to be regarded as mentally ill; it wasn't self-evident that the only thing done with a criminal was to lock him up; it wasn't self-evident that the causes of illness were to be sought through the individual examination of bodies.[89]

But if Foucault emphasized how ideas and knowledge were contingent social creations, he never rejected the importance of materiality. To the contrary, in some of his most influential work, he argued that ideas and state power can only be effectively instituted and made visible through material things. When discussing the evolution of the technology of the modern prison, for

---

[87] The seminal work was Edward W. Said, *Orientalism* (New York: Pantheon, 1978).

[88] Eley, *A Crooked Line*, 167.

[89] Quoted in Eley, *A Crooked Line*, 128. The original is Michel Foucault, "A Question of Method: An Interview with Michel Foucault," *Ideology and Consciousness* 8 (1981): 6.

example, Foucault gave great weight to the role of physical design and function.[90] However, as was often the case with the cultural turn in general, Foucault's materialist leanings received far less attention than did his more postmodern discursive and textual ideas. Perhaps this should come as no surprise. As Bjørnar Olsen notes, Foucault's empowering argument that social realities could be recreated through changes in discourse was surely more appealing to many humanists than his "somewhat dismal analysis of alienating disciplinary technologies."[91]

As already suggested, postmodernist theories also gained a powerful foothold among historians studying the history of science. As a discipline that had previously claimed to unproblematically reveal essential and enduring truths about the world, science was indeed ripe for some much needed deconstruction. Constructivist approaches were particularly influential among historians working under the rubric of Science, Technology, and Society studies, which often had strong connections to the more theoretically driven world of sociology. Beginning in the 1980s, a storm of articles and monographs appeared that sought to uncover what the historian of science Ian Hacking termed the "social construction of X," where "X" was the seemingly real thing or concept that the author proposed to carve open to demonstrate the sociopolitical forces hiding within.[92] Another approach rooted in sociology, the Social Construction of Technology (SCOT), became a powerful tool among historians of technology to push back against overly simplistic theories of technological determinism. By emphasizing how different social groups constructed or used technologies in unique ways, the advocates of SCOT argued that technology did not drive society – people and their institutions did. SCOT thus offered an (often deliberate) antidote to the modern fatalism that saw technological change as an unstoppable juggernaut, seeking instead to empower people to take greater control over the course of technological development.

As with other aspects of the cultural turn, there was much of value in SCOT. Humans do make decisions about technologies all the time and can shape its historical trajectory. However, the rise of SCOT also offers

---

[90] Michel Foucault, *Discipline & Punish: The Birth of the Prison*, trans. Alan Sheridan (New York: Vintage, [1975] 1995).

[91] Olsen, *In Defense of Things*, 46.

[92] Ian Hacking, *The Social Construction of What?* (Cambridge, MA: Harvard University Press, 1999), 5–7. See also the chapter "Do You Believe in Reality?" in Bruno Latour, *Pandora's Hope: Essays on the Reality of Science Studies* (Cambridge, MA: Harvard University Press, 1999), 1–23.

a good example of the limits of social constructivism. An excessive focus on a postmodern cultural constructivist framing could all too easily lead to a dangerous neglect of the real material nature of technologies and technical systems, which, if not autonomous, were also not always easily malleable abstractions. As the urban historian Chris Otter suggests in his recent critique of SCOT, the fundamental problem is in the largely unexamined assumption that material things like technologies are somehow clearly distinct from the culture that supposedly shapes them. To view society as shaping technology, Otter argues, "is to operate at a level of abstraction that obscures as much as it reveals" and which "introduces analytic partitions into a world typified by circulation and metabolism."[93] In a similar way, the cultural turn's emphasis on the importance of ideas and knowledge, with their nearly infinite possibilities for variation among individuals and societies at all scales, seemed to preclude older economic or structural explanations for history, including technological ones. "Previously attractive structuralisms," Eley observes, "now seemed 'reductionist' or 'reductive' in their logic and effects."[94] But if these earlier structural approaches had been too limited in their simplistic overconfidence, in their place came an equally problematic understanding of culture as a totalizing force that threatened to reduce all other aspects of human existence to its imperatives. As the historian Carolyn Steadman puts it: this hegemonic view largely ignored the nonhuman material world, suggesting instead "the notion of 'culture' as the bottom line, the real historical reality."[95]

It is with such a fundamentally anthropocentric view of humans and their place on the planet that neo-materialist approaches most sharply part ways with the cultural turn. As the geographer Sarah Whatmore argues, it is easy to exaggerate the idealism of the cultural turn. "Only the most vulgar of 'constructionist' accounts," she notes, maintained that the world was "'the product of an immaculate linguistic conception.'"[96] Yet if the extremes were perhaps rare, there can be little question that the cultural turn was in many ways a turn away from materiality and toward a concept of history in which an idealist culture with roots in a highly abstracted theory of language was the dominant if not hegemonic force.

---

[93] Chris Otter, "Locating Matter: The Place of Materiality in Urban History," in *Material Powers: Cultural Studies, History and the Material Turn*, ed. Tony Bennett and Patrick Joyce (London: Routledge, 2010), 25–37, here 54.

[94] Eley, *A Crooked Line*, 185.   [95] Quoted in Eley, *A Crooked Line*, 194.

[96] Whatmore, *Hybrid Geographies*, 1–2.

Indeed, if the cultural turn had been nothing more than a call to recognize the importance of human ideas and beliefs in shaping history, this was hardly a "turn" at all. As I noted earlier in Chapter 1, R. G. Collingwood had argued, way back in 1946, that abstract human thought or culture was the historian's sole legitimate topic. Hence the theoretical and methodological novelty of the cultural turn depended to a significant degree on its assertion that cultural forces played the leading role in determining the course of history, while the nonhuman material world was both shaped by and understood through discursive means that reflected social and cultural dynamics. While perhaps not the theoretical intent, the results tended toward an unapologetic and largely unexamined anthropocentrism that tended to marginalize the importance of the nonhuman material world, whether natural or anthropogenic. Frequently these were errors not of commission but of omission: scholars may not have deliberately denied the importance of material things in any theoretical sense, yet in practice the material was often ignored, since all the exciting insights were assumed to be found in the realm of culture, discourse, and ideas. Even scholars whose intent was to challenge older modernist dichotomies frequently replaced these with an equally problematic dichotomy between language and reality. How a human body, physical process, or technology actually functioned mattered less than how various social groups *believed* it functioned. Likewise, the idea that other nonhuman animals might also have a form of culture or creativity that influenced the course of history was largely ignored, as was the possibility that human ideas emerged at least in part from their engagement with that world and could not be accurately understood apart from this engagement. As the historian of science Paul Edwards has recently noted, postmodern constructivism of many stripes created a strange new type of Cartesian dualism: "It depicts physical reality as inaccessible and insignificant even while taking social realities – people's views and their ways of influencing each other – as transparently and directly knowable, not to mention all-powerful."[97] Thus the poststructuralist hope to collapse the wall between the cultural and material had instead often reinforced it, making it all but impossible to recognize the vital creative energy of a material world that had, after all, made humans and their ideas in the first place.

---

[97] Paul Edwards, *A Vast Machine: Computer Models, Climate Data, and the Politics of Global Warming* (Cambridge, MA: MIT Press, 2010), 437–8.

How can we account for the meteoric rise and broad influence of postmodernist thought among humanists and so many other scholars? Geoff Eley
argues that the cultural turn was at least in part a product of the growing
internal problems of the previously dominant social history, as its accepted
categories of structural analysis – race, class, and gender – came to seem
increasingly problematic.[98] No doubt many postmodern advocates were
also influenced by the rapid progress made by blacks, women, gays, and
other social groups, which suggested the immense power of ideas and action
to shape historic change as well as new ways of doing history. Likewise, the
fall of the Soviet Union and dissolution of the Eastern Block seemed to
suggest that grand overarching historical narratives were literally giving
way to a more fragmented and individually liberating world of possibilities.
Ironically, given the battles between scientists and constructivists in the so-
called science wars of the 1980s, the extraordinary accomplishments of
postwar science and engineering in curing disease, feeding a growing global
population, and even putting humans on the moon may have also helped to
engender an optimistic spirit of possibility, even in the face of the dark pall
cast by DDT, nuclear weapons, and other technologies. In this sense, the
postmodern faith in the power of ideas and discourse might well be understood as the ultimate outcome of the extraordinary postwar expansion of
real material wealth and abundance. Perhaps only scholars who were largely
distanced from the everyday demands of material sustenance and maintenance could begin to believe that discourse in some sense constituted reality.

However, the humanistic turn to idealism was also at least in part
a reaction against the overreach of some materially grounded biologists
and other scientists during the 1970s and 1980s. Many humanists were
alarmed by the rapid rise of the neo-Darwinian synthesis with its emphasis
on genes as determinative factors in animal behaviors, particularly when
the advocates of sociobiology tried to apply these insights to human
history and culture in ways that seemed to echo the genetic and environmental determinism of the first half of the century. Most famously and
notoriously the Harvard biologist Edward O. Wilson suggested in the final
chapter of his 1975 text *Sociobiology* that human behaviors like aggression and homosexuality were largely a result of genetics and could be
explained in terms of evolutionary fitness.[99] One of the best-selling

[98] Eley, *A Crooked Line*, 126.

[99] E. O. Wilson, *Sociobiology: The New Synthesis* (Cambridge, MA: Harvard University
Press, 1975). See also "History Meets Biology: Introduction," *American Historical
Review* 119 (2014): 1492–9, here 1494.

popular science books of the 1970s was the evolutionary biologist Richard Dawkin's *The Selfish Gene*. As the title suggests, Dawkins proposed that organisms were straightforward expressions of their genes and thus should be understood merely as the vehicles by which the eponymous "selfish genes" strove to maximize their own reproduction, including through hardwired cultural and social behaviors.[100] In the face of such neo-Darwinian arguments, the realm of "nature" seemed to be on the brink of eclipsing the realm of "nurture" that had long been the province of historians, humanists, and social scientists. In reality, the risk was probably not as great as it might have seemed. Even at the time, many other scientists were objecting to such an overly reductive gene-centered model. The evolutionary biologist Richard Lewontin, for example, insisted on the importance of nurture, or the material environment, in shaping the biological development of an organism. As the modern field of evolutionary developmental biology now fully recognizes, the material, social, and cultural environment deeply influences how genes are expressed in a living organism. Evolutionary natural selection acts on an embodied material being, not on an abstracted genetic code – a topic discussed in more detail in the next chapter.[101] In an early statement of what would later come to be known as niche construction theory, Lewontin also stressed that organisms adapt to and develop in an environment that they themselves have helped to create.[102] Organisms are, in some sense, their environments.

Despite these ongoing scientific debates, many humanists and social scientists were understandably concerned by what they viewed as an attempt to reduce their disciplines to branches of biology.[103] Some were perhaps equally worried that the rising influence of scientific experts in the public sphere commenting on cultural and social matter might come at the price of a decline in the influence of humanists. Given these and other factors, the postmodern cultural turn offered an attractive alternative to both genetic determinism and scientific hegemony, an

[100] Richard Dawkins, *The Selfish Gene* (Oxford, UK: Oxford University Press, 1976).

[101] See, for example, Andrews Wagner, *The Arrival of the Fittest: How Nature Innovates* (New York: Current, 2014), and Matt Ridley, *Nature via Nurture: Genes, Experience, and What Makes Us Human* (New York: Harper, 2003).

[102] Richard Lewontin, "Gene, Organism, and Environment," in *Evolution from Molecules to Men*, ed. D. S. Bendall (Cambridge, UK: Cambridge University Press, 1983), 273–85, and, Lewontin, *The Triple Helix: Gene, Organism and Environment* (Cambridge, MA: Harvard University Press, 2000).

[103] "History Meets Biology: Introduction," 1494–5.

alternative that emphasized the powerful role of ideas, culture, and other topics that the humanists were best prepared to study and explain. Postmodernism also suggested a more hopeful and optimistic view of human potentialities than the idea that humans were nothing more than robotic containers for their "selfish genes" fighting for survival. As the historian Carl Degler notes, "Ideology or a philosophical belief that the world could be a freer and more just place played a large part in the shift from biology to culture," and at its root lay "the will to establish a social order in which innate and immutable forces of biology played no role in accounting for the behavior of social groups."[104] At the same time a generation of historians who came of age in the revolutionary ferment of the sixties and seventies saw historical studies as a means of furthering these societal transformations. As Geoff Eley himself notes, "I wanted to become a historian because history really *mattered*; it was necessary for making a difference."[105]

At base, a strong antimaterialist stance made a great deal of sense if biology and other material factors were indeed understood as "innate and immutable forces" that were the antithesis of human social, political, and cultural creativity. And this understanding often prevailed at the time, even if the actual theoretical underpinnings of postmodern thought were more nuanced. However, as I will argue in the chapters to come, such a view now appears to reflect an entirely mistaken understanding of both our human biology and the wider material world within which we are intimately embedded. But this new understanding had to await the development of powerful new ideas in the sciences and humanities, the consequences of which we are only just beginning to grapple with today. Yet in offering an at times extreme idealism to counter an at times extreme biological reductionism, humanists ironically reinforced the deeper and more problematic distinctions between mind and body, culture and matter, and technology and nature. As the sociologist Peter Freund observed already in the 1980s, this effectively eliminated "any consideration of continuities between humans and the biological natural world."[106] Or, as Steven Pinker later noted, "It divides matter from mind, the material from the spiritual, the physical from the mental, biology from culture, nature from society, and the sciences from the social sciences,

[104] Quoted in Pinker, *Blank Slate*, 17.   [105] Eley, *Crooked Line*, ix.
[106] Quoted in Boivin, *Material Cultures*, 66. The original is Peter E. S. Freund, "Bringing Society into the Body: Understanding Socialized Human Nature," *Theory and Society* 17 (1988): 839–64, quote on 839.

humanities, and arts."[107] In their effort to avoid problematic genetic and environmental determinisms, postmodernists unintentionally marginalized a much-broader material world of creative things, both biotic and abiotic, that play a central role in making us human.

CONCLUSION

Precisely because many Western thinkers saw humans and their abstract minds as distinctly above and apart from the material world, they saw little reason to exercise much restraint in changing their environments or adopting new natural resources and technologies. As I will discuss in the next chapter, there have long been alternatives – the ideas of animist societies, for example, which viewed humans as emerging from their material world, not in opposition to it. In contrast with an idealist view of humans, a more materially grounded ontology tends to inspire a certain modest conservatism. If you believe that who you are as an individual or the qualities of the culture you live within emerges from the other creatures and things in your environment, you are perhaps more likely to avoid making reckless changes. Such a genuine conservatism seems entirely foreign to the modernist view that essentially worships human ingenuity and "disruptive" inventions. Those who call themselves conservatives today are often enthusiastic backers and defenders of transformative new technologies and massive engineering projects that promise to radically reshape the face of the planet. That these supposed conservatives believe they can fundamentally alter the way human beings live yet not fundamentally alter who they are, is yet further evidence of the bizarre modernist faith that the *true* spirit of the human resides in a transcendent mind or spirit or culture, not in an earthly material body and its environment. Ironically, while many postmodernists were perhaps politically opposed to the rise of neoliberal globalism in the later decades of the twentieth century, in some ways their theoretical focus on the primacy of discourse rather than materiality helped to enable the modern era of rapid global change driven by unfettered capitalism and free markets. If a disembodied and immaterial culture largely determines our fates, we need not worry excessively about the constant disruptions bred by new technologies and reconfigured environments.

In the pages to come, I will argue that this modern view is fundamentally and dangerously mistaken, as are other forms of idealism that deny

---

[107] Pinker, *Blank Slate*, 31.

the material nature of human existence. Because they believe they can use powerful material things largely as they wish, humans often become trapped into patterns that they did not intend but find it difficult to escape. Modern humans are, for example, a metallic species. We have long partnered with the earth's metals and minerals to survive and thrive. These human-mineral partnerships were never entirely inevitable. Certainly the minerals did not force themselves onto us, nor did they even choose us in the very specific ways in which wolves may have chosen to become domesticated because it benefited them. Nonetheless, we often tend to exaggerate our agency in these matters, always claiming active verbs for ourselves: humans discovered, or exploited, or used minerals. Less prone to brag, the minerals themselves speak through their extraordinary molecular abilities to transmit electricity, store the sun's energy, or perform countless other tasks essential to modern technological society. Sometimes they remind us in ways humans find less agreeable, as when copper arsenics poison our farmlands or coal carbon dioxides heat up the climate.

Just such a reminder is even now being offered at the Cradle of Humankind in South Africa. Having first nurtured the early hominin creatures who were capable of simple mining, the Cradle of Humankind itself is now threatened by some of the descendants of the *australopithecine* Mrs. Ples who have since learned to engage in mining at a much larger scale. As I noted at the start of the chapter, the Witwatersrand mines eventually proved to be the richest gold deposits in the world.[108] By the year 2000, more than half of the current supply of gold in the world, some 45,000 tons, had been extracted from its ancient rocks.[109] But the Witwatersrand gold ran deep, so mining engineers from all around the world converged there to develop technologies for sending humans farther down into the earth's crust than had ever been thought possible. Today, gold mines in the area sink nearly four kilometers (2.4 miles) below the surface. However, the Witwatersrand gold deposits have always been closely associated with the iron sulfide mineral called pyrite, which is often referred to as fool's gold because its shiny grains can easily dupe the unknowing. But perhaps the mineral is even more aptly named for the humans foolish enough to mine the gold and other valuable

---

[108] J. F. Durand, J. Meeuvis, and M. Fourie, "The Threat of Mine Effluent to the UNESCO Status of the Cradle of Humankind World Heritage Site," *TD: The Journal for Transdisciplinary Research in Southern Africa* 6 (July 2010): 73–92, here 78.

[109] Hilton-Barber and Berger, *The Official Field Guide*, 46.

minerals associated with it. When the pyrite in the Witwatersrand fool's gold comes into contact with water and oxygen, the sulfur dissolves out to produce the chemical H_2SO_4 – better known as sulfuric acid. Over the many decades when the deep mines were active, pumps kept them free of water. But when some were abandoned in the postwar era, the pumps were turned off and the mines began to flood. The chemical consequence has been a massive flow of acid mine drainage throughout the Witwatersrand subterranean rocks that releases dissolved heavy metals like cadmium, arsenic, and other toxins into both surface and ground-water. To completely flood the vast underground mine passages has taken decades. But in 2002, some of the low-lying surface springs near the mines that had been dry began to run again for the first time in a century – but now carrying heavy metal–laden acid mine water.

As you may remember, the early Dutch settlers called the cave where Robert Broom discovered the two million year old bones of the *Australopithecus africanus* Mrs. Ples at Sterkfontein, or "strong spring." The underground passages at Sterkfontein had always dripped with streams and pools of groundwater: the water made the caves in the first place, over the course of millions of years. But now the far more acidic groundwater created by the deep Witwatersrand gold mines is slowly but steadily flowing straight toward Sterkfontein and the entire Cradle of Humankind. The acid mine drainage has already reached some parts of the site, and it is beginning to dissolve the porous limestone cave passages and the many ancient fossilized bones and artifacts they contain.[110] The acid mine waste threatens both the human present and past, as the heavy metals are also contaminating ground water used for drinking and farming. In the Cradle itself, the results could be sinkholes, collapse, and irreparable damage to the unique paleoanthropological wealth still contained there. In the words of one report, the destruction of a site so "essential for our understanding of human evolution, may be considered to be a crime against humanity."[111]

If it is a crime, then it is obviously in some sense a self-inflicted one, as are so many of our modern problems. The acidic destruction of the Cradle of Humankind offers an apt example of what the philosopher Leif Wenar has termed the "crises of invention," which he predicts will increasingly plague humanity now that the earlier threats like disease and starvation

[110] Sheree Bega, "Acid Mine Water Threatens Cradle of Humankind," *Saving Water SA* (April 18, 2010).
[111] Durand, "Threat of Mine Effluent," 79–83, quote on 82.

have been sharply reduced. "Our science is now so penetrating, our systems are so robust," Wenar observes, "that we are mostly endangered by our creations."[112] Wenar is probably right about this, but we should also bear in mind that part of the reason humans are now endangered by their own technologies is because these were never solely ours in the first place. We can only be surprised that "our" technologies go their own way because we mistakenly believe that we *create* technologies out of a passive material world that is distinct from us, much like a god might create a garden and fill it with creatures. Yet such a view denies the reality that our technologies do not remove us from nature but rather embed us ever more deeply within its often-unpredictable powers. So it is that the age-old Western faith that humans left Eden has come full circle to destroy a genuine Garden of Eden. Western humans made an immense error when they concluded that their intelligence, creativity, and unprecedented power came from some mysterious divine spark or immaterial mind that set them apart from the very world that created and sustained these. Yet as the acid mine drainage literally dissolves the divide between the human and the natural at the Cradle of Humankind, perhaps it is not too late to realize that we never left Eden at all.

---

[112] Leif Wenar, "Is Humanity Getting Better?" *New York Times*, February 15, 2016.

3

Natural-Born Humans

A Neo-materialist Theory and Method of History

Do a Google search with the phrase "humans are natural born" and you will get back hundreds of hits for sites examining the degree to which humans are natural-born killers, liars, swimmers, explorers, artists, runners, nature lovers, and many more. A few will actually be about "natural-born humans" but only in the sense of natural versus assisted (and presumably less natural) ways of giving birth. Yet among all of these speculations about what is and is not natural about humans, you will have a hard time finding any serious claim that humans are *entirely* natural. To the contrary, the whole point of most of these discussions is that there are some things about humans that are natural and others that are *un*natural, and that we can and should figure out which is which.

This raises an interesting question: What did human beings do, and when did they first do it, to become unnatural? Everyone recognizes, of course, that modern humans have more-or-less natural bodies, a few titanium knees or ceramic teeth notwithstanding. And no one questions that we depend on natural things and processes to survive – just try growing corn without a corn seed. But as the only creatures that build towering concrete cities, explode atomic bombs, and rewrite genetic code, it also seems obvious that humans are very different from all the other animals around them. We routinely talk about artificial technologies or synthetic things, and we take it for granted that humans can behave in ways that are more or less natural. Yet if we were to go back far enough along the branching evolutionary path that led to our own species, we would eventually find ancestors that most of us would have no trouble deeming *entirely* natural – or at least as natural as modern-day chimpanzees, apes, and other primates. So what happened? What did our ancestors do to become the first creatures on the planet to get kicked out of the "100 Percent–Natural Club?"

Given how important this question is to our sense of what it means to be "human," you would be forgiven for assuming that there is a clear answer. But you would be wrong. Part of the problem is that our definitions of "natural" or "unnatural" are hopelessly circular. Something is natural because it exists or happens without any human involvement – because it comes from a separate nonhuman nature. But this obviously just brings us back to why we assume humans aren't part of nature in the first place. Arguing that we are unnatural because we aren't part of nature is a not very helpful tautology. Perhaps a more illuminating approach would be to focus on when humans became markedly *different* from other animals, leaving aside for a moment whether or not these differences actually made them unnatural. But there are no entirely clear answers here either. Some paleoanthropologists argue that anatomically modern humans living in Europe abruptly diverged from the rest of the natural world only about 40,000–50,000 years ago, a process that has been termed the human revolution.[1] Others argue that the divergence was a much more gradual process that began as long as 300,000 years ago among our more distant ancestors living in Africa.[2] Researchers also debate the degree to which these divergent behaviors were a result of significant anatomical changes, particularly in the size and abilities of brains.[3]

Still, most anthropologists do agree on one thing: that at some point in the past our ancestors began to do some unusual things. They made stone tools. They painted pictures and created symbols. They exploited their environment in ways that required foresight and planning. They talked. A bit prosaically, paleoanthropologists call this the advent of modern human behavior: how our ancestors became more like people today and less like the "natural" animals they had evolved from. It marked the

[1] A cogent explanation of the "human revolution" view is offered in Richard G. Klein, *The Human Career: Human Biological and Cultural Origins*, 3rd ed. (Chicago: University of Chicago Press, 2009). An earlier seminal use of the human revolution concept is L. R. Binford, "Human Ancestors: Changing Views of Their Behavior," *Journal of Anthropological Archaeology* 4 (1985): 292–327.

[2] Sally McBrearty and Alison S. Brooks, "The Revolution That Wasn't: A New Interpretation of the Origin of Modern Human Behavior," *Journal of Human Evolution* 39 (2000): 453–563.

[3] Klein argues that a genetic mutation in human brains about 50,000 years ago accounts for the rise of cognitively and behaviorally modern humans. See Richard G. Klein and Blake Edgar, *The Dawn of Human Culture: A Bold New Theory on What Sparked the "Big Bang" of Human Consciousness* (New York: Wiley, 2002), 24–5.

appearance of what we often call culture: art, technology, complex symbolic communication, and so on. Behaviors that are typically understood as predominately learned rather than instinctual. Probably every group of humans, or perhaps even protohumans, since that divergence began to take root has offered some explanation of how it came to pass that they did such strange things. Why do we paint pictures and make stone spearheads while gorillas and crows do not?

As I argued in the previous chapter, in the Western tradition one not unreasonable answer was that humans must have been created by supernatural beings, whether that was a god from the heavens or a big black alien monolith from outer space. Yet there is reason to believe that there has long been another widely used explanation, one that perhaps even predominated for much of the history of *Homo* on the planet. Among the modern peoples whose ways of life are perhaps somewhat similar to those of our more distant ancestors, many would still find the idea that humans are unnatural largely nonsensical. Not because they do not recognize the obvious point that humans do some things differently than other animals. But because they assume that these unusual behaviors came in significant part *from* a natural world that is dynamic, creative, and even intelligent. In other words, they would recognize that humans act differently, but reject the idea that these differences necessarily make humans unnatural. To their way of thinking, human beings don't belong in an entirely different box than all the other creative organisms around them.

Consider, for example, the Achuar people who live in the lush Amazonian jungles along the border between Ecuador and Peru, a fiercely independent tribe of the Jivaro Indians whose reputation for headhunting kept them largely isolated for centuries. After several years of living with them and mastering their language in the late 1970s, the French anthropologist Philippe Descola (a student of Claude Lévi-Strauss) eventually came to understand that Achuar women consider the plants they cultivate to be akin to their children. Achuar men regard the animals they hunt to be their brothers-in-law. These are not just metaphors or artifacts of translation. For the Achuar, many plants and animals have souls just like human beings and thus are social partners whose cooperation must be won through respectful treatment. They are as much a part of the Achuar culture as are their human relatives.[4] Like

---

[4] Philippe Descola, *Beyond Nature and Culture*, trans. Janet Lloyd (Chicago: University of Chicago Press, 2014), 3–6. The original French edition is *Par-delà nature et culture* (Paris, 2005).

many other animistic thinkers, the Achuar see the world as teeming with other sentient beings and things who to varying degrees understand and respond to human actions. Hence a good part of whatever it is that makes humans different or special comes *from* their intimate connections with a lively natural world that produces all sorts of other intelligent and creative beings – not from rising above it. "To say that the Indians are 'close to nature' is a kind of nonsense," Descola observes. "In order for anyone to be close to nature, nature must exist; and it is only the moderns who have proved capable of conceiving its existence, a fact that probably renders our cosmology more enigmatic and less sympathetic than the cosmologies of all the cultures that have preceded us."[5]

The Achuar have managed to maintain much of their independence and culture to this day. However, the discovery of oil, gold, and other valuable commodities in recent decades has increasingly brought the largely unwelcome attention of international energy, mining, and logging companies to the region. Many, though not all, of the Achuar have emerged as fierce and well-organized opponents of these attempts to exploit their homelands. As Germàn Freire, the president of the Achuar Nation of Ecuador, said in a speech to the United Nations, his people seek a more sustainable future: "We, the Achuar, were born in the forest, our traditions are still intact, our land untouched by logging or oil companies and our skies covered by flocks of colourful Macaws."[6] The Achuar protestors achieved a signal victory in 2012 when the Canadian oil company Talisman Energy announced it would cease all exploration projects not only in the Achuar territory but all of Peru.[7] Whether other companies will come if the extraordinarily low current price for oil eventually returns to its more typical historic highs remains to be seen.

From a historical perspective, however, the Achuar's success in protecting their land and culture is unfortunately somewhat exceptional. When animistic and Western peoples collided in the centuries past, the outcome was often sadly predictable. The Europeans were quick to demonstrate the supposed superiority of their own worldview by pointing out their big black ships, rattling their steel swords and tools, or making a lot of smoke and noise (or, worse, death and destruction) with their guns and cannons.

[5] Philippe Descola, *The Spears of Twilight: Life and Death in the Amazon Jungle*, trans. Janet Lloyd (New York: New Press, [1993] 1996), 406.
[6] Quoted in Gavin Armstrong, Nathan Lachowsky, and Alastair Summerlee, "The Achuar of the Amazon," *Queens Quarterly* 117 (2010): 516–29, quote on 518.
[7] Amazon Watch. "The Achuar of Peru." Amazonwatch.org, accessed on January 18, 2017. http://amazonwatch.org/work/achuar.

The Europeans believed that the people with the most impressive technologies were the most impressive people, as technology was a sign of their divine creation. Machines, as one historian of these encounters puts it, were supposed to be the measure of men.[8] Many in their intended audience were indeed impressed, and, as we will see, some quickly began to figure out ways they could get their hands on similar technologies, if for no other reason than to defend themselves. Still, that doesn't mean that it was clear to these animistic thinkers why having powerful machines meant that the Europeans had left the natural world behind. Animistic peoples had many technologies of their own – blow guns, deadly poisons, clever traps, and bountiful gardens. But that hardly meant that they were unnatural. A successful garden depended not just on human work and creativity but on the cooperative efforts of the plants themselves. Didn't the Europeans' big ships and noisy guns come from nature as well? Were these people – who certainly appeared to be mortal human beings like anyone else – really claiming that they were somehow *super*natural, above and apart from nature like a bunch of small white gods?

As I suggested in the previous chapter, this is exactly what they were claiming, or at least something very close to it. To the Achuar and other animistic peoples, such technological accomplishments could be understood as gifts from the dynamic and creative nature of which they were still very much a part. Whatever it was that made humans special came in significant part from the living world around them. It was a bottom-up theory. For centuries, most Western thinkers viewed such animistic ideas as primitive superstitions. As the descendants of Adam and Eve, who had left Eden and nature behind, their model was top-down: by definition, technological creativity and ability were unnatural because they were gifts from a supernatural God. Somewhat confusingly, Philippe Descola has termed this Western cosmology as the "naturalistic" view: naturalistic peoples believed that humans had parted ways with nature to become its unnatural masters. As a result, they could develop the singularly odd idea that there was a nature that was clearly distinct from humans and their cultures – a "naturalistic" rather than animistic view. To be sure, in the mid-nineteenth century Darwin would show that humans were biologically still animals – a serious blow to the idea that humans were unnatural but not, as it turns out, a fatal one. Even if humans were still animals, the defenders of human exceptionalism responded, their technology,

---

[8] Michael Adas, *Machines as the Measure of Men: Science, Technology, and Ideologies of Western Dominance* (Ithaca, NY: Cornell University Press, 1990).

language, and culture still gave them nearly god-like powers to reshape nature to their liking. For most naturalistic Western thinkers, animism was long seen as a sign of a primitive culture, one still ignorant of the truth that nature was a machine with universal laws that physics, chemistry, and biology could reveal. The key to becoming more powerful was to become more *unnatural*, to continually expand the gap between humans and the rest of the world. Plants and animals were not our relatives or a key source of human power, ideas, and culture. They were our tools.

Of course, the history of all this is more complicated than I can do justice to here. Both animistic and naturalistic ways of thinking are diverse and have changed over time, and they are only two among a variety of other ways of understanding the human place in the world. Likewise, some Westerners might agree that humans and their technologies are still natural, while even the most committed of animists might find it hard to accept a nuclear reactor as entirely natural. Nor do I mean to romanticize the Achuar as proto-ecologists who lived in perfect harmony with nature. The Achuar had some decidedly mistaken ideas about other animals: for example, Descola records that they believed that one whiff of flatulence from a great anteater could liquefy human bone marrow.[9] Still, it is worthwhile to begin here by highlighting the differences between naturalistic and animistic ideas because one of the main goals of this chapter is to convince you that people like the Achuar in some broad sense got it more-or-less right: humans still are members in good standing of the 100 Percent–Natural Club. This doesn't mean that we have to agree with the Achuar that plants and animals are literally our relatives, though we could do a lot worse than that, and have. Nor does it mean we should ignore all of the scientific and technological insights that the Western naturalistic worldview helped to generate. To the contrary, the extraordinary thing is that the Western tradition of scientific research has increasingly revealed a world that often looks more like the Achuars' than Descartes's.

In this chapter, I bring together recent insights from the humanities, sciences, and social sciences to develop a broad theoretical and methodological approach that better recognizes the many ways in which humans and their histories emerge from our engagement with the plants, animals, minerals, and other material things around us. In the past, the belief that humans were unnatural contributed to countless problems and tragedies we might have otherwise avoided. Today it keeps us from fully realizing

[9] Descola, *The Spears of Twilight*, 76.

the immense power of our material world simultaneously to endanger us and to make us better creatures. Ironically, at this perilous stage in human history when many assume we have never been less natural, our future might well depend on embracing the entirely opposite idea: that we are natural-born humans.

A MATTER OF THINGS

The time has come to talk of things – if not of ships and shoes and sealing wax, then definitely of Longhorns, silkworms, copper, and countless other material things great and small. As I argued in the previous chapter, for much of the past three decades, postmodern and social constructivist views have tended to dominate the academic solar system, at least on a theoretical level, tending to minimize the importance of the non-human world. But in more recent years the planets have begun to realign as scholars have rediscovered the importance of things, which is to say, the totality of the organisms, substances, and processes that constitutes the material environment. While no one questions that the human animal excels in inventing history-shaping stories and ideas, both founded and fantastic, the neglect of the materiality cloaked within these narratives has come to seem increasingly untenable. In his surprising 2009 manifesto "The Climate of History," the prominent postcolonial scholar Dipesh Chakrabarty rightly suggests that current scholarly approaches to understanding the past are inadequate to meet the challenges of the present. Historians, he argues, must begin to "look on human history as part of the history of life ... on this planet."[10] Grappling with the realities emerging from global climate change, revolutionary developments in epigenetic theory, and new scientific insights into the plasticity of both minds and brains, scholars from many disciplines are squarely challenging the modernist assumption that human culture is largely or entirely unmoored from matter. Scholars are beginning to recognize the power of material things and processes to shape the course of history in ways that were impossible

---

[10] Dipesh Chakrabarty, "The Climate of History: Four Theses," *Critical Inquiry* 35 (2009), 197–222, quote on 198. For further comments on the significance of Chakrabarty's ideas, see Timothy James LeCain, "Heralding a New Humanism: The Radical Implications of Chakrabarty's Four Theses," in "Whose Anthropocene? Revisiting Dipesh Chakrabarty's 'Four Theses,'" ed. Robert Emmett and Thomas Lekan, special issue, *Rachel Carson Center Perspectives: Transformations in Environment and Society* 2 (2016): 15–20.

to imagine just a decade ago. Even our current concepts of humanism may not survive the resulting intellectual upheavals intact.

In his recent career-defining magnum opus, Philippe Descola takes some inspiration from the Achuar people he had studied when he exhorts scholars to move "beyond nature and culture." Instead, he suggests we might do better to learn from the many non-Western peoples (Eurocentrism being a particularly virulent strain of anthropocentrism), like the Achuar, whose animistic worldviews make such dichotomies largely nonsensical. Anthropology, Descola writes, must come "to include in its object far more than the *anthropos*" and instead combine the traditional "anthropology of culture" with a new "anthropology of nature."[11] While tending to use the term "matter" rather than the impossibly fraught and contradictory term "nature," much of the recent rise in new materialist thinking is attempting a similar move, albeit in an array of different ways. Some new materialists seek to bridge the long-standing tensions between materialist and postmodern social-constructivist theories; others provide new insights into specific historical case studies where culture appears to be inextricable from matter; and still others, including humanists as well as scientists, go straight to the presumed first source of all human culture to argue that even our brains and minds are inseparable from the material world around us. Just to be wholly clear, none seeks to breathe new life into the corpus of crude determinist theories of the past that I discussed in earlier chapters, and none seeks to argue that a material world of "real" things drives the mere epiphenomena of culture, as some of the earlier advocates of the Annales school sometimes suggested. To the contrary, as is the case in this book, the new materialist goal is not to deny the importance of culture but rather to give culture greater depth and explanatory power by revealing the many ways in which it is created by the engagement of material human beings with a creative material world. I refer to my own approach as "neo-materialism" in part to distinguish it from the variety of recent approaches emerging from political ecology, literary studies, ethics, and other fields that can be loosely organized under the self-proclaimed banner of new materialism. As I will discuss shortly, despite its promising name, much new materialist thought tends to be oddly immaterial, often giving surprisingly little attention or weight to actual things. By contrast, what I term a neo-materialist approach puts considerable emphasis on the independent existence, creativity, and power of nonhuman organisms

---

[11] Descola, *Beyond Nature and Culture*, xix–xx.

and materials – what we might once have termed the realm of "nature" – as well as the deep bodily and cognitive embeddedness of humans within this material world.

As the quote from Dipesh Chakrabarty above suggests, the recent resurgence of interest in the material world reflects a growing dissatisfaction with the excessive idealism of the earlier cultural turn discussed in the previous chapter. While not denying the importance of human cultural constructs and the discursive creation of knowledge and power, a growing number of scholars argue that an overly narrow focus on the social has encouraged a dangerous neglect of the complex ways in which humans interact with a material world that is not simply a construct of human culture. As the political theorists Diana Coole and Samantha Frost note in their recent edited volume on the new materialisms, "The dominant constructivist orientation to social analysis is inadequate for thinking about matter, materiality, and politics in ways that do justice to the contemporary context of biopolitics and global political economy."[12]

It would be a mistake, however, to think of this rising neo-materialist tide as primarily reactionary, as many scholars take inspiration from earlier ideas whose potentials were perhaps not fully appreciated during the postmodern era. Posthumanist theory, for example, has long called for a shift away from the immaterial anthropocentrism of conventional humanistic analysis. Donna Haraway became one of the first scholars to seriously challenge the culture-matter or technology-nature divide when she argued in an influential 1985 essay that modern humans are best understood as "cyborgs" who literally and symbolically incorporate the technological into their bodily and mental existence, thus uniting the material and the discursive.[13] As a feminist theorist, Haraway also saw the idea of the cyborg human as a means to escape the modernist dichotomies that separate women and men, nature and culture, and body and technology. Unfortunately, as the feminist theorist Susan Hekman notes,

---

[12] Diana Coole and Samantha Frost, eds., *The New Materialisms: Ontology, Agency, and Politics* (Durham, NC: Duke University Press, 2010), 6. Coole and Frost suggest the term should be plural to better convey the diversity of recent materialist thinking.

[13] The 1985 essay first appeared in *Socialist Review* but was later republished in several venues, including as "A Cyborg Manifesto: Science, Technology, and Socialist Feminism in the Late Twentieth Century," in Donna Haraway, *Simians, Cyborgs, and Women: The Reinvention of Nature* (New York: Routledge, 1991), 149–81. For a useful overview and critique of posthumanist thought, see Langdon Winner, "Resistance Is Futile: The Posthuman Condition and Its Advocates," in *Is Human Nature Obsolete?: Genetics, Bioengineering, and the Future of the Human Condition*, ed. Harold Baillie and Timothy Casey (Boston: MIT Press, 2004), 385–411.

Haraway's goal of creating a more discursive materialism proved extraordinarily difficult to achieve in practice, leading many scholars to largely abandon the material aspects of her theories in favor of emphasizing solely discourse and social construction. One side effect was that the analytical distinction between fact and fiction became precariously porous, thus inviting criticism that the approach had become unmoored from reality altogether. Nonetheless, Haraway's groundbreaking work pointed toward what Bruno Latour would later call a "new settlement" that is proving more successful in its attempt to unite culture and nature, discourse and matter.[14]

Another early influence on new materialist thought was the emerging science of chaos theory and nonlinear self-organizing systems as pioneered by the meteorologist and mathematician Edward Lorenz in the 1960s. These ideas reached a much wider audience in the mid-1980s with the work of the Nobel Prize – winning chemist Ilya Prigogine and the biologist Lynn Margulis.[15] At the same time, a shift away from gradualism in evolutionary theory and toward an emphasis on more rapid change suggested a far less linear understanding of biological history. The theory of punctuated equilibrium suggests that evolution occurs in sudden leaps followed by long periods of relative stability. Likewise, Margulis's idea that complex cells formed in quick leaps through a symbiotic union of previously distinct organisms, which many scientists initially rejected, had achieved wide acceptance by the 1990s.[16] This grounding in such chaotic and nonlinear scientific theories sharply distinguished the new materialism from earlier materialist theories that promised to reveal the immutable laws of history – what Bruno Latour evocatively termed a "sound, table-thumping" insistence on material determinism.[17] The chaotic course of both human and nonhuman history may have a kind of order, but it definitely is not a linear or predictive one.

[14] Susan Hekman, "Constructing the Ballast: An Ontology for Feminism," in *Material Feminisms*, ed. Stacy Alaimo and Susan Hekman (Bloomington: Indiana University Press, 2008), 85–118, here 1–4.

[15] On Lorenz and the importance of chaos theory for ecological theory, see Donald Worster, "The Ecology of Order and Chaos," *Environmental History Review* 14 (1989): 1–18. See also Ilya Prigogine and Isabelle Stengers, *Order Out of Chaos: Man's New Dialogue With Nature* (New York: Bantam, 1984), and Lynn Margulis and Dorion Sagan, *What Is Life?* (New York: Simon and Schuster, 1995).

[16] Graham Harman, *Immaterialism: Objects and Social Theory* (Cambridge, UK: Polity Press, 2016), 45–6.

[17] Bruno Latour, "Can We Get Our Materialism Back, Please?" *Isis* 98 (2007): 138–42, here 138.

This growing scientific understanding of the ability of matter and complex systems to spontaneously organize in unpredictable ways suggested it might play a more important role in human intelligence and creativity than earlier, more linear models had allowed. In one of the first sustained attempts to incorporate these ideas into history, the philosopher Manuel De Landa argues in his important 1997 book *A Thousand Years of Nonlinear History* that what humans mistakenly and arrogantly view as their own self-evident creations – economics, language, technology – are better understood as the product of complex and unpredictable human interactions with a creative material world.[18] Somewhat similar ideas were suggested at roughly the same time by the German philosopher Klaus Meyer-Abich, who argued for what he termed a "physiocentric philosophy," an approach that put the *physis*, or nature, at the center of history rather than *anthropos*.[19] Taking inspiration from the work of the nineteenth-century geographer and naturalist Alexander von Humboldt, Meyer-Abich argues that other things "are essentially *with* us, not around or for us." There can be no fundamental division between the human spirit and body because reason itself "is a gift of nature" and language is "part of the natural history of mind."[20] The feminist theorist Elizabeth Grosz has recently argued that this unity between mind and matter is even inherent in the evolutionary ideas of Charles Darwin. "Language, culture, intelligence, reason, imagination, memory," Grosz suggests, "are all equally effects of the same rigorous criteria of natural selection: unless they provide some kind of advantage to survival, some strategic value to those with access to it, there is no reason why they should be uniquely human or unquestionably valuable attributes."[21]

Other new materialists have also dug deep into the intellectual past, taking inspiration from newly relevant insights in the work of Dewey, Husserl, Heidegger, Merleau-Ponty, and other philosophers. Among more recent philosophers, however, two French thinkers stand out: Gilles Deleuze and Félix Guattari. In widely influential but often-difficult works like *A Thousand Plateaus*, Deleuze and Guattari argue

---

[18] Manuel De Landa, *A Thousand Years of Nonlinear History* (New York: Zone Books, 1997).
[19] Klaus Michael Meyer-Abich, "Humans in Nature: Toward a Physiocentric Philosophy," *Daedalus* 125, no. 3 (1996): 213.
[20] Ibid., 214–15.
[21] Elizabeth Grosz, "Darwin and Feminism: Preliminary Investigations for a Possible Alliance," in Alaimo and Hekman, *Material Feminisms*, 23–50, quotes on 24, 44.

for a realist ontology in which things in and of themselves clearly can exist independently of the human mind. Language does not constitute reality, they insist, but rather reality is an emergent phenomenon that is produced in on our embodied experience of the material world, an engagement they term "practice." Crucially, they insist that the material world does not exist fully formed, a sort of preexisting stage or environment onto which the all-important human actors emerge and play out their histories. Rather, they argue for a so-called flat ontology in which no single entity is superior to all others or can alone be credited with bringing the others into existence. Typically, many Westerners have embraced the opposite of such a flat ontology, as for example in the belief that a divine being created the world as a preexisting habitat for humans to subsequently develop and dominate. Yet in a flat ontology, the world is constantly emerging and reemerging through the interactions with other things and actors, humans only one among them. The work of Deleuze and Guattari thus provided an important philosophical grounding for key new materialist concepts like the creative power of matter, the distributive nature of agency, and the rejection of anthropocentrism.[22]

The influence of Deleuze and Guattari is evident in the seminal 2010 collection *The New Materialisms* edited by the political ecologists Diana Coole and Samantha Frost.[23] In their introduction, Coole and Frost note that human beings "inhabit an ineluctably material world," yet that this essential materiality has been marginalized in recent decades. Coole and Frost argue that many researchers today have recognized that the previously dominant social constructivist methods are unable to effectively deal with key contemporary issues at the intersection of materiality, biology, and an increasingly integrated global political economy.[24] While the new materialism need not be antithetical to older constructivist methods, Coole and Frost call for a more vibrant role for matter in its interaction with humans and their social systems. Theirs is a matter that is "active, self-creative, productive, unpredictable," a matter that "becomes" rather than simply "is." Matter recognized in this way requires that we rethink conventional concepts of causation and agency that have long been simplistically anthropocentric. The human species, they argue, must be "relocated within a natural environment whose material forces themselves manifest certain agentic capacities and in

---

[22] Gilles Deleuze and Félix Guattari, *A Thousand Plateaus: Capitalism and Schizophrenia* (Minneapolis: University of Minnesota Press, 1987).
[23] Coole and Frost, *New Materialisms*.   [24] Ibid., 6.

which the domain of unintended or unanticipated effects is considerably broadened."[25]

Another powerful strand of new materialist thinking has emerged among feminist scholars over the past decade or so. This is somewhat surprising, as much feminist critical theory had previously been deeply suspicious of materiality. As Stacy Alaimo and Susan Hekman note in a penetrating introduction to their 2008 edited collection *Material Feminisms*, this suspicion was often warranted. Supposedly realist materialist views have long been used to justify the systematic marginalization and oppression of women, cultivating a dangerous biological essentialism that positioned women as inherently inferior to men. Given this history, the authors observe that "most contemporary feminisms require that one distance oneself as much as possible from the tainted realm of materiality by taking refuge within culture, discourse, and language." For several decades, this reliance on postmodern theory in feminist thought proved powerfully useful, as it revealed how patterns of discourse have worked to maintain women in positions that were subordinate and inferior to men, or rendered them all but invisible. For all its evident benefits, though, Alaimo and Hekman conclude that the turn to culture and discourse has increasingly become a liability for feminist critical theory. Ironically, by continuing to insist on a clear distinction between language and reality, postmodern feminist theory has undermined its broader goal of *transcending* these very same modernist dichotomies – a problem that has plagued the cultural turn more generally, as I noted in the previous chapter. While few have denied the existence of a material reality, most feminist scholars have focused their efforts largely on textual, linguistic, and discursive modes of analysis. Yet such an approach makes it nearly impossible to incorporate, for example, real material bodies or to "engage with medicine or science in innovative, productive, or affirmative ways."[26] As Karen Barad, another important critic of postmodern feminist thought, observed in 2003, "Language has been granted too much power," and "every 'thing' – even materiality – is turned into a matter of language or some other form of cultural representative."[27]

---

[25] Ibid., 9.

[26] Stacy Alaimo and Susan Hekman, "Introduction: Emerging Models of Materiality in Feminist Theory," in Alaimo and Hekman, *Material Feminisms*, 1–4.

[27] Karen Barad, "Posthuman Performativity: Toward an Understanding of How Matter Comes to Matter," *Signs* 28 (203): 801–31, here 801. See also Karen Barad, *Meeting the Universe Halfway: Quantum Physics and the Entanglement of Matter and Meaning* (Durham, NC: Duke University Press, 2007).

In lieu of bracketing the material off from the cultural, Alaimo, Hekman, and several other authors in the volume call on feminist scholars not to wholly abandon social constructivism but rather to better incorporate a dynamic material world into their understanding of discourse. One of the seminal thinkers in the field, Donna Haraway, today emphasizes what she terms the "material-discursive," an approach that recognizes the ways in which language and ideas emerge from the human engagement with matter, not in distinction to it. In a similar manner, Susan Hekman argues that discourse should not be understood as distinct from the material but rather as a means of disclosing a materiality which exists beyond it.[28] In keeping with the broader scholarly return to materialism, Hekman and many other new materialist feminists draw on the work of Bruno Latour, Andrew Pickering, and other scholars who argue that material things are not just passive social constructs but rather active and dynamic forces for historical change and the creative historical evolution of the social and cultural. As the feminist theorist Elizabeth Grosz puts it:

> The thing has a history: it is not simply a passive inertia against which we measure our own activity. It has a 'life' of its own, characteristics of its own, which we must incorporate into our activities in order to be effective, rather than simply neutralizing it from the outside. We need to accommodate things more than they accommodate us. Life is the growing accommodation of matter, the adaptation of the needs of life to the exigencies of matter.[29]

Grosz insists that it is absurd to neglect the nature of our own human biology and bodies, as these are the very material means which "enable cultural, social, and historical forces to work with and actively transform" our existence. Indeed, she concludes that "nature and culture can no longer be construed as dichotomous or oppositional terms when nature is understood as the very field on which the cultural elaborates and develops itself."[30]

Although he does not identify himself as a new materialist per se, the British anthropologist Tim Ingold has also been arguing since at least the 1990s for a more vigorous understanding of the material world. What we call culture, Ingold argues, is in significant part a collection of phenomena that emerge from the biological human body engaging with its material

---

[28] Hekman, "Constructing the Ballast," 85–118.
[29] Elizabeth Grosz, *Time Travels: Feminism, Nature, Power* (Durham, NC: Duke University Press, 2005), 132.
[30] Elizabeth Grosz, "Darwin and Feminism: Preliminary Investigations for a Possible Alliance," in Alaimo and Hekman, *Material Feminisms*, 23–50, quotes on 24, 44.

environment. Ingold offers the useful example of learning to play a stringed instrument like the cello. Typically, we view this process as a perfect example of a teacher transmitting a highly immaterial and abstracted aspect of "high culture" to a student. What could be more cultural than mastering a Bach cello suite? Yet Ingold notes the sheer impossibility of learning to play the cello strictly through abstract discursive means. A student might master all the essential musical theory of the cello, memorize all the finger positions, study the proper bowing movements, and so forth. Yet it seems obvious that she would be unable to begin learning truly to play the cello until she picked one up, pressed her fingers to the board, and felt the inimitable deep vibrations as she pulled the bow across the strings.[31]

Where then, we might ask, does "culture" reside? While we might debate the relative importance of the various parts, it seems evident that the culture of cello playing can only truly exist through the fusion of the human brain, body, and the cello itself. Culture is thus as much biological and material as it is an abstraction contained only in the ideas housed in a human brain. Given these realities, Ingold boldly challenges the old prohibitions against equating culture and biology discussed in the previous chapter by concluding, "There is nothing wrong with accounting for this or any other aspect of cultural form on a 'purely biological basis,' so long as the biology in question is of development, not genetics."[32] Rather than thinking of human and nonhuman biology in terms of genetics, Ingold argues we should recognize that the biological form develops through its unique course as a living organism interacting with an ever-shifting environment. (A theme I return to later in the chapter with my discussion of the extended evolutionary synthesis and human niche theory). Our failure to do so, he observes, "is the single major stumbling block that up to now has prevented us from moving toward an understanding of our human selves, and of our place in the living world, that does not endlessly recycle the polarities, paradoxes and prejudices of Western thought."[33]

In another oft-cited new materialist work, the 2009 book *Vibrant Matter*, the political ecologist Jane Bennett takes a related stance in arguing for what she terms a "vital materialism." Scholars, Bennett argues, should "readjust the status of human actants: not by denying humanity's awesome, awful powers, but by presenting these powers as evidence of our own constitutions

---

[31] Tim Ingold, "Beyond Biology and Culture: The Meaning of Evolution in a Relational World," *Social Anthropology* 12 (2004): 209–21.
[32] Ibid., 217.   [33] Ibid.

as vital materiality." In perhaps one of the most succinct statements of the potential significance of new materialist ideas to date, Bennett asserts that "human power itself is a kind of thing-power."[34] In part, Bennett's idea of "thing-power" derives from the distributive agency of human and nonhuman actants within actor network theory (discussed in more detail later in this chapter) and the "flat ontology" of Deleuze and Guattari – there is no distinction or hierarchy between structure and idea, the material and the cultural.[35] If, as these theories suggest, power and other seemingly sociocultural phenomena emerge only from the *interactions* between humans and other actants, then power obviously cannot reside merely within the human social sphere, much less solely in the realm of discourse and semiotics. In this sense, power *becomes* rather than *is*.[36]

Bennett also stands out among new materialist scholars for going beyond theorizing to engage with concrete material things. In one innovative chapter, she even attempts to capture the "life of metal" by exploring the role of copper wires in a recent failure of the electrical power grid in much of the northeastern United States.[37] Yet at this early stage, many other self-professed new materialists still seem more comfortable engaging abstract philosophy and theory than the actual stuff of the material world. Ironically, matter often makes far fewer appearances than one might expect and human ideas about matter far more.[38] As the philosopher Graham Harman notes in his recent book *Immaterialism*, quoting Levi Bryant, "materialism has become a *terme d'art* which has little to do with anything material. Materialism has come to mean simply that something is historical, socially constructed, involves cultural practices, and is contingent."[39] This troubling lack of attention to actual material things in much new materialist work suggests just how difficult it is to escape the powerful pull of anthropocentrism. Even when we deliberately set out to talk about other things, it is all too easy to lapse

---

[34] Jane Bennett, *Vibrant Matter: A Political Ecology of Things* (Durham, NC: Duke University Press 2010), 10.

[35] See Bruno Latour, "How to Keep the Social Flat," in *Reassembling the Social: An Introduction to Actor Network Theory* (Oxford, UK: Oxford University Press, 2007), 165–72.

[36] Bennett, *Vibrant Matter*, 10.   [37] Bennett, *Vibrant Matter*, 52–61.

[38] Another notable exception is the materially sophisticated article by Nancy Tuana analyzing what she terms the "viscous porosity" of Hurricane Katrina, which devastated the American city of New Orleans in 2005. See Nancy Tuana, "Viscous Porosity: Witnessing Katrina," in Alaimo and Hekman, *Material Feminisms*, 188–213.

[39] Quoted in Harman, *Immaterialism*, 13. The original is Levi R. Bryant, *Onto-Cartography: An Ontology of Machines and Media* (Edinburgh, UK: Edinburgh University Press, 2014), 2.

back into a more familiar and comfortable space where we mostly talk about ourselves. Further, by failing to grapple with real things in all their dimensions, many new materialists tend to emphasize only the positive and often human-like nature of things: matter is active, vibrant, dynamic, and even democratic but only much more rarely dull, recalcitrant, toxic, or dictatorial. Surely it is no coincidence that such a one-dimensional understanding of material things tends to help preserve the earlier optimistic view of constructivist postmodernism that many scholars are understandably, though perhaps not wisely, reluctant to give up.

Recognizing this ironic tendency of much new materialism to nonetheless still ignore the importance of "things in themselves," Harman and several other philosophers have recently attempted to bring things more squarely into the mix with an approach Harman terms "object-oriented ontology." Harman argues that an excessive focus on the *relations* between humans and things makes it impossible to discern the independent properties and potentialities of things that are never fully exhausted by their engagement with humans. Much of the work associated with the new materialism thus far, he rightly notes, neglects the reality that "the vast majority of relations in the universe do not involve human beings, those obscure inhabitants of an average-sized planet near a middling sun, one of 100 billion stars near the fringe of an undistinguished galaxy among at least 100 billion others."[40] To develop a truly materialist approach, Harman suggests we must not lose sight of the individual properties and potentialities of the many objects or things that interact with each other rather than just humans – an approach that surely points us toward a more ecological understand of things, though Harman does not use that term. Harman also takes issue with the tendency of many Latourian-influenced new materialist thinkers to focus solely on the ways in which objects *act* in relation to humans – a process that is always contingent and changing from moment to moment – rather than on the equally rich and enduring properties of the thing or object itself out of which such action necessarily emerges. Framing it as almost an antonym to the new materialism, Harman somewhat confusingly identifies his own approach as a type of "immaterialism," even though it is deeply rooted in the material nature of things.[41] Indeed, Harman's *im*materialism is a good deal more material than the supposed materialism of many other scholars.

---

[40] Harman, *Immaterialism*, 6.
[41] Harman, *Immaterialism*, 15. Timothy Morton has also played a key role in developing object-oriented philosophies. See Timothy Morton, *Hyperobjects: Philosophy and Ecology after the End of the World* (Minneapolis: University of Minnesota Press, 2013).

Scholars working in fields where material things have long been central to their theories and methods have also offered some stronger strains of materialism. Especially useful for historians are the new theories and methods emerging from history's estranged sister discipline of archaeology. As I discussed in the previous chapter, the professional academic division of the human past into "prehistory" and "history" was itself a symptom of the deeper split between matter and culture: true history only began when humans mysteriously (miraculously?) were supposed to have escaped the material world of "nature" to create a cultural world of writing, cities, and technologies entirely of their own devising. As Daniel Lord Smail observes, the result was that historians ended up with the letters and books in archives and archaeologists with the potshards and bones in the field.[42] As discussed in the previous chapter, archaeologists were also deeply influenced by the postmodern cultural turn, which tended to emphasize the centrality of culture and discourse over the importance of things. Bjørnar Olsen notes that by the late 1990s many archaeologists seemed to have concluded that the actual material properties of things in themselves mattered very little. As archaeologists began to treat things much like texts, they were pulled toward the same abstracted idea of culture that increasingly possessed other humanists. In his aptly titled 2010 book *In Defense of Things*, Olsen warns that the discipline's infatuation with a relational or semiotic theory of matter has produced a "hegemonic anti-material and social constructivist" theoretical approach that badly underestimates the power of things to create or constitute human culture.[43] An excessive focus on the relational, he argues, has "caused us to lose sight of the individual qualities of things, their intrinsic power."[44] Olsen calls instead for a more "symmetrical archaeology," an approach in which "all those physical entities we refer to as material culture, are beings in the world alongside other beings, such as humans, plants and animals."[45]

[42] Daniel Lord Smail, *Deep History and the Brain* (Berkeley: University of California Press, 2008), 3–9, and Andrew Shryock, Daniel Lord Smail, and Timothy K. Earle, eds., *Deep History: The Architecture of Past and Present* (Berkeley: University of California Press, 2011).

[43] Olsen, "Material Culture after Text: Re-Membering Things," 88.

[44] Olsen, *In Defense of Things*, 156.

[45] Bjørnar Olsen, "Material Culture after Text," *Norwegian Archaeological Review* 36 (2003), 87–104, quote on 88. On "symmetrical archaeology," also see Michael Shanks, "Symmetrical Archaeology," *World Archaeology* 39 (2007), 589–96.

The archaeologist Ian Hodder expresses a similar dissatisfaction. Hodder was one of the chief architects of the postprocessual school in the 1980s, which had been influenced by postmodern linguistic theory. Yet in his innovative 2013 book *Entangled*, Hodder sought to recover a more active role for material things that went beyond culture, discourse, and semiotics. Drawing in part on the concept of *tendance* developed by the French anthropologist André Leroi-Gourhan, Hodder argues that humans are entangled with things that both empower and trap them. "Entanglement," he writes, "is a mix of humans and things, culture and matter, society and technology."[46] All things, he argues, "are involved in complex flows of matter, energy and information," flows that also include the biological and cultural human beings who can all too easily be swept along by them.[47] The human relationship to even inanimate things, Hodder suggests, can best be understood as a form of domestication, as things like "clay, metal, oil, nuclear particles, water, and so on" become dependent on humans for their care and maintenance, much like domesticated cattle or cotton.[48] In this Hodder tends to overemphasize the degree to which the material world can no longer take care of itself without human aid. Echoing some of the recent thinking on the concept of Anthropocene, the supposed "Age of Humans," Hodder argues that increasingly "all aspects of the environment have become human artifacts" and the "whole environment (in the Anthropocene) is itself an artifact needing care, fixing, and manipulation."[49] As I will argue in the final chapter, an excessive emphasis on the human control of the earth can lead to a dangerous hubristic anthropocentrism. However, so long as we recognize that the domestication is always a two-way street, Hodder's idea highlights how deeply dependent humans become on the things they use. As he rightly notes, the human relationship with these domesticated things can lead "to entrapments in particular pathways from which it is difficult to escape."[50]

Because archaeology straddles the divide between humanistic and scientific disciplines, it offers a useful model for how historians and other humanists can incorporate more science-based materialist methods. If scholars are to effectively escape the matter-culture divide, it will

[46] Ian Hodder, *Entangled: An Archaeology of the Relationship between Humans and Things* (Malden, MA: Wiley-Blackwell, 2012), 208.
[47] Hodder, *Entangled*, 59.   [48] Hodder, *Entangled*, 86.
[49] Ian Hodder, "The Entanglement of Humans and Things: A Long-Term View," *New Literary History* 45 (2014): 19–36, quotes on 32–3.
[50] Hodder, "The Entanglement of Humans and Things," 19.

demand that they either form more research partnerships with scientists or develop at least a functional knowledge of the necessary scientific subjects themselves. That neo-materialism leans rather heavily on contemporary science does raise some problems. One of the achievements of cultural constructivism was to demonstrate that science is never an infallible or entirely objective source of universal truths about the material world.[51] For example, historians have revealed how science has been pervaded with a masculine and Eurocentric ethos, in terms of both its ideas about nature and its systemic exclusion of women and non-Western thinkers and ideas.[52] Furthermore, scientists are just as likely as humanists to assume there is a clear dividing line between culture and matter, though they tend to invert the priorities of their humanist colleagues by emphasizing the material over the cultural.[53] If left unchecked by a humble recognition of their own status as creations of the material world, scientists can easily succumb to the more Promethean impulses of their disciplines. Nor has the reductive drive to discover the supposedly enduring and universal laws of nature necessarily disappeared, although the evidence now suggests the material world is more chaotic and contingent than fixed and enduring. Nonetheless, at least in the peculiar realm of Western thought, science stands largely alone in offering a sophisticated methodology for minimizing anthropocentrism and studying the nonhuman world at least in part on its own terms. Indeed, in recent years some humanist scholars have also begun to embrace a "new empiricism" that brings the material back into science studies while preserving the useful elements of social constructivism.[54]

Nearly two decades ago, the human geographer David Harvey argued that "the artificial break between 'society' and 'nature' must be eroded, rendered porous, and eventually dissolved."[55] Yet absent a robust

---

[51] An insightful discussion is Paul S. Sutter, "Nature's Agents or Agents of Empire? Entomological Workers and Environmental Change during the Construction of the Panama Canal," *Isis* 98 (2007): 727.

[52] Alaimo and Hekman, *Material Feminisms*, 4.

[53] See Bruno Latour's discussion on this in his chapter, "Do You Believe in Reality?": Bruno Latour, *Pandora's Hope: Essays on the Reality of Science Studies* (Cambridge, MA: Harvard University Press, 1999), 1–23, especially 17–20.

[54] See, for example, Sandra Harding, *Objectivity and Diversity: Another Logic of Scientific Research* (Chicago: University of Chicago Press, 2015), and Helen E. Longino, *Studying Human Behavior: How Scientists Investigate Aggression and Sexuality* (Chicago: University of Chicago Press, 2013).

[55] David Harvey, *Justice, Nature, and the Geography of Difference* (Oxford, UK: Oxford University Press, 1996), 186.

methodology for analyzing the complex world of other organisms and things, humanists were ill prepared to achieve Harvey's goal. Whatever the limits of modern scientific thought, if historians and other humanists are going to stand any chance whatsoever of adequately analyzing the nonhuman "matter of history," they have little choice but to make careful and always critical use of the insights offered by science. At an even deeper level, we must move beyond the still-persistent tendency to place a supposedly fixed and deterministic substrate of the material in opposition to a supposedly malleable and indeterminate superstrate of the cultural, as such a polarization badly underestimates both the dynamic creativity of our material world and its inescapable entanglements with all things cultural. What new insights into the past might we achieve if we understood the material environment as neither a static substructure stolidly channeling human affairs, nor as a merely passive construct of a mercurial and ethereal human culture but rather as the very stuff that creates creative humans in the first place?

THE MATERIAL HISTORIANS

Even when the postmodern cultural turn was at its peak, many historians continued to recognize that material factors were an important influence on historical change, although few attempted to squarely challenge the conventional analytical divisions between the material and cultural. Nonetheless, scholars working in two historical subfields stand out for their stubborn and at times unfashionable insistence on the importance of material things: historians of technology and environmental historians.[56] While the recent call to incorporate more scientifically grounded insights into history may seem challenging to many of their colleagues, historians of technology and the environment have long depended on a working understanding of science and engineering to pursue their disciplines. Further, by recognizing the ways in which the technological should be understood as natural, and vice versa, scholars working at the intersection of these two disciplines have provided many compelling examples of the absurdity of the culture-matter divide by undermining several of its closely

---

[56] Recently scholars have also begun incorporating greater materiality into Marxist and World Systems theory. See especially Jason Moore, *Capitalism in the Web of Life: Ecology and the Accumulation of Capital* (London: Verso, 2015), and Alf Hornborg, John Robert McNeill, and Juan Martínez Alier, eds., *Rethinking Environmental History: World-System History and Global Environmental Change* (Lanham, MD: AltaMira, 2007).

related dichotomies: technology and nature, human and animal, and city and country.[57]

One of the most important and influential early challenges to the modernist division of matter and culture came with the actor network theory (ANT) developed by Bruno Latour, John Law, Michel Callon, and others in the 1980s. Much new materialist thought reflects the pioneering ideas of ANT, and the two also share some common intellectual ancestors, as both were influenced by the flat ontology of Deleuze and Guattari. While ANT had deep roots in postmodern constructivism and semiotic analysis (the parallel between relational actor-networks and Saussure's relational linguistics is evident), the theory also opened the door to a neo-materialist approach by including all manner of potential nonhuman "actants" in its complex networks and suggesting that agency was therefore distributive rather than confined to humans. Every thing within these networks could be understood as a "hybrid," a complex amalgam of many other material and immaterial parts of varying import.[58] With his bold declaration that "we have never been modern," Latour suggested that what was supposedly a clear line dividing the human and nonhuman was nothing but a modernist conceit.[59] "Consider things, and you will have humans," Latour argued. "Consider humans, and you are by that fact interested in things."[60]

---

[57] Several early works were seminal in bringing environment and technology together. See especially Richard White, "'Are You an Environmentalist or Do You Work for a Living?': Work and Nature," in *Uncommon Ground: Rethinking the Human Place in Nature*, ed. William Cronon (New York: W. W. Norton, 1996); White, *The Organic Machine: The Remaking of the Columbia River* (New York: Hill and Wang, 1995); and Mark Fiege, *Irrigated Eden: The Making of an Agricultural Landscape in the American West* (Seattle: University of Washington Press, 1999). The links between environmental history and history of technology are recognized in the development of a hybrid subfield called "envirotech." See especially the introduction to Sara B. Pritchard, *Confluence: The Nature of Technology and the Remaking of the Rhône* (Cambridge, MA.: Harvard University Press, 2011). See also Martin Reuss and Stephen H. Cutcliffe, eds., *The Illusory Boundary: Environment and Technology in History* (Charlottesville: University of Virginia Press, 2010), and Dolly Jorgensen, Finn Arne Jorgenson, and Sara Pritchard, *New Natures: Joining Environmental History with Science and Technology Studies* (Pittsburgh, PA: University of Pittsburgh Press, 2013).

[58] John Law and John Hassard, *Actor Network Theory and After* (Oxford, UK: Oxford University Press, 1999), and Bruno Latour, *Reassembling the Social: An Introduction to Actor-Network-Theory* (Oxford, UK: Oxford University Press, 2007).

[59] Bruno Latour, *We Have Never Been Modern*, trans. Catherine Porter (Cambridge, MA: Harvard University Press, 1993), and Latour, *Science in Action: How to Follow Scientists and Engineers through Society* (Cambridge, MA: Harvard University Press, 1988).

[60] Latour, *We Have Never Been Modern*, 20.

Some scholars attempted to discern the many material and cultural forces necessary to create and maintain what the American anthropologist Clifford Geertz had earlier termed "thick things."[61] Actor network theory provided a potentially powerful, if not always fully realized, means to escape a solely anthropocentric social constructivism and grasp how humans emerge from their engagement with things.

However, as a number of critics have since pointed out, the distributive nature of ANT also tends to minimize the ways in which the nonhuman world, whether natural or anthropogenic, exists and acts entirely independent of the human sphere. As Ian Hodder puts it: "To bring everything into the disperse human/non-human network risks losing one of the main motors of change – the limited unfixed nature of things in themselves and their relationships with each other."[62] The philosopher Graham Harman agrees but points to another critical weakness of ANT: its emphasis solely on how things "act" in relation with each other. The nature of an actor is always contingent and dependent solely on its interactions with other actors within a network, ignoring what Harman argues is the more essential and enduring independent existence of a thing. "Since an object must exist in order to act rather than act in order to exist," he observes, "it follows that all objects have a greater or lesser degree of *dormancy* prior to their first registering effects on the environment." The full potential agency of any object or thing, Harman insists, cannot be reduced to its interactions with other things, and certainly not just the other things that are humans. Indeed, he argues that this latter point was Kant's original ontological error, noted in Chapter 2: the anthropocentric notion that things "haunt human beings alone, so that the tragic burden of finitude is shouldered by a single species of object."[63]

Latour himself recognized this tendency for the social and discursive to overwhelm the material in the hybrid networks he had played such a central role in conceptualizing. In an influential 2004 essay, "Why Has Critique Run Out of Steam?" Latour challenges the excessive idealism of some postmodernist critiques of science and technology for fostering

---

[61] See the themed issue in *Isis* on "Thick Things," and Ken Alder's "Introduction," *Isis*, 98 (2007), 80–3. Despite the name, however, Geertz emphasized the symbolic nature of things far more than their material properties. See Clifford Geertz, *The Interpretation of Cultures: Selected Essays by Clifford Geertz* (New York: Basic Books, 1973), 5–6.

[62] Hodder, *Entangled*, 93. A similar point is made in Owain Jones and Paul Cloke, "Non-Human Agencies: Trees in Place and Time," in Knappett and Malafouris, *Material Agency*, 79–96.

[63] Harman, *Immaterialism*, 63–4, 29.

a scholarly environment in which it was no longer possible to even clearly identify *reality*, much less something resembling the truth. Latour lamented the misuse of the tools of postmodern social constructivism to undermine public belief in material realities like global warming and evolution by suggesting these were mere reflections of social or cultural ideas and values. The postmodern claim that all knowledge was a social construct had "sent us down the wrong path, encouraging us to fight the wrong enemies and, worst of all, to be considered as friends by the wrong sort of allies." The intent of actor network theory had never been to *get away from facts*, Latour wrote, but rather to *get closer to facts*. His goal was "not fighting empiricism but, on the contrary, renewing empiricism." Rather than striving to "debunk" or tear down the critically important insights of scientists and engineers, Latour argued that scholars must now learn to nurture and improve empirical investigations of the world by bringing together the cultural and the material.[64] Language and discourse should not be understood as being in opposition to the materiality of other things and creatures but rather as one means by which humans come to understand and reveal the power of a very real materiality that both creates and constitutes them.[65] A few years later Latour further refined his thinking on material objects and things in the aptly titled essay "Can We Get Our Materialism Back Please?" Earlier materialist concepts had in fact been idealist, he argues, as the supposed facts about a material world were only painfully thin descriptions that reflected not reality but merely a human *idea* of reality. The goal of a truly material materialism must be to recognize the difference between our ideas and representations of the parts of an object, while still realizing that "the parts themselves go their own ways and follow, so to speak, their own directions." Any adequate materialism must thus fully embrace the creativity and generativity of real matter, a dynamic materialism that "accounts for the surprise and opacity that are so typical of techniques-as-things."[66]

While they approached the issue from what might have once appeared to be the diametrically opposite direction, many environmental historians

---

[64] Bruno Latour, "Why Has Critique Run Out of Steam? From Matters of Fact to Matters of Concern," *Critical Inquiry* 30 (Winter 2004): 225–48, quotes on 231. See also the first chapter, "Do You Believe in Reality?" in Latour, *Pandora's Hope*.

[65] This point is well made in Hekman, "Constructing the Ballast."

[66] Latour, "Can We Get Our Materialism Back, Please?" 140–1. The historian of science Andrew Pickering has articulated a similar idea with his concept of a "mangle" of material and social agencies: Andrew Pickering, *The Mangle of Practice: Time, Agency, and Science* (Chicago: University of Chicago Press, 1995).

were also questioning the modernist concept of an immaculately immaterial culture through their insistence that human societies could not be
understood in isolation from the natural environment.[67] As one of the
founders of the field, Donald Worster, insisted in 2003 (a year before
Latour's own critique of the dangers of an excessive social constructivism)
the "unexamined cultural determinism which underlies mainstream his-
toriography is just as problematic" as any form of environmental or
materialist determinism.[68] The architects of actor network theory had
often focused on the human-built world of technologies, yet the theory
also had obvious affinities with the holistic ecological "networks"
embraced by many environmental historians, who included the broader
nonhuman world as a serious topic of study. Since postwar system theories and cybernetics influenced both the science of ecology and the
sociology of science and technology, the parallels are not surprising.
Indeed, actor network theory, and especially the key concept of hybridity,
has become increasingly influential in environmental history over the past
decade.[69]

Recognizing, however, that ANT and hybridity can underestimate
the independent agency of a dynamic natural world, some environmental historians have recently begun to develop approaches that preserve
a greater role for things in themselves. In his 2013 history of natural
resource management in Namibia, the historian Emmanuel Kreike suggests the concept of "environmental infrastructure" as a means to avoid

---

[67] See especially Donald Worster, "Seeing beyond Culture," *Journal of American History*
76 (1990); Worster, "History as Natural History: An Essay on Theory and Method,"
Pacific Historical Review 53 (1984); Worster, "A Transformation of the Earth: Toward
an Agroecological Perspective in History," *Journal of American History* 76 (1990). Much
of the work of John McNeill has been similarly materialist and critical of strong forms of
social constructivism. See J. R. McNeill, *Mosquito Empires: Ecology and War in the
Greater Caribbean, 1620–1914* (New York: Cambridge University Press, 2010);
J. R. McNeill, José Augusto Pádua, and Mahesh Rangarajan, ed., *Environmental
History: As If Nature Existed* (New York: Oxford University Press, 2010); and
J. R. McNeill, "Observations on the Nature and Culture of Environmental History,"
Theory and History 42 (2003): 5–43.

[68] Quoted in Richard C. Foltz, "Does Nature Have Historical Agency? World History,
Environmental History, and How Historians Can Help to Save the Planet," *The History
Teacher*, 37 (2003), 9–28.

[69] While recognizing the influence of hybridity in the field, Paul Sutter also critiques the
concept for potentially fostering moral relativism. See Paul Sutter, "The World with Us:
The State of American Environmental History," *Journal of American History* 100 (2013),
94–119. Linda Nash was among the first to embrace the concept of hybridity: Linda
Lorraine Nash, "The Agency of Nature or the Nature of Agency?" *Environmental
History* 10 (2005), 67–9.

the still-common idea that there is a middle ground or zone between human culture and the material world of nature. The environmental infrastructures that allow humans to survive on the planet, Kreike argues, do not reflect a *merging* of the two realms of nature and culture that had previously been clearly separate, but are rather the result of a constantly evolving *process* in which both nature and culture emerge together. Kreike's analysis is particularly adept at demonstrating how the old matter-culture divide has repeatedly been used to suggest that only "modern" Western peoples with their science and technology and capitalist markets have truly risen above nature to create a separate culture of their own devising. By consigning non-Western or "premodern" peoples and their knowledge systems to the supposedly passive and inferior realm of nature, Kreike observes, Westerners further justified their own dominance over non-Western peoples and environments.[70]

Other environmental historians have challenged the culture-matter divide by both historicizing the modernist belief that human bodies are largely distinct from their environment and by adopting a contrary stance as an analytical approach. Drawing in some cases on contemporary ecological and medical insights, Gregg Mitman, Linda Nash, Christopher Sellers, and others sought to develop an "embodied history."[71] In her examination of late-nineteenth century American ideas of health and the environment, Nash demonstrates that modernist physicians, captivated by the potential power of the new germ theory of disease, helped to create the belief in a "bounded" body that was isolated from its environment other than through a few medically determined disease pathways. This was a sharp departure from the previous belief in a more porous body whose health was thought to be inseparable from that of the material environment – what the historian Conevery Valençius

---

[70] Emmanuel Kreike, *Environmental Infrastructure in African History: Examining the Myth of Natural Resource Management in Namibia* (Cambridge, UK: Cambridge University Press, 2013), 1–5.

[71] Christopher Sellers, "Thoreau's Body: Towards an Embodied Environmental History," *Environmental History* 4 (1999): 486–514. Some other key works include Conevery Bolton Valençius, *The Health of the Country: How American Settlers Understood Themselves and Their Land* (New York: Basic Books, 2002); Gregg Mitman, "In Search of Health: Landscape and Disease in American Environmental History," *Environmental History* 10 (2005): 184–210; Mitman, *Breathing Space: How Allergies Shape Our Lives and Landscapes* (New Haven, CT: Yale University Press, 2007); and Brett Walker, *Toxic Archipelago: A History of Industrial Disease in Japan* (Seattle: University of Washington Press, 2010).

termed "the health of the country."[72] Nash and other scholars thus offered a radical new insight, as it suggested that what we typically consider to be a discrete and relatively stable human organism that manipulates an entirely separate environment should instead be understood as the product of a dynamic interchange with the material world. In this, the work of historians of medicine joins forces with the insights of contemporary science to suggest that we must set aside the modernist faith that who we are as individuals is clearly defined by the boundaries of our bodies. Humans do not inhabit their material environment so much as emerge from and with it. (As discussed below, current cognitive theories of an "extended" rather than "bounded" mind suggest a similar idea.) Or as Julia Adeney Thomas recently put it in a discussion of the postwar explosion of synthetic chemicals: "Our chemical environment *is* us," and the "old idea that there was a barrier between 'the body' and 'the environment' that could be policed by governments or by individuals no longer pertains as we have come to understand the interpenetratability of bodies and environments."[73]

In her insightful empirical study of the endocrine disrupter, diethylstilbestrol (DES), Nancy Langston provides a useful model for how historians can understand the material consequences of such a porous body as it inhabits and interacts with an environment awash in synthetic chemicals. The chemical DES can in many ways aptly be understood as a cultural construct, as its synthetic creation and medical use reflected deeply held postwar American ideas of femininity, beauty, and technological mastery. Yet as Langston demonstrates, DES also made real material changes in human bodies, embedding itself into the very "nature" of what makes us human. The chemical not only affected the pregnant women it was given to – often in the tragically mistaken belief it would prevent miscarriages – but also the women's children, sometimes causing cancer decades later. Langston thus demonstrates it is illogical to argue that such DES-human hybrids were somehow "constructing" a material world that was separate from them. Rather, the very humans who were supposed to be constructing material reality had already in significant part been constructed by it at a biological

---

[72] Linda Lorraine Nash, *Inescapable Ecologies: A History of Environment, Disease, and Knowledge* (Berkeley: University of California Press, 2006); Valençius, *The Health of the Country*.

[73] Julia Adeney Thomas, "History and Biology in the Anthropocene: Problems of Scale, Problems of Value," *American Historical Review* 119 (2014): 1587–607, quote on 1601.

level.[74] "Whatever humans do to the natural world finds its way back inside our bodies, with complex and poorly understood consequences," Langston writes. "And in turn, what happens inside our bodies makes its way back into the broader world, often with surprising effects."[75] Beyond DES, Langston notes that in the postwar period all but the most isolated populations of humans have been exposed to vast numbers of synthetic chemicals that their bodies had no previous exposure to and thus could not have evolved effective means of safely metabolizing. Langston quotes the insightful words of a report by the Greater Boston Physicians for Social Responsibility: "We are engaged in a large global experiment. It involves exposure of all species of plants and animals in diverse ecosystems to multiple manmade chemicals."[76]

Langston is also among the first historians to consider the potentially enormous consequences of the emerging epigenetic revolution that I discussed briefly in Chapter 1. Historians have long recognized, of course, that germs, viruses, chemicals, and other materials in the environment can influence human health and well-being, and thus the course of history. Alfred Crosby's influential *Ecological Imperialism*, for example, made a compelling case that the diseases they brought with them played a central role in the European conquest of new lands. However, epigenetic science is now demonstrating that material things in our environment not only cause disease or famine but can fundamentally alter the very nature of humans and other animals. Contrary to popular belief, DNA does not contain a "blueprint" in which there is always a straightforward connection between every gene or genotype and the resulting organism or phenotype. Rather, it is now recognized that there are secondary, or "epigenetic," processes in which environmental influences can be passed on to offspring through pathways other than DNA. At a basic and largely uncontroversial level, epigenetics can be understood as the processes that regulate the expression of the genes in our DNA, turning genes on or off at various points, typically through a sort of chemical gene-capping process called methylation. In order to form the fetus and to make sure that heart cells in children and adults do not suddenly start reproducing themselves as eye cells, epigenetic mechanism must cause certain areas of the genetic code to be expressed while others are repressed. But chemicals like DES that mimic hormones can affect humans by interfering with this critical

---

[74] Nancy Langston, *Toxic Bodies: Hormone Disruptors and the Legacy of DES* (New Haven, CT: Yale University Press, 2010.
[75] Langston, *Toxic Bodies*, 136.   [76] Quoted in Langston, *Toxic Bodies*, 15.

epigenetic process, causing genetically coded cell processes to be turned off and on in ways that can cause devastating diseases. If a pregnant woman is exposed to chemicals like DES, the epigenetic effects may cause reproductive cancers in her daughter that will only show up many years later when she reaches sexual maturity. "Development is no longer envisioned as an inevitable chain of events dictated by genes alone," Langston observes. "Rather, developmental biologists now describe a complex symphony between cells, genes, organs, individuals, and environment, all influencing one another's melodies and harmonies."[77]

More controversially, a growing body of evidence suggests that epigenetic changes caused by environmental factors may in certain cases be heritable through multiple subsequent generations, even though there is no change in the permanent genetic information coded in DNA. While not exactly a vindication of the Lamarckian theory of inheritance of acquired traits, epigenetic theory does challenge the long-standing belief that DNA is the sole mechanism of heredity. Transient and often culturally generated changes in the environment produce epigenetic changes that can be passed down for several generations and perhaps longer. During the infamous Dutch Hunger Winter of 1944–45, a German military blockade drastically cut food shipments to the western Netherlands, resulting in a devastating famine that killed more than 20,000 people. To the initial astonishment of later researchers, detailed longitudinal statistical studies revealed that not only the children but also the *grandchildren* of women who were pregnant during the Hunger Winter suffered from higher rates of obesity and other physical and mental problems.[78] The recent study of the isolated Swedish village of Överkalix offers another example of a historically rooted epigenetic effect, revealing that whether or not men experienced periods of famine as growing boys in the village could influence the degree to which their grandsons subsequently suffered from diabetes and heart disease.[79] A recent study by a Danish team offered further support for these transgenerational epigenetic effects, as it found clear epigenetic differences between the sperm of obese and slim men as

[77] Langston, *Toxic Bodies*, 11–12.
[78] R. C. Painter et al., "Transgenerational Effects of Prenatal Exposure to the Dutch Famine on Neonatal Adiposity and Health in Later Life," *BJOG: An International Journal of Obstetrics and Gynaecology* 115 (2008): 1243–9; Nessa Carey, *The Epigenetics Revolution: How Modern Biology Is Rewriting Our Understanding of Genetics, Disease, and Inheritance* (New York: Columbia University Press, 2010), 2–3.
[79] See Judith Shulevitz, "Why Fathers Really Matter," *New York Times*, September 9, 2012.

expressed in the way some nine thousand different genes were "methylated" or turned off or on. These epigenetic patterns in the sperm could also be rapidly changed by environmental factors, as when obese men quickly slimmed down by undergoing gastric-bypass surgery. Further, the researchers found that at least some of the genes that were regulated were epigenetically related to the ways in which the brain governs appetite and metabolism.[80]

While such studies reveal that epigenetic effects clearly affect sperm production, precisely how or even if this information might be passed on to subsequent generations is not yet fully clear. It was long believed that any such epigenetic coding would be entirely erased during fertilization so that only pristine copies of the male and female DNA were passed on to offspring. Yet it now appears that at least some of this environmentally influenced epigenetic information can be passed on, most likely through interchanges between sperm, ova, and the female placenta.[81] For example, the environment can affect genes from the father's sperm that subsequently influence the growth of the mother's placenta in ways that affect the development of the fetus. Regardless of the mechanisms, though, researchers speculate that the transgenerational epigenetic inheritance found in the Dutch and Swedish famine studies makes evolutionary sense, as it would provide a rapid means of preparing the next generation for either a scarcity or abundance of food that would be impossible through the slow process of conventional genetic evolution.[82] Recent research suggests that there may be transgenerational epigenetic effects for a wide variety of other environmental chemicals, like DDT, dioxin, and plastic additives like BPA, among others. This raises the haunting possibility that modern technological changes to the environment could be causing long-term changes to the material nature of the human species over the brief course of just a single generation, placing epigenetic effects squarely within the shorter time spans typically of interest to historians.[83]

Yet as intriguing as this research is for our understanding of the human place in the material world, we should keep in mind that many of these findings remain controversial. For example, an epigenetic effect observed

---

[80] Ida Donkin et al., "Obesity and Bariatric Surgery Drive Epigenetic Variation of Spermatozoa in Humans," *Cell Metabolism* 23 (2016): 369–78.

[81] Mitch Leslie, "Are You Inheriting More Than Genes from Your Father?" *Science Magazine*, December 31, 2015.

[82] Ida Donkin et al., "Obesity and Bariatric Surgery Drive Epigenetic Variation of Spermatozoa in Humans," *Cell Metabolism* 23 (2016): 1–10.

[83] Jocelyn Kaiser, "The Epigenetic Heretic," *Science* 343 (2014): 361–3, here 363.

only over three generations may not truly be passed down serially between generations in a way analogous to the genetic information in DNA. If a mother is epigenetically affected while pregnant, this single change could influence three generations at once: the mother, her unborn child, *and* that child's own reproductive information that could influence the third generation. A pregnant woman is in this sense three generations at once. For these reasons and others, transgenerational epigenetic theory remains a topic of hot scientific debate. As one researcher observed in 2014, it "is either going to be blown away or it's really going to be confirmed and expanded on and that's what I find exciting."[84]

Nonetheless, while the field is still rapidly evolving and in some aspects controversial, epigenetic theory offers some scientific grounding for understanding the many ways in which the fundamental nature of human bodies, minds, and thus cultures are intimately connected to their material surroundings. In the past, evolution could only happen very slowly through the gradual accumulation of random mutations in DNA, requiring thousands of generations for significant physiological changes to occur in a species. Epigenetic changes, however, can happen very quickly in response to changes in the material environment and can occur in many individuals at the same time. The flexibility of the epigenome allows an organism to continually and rapidly adjust to a changing environment without having to undergo the slow process of natural selection acting on DNA code. If transgenerational epigenetic theory is also proven true, the implications are profound. As one recent overview from the perspective of historians suggests, "We are faced with the prospect that the entire domain of historical action – the ever-changing 'niches' that we construct, reconstruct, and occupy – has subtly shaped and reshaped our biological substrate."[85]

In addition to this emerging new epigenetic understanding, historians are also beginning to develop a much richer sense of how the material environment generates conventional genetic changes even in the relatively brief time spans typically of interest to historians. As the historian of technology and environment Edmund Russell has argued, evolution is not something that only took place hundreds of thousands or millions of years ago – rather, it is a process that happens on a much shorter historical time scale. For example, archaeological evidence suggests that the first

---

[84] Kaiser, "The Epigenetic Heretic," 363.
[85] "Introduction: History Meets Biology – AHR Roundtable," *American Historical Review*, 119 (2014): 1492–9, here 1498.

modern humans arrived in Europe about 45,000 years ago. For 35,000 years they lived as hunter-gatherers, but by 10,000 years ago some had begun to practice farming and settle in permanent villages in what is now Turkey. The shift to farming and pastoralism created an environment that selected for a wide variety of new traits, including the ability to digest milk into adulthood (though curiously this trait only clearly emerged about 4,000 years ago), metabolize a critical amino acid from wheat and other grain crops, and to absorb more vitamin D from the sun through lighter skin when the previous source – animal meat that was rich in the vitamin – was replaced by grains that had very little. Another well-known example of such "rapid evolutionary change" is the development of a genetic mutation for sickle-cell-shaped red blood cells among early farmers in West Africa. These Sahelian peoples began to farm yams on the edge of rainforests, creating abundant open pools of water that were ideal breeding grounds for mosquitoes carrying malaria. If an individual received a copy of the genetic mutation for sickle cells from *both* of her parents, she would develop a potentially deadly sickle-cell anemia. But if only one copy was received, it would not result in serious health effects yet would provide some protection from a potentially fatal malarial infection.[86] Just in the past eight thousand years – a blink of the eye in geological time – Europeans and presumably many other humans were thus genetically reshaped by the material changes wrought by the shift to farming.[87] In a biological sense, not just a cultural one, these humans quite literally became "farm people."

The emerging concept of human niche construction offers another useful way of understanding how humans interact with their environment, whether through epigenetic, genetic, or external material means. As noted in the previous chapter, the evolutionary biologist Richard Lewontin suggested the idea of niche construction in the 1970s, in part as a response to what he saw as an excessively gene-centric understanding of evolution that neglected the way in which organisms grew and developed in an environment that they themselves shaped.[88] Since then, evolutionary biologists have further developed the concept to better take into

---

[86] John Brooke and Clark Spencer Larsen, "The Nurture of Nature: Genetics, Epigenetics, and Environment in Human Biohistory," *American Historical Review* 119 (2014): 1500–13, here 1504.

[87] Iain Mathieson et al., "Genome-Wide Patterns of Selection in 230 Ancient Eurasians," *Nature* 528 (2015): 499–503.

[88] Richard Lewontin, "Gene, Organism, and Environment," in *Evolution from Molecules to Men*, ed. D. S. Bendall (Cambridge, UK: Cambridge University Press, 1983), 273–85,

account that every organism changes the environment in which it lives and evolves. An often-cited example is the North American beaver (*Castor canadensis*), a large semiaquatic rodent that clearly does not just evolve to fit a distinctly separate and largely static environment but rather shapes its own niche by deliberately building dams and ponds – indeed, this "niche" must be understood as an inextricable part of what defines the species.[89] Some historians have suggested niche construction offers a useful way to understand human technological change. The Agricultural, or Neolithic, Revolution, for example, might be understood as a type of niche construction, which in turn shaped humans both biologically and culturally.[90]

More recently some scholars from evolutionary biology, evolutionary developmental biology, genomics, ecology, social science, and other fields have argued that standard evolutionary theory should be replaced by what they term the extended evolutionary synthesis (EES). Central to the earlier "modern synthesis" of Darwinian evolution and genetics was the belief that random mutations in genes offered the sole source of variation in organisms. Because very little was then understood about how genes were actually expressed in the development of a living organism – a subject studied within the discipline of developmental biology – scientists simply assumed there was a relatively straightforward correlation between genes (the genotype) and the organism (the phenotype). Hence, whether a random mutation in genetic code would survive in a population depended on whether it happened to improve the fitness of the organism in its existing environment through the Darwinian process of natural selection. This synthesis between Darwinian natural selection and genomics created a powerful theory, as it permitted evolutionary biologists to understand evolution in terms of quantifiable genetic variations in a population that could be analyzed and described using mathematical tools. In more recent decades, however, evidence has steadily accumulated

---

and, Lewontin, *The Triple Helix: Gene, Organism and Environment* (Cambridge, MA: Harvard University Press, 2000).

[89] Key works include Kevin Laland, John Olding-Smee, and Marcus Feldman, "Niche Construction, Biological Evolution, and Cultural Change, *Behavioral and Brain Sciences* 23 (2000): 131–75, and Kevin Laland, "Cultural Niche Construction and Human Evolution," *Journal of Evolutionary Biology* 14 (2001): 22–33.

[90] Brooke and Larsen, "The Nurture of Nature," 1507. See also Nicole L. Boivin et al., "Ecological Consequences of Human Niche Construction: Examining Long-term anthropogenic Shaping of Global Species Distributions," *Proceedings of the National Academy of Sciences* 113 (2016): 6388–96. My own thinking on human niche construction was influenced by a 2015 workshop organized by Maurits Ertsen and Edmund Russell at the Rachel Carson Center in Munich, Germany.

that suggests the standard model is too simple. As Kevin Laland, one of the leading advocates of EES argues, "We hold that organisms are constructed in development, not simply 'programmed' to develop by genes." In addition to the importance of niche construction, Laland and others point to the plasticity of organismal development that allows, for example, the color of butterflies or the shape of tree leaves to change during the lifetime of a single organism in response to environmental factors. Advocates of EES also embrace the possibility of extra-genetic inheritance through epigenetic factors, social learning, and transmission through structural changes in the environment – such as a beaver dam or termite mound – that constitute the niches that subsequent generations will develop within and be shaped by.[91]

Not all evolutionary biologists agree that these new insights into the role of development, plasticity, and niche construction warrant the creation of a new synthesis. Rather, while acknowledging the importance of developmental factors, they argue that these have already been effectively incorporated into the existing model. Moreover, they insist that genetic transmission remains the central explanatory insight. To lose sight of the genes "would de-emphasize the most powerfully predictive, broadly applicable and empirically validated component of evolutionary theory."[92] As both sides suggest, the ultimate resolution of the debate will turn on the further accumulation of empirical evidence. But regardless of whether it justifies a new synthesis, this increased emphasis on the development of the organism within a niche that the organism itself plays a role in creating suggests a somewhat different understanding of evolutionary biology than the one that dominated during the earlier reign of the "selfish gene," discussed in the previous chapter. The move toward "extragenetic inheritance," for example, suggests how organisms shape the biology of their descendants by making enduring changes in the environment in which they will develop. Observed similarities between parents and their offspring are a product not just of genetic heritage, they argue, but also of the ways in which the parents have reconstructed or maintained the environments that they themselves had developed in for their offspring.[93] Given this, what in the humanities is often termed

[91] Kevin Laland et al., "Does Evolutionary History Need a Rethink?: Yes, Urgently," *Nature* 514 (2014): 161–4, quote on 162.

[92] Gregory A. Wray and Hopi E. Hoekstra, "Does Evolutionary History Need a Rethink?: No, All Is Well," *Nature* 514 (2014): 161–4, quote on 163.

[93] Laland, "Does Evolutionary History Need a Rethink?" 162.

material culture can be understood as having an evolutionary component: when humans make enduring changes in their environments, as when they build concrete cities or increase global temperatures, they also are shaping the evolution of later generations, who will develop and live in these environments. Importantly, in this case the evolutionary process stems not from genetic changes but rather from the way anthropogenic niches affect the biological development of individual organisms during the course of their lifetimes. When we change our environments, we change ourselves.

Obviously humanistic scholars must exercise care in applying these ideas to their understanding of human history, culture, and society. Yet in contrast to the more gene-centric approach that had previously dominated, the concept of extended evolution potentially complements the humanist emphasis on the importance of social and cultural phenomena rather than reducing them to mere byproducts of deeper genetic factors. From the perspective of the developmental model, the old "nature-versus-nurture" debate appears hopelessly flawed, because by "nature" it typically meant only genes and by "nurture" it typically meant only an abstracted idea of culture as transmitted by social learning. It seems extraordinary in retrospect that so little attention was given to the complex process by which humans and other organisms actually grow and develop in a vast material environment that creates, sustains, and shapes them. In the emerging neo-materialist view, the environment is understood to shape human biology and culture not just through the slow process of Darwinian selection on genes (though this obviously still plays an important role) but rather through the real-time effects of food, toxins, buildings, machines, and other material things acting on the bodies and brains of individual and groups of human beings at every stage of their lives. Such a view is the antithesis of the genetically based environmental determinism of earlier racist theories. Instead, neo-materialist theory strives to move beyond the old culture-matter division to better understand how each individual emerges from our complex and historically contingent interactions with a dynamic material environment.

But if a neo-materialist environmentalism eliminates the risks of genetic determinism by emphasizing developmental processes, it may court other dangers. Robert Stolz, a historian of Japanese political thought and the environment, rightly observes that returning humans to nature has potentially profound political implications. The earlier modernist separation of the human from the natural was an essential precondition for the emergence of the liberal political subject, "an autonomous, individual conscience protected from outside interference, first from nature and then from the state."[94] This separation in turn enabled societies like the United States and Japan to develop an instrumentalist understanding of nature as nothing more than a passive source of raw materials and forces to be exploited and controlled for human ends. As discussed earlier, the anthropologist Philippe Descola calls such a dichotomous and instrumental view "naturalistic," contrasting it with animistic views that avoid any ontological separation between humans and a creative natural world.[95]

In Japan, for example, nature was increasingly reduced to a source of minerals and energy needed to create what the late-nineteenth-century Meiji government termed a "rich nation with a strong army."[96] Yet when massive environmental disasters like the Ashio mine pollution case discussed later in this book occurred, they challenged this separation, demonstrating instead that humans were inescapably embedded in a surprisingly powerful natural material world. "Being part of an inescapable ecology," Stolz notes, "also meant that humans were not only the *subject* of evolution but also its *objects*."[97] Yet if the natural material world made humans, how could they claim to be the autonomous individuals that the liberal economic and political order required?

There is a disconcerting tension at work in this. On the one hand, as the German scholar Ulrich Beck has observed, the ability of environmental threats to break down the conventional boundaries between humans and nature can have the positive consequence of revealing the deeper commonality between humans and all other organisms and things. "The toxic threat makes them sense that they participate with their bodies in things," Beck notes – that they are akin to a "metabolic process with consciousness and morality."[98] Yet as Stolz rightly observes, the idea of the clearly bounded autonomous individual has also been central to the development of modern liberal democracy and its persuasive and often-effective defense of inalienable individual human rights. To undermine this concept runs the risk of giving support to fascist, communist, or other totalitarian political systems that have often degraded individual autonomy and rights in the name of the supposed greater good of the whole.[99]

---

[94] Robert Stolz, *Bad Water: Nature, Pollution, and Politics in Japan, 1870–1950* (Durham, NC: Duke University Press, 2014), 25.

[95] Descola, *Beyond Nature and Culture*, 63–4.   [96] Stolz, *Bad Water*, 22.

[97] Stolz, *Bad Water*, 9.   [98] Quoted in Stolz, *Bad Water*, 86.

[99] Others have made a similar point in critiquing new materialist theory, though their understanding of materialist thinking has at times been weak. See, for example, the recent discussion of Hodder's book: "Entangled Discussions: Talking with Ian Hodder about His Book *Entangled*," *Forum Kritische Archäologie* 3 (2014): 151–70, especially 156–7.

This is an issue both humanistic and scientific scholars should take seriously. However, as I will suggest in the pages to come, to recognize the unity of humans with their material environment does not require that the individual and their attendant human rights disappear into a sort of collective social and material whole. To the contrary, by undermining the old liberal autonomous self, the recognition of the materiality of all humans has the potential to create a deeper and more robust concept of the individual. All humans may emerge from nature, yet contrary to the modernist view, this material world is not a static realm of fixed and uniform properties but rather a lively and creative place filled with an inherent "individualism" of its own. Biological evolution is predicated on variation between individual organisms, the essential material wildness that has created our world and us.[100] To suggest that a static, uniform natural world stands in opposition to human individuality points to a deeper modernist misunderstanding of both. Individuality is character-istic of all organisms, and humans are no exception. Further, we do not all respond to these creative material possibilities in the same way. Human metabolisms, to name but one firmly material yet exceedingly complex example, are all extraordinary unique, as any doctor knows who has witnessed how a course of treatment cures one patient yet scarcely helps or even harms another. This fundamental biological diversity is even greater at the level of our individual cognitive systems that are a result in significant part of our unique historical development as embodied biolo-gical beings in a particular material environment. From a neo-materialist perspective our environments are a powerful influence over this historical process but in a creative rather than a determinative sense.

This new understanding of the human commonality with all other organisms has also been one of the critical insights offered by another new historical field: animal history. Historians of animals have developed a growing body of historical evidence that clearly challenges the absurdity of both conventional anthropocentrism and the culture-matter divide.[101] In her history of the role of animals in the British colonization of North America, Virginia DeJohn Anderson makes a compelling case that cattle

---

[100] Elizabeth Grosz makes this point well with her useful effort to bring Darwinian theory into feminist critical theory. See Elizabeth Grosz, "Darwin and Feminism: Preliminary Investigations for a Possible Alliance," in Alaimo and Hekman, *Material Feminisms*, 23–50.

[101] For a recent consideration of the field, see Susan Nance, "Animal History: The Final Frontier?" *The American Historian* 6 (November 2015), 28–32. Older but still useful is Harriet Ritvo, "On the Animal Turn," *Daedalus* (Fall 2007), 118–22.

and pigs were active, and to some degree self-directed, "agents of empire." As these animals literally crossed the geographical boundaries that were supposed to separate colonists and native peoples, Anderson suggests they also crossed conceptual boundaries meant to separate humans from nature.[102] While perhaps not typically seen as a work of animal history, John McNeill's *Mosquito Empires* suggests another role for nonhuman animals in history. McNeill demonstrates that the ecological disruption caused by the first wave of Spanish and English imperialism in the region from the Chesapeake to Suriname caused an explosion of mosquitoes carrying yellow fever and malaria. Early settlers were thus forced to adapt and build bodily resistance to these diseases, which allowed them to more effectively resist the efforts of subsequent empires to displace or control them with armies of men, who were, by contrast, easily decimated by mosquito-borne diseases. McNeill's evidence and argument accords well with the concept of human niche construction: while noting that the disease conditions were certainly in part the result of culturally driven human actions, McNeill demonstrates that these ecological and animal effects inherited from the past shaped human history every bit as much as intellectual or cultural inheritances. Expanding on Karl Marx's famous phrase, McNeill observes that "humankind and nature make their own history together, but neither can make it as they please."[103]

Other historians have drawn on animal histories to squarely challenge the common assumption that what we call a technology must be an inherently unnatural machine or process. If, as the historian Edmund Russell and other scholars convincingly assert, a cow deliberately bred by humans to serve a specific instrumental purpose is best understood as a technology, the line between the technological and the natural blurs.[104] Nor is the point just semantic. Rather, as Russell notes in his call for an "evolutionary history," the genetic structures of organisms like dogs, cattle, and cotton have all coevolved with human sociocultural phenomena. Russell argues that domestication is always a two-way street: "Rather than forcing us to choose one partner or the other as initiator, as the common understanding of domestication does, coevolution enables us to

---

[102] Virginia DeJohn Anderson, *Creatures of Empire: How Domestic Animals Transformed Early America* (Oxford, UK: Oxford University Press, 2006).

[103] McNeill, *Mosquito Empires*, 6.

[104] Philip Scranton and Susan R. Schrepfer, eds., *Industrializing Organisms: Introducing Evolutionary History* (New York: Routledge, 2004).

focus on the actions of both partners in evolving a relationship."[105] In this coevolution, human cultural practices – say, a preference for meaty but docile animals – became embedded in the appearance, behaviors, and genes of the cattle.[106] Even more importantly, these new types of cattle subsequently affected human biology and culture, as for example by facilitating the spread of a genetic mutation enabling adults to digest milk.[107] Thus, while understanding animals as technologies might at first seem to support Descartes's reductionist claim that all nonhuman animals are machines, the more significant point is to recognize that important aspects of human intellect, culture, and creativity emerge from our interactions with these animals. Far from being passive machines, these animal technologies are part of the material niche from which humans emerge – a point I develop at length in the next two chapters discussing the intelligence and creativity of Longhorns and silkworms.

By forcing historians to grapple with other organisms that clearly possess at least some level of consciousness and will, animal history is an effective means to pull historians out of our default position of anthropocentrism. However, from a neo-materialist perspective we must also take care not to simply replace anthropocentrism with a narrow focus only on other animals, thus continuing to ignore the equally important role of plants, minerals, and other things, both biotic and abiotic. In another example of evolutionary history, Russell deals an even more powerful blow to anthropocentrism with his argument that a plant – a strong long-fiber strain of cotton that had coevolved with several native peoples of the Americas and could handle the stress of mechanized spinning – was at least as important to the rise of the British industrial revolution as were human inventions or social relations.[108] That the critical role of the cotton itself has been mostly ignored by generations of earlier historians offers a telling example of the discipline's tendency to

---

[105] Edmund Russell, "AHR Roundtable: Coevolutionary History," *American Historical Review* 119 (2014): 1514–28, quote on 1520.

[106] For a discussion of how properties of plants pulled humans into certain relations, see D. Q. Fuller, "Contrasting Patterns in Crop Domestication and Domestication Rates: Recent Archaeobotanical Insights from the Old World," *Annals of Botany*, 100 (2007), 903–24, and, M. A. Zeder, "Central Questions in the Domestication of Plants and Animals," *Evolutionary Anthropology*, 15 (2006), 139.

[107] A good summary is Andrew Curry, "The Milk Revolution," *Scientific American* 500 (August 1, 2013), 20–2.

[108] Edmund Russell, *Evolutionary History: Uniting History and Biology to Understand Life on Earth* (Cambridge, UK: Cambridge University Press, 2011), especially 103–31.

marginalize the material in favor of celebrating – or bemoaning, depend-ing on the author's perspective – a largely abstract understanding of human creativity and initiative.

Finally, other historians have made similar progress in breaking down the modernist distinction between the city and nature.[109] The Western belief that the city is the antithesis of the natural is perhaps even older and more powerful than the idea that technology is inherently unnatural.[110] Yet as some urban environmental historians embraced a more material approach, they began to perceive the city as a place of material flows and processes in which the human and nonhuman are inextricably tangled. Likewise, scholars focusing on human health have brought environmental history indoors to study human-built spaces like offices and mobile homes, further erasing the distinction between the natural and built environment.[111] As one of the founders of urban environmental history, Martin Melosi, recently asserted, historians must move beyond the idea that humans and their cities constitute "a separate category from the rest of living things."[112] These ideas also resonate with recent thinking in fields like art and architecture. The art historian Annabel Jane Wharton, for example, recently took issue with the long-standing postmodernist

[109] Some key works are: Martin Melosi, *The Sanitary City: Urban Infrastructure in America from Colonial Times to the Present* (Pittsburgh, PA: University of Pittsburgh Press, 2008); Craig Colten, *Transforming New Orleans and Its Environs: Centuries of Change* (Pittsburgh, PA: University of Pittsburg Press, 2001), and Colten, *An Unnatural Metropolis: Wresting New Orleans from Nature* (Baton Rouge, LA: LSU Press, 2005); Adam Rome, *The Bulldozer in the Countryside: Suburban Sprawl and the Rise of American Environmentalism* (Cambridge, MA: Cambridge University Press, 2001); Christopher C. Sellers, *Crabgrass Crucible: Suburban Nature and the Rise of Environmentalism in Twentieth-Century America* (Chapel Hill, NC: The University of North Carolina Press, 2012); Matthew Gandy, *Concrete and Clay: Reworking Nature in New York* (Cambridge, MA: MIT Press, 2002); Matthew Klingle, *Emerald City: An Environmental History of Seattle* (New Haven, CT: Yale University Press, 2007); and Andrew C. Isenberg, ed., *The Nature of Cities: Culture, Landscape, and Urban Space* (Rochester, 2006).

[110] Raymond Williams, *The Country and the City* (Oxford, UK: Oxford University Press, 1975).

[111] A seminal work is Michelle Murphy, *Sick Building Syndrome and the Problem of Uncertainty: Environmental Politics, Technoscience, and Women Workers* (Durham, NC: Duke University Press, 2006). More recently Janet Ore has proposed the useful concept of "domestic ecology": Janet Ore, "Mobile Home Syndrome: Engineered Woods and the Making of a New Domestic Ecology in the Post-World War II Era," *Technology and Culture* 52 (2011): 260–86.

[112] Martin V. Melosi, "Humans, Cities, and Nature: How Do Cities Fit in the Material World," *Journal of Urban History* 36 (2009), 3–21, quote on 7. Similar ideas are also articulated in Melosi, *The Sanitary City*.

tendency to see the buildings that make up our cities as "texts." Buildings, Wharton argues, "exert a force on the world independent of human intention or even human consciousness," a force that emerges from their irreducible material natures. Striking a useful contrast to the tendency of many new materialists to see things solely as vibrant and creative actors for good, Wharton argues that buildings can also in some limited sense be understood as behaving badly, as their material and spatial nature play a significant role in shaping pathological human behaviors like murder or addiction. We are not so much creatures of an abstract realm of ideas and culture, Wharton argues, as we are creatures of the built environment we live in and interact with.[113] Given that many of us spend the vast majority of our time inside buildings, this should not really be a surprise, yet it is a measure of our allegiance to an abstracted idea of ourselves, our "Soul 2.0," that we have only recently begun to recognize and grapple with this reality.

By collapsing the conventional analytical distinctions between the city and nature, or the technological and natural, urban historians thus suggest how we can begin to think of cities – indeed, any space that humans occupy on the planet – as simply *material* environments. They arrive at this position not primarily because city and nature are texts or cultural constructs, and thus that there are no grounds by which we can make analytical distinctions. Rather, in keeping with a neo-materialist position, these urban environmental historians suggest that city and nature are united by their equivalently material basis, focusing our attention on the productive role these material environments play in creating human culture, actions, and history. The question then becomes not which material system is more-or-less "natural" – a largely meaningless term within neo-materialist theory – but rather how these help to create certain ways of being, some of which we may prefer over others.

In sum, groundbreaking empirically driven research that challenges the modernist divisions between technology and nature, human and animal, and city and country, all suggest the need to radically rethink our understanding of the human place in the material world. My focus on these three topics is, however, far from exhaustive. Historians working outside the realm of what are considered to be the traditional topics of environmental history have also begun to move beyond the material-cultural divide. Several are well worth highlighting here. Transcending the tired

---

[113] Annabel Jane Wharton, *Architectural Agents: The Delusional, Abusive, Addictive Lives of Buildings* (Minneapolis: University of Minnesota Press, 2015).

old theoretical debates about whether the slavery economy of the American South was truly "capitalist," the historian Walter Johnson in his recent book *River of Dark Dreams* stresses instead that the power, wealth, and culture that supported a transatlantic capitalist system emerged from brute material realities. "The Cotton Kingdom," Johnson writes, "was built out of sun, water, and soil; animal energy, human labor, and mother wit; grain, flesh, and cotton; pain, hunger, and fatigue; blood, milk, semen, and shit." Whether slavery was theoretically "capitalist" is a largely meaningless question, Johnson argues. The important insight is that American power and wealth were a direct product of the vast amount of material labor extracted from the four million human beings who were enslaved by 1860. This labor was turned to exploiting the equally immense material power of the southern land, leveling ancient forests to grow cotton and fuel steamboats and turning the Mississippi into an organic machine where dangerously explosive high-pressure steam engines moved bales of cotton that were the physical embodiment of soil, trees, plants, and enslaved men, women, and children.[114]

In a similar way the historian Mark Fiege has recently demonstrated that an environmental or materialist element underlies *every* aspect of human history, not just the traditional environmental history topics, such as national parks or industrial pollution. In *The Republic of Nature*, Fiege offers a series of bold reinterpretations of iconic chapters in American history that reveal their previously unrecognized material foundations. The famous Salem witch trials, Fiege notes, grew out of the pathetic inability of the colonists to grow the crops they needed to feed themselves in the unfamiliar ecologies of New England, "a biophysical environment in which nothing was stable." Unable to exert the magisterial control over nature that they believed was their divine right, the colonists instead concluded that some of their own number – a few men, but mostly women whom they believed were already inclined by their bodily natures to be closer to the unruly forces of wild nature – were deliberately under-mining the colony through their allegiance with the satanic forces of dark woods and malevolent Indians. Taking "nature" both as a way of think-ing and as a material reality, and at times blending these seamlessly, Fiege charts the central importance of the material world in American history from the framing of the Constitution and the rise of cotton slavery all the

---

[114] Walter Johnson, *River of Dark Dreams: Slavery and Empire in the Cotton Kingdom* (Cambridge, MA: Harvard University Press, 2013), quote on 9.

way up through the earthshaking events of the Manhattan Project and the case of *Brown v. Board of Education.*[115]

Finally, two historians have recently called for a return to the Annales school concept of the *longue durée*, an approach that has often been praised though it was less frequently applied, particularly after the cultural turn of the 1980s. In their 2014 book *The History Manifesto*, Jo Guldi and David Armitage argue that the postmodern focus on short-term "microhistories" has crippled the profession's ability to address the pressing big questions of both the past and the present.[116] The authors' assertion that there has been a measurable decline in the span of time examined in historical studies has been questioned, as has their assumption that a longer-term frame necessarily reveals matters of greater significance.[117] But from a neo-materialist perspective what is striking about the authors' manifesto is that it emphasizes the Annales school's penchant for long or deep history yet says much less about its call for a more materialist or environmental understanding of the past. As I have already suggested, what is potentially revolutionary at this moment is not so much a return to the *longue durée* or "deep history" but rather the shift away from the postmodern focus on an abstracted idea of culture as the driving factor in human history. On timescales both long and short, humans in all their dimensions emerge from the material world around them, and important insights can be found at both the macro and micro level of analysis. As the works in this section suggest, many historians are already moving in this direction. Relatively few, however, have fully embraced the emerging scientific and humanistic realization that much of what we consider to be *our* human nature resides not just in ourselves but in the other animals, objects, buildings, and materials we live with and through. The time seems ripe, then, to offer a broader and more radical neo-materialist theory and method of history.

THE MATTER OF CULTURE

In piercing the boundaries between city and nature, humans and animals, and technology and the environment, the material historians have, whether

[115] Mark Fiege, *The Republic of Nature: An Environmental History of the United States* (Seattle: University of Washington, 2012), quote on 27.
[116] Jo Guldi and David Armitage, *The History Manifesto* (Cambridge, UK: Cambridge University Press, 2014).
[117] Deborah Cohen and Peter Mandler, "The History Manifesto: A Critique," *The American Historical Review* 120 (2015): 530–42.

by design or not, revealed the intimate connections between the cultural and the material. Yet to speak of connections is, of course, to continue to presuppose the existence of separation, of a divide. The challenge now is to squarely recognize that the divide itself never existed, to go beyond pointing out the many ways in which material things are intimately *connected* to culture to fully recognize what this ever-growing mass of empirical evidence seems to be telling us: in many cases, material things simply *are* culture. Much of what makes us most deeply and uniquely human comes not from within us but from the organisms and things around us.

Perhaps the clearest example of the essential materiality of what is usually seen as a largely cultural phenomenon concerns a topic many historians have long taken as central to their discipline: social power. Typically, the power that individuals, groups, and states wield over one another is understood largely as a socially constructed phenomenon. To be sure, everyone recognizes the material nature inherent in the coercive power of a state's military or police force, or even of individual violence. Yet as Michel Foucault argued, much human social power – in the sense of the ability to make others act as desired – is a product of discourse and knowledge creation, the cultural cues that establish the boundaries of acceptable ways of thinking and acting. The state or an elite need not physically force weaker subjects to act as they are told, Foucault suggests, because most are already unable to imagine acting any differently. This understanding of social power has much to recommend it, and it even anticipates the neo-materialist emphasis on the distributed and fluid nature of human cultural phenomena.[118] However, like much postmodernist thought, to emphasize only a semiotic or relational understanding of power fails to adequately account for the essential materiality of power and the ways ideas are conceived from, created with, and embedded in material things. Indeed, as I noted in the previous chapter, Foucault himself stressed the importance of disciplinary things and technologies like prisons and mad houses in crystallizing discursive power and marshaling the "biopower" generated by human bodies. Despite this, many who have used Foucault's ideas have often been mostly interested only in discussing discourse, culture, and society, leaving things to languish as little more than passive reflections of their human users and creators.

---

[118] Foucault explores this concept of power in a variety of works, but perhaps the most well developed articulation is: Michel Foucault, *Discipline and Punish: The Birth of the Prison*, trans. Alan Sheridan (New York: Vintage, 1977).

How then can we better understand the ways in which human power, as Jane Bennett suggests, is also a type of thing-power?[119] Foucault's concept of power as something that flows through societies *and* things suggests the most readily evident way in which matter constitutes power: the physical energy that humans derive from plants, coal, or atoms, which literally does flow through human bodies, machines, and cities. As Edmund Russell and several colleagues have recently argued, the ability of some humans to control and direct the planet's finite flows of energy provides the essential material basis for their ability to exert control over other humans. "All power, social as well as physical," they argue, "derives from energy." The social power wielded by the owner of a network of grain silos emerges from the degree to which the owner is able to control how the caloric energy stored in wheat or corn flows through a society.[120] Indeed, in Foucauldian terms we should recognize that even the discursive construction of social power depends significantly on the differential ability of some humans to control the physical energy necessary to print books, manufacture paper, broadcast television signals, build prisons, and feed workers – even the seemingly abstract power of the modern Internet depends on very real computer server farms powered by huge amounts of electricity, much of it generated by the burning of coal and gas. The urban historian Patrick Joyce makes a somewhat similar point for an earlier age in his perceptive analysis of the central role of pens, ink, and paper in creating the power of the British state within India. Since all states depend heavily on writing, Joyce argues that state power is best understood as operating as an "embodied practice, in pre-discursive and pre-cognitive ways."[121] Ultimately, Edmund Russell captures the broader point: "Social power might have multiple sources, such as access to knowledge, but nothing social happens without some physical action, at minimum by human bodies."[122]

---

[119] Bennett, *Vibrant Matter*, 10.
[120] Edmund Russell et al., "The Nature of Power: Synthesizing the History of Technology and Environmental History," *Technology and Culture* 52 (2011): 246–59, quote on 248.
[121] Patrick Joyce, "Filing the Raj: Political Technologies of the British Imperial State," in *Material Powers: Cultural Studies, History, and the Material Turn*, ed. Tony Bennett and Patrick Joyce (New York: Routledge, 2010), 102–23, quote on 14. See also Ben Kafka, *The Demon of Writing: Powers and Failures of Paperwork* (Cambridge, MA: Zone Books, 2012). Raymond Williams's attempts to move beyond the limits of Marxist dialectical processes also led him to emphasize the materiality of cultural production by insisting that even writing is not solely a semiotic phenomenon but involves a physical process of "notations" on the page. See Frow "Matter and Materialism," 26.
[122] Russell, "Coevolutionary History," 1523.

Nor are these energetic and other material means of manufacturing consent merely malleable carriers whose material properties are irrelevant to the content. Rather, when humans use things like coal or electricity to generate social power – when they are domesticated, to use Ian Hodder's useful observation – these things demand that humans conform to *their* material demands, thus deeply influencing the way power is created and exercised. In *Killing for Coal*, his much-admired revisionist take on the American Ludlow Massacre of 1914, Thomas Andrews takes Marx's ideas about factory work creating class consciousness underground, arguing that the material nature of coal – the demands it exacted and the possibilities it created among the men who worked in and with it every day – was a key force in creating solidarity and social power among coal workers.[123] Pursuing a related vein, in the provocative 2011 book *Carbon Democracy*, Timothy Mitchell argues that the material nature of coal not only helped create modern democracy, but also in a deeper sense *constitutes* democracy.[124] Democratic thought and practice, Mitchell suggests, are not primarily a product of the spread of an abstract idea, but are rather *in and of themselves* inescapably material phenomena. To transform coal into useful and profitable commodities involved "establishing connections and building alliances," Mitchell argues, "connections and alliances that do not respect any divide between material and ideal" or even between the "human and nonhuman."[125]

Some philosophers and other humanists had been arguing for a similar position for at least a century. The American pragmatist philosopher John Dewey, for example, rejected Cartesian dualism to argue that human thought and other "cerebral events" are inseparable from the material. Instead, Dewey proposed a sort of instantaneous dialectic between mind and matter that bears some resemblance to the flat ontology later proposed by Latour, Deleuze, and others.[126] In more recent years these ideas

---

[123] Thomas G. Andrews, *Killing for Coal: America's Deadliest Labor War* (Cambridge, MA: Harvard University Press, 2008). A related point is made for strip mining of coal in Chad Montrie, *Making a Living: Work and Environment in the United States* (Chapel Hill: University of North Carolina Press, 2008).

[124] Timothy Mitchell, *Carbon Democracy: Political Power in the Age of Oil* (London: Verso, 2011).

[125] Mitchell, *Carbon Democracy*, 7.

[126] See especially John Dewey, *Essays in Experimental Logic*. Good summaries of Dewey's thought are found in Robert B. Westbrook, *John Dewey and American Democracy* (Ithaca, NY: Cornell University Press, 1993), and James T. Kloppenberg, *Uncertain Victory: Social Democracy and Progressivism in European and American Thought, 1870–1920* (Oxford, UK: Oxford University Press, 1988). The anthropological theorist

have found support from a significant number of cognitive scientists and theorists who argue that even our much-vaunted human intelligence – presumably the first source of what we typically think of as culture – must also be understood as a material phenomenon. By this they mean not merely the largely undisputed point that all thought and consciousness emerge from entirely physical biochemical processes. Rather, some cognitive scientists and philosophers argue that the human mind is not confined to our skulls, or even our bodies, but is rather *extensive* with its surrounding environment.[127] Andy Clark, the most prominent advocate of this "extended mind" thesis, argues that human cognitive abilities can be distributed in a network of external props and aids like notes, maps, and files, aspects of our material surroundings without which some fundamental part of what we consider to be our intelligence would vanish.[128] While the cognitive processes of all animals may be similarly distributed in their environments to an extent (the example of beavers and dams again comes to mind), Clark notes that humans are unique in the pronounced degree to which they also incorporate tools, technologies, and other "things" into their thinking. In this sense, he suggests humans are "natural-born cyborgs," seamlessly and efficiently fusing the material and the cognitive. Clark offers the example of writing an academic paper. From a modernist point of view, completing a paper is typically seen as the product of the scholar's brain alone: entirely a result of abstract cognition. Yet Clark argues that in reality the brain and body have worked together

Gregory Bateson also argued in the 1970s that scholars should understand both cognition and culture as materially situated processes that emerge from the encounter between embodied human senses and the environment: Gregory Bateson, *Mind and Nature: A Necessary Unity* (New York: Hampton Press, 1979). The American psychologist James Gibson suggested a similar model: James J. Gibson, *The Ecological Approach to Visual Perception* (New York: Psychology Press, [1979] 2015).

[127] The seminal article is Andy Clark and David J. Chalmers, "The Extended Mind," *Analysis* 58 (1998), 7–19. The extended-mind thesis is closely related to the psychological and philosophical theory of embodied cognition, but the latter puts more emphasis on how the biological nature of the body shapes or constitutes the mind. See, for example, George Lakoff and Mark Johnson, *Philosophy in the Flesh: The Embodied Mind and Its Challenge to Western Philosophy* (New York: Basic Books, 1999), and, Anthony Chemero, *Radical Embodied Cognitive Science* (Boston, MA: MIT Press, 2011).

[128] Andy Clark, "Where Brain, Body and World Collide", in Knappett and Malafouris, *Material Agency*, 15. See also Andy Clark, *Being There: Putting Brain, Body, and World Together Again* (Cambridge, MA: MIT Press, 1997); Clark, *Natural-Born Cyborgs: Minds, Technologies, and the Future of Human Intelligence* (Oxford, UK: Oxford University Press, 2003); and, Clark, *Supersizing the Mind: Embodiment, Action, and Cognitive Extension* (Oxford, UK: Oxford University Press, 2008).

with the environment to create the paper by reading printed materials, formulating ideas, jotting down computer or printed notes, reprocessing these for further writing, and so on. What seems to be an entirely abstract intellectual process actually owes a great deal to the material world, a "wideware" which Clark argues operates in tandem with our brain's biological "wetware" and cognitive "software."[129]

Many might reasonably object that these external material things are merely tools or scaffolding for an internal mind located solely in the brain.[130] Yet Clark insists there are good reasons to embrace the idea that the mind is literally extensive, as "it drives home the degree to which environmental engineering is also self-engineering." In changing our material physical environment, he argues, we also reconfigure "our minds and our capacities of thought and reason."[131] Clark, of course, does not intend to deny that the human brain is the indispensable organ in this process – if I suffer a severe injury to my frontal lobe, no number of notes, files, and papers are going to compensate. Likewise, few researchers now seriously question that the "mind" emerges from entirely material biological functions. Ironically, though, the recent explosion of new insights into the internal functioning of the brain has tended to resurrect the Cartesian dualism between mind and body. Recall, for example, Hayworth and other transhumanists discussed in the previous chapter who believe that the mind simply *is* the brain: if you replicate the connectomes in the brain in a computer you will replicate the mind. Clark, however, argues a biological brain evolved to interact with a material world through a material body with an intimately connected sensory system, and to isolate it from the environment in which it came to exist would be to lose its essential nature. The mind, he concludes, "is best understood as the activity of an essentially *situated* brain: a brain at home in its proper bodily, cultural and environmental niche."[132] The implications of this, Clark argues, are profound:

We must abandon the image of ourselves as essentially disembodied reasoning engines. And we must do so not simply by insisting that the mental is fully determined by the physical, but by accepting that we are beings whose neural profiles are profoundly geared so as to press maximal benefit from the opportunities afforded by bodily structure, action and environmental surroundings.[133]

[129] Clark, *Supersizing the Mind*, 12–13.   [130] Ibid., 76.   [131] Ibid., xxviii.
[132] Clark, "Where Brain, Body and World Collide," 1.   [133] Ibid., 13–14.

These ideas have also begun to provide an alternative to the Saussurian, postmodern theories of language and discourse. No one, of course, denies the immense importance of language, both spoken and written, to the development of humans and their histories. In many ways, language is the most powerful technology the human species has developed. Likewise, we not only speak and write through words but to some degree we also think with and through them. Given this, the postmodern semiotic turn in many ways made sense – twenty years ago. However, since then our understanding of human language capabilities has grown immensely and in ways that demonstrate that the earlier views of language as largely or entirely an abstract and even self-contained system of symbols were largely mistaken. An increasingly influential theory of meaning called embodied cognition posits that meaning in our internal language of thinking emerges from our material sensory experience of the world. As discussed briefly in the previous chapter, the cognitive linguist Benjamin Bergen argues that we understand the meaning of the word or thought "dog" because we have had some experience of the dog mediated through our senses – eyes, ears, touch, smell, and perhaps even taste. Thought is, at base, not an abstraction but an engagement with the material things around us. But the theory goes a step further. Neurological tests have shown that when we think of words and their meanings, we use the actual parts of the brains dedicated to processing the sensory input from our eyes, ears, nose, tongue, and skin. Language in this sense is not a product of a wholly new area of the brain evolved specifically for that purpose, but rather it involves a repurposing of existing brain systems honed by millions of years of Darwinian natural selection to perceive and interact with the material world in a reasonably accurate manner. If that had not been the case, competitors that perceived the world more accurately would probably have quickly eliminated the ancestors of modern humans. "As far as meaning goes," Bergen argues, "we are distinguished from other animals not in that we've evolved a brand new mental organ but rather that we have recycled older systems for a new purpose."[134] The phrase to "see with the mind's eye" acquires new meaning, as we imagine things that do not exist in the real world to some degree through that part of the mind that evolved to process visual information. This is also why it is so difficult to speak and engage in a complex activity at the same time, as when attempting to drive while talking on a cell phone. Brain circuits that have evolved to perceive the visual world are taxed both by driving and talking.

[134] Bergen, *Louder Than Words*, 253.

Of course, merely because the roots of meaning derive from our physical experience of things in the world does not mean that we are therefore capable only of thinking about things or concepts we have previously encountered. As Bergen argues, humans are able to use language to imagine and talk about all sorts of things, like flying pigs and many even more novel chimeras and ideas. Unlike all other animal communication systems (at least so far as we understand these at the moment), human language is almost infinitely open-ended. We can of course talk about things that do exist, Bergen notes, but also "even things that don't, like Martian anthropologists or vegetarian zombies." How different people do this will, of course, be influenced by their own experiences, including the cultures they live in. However, it seems readily apparent that if the things and organisms a person experiences significantly change, then so does the way in which they can think. If I have never seen a real pig but only drawings, my imagined picture of what a *flying* pig looks like will obviously be different than that of someone who has seen a pig in the flesh. The difference will likely be all the more pronounced if the comparison is made to someone who has spent 25 years raising pigs. Theirs will be a vastly richer embodied experience of "pig" than would mine, and thus provide them with a much wider array of things and properties for thinking with. If this is true, then as once-diverse societies converge toward increasingly similar material states, perhaps their ways of thinking and ideas will become increasingly similar too. As the British writer Robert Macfarlane pointed out in a recent essay, the Gaelic speakers of the Outer Hebridean island of Lewis once had more than 120 distinct words to describe the wonderfully useful material that we today typically clump together under the single word "peat." This decline in words, of course, reflects the declining degree to which the inhabitants of Lewis interact with peat, a material that had once been essential to their daily lives. But as we lose these intimate material engagements, Macfarlane suggests, we also lose the raw materiality from which we can imagine and create new sympathies and possibilities. "As we deplete our ability to denote and figure particular aspects of our places," Macfarlane writes, "so our competence for understanding and imagining possible relationships with nonhuman nature is correspondingly depleted."[135]

Embodied cognition also supplies a plausible cognitive explanation for how humans develop new technologies. As I noted in my discussion of

---

[135] Robert Macfarlane. "The Word-Hoard: Robert Macfarlane on Rewilding Our Language of Landscape." *The Guardian*, February 27, 2015.

Mrs. Ples and Sterkfontein Cave in the previous chapter, humans have long believed that their ability to invent entirely new technologies offers the clearest evidence that they have risen above nature. Innovation is seen as primarily the product of an abstract symbol-manipulating mind that can imagine what does not yet exist. In reality, though, historians of technology have long recognized that most innovations are incremental and emerge from an often-random or serendipitous engagement with the existing material world at any moment. The popular idea of a light bulb going off above our skulls notwithstanding, Thomas Edison did not invent the incandescent light bulb by first imagining it as an abstract idea and then creating it in the real world. Rather, the basic idea of the light bulb had become readily obvious as soon as batteries were able to produce sufficient electrical current to make a conductive metal wire glow. In 1810, some seventy years before Edison's famous invention, the British scientist Sir Humphrey Davy staged a public demonstration of incandescent light to the Royal Society in London by passing a current through a platinum wire.[136]

The historian of technology, Eugene Ferguson, also anticipated the idea of embodied cognition with his often-forgotten argument that invention occurs in the "mind's eye." Among artisans and engineers, Ferguson notes, "the design starts with an idea – sometimes distinct, sometimes tentative – which can be thrown on the mind's screen and manipulated by the mind's eye." While artisans might immediately engage with their materials, driven only by models in the "mind's eye," engineers will typically express their models first on paper, further refining their thinking. Yet how is it that engineers are able to perform such a neat cognitive trick of manipulating nothing more than an *idea* of a thing? Ferguson reminds us that while an engineering drawing may look abstractly precise, this "precision conceals many informal choices, inarticulate judgments, acts of intuition, and assumptions about the way the world works."[137] As Bergen suggests, this seemingly abstract process is actually deeply embedded in the material nature of the human body as it interacts with the world. As engineers imagine their designs, this "mind's eye" is literally

[136] Ernest Freeburg, *The Age of Edison: Electric Light and the Invention of Modern America* (New York: Penguin, 2013), 15–16. On the precursors to Edison's incandescent lighting system, see especially Michael Brian Schiffer, *Power Struggles: Scientific Authority and the Creation of Practical Electricity Before Edison* (Cambridge, MA: MIT Press, 2011).

[137] Eugene S. Ferguson, *Engineering and the Mind's Eye* (Cambridge, MA: MIT Press, 1994), 3–4.

engaging those parts of the brain used for visualization and touch. Engineers can "see" what inventions might do because they have seen countless other similar real machines that have left marks on the way their brains process visual information. The mind's eye can imagine what is not yet real, but it does so at least in part through its embodied engagement with what *has* been real up until that point. Invention is always incremental, building on what already exists – a point I will explore in more depth in Chapter 6.

Embodied cognition thus fundamentally challenges any claim that language is a largely self-referential, abstract system that creates meaning solely within the brain. Instead, language and the brain are increasingly understood as bodily phenomena that cannot be separated from our sensory experience of material things. From an evolutionary perspective, this is entirely to be expected. As the cognitive linguist George Lakoff observes, "Our brains evolved to allow our bodies to function in the world, and it is that embodied engagement with the world, the physical, social, and intellectual world, that makes our concepts and language meaningful." The abstract idea of "dog" is not abstract at all. Rather, its meaning will be inextricable from your personal physical experience with dogs – that unique doggy smell, the feel of their fur, the shape of their ears and eyes. Likewise, someone whose environment has no dogs can never have the same meaning for the word "dog" as you do, no matter how many definitions they read or pictures they might see, as these will never capture the flood of physical sensory engagements that come from the actual experience of a real dog. Meaning at *every* level comes from our bodily engagement with the world, even when thinking about seemingly entirely abstract concepts. As Lakoff writes, "The way our mind works, from the nature of our thoughts to the way we understand meaning in language, is inextricably tied to our bodies – how we perceive and act in the world."

In a somewhat similar way, other psychologists and cognitive thinkers put more emphasis on the internal cognitive parts of the brain as generative of human thought and creativity. Human behavior does not come directly out of culture or society alone, the psychologist Steven Pinker argues, but emerges from "an internal struggle among mental modules with differing agendas and goals." Further, since these mental modules are shared by all human beings, they help to explain the deeper commonalities that unite the astonishing variety of behaviors seen around the globe. "People may dress differently, but they may all flaunt their status via appearance," Pinker observes. "They may respect the rights of the members of their clan exclusively or they may extend that respect to everyone in their tribe, nation-state, or species, but all divide the world into an in-group and an out-group."[138] These are reasonable points, yet we should also take care not to overemphasize the importance of brain structures at the price of neglecting the brain's interaction with a social and material environment. As Cordelia Fine notes in her devastating critique of recent claims from some neuroscientists (or more often their popularizers) that differences between male and female brains can explain supposed differences in behaviors and abilities, these ideas can all too easily serve as the latest in a long series of supposedly scientific justifications for gender inequality, what Fine terms "neurosexism." Confident comparisons between the "female mind" and the "male mind," Fine notes, often ignore the key role of the environment in shaping gender and many other aspects of who we are. "There *are* sex differences in the brain," Fine acknowledges, yet we know very little about how these might translate into differences in behaviors between men and women, which are, in any event, becoming increasingly similar as barriers limiting opportunities, and thus material experiences, continue to fall for women. Whatever the nature of the brain structures we are born with, the environment plays an outsized role in shaping the ongoing development of our highly plastic and adaptable brains and minds throughout our lives. Fine stresses the social and cultural aspects of this environment, whereas my own approach is focused more on the often-neglected material aspects that I argue are inseparable from these.[139] Regardless, the concepts of embodied or extended cognition suggest that the gray stuff inside our heads, whatever its structural nature, has evolved to engage and work with the stuff outside of our heads. At least until we know far more about the complex nature of our brain's internal functions, we might do better to focus our analysis on the more accessible material environment that shapes its development.

As we understand more about how ideas emerge from an embodied or even extended brain, we are also approaching a cognitive theory of consciousness itself. Until recent years, attempts to find a biologically based explanation for human consciousness were viewed with deep suspicion in scientific communities, not to mention among humanists. Most assumed that consciousness – defined as an awareness of our own existence and

---

[138] Pinker, *Blank Slate*, 39.
[139] Cordelia Fine, *Delusions of Gender: How Our Minds, Society, and Neurosexism Create Difference* (New York: Norton, 2010), quotes on xxvi, xxvii.

thought processes – was likely rooted in the biochemical functions of our brain, but they argued the scientific understanding of these functions was still too paltry to take on such a grand concept. However, with the recent insights into the neurobiology of the brain, researchers are now beginning to suggest possible models for consciousness.[140] Bergen's idea of the evolution of a secondary cognitive system on the substrate of an older sensorial system suggests one possibility. Thought and meaning *feels* distinct from these merely materially rooted sensory systems, providing humans with a sense that they are conscious. The cognitive basis of human consciousness remains a topic of intense research and debate, and no doubt many other ideas will emerge as further evidence is uncovered. Yet what evidence we do have today is more than adequate to demonstrate that the old models of an abstract, symbol-making brain that provided much of the intellectual underpinning of the postmodern cultural turn were simply wrong. As one of the pioneering posthumanist scholars, Katherine N. Hayles, had already begun to suspect in the 1990s, abstract human thought and consciousness should not be taken as evidence that humans are separated from the world around them. Rather, Hayles argues we would do better to ask: "What happens if we begin from the premise not that we know reality because we are separate from it (traditional objectivity), but we can know the world because we are connected with it?"[141]

In applying theories of cognition and the mind to the analysis of the past, archaeologists are again doing much pioneering work. The prominent British archaeologist Colin Renfrew and several of his students have become leaders in exploring how ideas like the extended mind can inform bold new understandings of the past.[142] In his 2013 book *How Things Shape the Mind*, Lambros Malafouris draws on Clark and others to further develop what Renfrew had first termed "material engagement theory," an analytical approach that views human intelligence as a phenomenon that spreads out "beyond the skin into culture and the

---

[140] David P. Barash, *Homo Mysterious: Evolutionary Puzzles of Human Nature* (Oxford, UK: Oxford University Press, 2013), 268–69.

[141] Quoted in Whatmore, *Hybrid Geographies*, 1.

[142] See Colin Renfrew, "Towards a Theory of Material Engagement," in *Rethinking Materiality: The Engagement of Mind with the Material World*, ed. Elizabeth Demarrais, Chris Gosden, and Colin Renfrew (Cambridge, UK: Cambridge University Press, 2005); Colin Renfrew, *Prehistory: The Making of the Human Mind* (London: Modern Library Chronicles, 2008); and Colin Renfrew, Chris Frith, and Lambros Malafouris, eds., *The Sapient Mind: Archaeology Meets Neuroscience* (Oxford, UK: Oxford University Press, 2009).

material world." Within this frame, Malafouris offers a compelling new understanding of "how human minds came to be" in which material things play a central role in creating and shaping both the extended human mind and the evolution of the organic human brain within the skull.[143]

Another sign of the growing influence of the extended or embodied brain can be seen in new ways of understanding the evolution of human tool use. Reversing the usual causalities, scholars have increasingly asked not how a stone tool serves simply as an indicator of improved cognitive ability but rather how the stone tool itself might have *driven* that cognitive evolution. The neuroscientist Terrence Deacon, for example, points to some evidence that suggests stone tools may have preceded the increased brain size in the *Homo* genus. The resulting shift to intensive foraging made possible by these stone tools could have been the driver for cognitive evolution rather than a result of it – a sort of coevolutionary process between tools, language, and brains.[144] Other anthropologists have focused their attention on the human use of fire, the evidence for which emerges about one million years ago and is associated with the hominin species *Homo erectus*. The ability of humans to spread into the colder regions of northern Eurasia may have depended on fire simply in terms of its practical utility. But the anthropologist Richard Wrangham has argued that the use of fire and cooking might also have been critical to the evolution of physical and social changes in *Homo erectus*. By making it possible to cook plants and meat, Wrangham points out that fire reduced both the caloric energy needed to eat and digest these foods and thus the need for large powerful jaws.[145] The increased energy available through cooking would have permitted more bodily energy to be channeled into supporting bigger brains and the related development of an increasingly complex social environment.[146] (As I will discuss in the final chapter, modern humans use about 20 percent of their bodily calories simply to support their big energy-hungry brains.) Wrangham's thesis remains

[143] Lambros Malafouris, *How Things Shape the Mind: A Theory of Material Engagement* (Boston, MA: MIT Press, 2013), 2, 8. See also Malafouris, "At the Potter's Wheel: An Argument for Material Agency," in Knappett and Malafouris, *Material Agency*, 19–36.

[144] Boivin, *Material Cultures*, 190–2; Terrence W. Deacon, *The Symbolic Species: The Co-evolution of Language and the Human Brain* (London: Penguin, 1997).

[145] Richard W. Wrangham, J. H. Jones, G. Laden, D. Pilbeam, and N. Conklin-Brittain, "The Raw and the Stolen," *Current Anthropology* 40 (1999): 567–94.

[146] Richard W. Wrangham, *Catching Fire: How Cooking Made Us Human* (New York: Basic Books, 2010).

contested – the archaeological evidence of widespread use of fire for cooking by early humans like *Homo erectus* has yet to be found. However, some recent discoveries like those made at the Cradle of Humankind in South Africa – not far from the site where the skull of the *australopithecine* Mrs. Ples was found – have begun to suggest the controlled use of fire may have occurred much earlier than previously believed, lending some support to Wrangham's theory.[147]

Among humanists, the recent development of "neurohistory" also suggests the importance of considering cognition in our analysis of the past. Rather than pursuing the idea that the mind (in distinction to the brain) is extensive with the material environment, Daniel Lord Smail and other advocates of neurohistory focus more on the biological brain itself. Nonetheless, their concept of the brain is similarly linked to the material world. Drawing on recent insights from neuroscience, they point out that the brain is highly plastic, capable of both shaping and being shaped by its material environment. As humans use their intelligence and culture to change their material surroundings, Smail argues that they practice new patterns of behaviors that in turn "generate new neural configurations or alter brain-body states."[148] Further, Smail notes, "The existence of brain structures and body chemicals means that predispositions and behavioral patterns have a universal biological substrate that simply cannot be ignored." These brain structures and chemicals generate basic social emotions that are nearly universal among humans, although "they do different things in different historical cultures."[149]

Epigenetic studies have also begun to suggest that these materially driven changes in brains might even be passed down for at least a few subsequent generations. For example, it has been recognized for some time now that the children and grandchildren of Holocaust survivors are more likely than average to suffer from problems like posttraumatic stress disorders, even if they have not personally experienced unusually high levels of stress. For decades, researchers speculated that these correlations were a result of a family culture of poor parenting behaviors that were learned by subsequent generations – a good example of an abstract ideational model of cultural transmission. However, new research has found

---

[147] Rachael Moeller Gorman, "Cooking Up Bigger Brains," *Scientific American* 22, no. 1 (Winter 2013): 36–7.

[148] Smail, *On Deep History and the Brain*, 155.

[149] Smail, *On Deep History and the Brain*, 114. For a balanced discussion of the potential of neurohistory, see Lynn Hunt, "The Self and Its History" in the roundtable on "History and Biology," *American Historical Review* 119 (2014): 1576–86.

that the very same epigenetic changes found in Holocaust survivors are also found in their children, suggesting that severe stress changes the chemistry of the body in ways that are passed to the next generation.[150] Other studies in mice and rats indicate that environmental stress alters the expression of a gene that plays a critical role in how the body and brain deal with stressful events. In mice, too much stress leads to permanent changes in the way this gene is expressed that in turn renders the mice apathetic, lethargic, and timid – behaviors that we might identify with depression in humans.[151] Even more surprisingly, it appears that these epigenetically mediated changes in brain functions are inherited by subsequent generations, possibly through molecular changes in the ova, or "eggs," of the female rats who suffered the initial stress. This epigenetic inheritance did not *guarantee* that that rat's offspring would also suffer from stress-related problems – neither genetic nor epigenetic factors determine such behaviors absent critical environmental factors. Rather, it simply increased the probability that such problems would occur, particularly if the rat's offspring also experienced significant stress in their own lives. In sum, the transmission of these stress-related problems was probably not primarily the result of learned transgenerational cycles of poor parenting (though this could still be part of the explanation – depressed parents may not be the most effective parents) but rather of epigenetically mediated changes in brain functions that could be passed on for several generations.[152]

Studies in mice and rats do not necessarily apply seamlessly to humans. Though as Nancy Langston notes, we have too often wrongly dismissed the relevance of animal studies to our own biology and health from a mistaken confidence that humans are superior to and thus distinct from other animals.[153] Regardless, given that it is ethically and practically impossible to conduct such controlled experiments on people, these studies of other mammals offer at least highly suggestive explanations for

[150] Rachel Yehuda et al., "Holocaust Exposure Induced Intergenerational Effects on *FKBP5* Methylation," *Biological Psychiatry* 80 (2016): 372–80.
[151] Intriguingly, treating the mice with antidepressant drugs can reverse the effect. See Evan Elliott et al., "Resilience to Social Stress Coincides with Functional DNA Methylation for the *Crf* gene in Adult Mice," *Nature Neuroscience* 13 (2010): 1351–3.
[152] Hiba Zaidan, Micah Leshern, and Inna Gaisler-Salomon, "Prereproductive Stress to Female Rats Alters Corticotropin Releasing Factor Type 1 Expression in Ova and Behavior and Brain Corticotropin Releasing Factor Type 1 Expression in Offspring," *Biological Psychiatry* 74 (2013): 680–7. For an accessible summary, see Inna Gaisler-Salomon, "Inheriting Stress," *New York Times*, March 7, 2014.
[153] Langston, *Toxic Bodies*, xi.

observational research that might identify similar patterns in humans. Again, such theories do not obviate the crucial rule of subsequent environments. The horrors of World War II might well have caused epigenetically related changes in millions of people, yet if their children and grandchildren grew up and lived in a safer and less brutal world, the transgenerational effects might well be sharply mitigated or eliminated altogether. But regardless of whether the material environment causes hereditable changes in the brain or it simply changes the way brains work – and thus how people feel, think, and act – at any particular historical moment, it seems clear that historians can no longer safely assume that a largely abstract ideational concept of culture has significant explanatory power. Instead, we must begin to develop new and better methods for analyzing the inescapable materiality of human ideas, technologies, practices, and cultures that are rooted in both scientific and humanistic approaches.

A NEO-MATERIALIST THEORY AND METHOD

Whether we accept the idea that things literally change our brains and bodies, or that we coevolve and become entangled with powerful things, or simply that the cultural and material are inextricably mixed in all sorts of unexpected ways, or yet some other possible permutations of these, the time has clearly come to move beyond the long-standing humanistic suspicion and neglect of the material world. What then might a neo-materialist historical approach look like? At the inevitable risk of missing or mischaracterizing what promises to be a very fertile new way of thinking, let me offer several key ideas and observations which will be put to work in the empirically driven chapters to come.

At the broadest level, a neo-materialist method suggests a significantly different theory of historical change than has heretofore dominated. At least in some cases, what we typically identify as abstract and solely human-generated intellectual, cultural or social phenomena are more accurately understood as emerging from countless encounters between porous human minds, bodies, and cultures and a creative and even in some cases intelligent material world. In this model, humans figure less as the masters and manipulators of a static world and more as the products of a vibrant world. Such an approach may help us to escape what I argue is a dangerous overestimation of the human ability to understand and control the material things we partner with, a mistake that also too often grants an exaggerated sense of our ability to find technological fixes for subsequent problems. Things do not, of course, *determine* who we may become as individuals, groups, or citizens. We emerge as we develop and grow in a constantly changing world of other things and people, and our individual and group histories change as a result. But it is intellectually vapid to deny that our fundamental material state as living, breathing, and embodied creatures plays no significant role in explaining how we have become what we are. Among the greatest intellectual achievements of the modern age has been the discovery that matter gave rise to all life on the planet and created human beings in all their dimensions. Among the greatest intellectual mistakes was to then turn around and suggest that humans were nonetheless the sole creative species and thus reduce the material world that made us to a mere source of raw materials. The created, some insisted, must infinitely surpass its humble creator. Again, my intent is not to deny the accomplishments of humans with their complex languages and ideas. Rather, observing that for hundreds of years most humanists have focused all their efforts on celebrating, critiquing, and analyzing every possible detail of human accomplishments and failures, I simply conclude that it is high time we escape our obsession with ourselves to consider the possibility that to the degree humans are indeed special it is because they are the creation of countless other special creatures and things. In sum, without doing too much damage to its larger complexities, a neo-materialist approach to analyzing the past might be said to rest on two essential assertions. First, that humans in all their dimensions are far more embedded in the material world around us than previously understood. And second, that this material world in which humans are so deeply embedded is far more dynamic and creative than previously understood.

Within the intellectual space carved out by this broader theory of historical change, a number of specific neo-materialist concepts and methodologies emerge. While common threads link all, four strike me as the most distinct and important: the material environment, thing-power, the matter of culture, and the end of anthropocentrism. These four are not meant to be definitive but rather to serve as starting points that others might usefully apply, develop, or challenge as they pursue their own research. Further, these ideas will drive the empirical analysis in the chapters to come, where the concrete material dynamics of cows, silkworms, and copper will serve both to more clearly explain the principles at hand and demonstrate their methodological utility.

1) The Material Environment

The distinctions historians and others typically make between the technological and the natural are rooted in the destructive modernist conceit that humans have somehow left the natural world behind, itself in part a product of the religiously perfused "sacred history" in which the human adoption of supposedly unnatural technologies stands as a thinly veiled version of the Christian fall from grace and departure from Eden. In contrast, neo-materialist theory suggests that humans never left Eden, that no cultural or technological development could ever strip them of their state as entirely natural creatures. By rejecting any essential analytical or ontological difference between human-related artifacts or technologies and "nature," it becomes feasible and preferable to instead conceive of a singular and holistic material environment or niche, one that humans (like all organisms) participate in creating. Historians and other humanists, as well as scientists, may still find it useful to try to identify the degree to which an artifact or process is anthropogenic. However, we should soundly reject the still-common belief that even the lightest of human touches somehow transforms matter into an unnatural technology entirely stripped of its own powers and capabilities. Rather than seeing humans as creating and dominating the material, we should recognize the possibilities inherent in things that may be both helpful and dangerous, what the psychologist James Gibson called "affordances" or Heidegger referred to as the "ready to hand." Further, since human cultures and brains are understood as having been at least in part created by their previous history of material alliances, attempting to discern precisely where the material thing stops and the human starts will inevitably prove very difficult, and probably the wrong approach to take in any event. By thinking instead in terms of a holistic material environment of flows and interactions, we can better recognize the many ways in which humans are continually forming partnerships with or "domesticating" dynamic things that demand our sustained attention and continually act to shape who we are. Indeed, since things play an important role in every historical period and field of study, historians might add "matter" or "material history" to the standard and highly anthropocentric list of categories of social analysis like race, class, and gender. Like these, matter can be both a category of analysis and a subject of historical investigation in its own right.

One possible consequence of embracing the concept of a unitary material environment is that many of the disciplinary and topical divisions we now accept as self-evident may appear mistaken or counterproductive. In one of my own fields of study, the environmental history of mining, scholars (myself included) have typically focused most of their efforts on the effects of extracting and processing a mineral – copper minerals, for example – implicitly accepting an anthropocentric division between the nonhuman geological and biological environment of extraction and the human cultural environment where the resulting copper is used. A neo-materialist approach would instead suggest that we pursue a more holistic "material history of copper" which would encompass all the many ways in which the mineral itself helped to form human practice and culture, from extraction to use to recycling to disposal. For almost a century now, many people and other organisms living in the industrial world have spent their entire lives in a material environment where they were rarely more than a few yards away from a substantial mass of nearly pure copper, yet historians have paid scant attention to this extraordinary fact. By focusing our attention on the copper itself, we can better recognize how this material thing helps to create the cultural phenomena associated with (to name but a few) electric light and power, telephony and telegraphy, and our own digital age that are typically treated as largely unrelated topics of study.

Put differently, my aim is to argue for a renewed environmentalism – not in the modern sense of the word as a movement to protect the environment but rather in the older sense regarding how our environments help to make us who we are. Obviously I do not intend to revive the racist environmental determinism of Grant, Huntington, and others discussed in the previous chapter, most notably the supposed "biological" determinism of the dark fascist minds that even at the time owed more to myth and superstition than to the actual biological sciences. To the contrary, a new form of environmentalism has no room for such simplistic determinisms. Nor do I ascribe to the recent attempts by some to reduce history to a type of science, as for example with Ian Morris's assertion that "history is a subset of biology is a subset of chemistry is a subset of physics."[154] Rather than making history into science – an impossibility in any event – we should ask how a dynamic, creative, and even intelligent material world helps to create dynamic, creative, and at least intermittently intelligent human beings. While I do not doubt that humans construct the world around them, my goal is to point out the many ways humans have often already been constructed by the world they claim to create.

---

[154] Quoted in Thomas, "History and Biology in the Anthropocene," 1587.

If humans are indeed embedded in their material world, as the evidence now powerfully suggests, postmodern social or cultural construction is at least in part also a form of material construction, a product not just of our minds but of our bodies and the things with which they interact. We are surrounded by infinite numbers of fellow travelers, or what Latour calls "mediators," the things whose material properties serve not just to reflect or symbolize social meaning and thought but to usher these into existence.[155]

2) Thing-Power

We derive much of what we consider to be our essential humanity from the power of material things around us – what Jane Bennett aptly calls "thing-power." Coal, as already suggested, is not just a passive raw material that union members or democratic states mine and process but itself an inseparable part of the worker solidarity and democratic practices that we often mistakenly viewed as largely abstract ideas or entirely sociocultural phenomena. Social power is a type of thing-power, which can in turn often be a form of physical energy. However, things have other forms of power that cannot be reduced to a physical measurement like energy. As Thomas Andrews shows, when miners found solidarity in the dangerous passages of underground coal seams, it emerged not from the energetic content of the coal but rather from the material demands and possibilities inherent in mining the coal itself. Or consider the power of domesticated cows, bulls, and steers to help create an entire industry and cultural mythos in the American West, the topic of the next chapter. If animals like Longhorns had not already possessed the social intelligence to survive largely on their own, yet to also cooperate with humans when asked to do so, the history of the United States would have been significantly different. Humans did not socially construct cows so much as socially cooperate and communicate with them, which in turn was only made possible by the long coevolutionary history between these two similarly social animals. Why is it, then, that historians typically credit their own species with "inventing" and "creating" the western open-range "cattle industry" when the animals themselves so clearly played a central role?

---

[155] Bruno Latour, *Reassembling the Social: An Introduction to Actor-Network-Theory* (Oxford, UK: Oxford University Press, 2005), 39–40.

In a sense, we are surrounded by nonhuman technologies that we constantly interact with and borrow from but did not in any sense create. The natural material world is awash in extraordinary technological breakthroughs, from the work-hardening abilities of copper to the protein recombinations of silkworm synthesis – topics I will discuss in depth in the next three chapters. Some, of course, will object that these are not technologies at all: they are natural systems that simply emerge out of material properties or evolve from living things. Yet this begs the question again of why we assume that other human technologies are fundamentally different from this, that humans have somehow left Eden and risen above nature. Yet if we set aside such overt human exceptionalism to assume, as it seems to me we only can, that even our most abstracted technological abilities are in some logical sense creations of our natural cognitive functions interacting with the inherent creative material possibilities of the world, then the line between anthropogenic and "natural" technologies vanishes.

While not necessarily denying Marx's key argument that capitalist commodification may alienate workers from the products of their labor, I would argue that both workers and consumers need not be alienated from the commodities they interact with in any bodily sense. The power or value of a commodity or other thing inheres not just in the labor invested in its production, but in the material attributes of the thing itself. As the anthropologist Janet Hoskins notes, material things can have immense emotional power, as humans "attach themselves to ordinary objects and fix them in memory as markers of the extraordinary."[156] We grow fond of technological objects like cars or tools, and new technologies that threaten to replace them can inspire the same distrust as humans sometimes feel toward human strangers.[157] Such sentiments are often dismissed as anthropomorphizing, as attributing human or biological traits to inanimate things. In a similar way, Western thinkers once criticized the "primitive," animistic peoples of the globe, who indulged in what they saw as an immature "fetishism" that mistook mere stone or wood representations of gods to be the real thing.[158] As Daniel Miller notes, many later critics of modern mass consumerism also continued to "assume that

[156] Janet Hoskins, *Biographical Objects: How Things Tell the Stories of People's Lives* (New York: Routledge, 1998), 194.

[157] Michael Jackson, "Familiar and Foreign Bodies: A Phenomenological Exploration of the Human – Technology Interface," *Journal of the Royal Anthropological Society* 8 (2002): 333–46.

[158] Olsen, *In Defense of Things*, 92–94.

the relation of persons to objects is in some way vicarious, fetishistic, or wrong" and thus shifts our attention away from the truly important social relationships between people.[159] All of these powerful academic trends conspired to once again focus attention solely on the social realm while reducing the material to a collection of passive things stripped of any vibrant power or lives of their own. Of course, a favorite car or a well-used carpentry hammer are not "alive" in a biological sense, yet the point I would stress is that we humans come alive or live *through* these things. It is not unreasonable then to grant them some measure of respect and admiration (or fear, as their powers can equally court danger) as central players in making us human. Likewise, an affection for a trusty automobile arises from its efficient functionality and reliability, which in turn is a product of thousands of engineers and workers who designed and assembled the car, imbuing it in the process with some part of who they are. This labor might well be understood as alienated in a capitalist system, yet the things in themselves will always constitute much more than solely their human input. Finally, to have affection for a car is to also have a certain wonder at the natural material world that helped to create it and power it. As Leif Wenar puts it regarding a modern cell phone, our technologies are "set on the periodic table" whose "flow of soul rush through the earth, the mother of all our inventions."[160] Humans did not create the molecular properties of iron and steel, nor the ability of vaporized hydrocarbons mixed with oxygen to explode with an electric spark. A car is not alive, yet it uses some of the same basic chemical and material things and physical phenomena to operate – carbon, oxygen, electricity – that a human uses to live. Is it so foolish, then, to transcend the modernist view of a car as a mere thing and embrace a more animist view which sees it as something more intimately bound up with a lively material world?

In part, understanding the power of our material environment simply asks historians to better recognize the inherently fascinating and often-stunning history of a dynamic and creative nature that we too often dismiss as little more than a passive reservoir of "raw materials" or "natural resources." As the philosopher Edward McCord notes in his passionate defense of the value of species, every living creature is a marvel of millions of years of evolution so astounding in its individual

---

[159] Daniel Miller, *Material Culture and Mass Consumption* (Oxford, UK: Blackwell, 1987), 11.

[160] Leif Wenar, *Blood Oil: Tyrants, Violence, and the Rules That Run the World* (New York: Oxford University Press, 2016), ix.

properties as to richly merit human appreciation and respect. "The propensity to astound us intellectually is beyond our control," McCord writes. "Somehow we of all creatures have brains capable of such a response – in many ways this sense of wonder for the other is what makes us most human." For the human animal, McCord rightly notes, "an interest in any living thing is an interest in the same dimensions that constitute our own nature."[161] In this I would argue that McCord's argument for the essential value of living creatures should also be extended to the material world as a whole, both biotic and abiotic, as well as the many things humans craft from these. The creative powers of spruce and maple trees do not suddenly cease when they are cut down and shaped into an instrument like a cello – they are beginning a new and fascinating form of creativity. There are, to be sure, very significant differences between living and nonliving things. Yet rather than embracing a fundamental conceptual divide where living matter is understood as free and creative while nonliving matter is determined and passive, we should preserve a conceptual space in which we examine the interactions of things without any prior judgment of categorical difference.[162]

To tell these stories effectively, to capture the countless wonders of this marvelous and ever-changing world around us, conventional disciplinary boundaries may need to shift. Environmental history and the history of technology, for example, might converge toward something more like "material history." To be effective, such a material history would also need to engage with cultural, social, and even intellectual history. Some might well respond that this approach asks historians to undertake the nearly impossible task of doing a history of *everything*. Indeed, as Julia Adeney Thomas rightly notes, "the difficulties of analyzing the organic and inorganic substrates of history dwarf the difficulties posed by reconfigured concepts of context and text."[163] Yet to shrink from this challenge

---

[161] Edward L. McCord, *The Value of Species* (New Haven, CT: Yale University Press, 2012), 11, 16.

[162] Some critics of symmetrical or flat ontologies have argued these go too far in rejecting a categorical difference between biotic and abiotic things. See, for example, Paul Graves-Brown, "Review of *In Defense of Things*," *Journal of the Royal Anthropology Institute* 19 (2013): 183–4, and John Barrett, "The Material Constitution of Humanness," *Archaeological Dialogues* 21 (2014): 65–74. For an effective response, see Bjørnar Olsen and Christopher Witmore, "Archaeology, Symmetry, and the Ontology of Things: A Response to Critics," *Archaeological Dialogues* 22 (2015): 187–97, especially 188–90.

[163] Julia Adeney Thomas, "Comment: Not Yet Far Enough," *American Historical Review* 117 (2012): 794–803, quote on 802.

would be to accept what increasingly appears to be a dangerously narrow and misleading understanding of both past and present. As already noted, to give this material world its due, historians must become more versed in science or, like archaeologists, form more partnerships with scientists. Still, in reckoning with this universe of powerful things, much of what historians have to offer of value remains largely the same: a nuanced, detailed, empirically rigorous analysis of the past in all of its complexities. Recognizing and capturing the power of things does not challenge this so much as extend it into promising new areas of inquiry, to raise new questions and subjects of study, and to seek previously unrecognized explanations for well-recognized phenomena.

3) The Matter of Culture

Perhaps the single biggest stumbling block to a clearer understanding of both past and present is the pervasive but often-unexamined belief that culture and matter are separate things. As I have argued throughout this chapter, what we typically call culture is not an abstract, disembodied phenomenon that resides in an immaculately immaterial human spirit or its modern variant, an isolated brain with fixed and supposedly genetically determined properties. Rather, human culture increasingly appears to be intimately connected to the material world around us, and in some cases simply *is* material. Matter can constitute culture in many ways: it may physically change the human body and a highly plastic brain; or it might be an inseparable part of a mind that extends beyond the skull; or it could simply be the essential stuff that shapes both the possibilities and the boundaries of how and what we can effectively think. Regardless, if neo-materialist theory is correct that humans and their variegated cultures are at least in some cases analytically inseparable from their environments, then three related framing or methodological approaches emerge.

First, historians should continue to challenge any reductionist theories, historical or otherwise, that seek to identify a fixed and permanent human "nature." However, they should do so not by substituting an equally reductive and modernist social constructivist explanation that pretends that human beings are "blank slates" to be entirely determined by cultural forces. Instead, we should reject altogether this false distinction between matter and culture, nature and nurture, and understand that humans, like all organisms, emerge from a process of growth in which there is a constant interchange between the categories that we term bodies, matter, and culture. Thus what is sometimes misleadingly termed human nature has a material history – not just our *ideas* about human nature but rather that human nature which is coextensive with and develops out of the material environment of landscapes, organisms, buildings, technologies, and artifacts.

Second, historians should pay much more attention to the history of changes in that material environment. As Andy Clark suggests, to reengineer our environment may be to reengineer the minds, brains, bodies, and cultures of humans, as well as countless other organisms that interact with these changes. Historians have an unparalleled opportunity to see if this idea really bears out in the past through careful empirical investigations of the relationships between material and sociocultural change.

Third, historians might practice a sort of "materialist reconstruction" in which we recover the ignored or overlooked material aspects of sociocultural phenomena that had been previously assumed to be mostly or entirely abstract, cultural, or semiotic. Again, to seek the material in the cultural is not to embrace some sort of crude biological or environmental determinism. Rather, it is to add new depth and weight to our concept of culture, to discover another facet of what Smail terms "a deep cultural history," yet one that operates on all timescales.[164]

As already noted, many ecologically or environmentally oriented scholars have been pursuing these approaches for some time now. However, an emphasis on an ecological perspective often tends to erect its own divisions by juxtaposing a clearly separate natural environment against an artificial human-built world and culture. Scholars might, for example, use the recent scientific concept of ecosystem services to highlight the dependence of a city or a technology on ecological systems. But the concept is rarely, if ever, used to analyze the material nature of phenomena like art, cooking, and music that are still assumed to be entirely cultural, and thus outside the realm of ecology. As the anthropologist Tim Ingold observes, the material properties of a cello play a critical role in creating the musical culture associated with the instrument, and the cultural power of the cello in turn derives partly from the biological properties of the spruce and maple woods from which cellos are traditionally crafted.[165] This is indeed a type of ecosystem service, yet it is only rarely recognized as such. The contemporary idea of "ecology" is too pinched to include the ways in which supple pieces of spruce and maple wood served to help humans create the rich musical culture associated

---

[164] Smail, *On Deep History and the Brain*, 156.
[165] Ingold, "Beyond Biology and Culture," 209–21.

with the cello. In focusing solely on the instrumental ecological functions of the trees from whence the woods came, we hear but one note of a much larger material symphony.

4) The End of Anthropocentrism

If historians accept any of the previous points, it seems evident that we must also move beyond the traditional practice of placing humans largely alone at the center of our historical narratives. Philosophers and ethicists have made great strides in developing a less anthropocentric understanding of the world.[166] Likewise, environmental and animal historians have begun shifting our narratives toward the nonhuman. However, my meaning here is somewhat different in that it encourages historians to recognize the critical role of the material world even in the stories that we have previously assumed were solely human. Indeed, while humans obviously at times make choices about which things to ally themselves with, historians too often overstate the consciousness of these choices, thus failing to recognize how we may at times be swept along by powerful material forces that humans only imperfectly perceive and understand. A neo-materialist approach rejects any simplistic determinism, but it also suggests a means for moving beyond the merely descriptive and narrow particularism of much postmodernist work to again seek broader patterns of historical causality. There is always an element of wildness in the human animal and the material world. No course, no matter how deeply embedded in the materiality of past and present, is entirely inevitable. But a neo-materialist approach also points out that the path not taken may not be easily recognized, much less followed. Since humans are entangled in a material world that creates and facilitates certain ways of acting and thinking, we should not expect that very many will easily or painlessly learn to act or think in ways that contradict this. Global climate change offers an obvious contemporary example, as the desire of some humans to generate social power from the immense energetic power of coal and oil has created cultural patterns that we did not entirely intend and yet now find exceedingly difficult to escape. As I discuss in detail in the

---

[166] See, for example, Dale Jamieson, ed., *A Companion to Environmental Philosophy* (Malden, MA: Blackwell, 2001); Andrew Light and Holmes Rolston III, ed., *Environmental Ethics: An Anthology* (Malden, MA: Blackwell, 2003); and David Schmidtz and Elizabeth Willott, eds., *Environmental Ethics: What Really Matters, What Really Works* (Oxford, UK: Oxford University Press, 2002).

final chapter, the Australian philosopher Clive Hamilton has recently suggested that the illusory belief that humans somehow created this carbon-based civilization entirely on their own is now matched by what may prove to be an equally illusory belief that we can solve the problem through unprecedented geoengineering projects of a breathtaking scale.[167] Rather than continuing to imagine that we can do what we like with a material world that is categorically distinct from us, we would do better to recognize the immense part that the world plays in creating us – biologically, culturally, and socially – both in the past and the present.

If we humans wish to change our ways, then we might first begin by striving to change the material alliances that help to create who we are. Indeed, in this now much broadened sense, Marx and other earlier materialists were correct: people and societies change not so much because of new ideas but rather because their material circumstances permit them to imagine new ideas and enable new ways of acting. Neo-materialist theory departs from the Marxist claims to reveal the laws of history, and its farless linear approach has no room for an inevitable dialectic of progress or conveniently foreordained revolutions. Nonetheless, perhaps by better recognizing the many ways in which a powerful and often-dangerous material world shapes us, we can summon the will to change our environments in ways that foster the kinds of ideas, cultures, and societies we wish to have. Making such changes will require the political will to act, which (at least in a nominally democratic state) in turn requires convincing enough people that it is necessary to act. The hope lies in the possibility that even small initial changes in the material fabric of society may eventually have big results. Once we move beyond anthropocentrism we may realize that we do not change our societies so much as we nurture and grow them, bending the current and future material possibilities in new directions.

On a practical methodological level, the end of anthropocentrism concept encourages historians to make nonhuman organisms and things more central to their narratives. In the past, historians have been understandably focused on their own species because they believed that their human stars lived in and manipulated a separate material world to their own ends. If neo-materialist theory is correct that dynamic and unpredictable material things play an indispensable role in creating human ideas, intelligence, and power, then it seems reasonable to make the story of these

---

[167] Clive Hamilton, *Earthmasters: The Dawn of the Age of Climate Engineering* (New Haven: Yale University Press, 2013).

things more central to our analysis and narratives. Escaping the powerful pull of anthropocentrism is not easy, especially for historians who focus their research solely on written documents that were created by humans who were themselves anthropocentric. We cannot expect that our historical subjects will often recognize or write about the importance of the material things around them. To avoid falling back into the anthropocentric trap will demand that historians make a deliberate and conscious effort to look for the critical nonhuman actors in their research. We might, for example, adopt a kind of simulated archaeological method in which we begin by approaching our subject *as if* there were no written evidence available. What might we learn solely by analyzing the material environment of our subjects before subsequently turning to the documentary record?

Modern humans are probably constitutionally averse to modesty. Yet a key task of the neo-materialist historian is to provide the insights and stories that might yet temper the narcissism and hubris that may now threaten humans with annihilation. For thousands of years we have been obsessed with nothing so much as ourselves. Now, when the human partnership with powerful things like copper, coal, and oil may have led us into a new geological epoch that we nonetheless propose to name solely after ourselves, the time has indeed come for historians to talk of other things, to escape the intellectual and analytical narcissism that brought us to this existential precipice, and to finally give some long-overdue attention to the many other fellow travelers around us. If we do, we may yet discover that the fault really is not entirely in ourselves but in our stars and the vast multitude of nonhuman things that constitute the ocean in which we swim.

CONCLUSION

In 1936 the British zoologist James Gray – later to be Sir James Gray – identified a seeming paradox that would puzzle researchers for decades to come. Gray was an occasional student of animal locomotion. Like many before him, he had been amazed at the ability of some sea creatures to swim at extraordinarily high speeds and to change directions on a dime. Dolphins, for example, appear to delight in leaping and darting through the wakes of big ships and can speed along as fast as 20 knots. To Gray, the dolphins' high-speed maneuvers seemed effortless compared to the stolid slog of human ships through the viscous water. Intrigued, he calculated how much drag the dolphin's shape would generate as it moved through the water. He then made a rough estimate of the power the dolphin's musculature could theoretically deliver through its tail at peak performance. Based on these numbers, he concluded that dolphins were too weak by a factor of *seven* to be able to swim as fast as they did. Yet since dolphins obviously did reach speeds of 20 knots or more, Gray speculated that the mammals might have some special mechanism through which they dramatically decrease the drag of water on their bodies.[168]

Gray went on to become a highly respected Cambridge professor of cell biology, which in turn earned him his knighthood. But beyond the world of cytology he perhaps remained best known for this somewhat back-of-the-envelope analysis of swimming dolphins that came to be called Gray's Paradox. It inspired a good deal of research on the biomechanics and hydrodynamics of dolphins and similar animals, but the paradox remained largely unresolved for more than half a century. However, in the summer of 1989 two brothers, Michael and George Triantafyllou, who had both earned doctorates in ocean engineering at MIT, were working together at Woods Hole Oceanographic Institution on Cape Cod. In talking with their colleagues, the Triantafyllous wondered if Gray's Paradox might suggest a way to improve the speed and efficiency of human-made ships and submarines. To better understand how dolphins and similar creatures swim so well, they built a robotic replica of another superb swimmer, the bluefin tuna (*Thunnus thynnus*). Unlike Gray's static model, this "RoboTuna" had an articulated body that could approximate the undulating motion of the tuna's body and tail as it sliced through the water. By carefully measuring the RoboTuna's movements in a tank of water, the brothers made a critical breakthrough. They discovered that the water was not just a source of drag that was slowing the fish down – rather, the water was actually helping to make the fish go faster.

Subsequent work observing small tropical fish swimming in a sort of liquid "wind tunnel" confirmed the robotic data: contrary to seeming common sense, fish can actually *gain* energy from swimming through highly viscous water. But how? The Triantafyllous' data showed that, as a tuna sweeps its tail through the water, it creates whirling vortices and pressure gradients that help push its body forward more quickly and

---

[168] James Gray, "Studies in Animal Locomotion VI: The Propulsive Power of the Dolphin," *Journal of Experimental Biology* 13 (1936): 192–9; Michael S. Triantafyllou and George S. Triantafyllou, "An Efficient Swimming Machine: Instinctive Control of Vortices Lets Fish Swim the Way They Do," *Scientific American* 272, no. 3 (March 1995), 64–71.

efficiently. An initial powerful flap of the tail creates a large vortex spinning in one direction and a second flap then creates a vortex spinning in the opposite direction. When the two vortexes meet, they create a jet of moving water that pushes the tuna forward: the tuna, dolphin, and other super swimmers "instinctively exert precise and effective control of the flow around their bodies to extract energy from waves, turbulence, and even their own wakes."[169]

Gray had imagined that the explanation for the dolphin's extraordinary swimming abilities must be entirely contained in the animal itself: in its muscular power, shape, and skin. But the solution to Gray's Paradox was to realize that the dolphin's watery material environment was equally important. What makes the dolphin a dolphin – its quicksilver speed and maneuverability – emerges not only from the animal, but from the water that the animal lives in. I first encountered Gray's Paradox in reading the cognitive philosopher Andy Clark, whose work I discussed earlier. Clark argues that the Triantafyllous' tuna offers a good analogy for how a human brain interacts with the surrounding environment. Just as the tuna cannot be understood outside of its material environment, so is human intelligence "best understood as the activity of an essentially *situated* brain: a brain at home in its proper bodily, cultural and environmental niche."[170] The tuna obviously evolved with and from the water in which it swam, just as our brains evolved in a terrestrial environment – yet why then do we tend to think that only the muscular fish and the brainy human really matters while the environment is nothing but a passive stage on which they act?

The Triantafyllou brothers' solution to the mystery of the dolphin also provides a useful way of understanding the neo-materialist approach to understanding humans and their histories. Just as the extraordinary speed and power of the dolphin emerges from its material surroundings, so too should we understand that the many extraordinary abilities of humans emerge not solely from ourselves but from the material world around us. Reduced to its essence, such a neo-materialist theory and method asks that historians and others pay more attention to the material environment because it plays a much bigger role in creating history than previously recognized. Absent the material things, organisms, and processes from which we conspire to create the amalgam that we term human, our stories about the past are only half told, vaporous in their abstract immateriality.

---

[169] Triantafyllou and Triantafyllou, "An Efficient Swimming Machine."
[170] Clark, "Where Brain, Body, and World Collide," 1.

The neo-materialist game is not to find the decline of the Roman Empire in a lead pipe or the kingdom lost for want of a horse. Rather, it asks historians and humanists to develop a more holistic understanding of the human past, one in which we emerge from and with the things around us, and we forge new chains in every claim of mastery. It is to find history in those things from which human power, ideas, and visions emerged, to explain how coal could create the possibility of democracy or a cotton plant could weave an industrial revolution into existence. And it is to escape the dangerous delusion that we humans chart our course alone, limited only by our imagination and our will to triumph.

In the chapters to come, I will tell the stories of copper mining and smelting pollution at the American Anaconda mine and the Japanese Ashio mine, analyzing the complex material and social ways in which pollutants interacted with the cattle and silkworms in the surrounding environments. While Anaconda and Ashio were in many ways very different places, both materially and culturally, I argue that with the advent of copper mining they were subject to strikingly similar material processes. In both cases, human social power, intelligence, creativity, and cultural diversity had previously emerged from the material possibilities afforded by nonhuman creatures – cows and silkworms. When a different source of human power and culture – copper – began to destroy these organisms, it could not help but also destroy the human cultures so intimately associated with them, forever changing both the American and Japanese people and their nations. Key to the success of this neo-materialist argument is that we come to understand that Longhorns were not just passive resources – rather, they were intelligent social animals that coevolved and interacted with humans to create an entire industry and culture that was central to the American identity. Likewise, that silkworms were far more than mere reflections of Japanese creativity – rather, their ability to evolve rapidly and the demands they placed on humans played an indispensable role in creating a unique Japanese culture, and perhaps even a unique Japanese industrial path. As cattle and silkworms died from the poisons created by copper, some important part of what we mistakenly think of as solely human intelligence, creativity, and other cultural phenomena – of history – died with them. American cattle people and Japanese silkworm people thus began to converge toward an increasingly homogenous global society of copper people.

4

The Longhorn

The Animal Intelligence behind American Open-Range Ranching

In the fall of 1902, many of the cows, horses, and sheep living in the Deer Lodge Valley of southwestern Montana suddenly became ill, bleeding from their noses, staggering aimlessly, and collapsing. Within days, thousands were dead. When veterinarians cut their corpses open, instead of firm, functional livers, kidneys, and hearts, they found bloody lesions and soft collapsing organs. The owners of the animals, small and middling farmers and ranchers, as well as several powerful "cattle kings," demanded to know why, though many suspected they already knew. Their veterinarians offered the best answer that theory and practice then afforded them: arsenic poisoning.[1]

Even a century later, forensic pathologists would not quibble much with their diagnosis, though they could better explain the etiology. Because of its chemical resemblance to phosphorous, arsenic interferes with the production and transport of energy in the cells of all animals, cows and humans alike. The energy-starved cells soon die en masse, and the delicate internal membranes of vital organs disintegrate and rupture. A complex cascade of painful biochemical events ends with heart failure and what is probably by that point a welcome death for the suffering cow or bull.

This much is clear. But scarcely had the word "arsenic" been uttered when the ranchers and veterinarians rose and turned away from the dead animal at their feet, perhaps wiping the blood and gore from their hands as they walked away, already pondering the *true* cause. Arsenic, a merely

---

[1] Montana Historical Society Archives, "Anaconda Copper Mining Company Records," Collection 169, *Bliss v. Washoe*, Box 22, Folder 1, "Opinion," January 25, 1909, 202.

inanimate "thing," could not be the real killer. The more important question was from whence had the arsenic come? Here, too, the answer seemed clear, as they had only to look south to a low ridge at the valley's edge to see the huge clouds of white smoke rising from the Anaconda Copper Mining Company's newly opened Washoe smelter. Scattered among the sulfur dioxide and other noxious gases in the plume were white particles of arsenic trioxide. On days when the wind was calm, the arsenic trioxide would gently settle out of the smoke, falling like a poison snow across the valley range grass. The livestock ate it as they grazed. If they ate enough, they suffered acute arsenic poisoning and died.

To the ranchers at the time, the Anaconda Company was the truly guilty party, and most historians have since agreed. Some scholars have focused their blame on power politics, arguing that the Anaconda's domination of the Montana legislature and economy offers the deepest explanation for the poisonings.[2] Others adopted a wider lens, suggesting that corporate capitalism or perhaps the American consumer's fondness for the blessings of electrification were the root causes.[3] And so on. What unites all of the varied historical explanations, however, is the alacrity with which they move from thinking about things – creatures like cows and molecules like arsenic trioxide – to thinking mostly about humans. Like the ranchers and veterinarians who turned away from their dead cows and fixed their gaze on the human-built smelter, we historians almost reflexively shift our collective analytical gazes away from the material to the social, assuming that, while these two factors might influence each other, they remain fundamentally distinct, and that the latter is usually the most important.

However, to really understand who or what killed the cows in the Deer Lodge Valley, I argue we must instead turn away from our obsessions with ourselves and back to the animals themselves. Let us imagine one in particular, a dead Longhorn cow, as she lies already nearly forgotten by her human keepers, her ravaged entrails now laid bare to the Montana sky. Look closely at the size and shape of that cow, the treacherous sharp hook of her thick wide horns, her lean muscular body, the lanky length of

---

[2] See, for example, Donald MacMillan, *Smoke Wars: Anaconda Copper, Montana Air Pollution, and the Courts, 1890–1924* (Helena: Montana Historical Society Press, 2000), and more broadly, Michael P. Malone, *The Battle for Butte: Mining and Politics on the Northern Frontier, 1864–1906* (Seattle: University of Washington Press, 1981).

[3] I include some of my own earlier work in this category. See Timothy J. LeCain, *Mass Destruction: The Men and Giant Mines That Wired America and Scarred the Planet* (New Brunswick, NJ: Rutgers University Press, 2009).

her legs, and we can begin to see an animal that evolved with and helped to create a culture that we wrongly think of as entirely human: the "cattle king," the cowboy, the evocative dream of the open range are all among its products. If we could look even deeper into the cow's cells ruptured by arsenic, if we could actually *see* the element's perilous affinity for bonding not only with the mitochondrial chemicals that keep both cows and humans alive but with the copper that humans find so useful – then we might also begin to glimpse a very different material form of human culture and power, one associated with the occult hum of distant dynamos and the bright glow of electric lights in the night. Neither of these human foci of culture and power could logically exist apart from the material things in and of themselves, yet humans, then and now, have insisted on drawing clear lines between them in what increasingly looks to be shifting sands. Yet if we do let the lines shift and fade, as they are wont to do, we can begin to suspect the heretical: that what killed that Longhorn cow and the others like it was nothing so simple as politics, capitalism, consumerism, or any other human-centered explanation alone. Rather, the Longhorn was the victim of a fatal collision between very different material things and powers that humans benefited from but only vaguely understood and imperfectly controlled. It was from their engagement with inherently powerful *things* like cows and copper that these diverse and surprising human sociocultural phenomena evolved. In one of them, critical aspects of human power and intelligence emerged from the intimate material and social relationships between humans and the animals they called cattle. In the other, they emerged from a very different but no less intimate relationship with copper. At base, I argue that the conventional histories of these events, and many others like them, have to a significant degree often put the historical causalities backwards. That rather than focusing our attention solely on how the people of the Deer Lodge Valley made cows and copper, we need to also think much more deeply and clearly about how the cows and copper made those people and their ways of life. In this sense, the history of the stock deaths in the Deer Lodge Valley should be understood as a collision between two very different material systems for generating human power and culture. To be sure, these material systems might to greater or lesser degrees be reconciled through politics, laws, and technologies, but even these seemingly wholly anthropogenic matters make little sense unless we first recognize the primal creative and destructive powers of the animals, molecules, and other material things from which they had emerged in the first place.

THE VALLEY OF THE DEER LODGE

Traditional anthropocentric accounts of the settling of Montana's Deer Lodge Valley often stress the story of ranchers and farmers struggling to overcome the challenges of a wild and often-inhospitable frontier land and create civilization. Yet even these predictable pioneer stories implicitly recognize that the valley itself actually played some role in human success. In 1912, looking back at nearly half a century spent in Montana and the Deer Lodge Valley, the early rancher Conrad Kohrs told a journalist: "Nature, while imposing some handicaps, has done much for humanity in this vast region and humanity has ever manifested an ability to make the most of nature's lavishness."[4] Others recorded that the valley "was a rich and fertile farming country, well watered and adapted to raising sheep, cows, horses, swine and all livestock."[5] While the pioneers would have been unlikely to put it in these contemporary terms, they nonetheless understood that the valley itself had a certain measure of material power that derived from the energy stored in those "nutritious" grasses. Further, to tap into those vast yet widely spread stores of solar energy, they knew they would need the assistance of other creatures, animals that possessed powers of their own that went well beyond their crucial ability to turn plants into meat and milk.

The first Longhorns to arrive in the Deer Lodge Valley would have found a ruminant grazer's paradise. As Kohrs observed, it was "one of the best, if not the best valleys in Montana, because the bunch grass was long and very nutritious."[6] Today, the Deer Lodge Valley is classified as part of the Montana Valley and Foothill grasslands ecoregion, an area of river valleys and hills threading through steep mountains that encompasses much of southwestern Montana, as well as a twisting narrow tendril of territory that reaches all the way up into southern Alberta. The Deer Lodge Valley is drained by the Clark Fork River, whose headwaters begin at the base of the Continental Divide just to the southeast near Butte, Montana. Compared to the extreme cold and heat of the northern plains of eastern Montana, the Deer Lodge Valley is relatively temperate, though winter temperatures can occasionally drop to 30 to 40 degrees Fahrenheit below zero (roughly -35 to -40 degrees Celsius). Annual rainfall is sparse, rarely much above 10–12 inches (25-30 cm), and

---

[4] Quoted in Anna Fay Rosenberg, "Hard Winter Endurance: Conrad Kohrs' Cattle Raising Operation, 1887–1900" (MA thesis, University of Montana, 1996), 42.

[5] "Farmers Bring Action," *Anaconda Standard*, May 21, 1905.

[6] "Washoe and Anaconda Are Good Customers," *Anaconda Standard*, February 18, 1906.

significantly less during periodic droughts. The surrounding high mountain peaks capture much of the winter snowfall, helping to keep the valley's grasses exposed for grazing. Prior to the invasion of cows, sheep, and horses, the Deer Lodge was home to several of their ruminant cousins, such as bison, elk, and deer, whose grazing patterns helped to create and maintain the wide open-range lands Kohrs and others came to depend on. Appropriately enough, the valley actually took its name from the white-tailed deer that in winter clustered around the warmth and mineral salts provided by a prominent geothermal cone which had been created by the same geological forces that made the geysers and hot springs of Yellowstone National Park two hundred miles to the southeast. Many different tribes traveled through the valley, including the Flatheads, Nez Perces, Pend d'Oreilles, Spokanes, Snakes, Bannocks, and Kootenais, but by the early nineteenth century the aggressively expansionist Blackfeet regarded it as theirs. Many tribes remarked that in winter the steam rising from the pyramidal cone resembled smoke rising from their own lodges or teepees, but it was the Snakes who named the area *It soo ke en car ne* – the lodge of the white-tailed deer.[7] Though the Euro-Americans who came later would push out the native people and force the animals to seek refuge in the surrounding mountains, the white-tailed deer and their "lodge" nonetheless lived on in the valley's name.[8]

The Deer Lodge Valley range was dominated by several different types of hardy fescues and bunchgrass. Bluebunch wheatgrass (*Pseudoroegneria spicata*) was a member of the immense *Poaceae* family of grassy plants thought to have first evolved some 60 to 70 million years ago. As the name suggests, bunchgrasses grow in scattered clumps rather than forming a dense contiguous mat like Kentucky blue or other lawn grasses. The plants can also develop extraordinarily deep root systems, up to six feet or more, that help them to tap into groundwater during the long Montana dry seasons. Unlike the more familiar eastern range plants like bluegrass, bunchgrass also has the unusual ability to retain much of its high-calorie store of proteins even after the leaves have dried out in late summer, resulting in a type of wild hay. Rice,

---

[7] Mary C. Horstman, "Historical Events Associated with the Upper Clark Fork Drainage," Montana Department of Fish, Wildlife, and Parks, Project #8241 (August 15, 1984): 3–4. See also Virginia Lee Speck, "The History of the Deer Lodge Valley to 1870" (MA thesis, Montana State University, 1946).

[8] Taylor H. Ricketts et al., *Terrestrial Ecoregions of North America: A Conservation Assessment* (Washington, DC: Island Press, 1999), 285–7; "Intermountain/Foothill Grassland Ecotype," in Montana Fish, Wildlife, and Parks, *Comprehensive Fish and Wildlife Conservation Strategy*, (Helena, MT: 2012), 37–42.

wheat, and other cereal grains are also in the *Poaceae* family and are distant evolutionary relatives of bunchgrasses. Humans and cows depend on the same family of plants for much of their energy intake, though humans are only able to digest the tiny seeds whereas cows can consume much of the plant. Without cows or some other ruminant animal, the settlers of Deer Lodge Valley would have had no way to efficiently tap the immense supplies of solar energy stored each year in the valley grasses.[9]

The first cows arrived in the Deer Lodge Valley in the 1860s. They were not just "cows," of course, but rather, according to the terminology of the cattle industry, were a mixture of female cows, castrated males termed "steers," and, more rarely, uncastrated male "bulls." However, to avoid using the dismissive term "cattle" with its misleading sense of total human ownership and domination, I will follow the good example of the historian Reviel Netz and use the term "cows" to refer to a group of *Bos taurus* regardless of their sex, though I will still use the word cattle when historical context or clarity suggests it.[10] Many of the pioneering cows were led into the valley by Euro-Americans like Johnny Grant and, a few years later, by Conrad Kohrs, who were betting that the same grass and environment that supported bison and deer could also keep cows alive. Kohrs's interest in ranching began when he took a job as a butcher in the Montana mining boomtown of Virginia City. He eventually took over and expanded the business and started to purchase local cows to supply his growing number of butcher shops. By 1866 he owned most of the cows in the valley and several sizable properties. These early cows were often a mixture of eastern breeds that had accompanied overland emigrants on their trek to the Northwest along the Oregon Trail. By the time these animals reached southern Idaho, they were often worn down to little more than skin and bones. Many could not go on, and the emigrants could not pause long enough for the animals to graze and recover their strength. Seeing an opportunity, enterprising traders and former mountain men bought the animals cheap, fattened them up for a year in the neighboring Beaverhead and Deer Lodge Valleys, and then sold them to the next wave of Oregon emigrants, or increasingly to the growing numbers of miners seeking gold and silver.

---

[9] The seminal discussion of the energetic basis of the open-range stock industry is Richard White, "Animals and Enterprise," in *The Oxford History of the American West*, ed. Clyde A. Milner, Carol A. O'Connor, and Martha A. Sandweiss (New York: Oxford University Press, 1994),237–74, and especially 252–7.

[10] See Reviel Netz, *Barbed Wire: An Ecology of Modernity* (Middletown, CT: Wesleyan University Press, 2004), 239–40, fn. 7.

FIGURE 4.1 The dangerous horns, powerful long-legged body, and sharp social intelligence of the Texas Longhorns equipped them to fend off predators and survive without human assistance even in challenging semi-arid ecosystems. University of North Texas Library, George Ranch Historical Park (c. 1940).

Having found that the local supply of animals increasingly fell short of demand for beef, in 1871 Kohrs's half-brother and business partner John Bielenberg traveled down to Texas to take advantage of the large population of inexpensive Longhorns. Bielenberg drove about one thousand of the Longhorns back up to Montana, though he appears to have acquired some additional "high-grade" Durham cows along the way. Once they arrived in the Deer Lodge Valley, the Texas Longhorns gradually interbred with the Durham and other eastern breeds, resulting in animals that were particularly well-suited to the northern environment of the Deer Lodge Valley. Yet even as late as 1892, there were some 26,000 recently arrived Texas Longhorns grazing on the same open-range regions that Kohrs was using.[11]

As Kohrs observed in 1885, open-range grazing demanded a huge amount of land. "It takes 20 acres on a new range to feed one cow," he noted, and twice that amount after the range had been grazed for six years.[12] To transform the range's bunchgrass into something humans could consume, the ranchers relied on one of the earliest and perhaps

[11] Rosenberg, "Hard Winter Endurance," 5–15.
[12] Rosenberg, "Hard Winter Endurance," 39.

most successful animal-human partnerships in history. Domesticated since the early Neolithic period, cows have been critical to the survival and expansion of humans around the globe. Their ability to digest complex fibrous plant material like the cellulose of bunchgrass and turn it into muscle and milk provided humans with a convenient source of highly concentrated caloric energy. However, Kohrs, Grant, and other ranchers were able to *efficiently* harness the energy of the Deer Lodge Valley grass only because their cows were willing to work with them in doing so. The material power of the cows thus resided not only in the caloric content of its meat but also in their genetically rooted ability to cooperate with humans that had resulted from domestication and the heritage of centuries of human-animal interaction and accommodation.

THE COEVOLUTIONARY HISTORY OF COWS

The ability of cows to digest plant material like bunchgrass cellulose was a powerful evolutionary development shared with other ruminants such as sheep, goats, bison, deer, and elk. Based on genetic studies, evolutionary biologists believe that this ability first emerged sometime in the mid-Eocene age, some 45 to 50 million years ago, among a group of small forest-dwelling mammals.[13] The modern ruminants' ability to eat grass depends on the evolution of a four-chambered stomach and a symbiotic relationship to a complex and highly adaptable mixture of bacteria, fungi, protozoa, and yeasts. This creative and fast-evolving gut microbiome has the ability to produce cellulase enzymes that break down the cellulose-based walls of many plants through fermentation, thus releasing the critical fatty acids therein to fuel the animals' biology. As one author suggests, the process is somewhat akin to "a big complicated brewery, turning out food instead of beer."[14] In this sense, it was not just the cows that humans would eventually find so useful but also the microbiomes of those cows. At least some of the critical genetic creativity was neither human nor bovine, but bacterial.

The ancestors of modern species of cows are believed to have coevolved with the abundant new temperate-area grasses that first appeared about 23 million years ago. Their coevolution is evident in the way these range

---

[13] T. J. Hackmann and J. N. Spain, "Invited Review: Ruminant Ecology and Evolution: Perspectives Useful to Ruminant Livestock Research and Production," *Journal of Dairy Science* 93 (2010): 1320–34;

[14] M. R. Montgomery, *A Cow's Life* (New York: Walker and Company, 2004), 142–3.

grasses grow from the base of the leaf rather than at the tip of the leaf. This growth pattern permits animals to bite off much of the leaf without destroying the plant's ability to quickly regenerate – the same growth pattern that enables us to mow lawns today without killing the grass. One line of these grazing mammals eventually gave rise to the prehistoric mother of all modern cows, the aurochs, whose image is perhaps most famously painted on the cave walls of Lascaux, France.[15] A Paleolithic artist portrayed the aurochs (the plural form is also used for a single animal) at Lascaux as 17 feet long, which was surely an exaggeration, but perhaps not by all that much. Julius Caesar recorded some 15,000 years later that the surviving aurochs of his era (isolated small herds survived in northern Europe into the early modern period) were "a little smaller than an elephant."[16] Their actual size varied, but skeletal remains indicate the bulls were nearly twice the size of the biggest of their modern descendants. These were fearsome and dangerous beasts with massive, sharp horns, and it is little wonder that the Lascaux artist painted them, either in homage or in supplication. At one of the best explored Neolithic sites in Eurasia, Çatalhöyük in south central Turkey, archaeologists have excavated statues and shrines that suggest the inhabitants worshipped the aurochs with its mighty horns, a creature that was both a source of protein and a symbol of fearsome strength. The excavations have also revealed the remains of a man who had been gored in the groin.[17] Great power seems to have also carried great risks.

With the aurochs, biological evolution created an animal and a microbiome that could efficiently transform immense swaths of dispersed low-calorie grasses into a dense high-calorie meat that humans could digest. To slay just one of these great beasts would have provided enough meat to feed a good-sized band of humans for many months. Yet to focus solely on the paths of energy transfer here is to miss other critical aspects of the material power of the aurochs and its descendants. Kohrs, Grant, and other ranchers were able to efficiently harness the energy of the Deer Lodge Valley grass only because their Longhorn – and later, Shorthorn and Hereford hybrids – were willing to cooperate with them in doing so. Paleolithic humans obtained the high-calorie meat of aurochs

---

[15] D. G. Bradley et al., "Genetics and Domestic Cattle Origins," *Evolutionary Anthropology* (1998): 79–86.

[16] Montgomery, *A Cow's Life*, 3.

[17] Stephen L. Sass, *The Substance of Civilization: Materials and Human History from the Stone Age to the Age of Silicon* (New York: Arcade, 1998), 436.

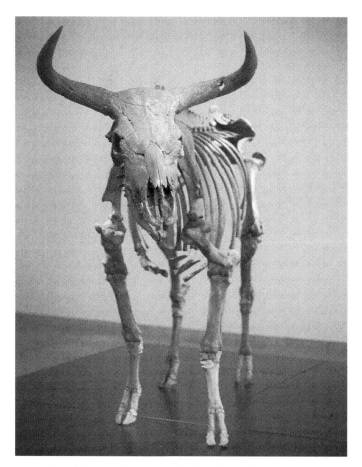

FIGURE 4.2 The skeleton of an aurochs that lived about 10,000 years ago in northern Europe is on display at the National Museum of Denmark in Copenhagen. This enormous animal weighed in at about 1,000 kilograms (2,200 pounds) and measured nearly 2 meters (6.5 feet) at the shoulder. Photograph by Marcus Sümnick.

through the haphazard and hazardous method of hunting. But nineteenth-century ranchers like Kohrs were the unknowing beneficiaries of the material power that had emerged from the centuries-long process of domestication and cooperation.

Just how humans domesticated such a large and dangerous animal as the aurochs is something of a mystery. Caesar noted that the Germanic tribes hunted aurochs for their meat but observed that the beasts were far too aggressive to "be tamed or accustomed to human beings."[18] Scholars of animal domestication point out that of all the earth's thousands of moderately large and potentially useful animals, only a handful have become domesticated. This is not necessarily from a lack of a human effort but rather because the majority of animals have little interest in being domesticated. Some of the native peoples of North America, for example, might very well have coevolved with the abundant Plains bison into some pattern of domesticated cooperation had it been possible. The resulting ease of access to high-calorie meat and (perhaps) milk would likely have been a boon. However, despite the efforts of many to this day, purebred bison (in distinction to the hybrid bison-cow cross) remain distinctly wild animals, even if they are nominally confined and controlled on a bison ranch. They are commensal – that is, willing to tolerate the company of humans – but not really domesticated.

Successful domestication is a two-way coevolutionary process that demands changes in both the human and animal partner. It typically requires an animal species with an inherent capacity to be tamed – in other words, an animal with the ability to tolerate close proximity and cooperation with human beings long enough for the powerful forces of coevolution to kick in. Big terrestrial herbivores that could be candidates for domestication are relatively rare – perhaps about 148 animals. Of these, though, humans have only domesticated 14. For a variety of different reasons, all of the others proved too difficult to domesticate. Cheetahs, which would otherwise have been useful for hunting, simply will not breed in the conditions typically associated with captivity. Bears and hippos, which offer immense amounts of meat, are so dangerous that even careful attempts to control them often ended in disaster well before they could evolve more peaceable temperaments. Perhaps above all else, to be successfully domesticated a species had to share a key trait with their human partners: sociability. Many of the most important domesticated animals – cows, sheep, goats, horses, dogs – were already social creatures before they ever came into contact with humans. Social animals organize themselves into herds or packs in which individuals have a clear place in a hierarchy of power and influence, a type of group culture similar to those formed by humans. Humans are able to exercise some limited influence over these animals because they can take over the top spot in the herd or pack structure. In effect, the animals may well perceive their human partners as strange but still reasonably acceptable versions of themselves.

---

[18] Quoted in Montgomery, *A Cow's Life*, 11.

This may especially be the case with many herd animals, where their young are biologically primed to imprint on the other animals around them. To a calf, a human can for all practical purposes become a cow.[19]

The prominent evolutionary biologist W. D. Hamilton argues that the early ancestors of modern cows (various subspecies of the aurochs, *Bos primigenius*) likely developed just this type of social herding behavior as a defensive measure. As weak-eyed animals that must spend most of their day with their heads down grazing, cows are always vulnerable to attack by predators. By gathering in herds they increase the likelihood that a predator will be spotted before it can attack. The strongest and most dominant animals are also able to claim the safest possible spot at the center, leaving the weaker animals to be sacrificed at the edge.[20]

Why some human farmers in southwest Asia and India, where studies suggest domesticated cows evolved independently about 8,000 years ago, would even attempt close cooperation with the fearsome aurochs is a bit hard to imagine.[21] One theory suggests that the aurochs made the first step. In the centuries following the development of agriculture in the Neolithic age, the big sharp-hoofed beasts congregated around human settlements to graze on their lush fields of wheat, barley, rye, and oats, often doing considerable damage. At first, farmers probably tried to kill them immediately or chase them off. But perhaps some eventually realized that the beasts could be penned and kept to be slaughtered when convenient. If so, the humans might well have killed and ate the most aggressive and troublesome animals first, thus beginning a slow and entirely unintentional process of coevolution that led to calmer more tractable animals.[22]

Regardless of the precise coevolutionary history of the aurochs's domestication, its success depended on the inherent abilities and genetic plasticity of the animals themselves. Likewise, humans changed their own behaviors and genes in order to conform to those of the cows. The unusual human practice of consuming milk after infancy is one of the more striking

---

[19] Jared Diamond, *Guns, Germs, and Steel* (New York: Norton, 1999), 162–7,

[20] W. D. Hamilton, "The Genetical Evolution of Social Behavior (Parts I and II)," *The Journal of Theoretical Biology* 7 (1974): 1–52.

[21] Diamond, *Guns, Germs, and Steel*, 161.

[22] Useful overviews are offered in Ian Mason, *The Evolution of Domestic Animals* (London: Longman, 1984), and A. Smith, "Review Article: Cows Domestication in North Africa," *The African Archaeological Review* 4(1986): 197–203. See also the discussion of domestication in Alfred Crosby, *Ecological Imperialism: The Biological Expansion of Europe, 900–1900* (Cambridge, UK: Cambridge University Press, 1986).

examples of the coevolutionary history some modern humans share with cows. Like all mammals, human babies possess a special enzyme lactase that makes it possible for them to digest the lactose sugars in mother's milk. But babies are not overly picky about whether the milk comes from humans or cows (though mother's milk offers a better source of key nutrients needed by babies younger than one year). The ability to supplement human milk with cow's milk greatly increased the calories available to small children and thus their survivability. However, today, as in the Neolithic age, most humans lose their ability to consume milk by adulthood. The roughly 25 percent of the global population that is descended primarily from north-central European and East African ancestors are an exception, reflecting the intimate bonds these peoples developed with cows. Compelled by hunger, many of our Neolithic ancestors probably tried to drink milk as adults. It would have been an obvious food source, and many might well have already successfully experimented with feeding it to their infants. Thus when a chance genetic mutation occurred that permitted the bodily production of the lactose-digesting enzyme to persist into adulthood, these cow-humans were already primed to take advantage of it, consuming it not only as milk but also eventually as cheese, butter, and other dairy products. According to some recent studies, the caloric benefits from drinking milk would allow those who had this genetic mutation to produce as many as *ten times* the number of surviving descendants as their non-milk-drinking counterparts, ensuring that the gene quickly became a dominant trait among humans who lived with cows.[23]

In sum, it was not just that humans encouraged certain genes and cultural traits to develop in cows but that the cows encouraged certain genes and cultural traits in humans. Cows made some humans as much as those humans made them. This coevolution of cows and humans in many ways proved beneficial for both. With the additional calories made possible by the meat and milk of domesticated cows, humans were able to expand their populations beyond that of typical hunter-gatherer societies that they often replaced, either by out-competing them or through war. For their part, the number of cows on the planet increased rapidly as domestication spread, as for example when their human partners helped cows to replace the previously dominant bison on the North American plains. This powerful material partnership was not without its dangers,

---

[23] A good recent summary of the research is Andrew Curry, "The Milk Revolution," *Scientific American* 500 (August 1, 2013): 20–2.

however. In addition to having to devote considerable time, energy, and resources to raising their cows, humans suffered from the many devastating zoonotic diseases that made the evolutionary jump from cows to humans. Measles, tuberculosis, and smallpox all likely originated from the close human association with the cows they supposedly controlled.[24]

Despite these very real dangers, this human partnership with cows and other animals would eventually help power the European rise to global dominance. Even the zoonotic diseases proved to be a powerful tool of conquest. Europeans eventually evolved resistance to cow-borne diseases, but the native people of the New World who had no domestic cattle were devastatingly vulnerable. It is perhaps not too much to say that the most powerful weapon the Europeans brought to bear in their conquest of the Americas was a biological one: the diseases given to them by their cows and other domestic animals. Cows, pigs, horses, and other animals gave the Europeans many other advantages, and had the New World peoples had their own large domestic animals, the history of the world might well have been very different. This Eurasian advantage, however, was largely the product of sheer luck. As Jared Diamond points out, there were far fewer candidates for domestication in other parts of the world than there were in Eurasia. In North America, as recently as 15,000 years ago, there had been a wide variety of big mammals, including species of horses and camels that might well have been good candidates for domestication by the North American Indians. However, during the subsequent 5,000 years many of these species went extinct, most likely because of a combination of over-hunting by humans and climate change.[25] Yet whatever the causes, the loss of this immensely rich reservoir of species severely constrained the ability of the indigenous peoples of North America to benefit from the material power of other intelligent social animals, significantly undermining their ability to resist the later European invaders.

THE LONGHORNS

When Conrad Kohrs first began ranching Texas Longhorns in the Deer Lodge Valley in 1866, he could not have known that he was benefitting from a six-thousand-year-old history of humans living and dying in close cooperation with these extraordinary animals. Yet what Kohrs knew or

---

[24] Diamond, *Guns, Germs, and Steel*, 199, and Alfred Crosby, *Plagues and People* (Garden City, NY: Doubleday, 1976).

[25] Diamond, *Guns, Germs, and Steel*, 46.

thought he knew about his Longhorns in some ways mattered very little in comparison to the immense material power they possessed, and he would spend much of his adult life cooperating with the animals in order to harness this "thing-power" for his own ends. Even if Kohrs only dimly comprehended its origins and nature, the power of his cows would nonetheless make him into one of the state's most influential men. In the usual way we often like to tell stories about ourselves, Kohrs would likely be presented as a self-made man. But he might better be thought of as a cow-made man. Or perhaps a Longhorn-made man.

A good part of the early cows that migrated to Montana's Deer Lodge Valley were Texas Longhorns, lean and long-legged animals whose great sharp horns could stretch as much as seven feet from tip to tip in some steers, an echo of the mighty aurochs from whence they had come. As noted earlier, Kohrs's initial herd of mixed-breed eastern cows received a big infusion of Longhorns when his half-brother John Bielenberg drove a herd of about a thousand of the animals up to the Deer Lodge Valley from Texas.[26] These Texas Longhorns were the descendants of Spanish and Portuguese breeds, most likely from the southern Andalusian region of the Iberian peninsula, shipped to the New World by the conquistadors in the sixteenth century. Recent genetic research, however, suggests that these Spanish and Portuguese cows may themselves have had genetic roots with Brahman or Zebu cows from India (*Bos indicus*) rather than the separately domesticated line of European cows (*Bos taurus*). This evolutionary history of adapting to the more tropical Indian climate may explain the Longhorn's ability to better tolerate drought and food stresses, as well as their relative inability to quickly gain weight.[27]

Regardless of their precise genetic lineage, the animals thrived in the scrubby woodland of southeast Texas, where their Spanish and later Mexican "owners" let them run free to fend for themselves. Some developed what were essentially wild herds that survived with no human care. Indeed, the Spanish and Mexicans may well have deliberately used these semiferal Longhorns as a powerful material tool for extending the ragged and contested edge of their northern frontier. As the historian Virginia DeJohn Anderson has shown, the American colonists used cows, pigs, and other "creatures of empire" as an animal avant-garde that pushed their

---

[26] Rosenberg, "Hard Winter Endurance," 15.

[27] E. J. McTavish et al., "New World Cows Show Ancestry from Multiple Independent Domestication Events," *Proceedings of the National Academy of Science* 110 (2013): E1398–406.

claims westward into native territories well in advance of actual human settlement.[28] Whether by intent or accident, the wandering Longhorns did similar work for the Spanish. Intelligent, fast-breeding, and well-armed, the Longhorns could protect themselves and their offspring from many predators and survive the winter without being fed by humans. In this they resembled the American bison, which in the sixteenth century were as yet still the most populous large herbivore on the planet. Nonetheless, these semiferal Longhorns still carried the genetic markers of their earlier coevolutionary history with human beings in India and Iberia. When horseback mounted men took a renewed interest in them in the second half of the nineteenth century, the Longhorns were not so skittish or aggressive that they saw the men as mortal threats to be attacked or resisted at all costs. The Longhorns could be herded, albeit reluctantly and still dangerously, up to lucrative markets at the rail terminals of the newly sprouted Midwest "cattle towns" like Dodge City and Abilene. Eventually, the hardy animals would even walk all the way north to ranches in the central and northern Great Plains, including Kohrs's ranch in Montana's Deer Lodge Valley. While perhaps a source of considerable annoyance to the individual cows themselves, this human-assisted territorial expansion would soon after allow these adaptive animals to replace the bison as the dominant North American herbivore. Many of the histories chronicling the foundation of the western stock industry celebrate, or sometimes bemoan, the humans who "drove" the animals north and "raised" them on vast swaths of public land. Yet what is often less recognized and understood is the crucial fact that thousands of these semiferal cows were willing and able to make the trip. In this the ranchers owed their eventual power and success to the social hierarchy and herding practices of the cows themselves, as well as the animals' ability to traverse large distances quickly and process almost any available woody or grassy forage for caloric intake.[29] The abilities of these cows and steers to harness the

---

[28] Virginia DeJohn Anderson, *Creatures of Empire: How Domestic Animals Transformed Early America* (New York: Oxford University Press, 2006).

[29] The literature on the history of the western cattle industry is vast and ranges from romantic popularizations to serious scholarly studies. But some key works include Don Worcester, *The Texas Longhorn: Relic of the Past, Asset for the Future* (College Station: Texas A&M University Press, 1987); Maurice Frink, W. Turrentine Jackson, and Wright Spring, *When Grass Was King: Contributions to the Western Range Cattle Industry Study* (Boulder: University of Colorado Press, 1956); Edward Everett Dale, *The Range Cattle Industry: Ranching on the Great Plains from 1865 to 1925* (Norman: University of Texas Press [1930] 1960); James A. Young and B. Abbott Sparks, *Cattle in the Cold Desert* (Logan: Utah State Press, 1985),

energy-rich grasses of the southern and northern plains is captured in the words of a successful rancher of the time: "A three year old fat steer in the South of Texas weighs 900 to 950 pounds; in the north of Texas, 1,100 pounds; in New Mexico and south and middle Colorado, 1,100 pounds; while in Wyoming, and still farther north in Montana, 1,200 to 1,300 pounds."[30]

In the Deer Lodge Valley of the latter years of the nineteenth century, ranchers depended on a delicate balance between the Longhorns' hardy independence and their willingness to tolerate humans. On the high plains, a mother cow has to be aggressive enough to protect her calf from danger – wolves, mountain lions, and other predators – but not so aggressive that she attacks any human who comes near her and her calf. In this sense, the Longhorns and later hybrid breeds of range cows all had to remain somewhere in the imprecise borderlands between domestication and wildness. In this the animals fit Frederick Jackson Turner's belief in the character-forming force of the frontier better than most humans. As one student notes of the Aberdeen Angus, a similarly hardy and successful open-range breed, the ability of any cows to take care of themselves largely depends on tapping into the animal's own highly evolved social behaviors and hierarchies within the complex system of a herd:

If [a rancher] wants a cow that will protect its calf (up to a point and when appropriate), a cow that will range widely in a summer pasture, exploring to the fence lines for particularly choice morsels of grass and brush and in springtime for the delectable flower stalks of the soap yuccas; if he needs a cow that can stand stoically next to her calf in a blizzard and not drift with the wind, then he has also to accept the bullying, the chain of dominance."[31]

Though they originated in much-warmer climates, Longhorns also proved surprisingly adaptive to the cold weather of the central and northern plains. Pioneer ranchers like Kohrs were able to snap up the most favorable sites, well-watered and sheltered valleys and drainages with abundant grasses. For several decades, their cows seemed to survive the winter with relatively few deaths.[32] Still, a harsh winter where layers of

---

A. H. Sanders, *Shorthorn Cattle* (Chicago: Sanders, 1916); and James Frank Dobie, *The Longhorns* (Austin: University of Texas Press, 1980).
[30] Walter Von Richthofen, *Cattle-Raising on the Plains of North America* (New York: Appleton, 1885), 56–7.
[31] Montgomery, *A Cow's Life*, 211–2.
[32] Mary C. Horstman, "Historical Events Associated with the Upper Clark Fork Drainage," 29.

thick snow and ice might cover the bunchgrass could still be deadly. The infamous winter of 1886–87 (discussed in more detail later in the chapter) killed tens of thousands of Montana Longhorns and related hybrid breeds, many of them dying in masses along the barbed wire fences that were by then already beginning to limit their ability to range widely in search of food and shelter. Even those that did manage to survive a hard winter might later die from disease or predators that they were by then too weak to resist. In some areas, the over-winter losses could be as high as 90 percent, a death rate that early ranchers tolerated because the rangeland was free and their Longhorn could regenerate quickly.[33] In some areas, ranchers would still run Texas Longhorns on open ranges without any supplemental feeding until nearly the end of the century. Increasingly, though, many stock growers realized that the costs of growing and storing summer hay for winterfeed could easily pay for itself in increased survivability and growth rates. Yet if ranchers were to go to the trouble and expense of winter-feeding, then the value of the Longhorn's ability to fend for itself decreased, while its shortcomings in rates of meat production and difficulties in handling became more apparent. Even when shipped to stockyards where they were fed a rich diet of corn and sweet-clover hay, Longhorns did not fatten quickly to produce the kind of richly marbled beef that many Americans increasingly favored. Likewise, the aggressive traits and sharp horns that had helped Longhorns fend off predators and take care of themselves on the open plains became downright dangerous in the confined spaces of a feedlot or slaughterhouse.[34] By the final decades of the century, ranchers like Kohrs and others around the West had begun looking to fatter and gentler breeds to exploit their immense ranges of bunchgrass.

The English and Scots had enjoyed considerable success in breeding new strains of cows to maximize the animals' ability to turn forage into meat, particularly the Shorthorn (Durham), Hereford, and Aberdeen Angus breeds. In the early eighteenth century, cows sold on the London beef markets averaged only around 370 pounds. Yet within a century, aggressive breeding efforts had almost doubled the size of the animals, and truly massive Shorthorns could weigh more than 2,000 pounds. Other

---

[33] The role of barbed wire fences in increasing winter fatality rates is discussed in David L. Wheeler, "Winter on the Cows Range: Western Kansas, 1884–1886," *Kansas History* 15 (Spring 1992): 1–17.

[34] James A. Young and Charlie D. Clements, "Durham Cattle on the Western Range," *Journal of the West* 45 no. 1 (Winter 2006): 35–42, here 7.

breeders focused their efforts on dairy cows, seeking to maximize milk rather than meat production. The resulting Jerseys and Holsteins were distinctly different from their cousins destined for the table, marking one of the first major instances of human-animal genetic specialization.[35] Specific strains of cows were now being consciously designed to serve as organic machines for maximizing the transformation of grass into either meat or milk. General-purpose all-around cows like Longhorns began to fade in importance.

The first Shorthorns were imported to Virginia shortly after the Revolutionary War. However, for almost a century, few ranchers west of the Mississippi had much interest in the animals. Despite their obvious superiority in producing profitable meat, British purebred Shorthorns did poorly even in the warmer southern plains, perhaps in part because they were vulnerable to tick-borne diseases. The solution lay in crossbreeding the Shorthorns with the hardy Longhorns, either deliberately or accidentally. The resulting animal was larger and meatier than a Longhorn, yet better able to survive disease and harsh conditions than purebred Shorthorns. Critically, the hybrid heifers (young females who have yet to produce offspring) also soon proved to be exceptionally good frontier mothers, producing both bigger calves and the increased milk needed to feed them.[36]

Where ranchers had the interest and the resources to care for them in the winter, Anglo-European purebreds also began to be introduced, including Shorthorns, as well as the white-faced Herefords and the black square-backed Aberdeen Angus imported from Scotland. Indeed, short or hornless (what ranchers refer to as polled) cows were actually better adapted to withstand the cold winters of the northern plains. Unlike the antlers of deer or elk, which grow during the spring but subsequently become dead bone, the living horn of a steer or cow is constantly supplied by blood from within. The thin sheath of the horn provides little insulation, so large-horned cows like Longhorns lose a great deal of body heat through their horns. This may have been an acceptable and even useful trait in southern Spain or Texas, but it was a disadvantage in northern climates.[37]

Breeding for maximum meat production also has its downsides. Breeders have often been tempted to select for "deep" bodies – thickness

---

[35] Montgomery, *A Cow's Life*, 33–4.
[36] Young and Clements, "Durham Cattle on the Western Range," 39–40.
[37] Montgomery, *A Cow's Life*, 131.

measured top to bottom – as this increases the relative amount of the more valuable cuts of meat carried by any animal. Deep bodies, though, came at the price of shorter legs, which in turn limits the ability of a cow to forage for food efficiently over large areas of range only sparsely covered with forage. Shorter legs meant more energy expended in walking, which in turn meant more calories burned for less fodder consumed. In some cases, extremely large animals, especially steers, even outgrew the strength of their feet to hold up under all that weight, leading to frequent foot injuries that severely limited their ability to graze.[38] Very large cows also tended to bear very large calves, and the fetus sometimes became so big that an unassisted birth was impossible. If no ranchers or cowboys happened to be present during the birth to help pull the over-sized offspring out, both the mother and the calf could die.

In the transition from the wily and independent Longhorns to breeds that were so grotesquely overgrown that their cows could not even give birth without a cowboy midwife, it is evident that humans played an ever more intimate role in shaping the cows they raised. Indeed, the more deeply humans tapped into the inherent material powers of cows, the more tightly bound they became to them. But while the success of the open-range cattle industry was a result of cooperation between human and animal abilities, in the end this was of course a system designed to benefit humans, not cows. As the historian Reviel Netz notes, open-range ranching in essence turned the intelligent social nature of cows against them, exploiting their cooperative herding nature to more efficiently prepare them for slaughter in the meat-packing plants to the east. If a herd of Kohrs's cows had somehow realized this, the rational decision would have been to break up the herd and spread out so widely across the landscape that no number of cowboys could ever efficiently round them up.[39] But their practice of congregating in herds had effectively protected cows from predators for hundreds of thousands of years, while several thousand years of coevolution with humans had made them more trusting than they should have been. Nor was the open-range industry without other stark elements of violent coercion. Consider, for example, the description of the often-romanticized process of branding a cow, offered by a pair of western authors in the 1940s. As the red-hot branding iron literally burns the cow's flesh, "there is an acrid odor, strong, repulsive," and the cow

---

[38] Montgomery, *A Cow's Life*, 159–60. [39] Netz, *Barbed Wire*, 18.

"will go BAWR-R-R-R, its eyes will bulge alarmingly, its mouth will slaver, and its nose will snort."[40] It was also during the roundup that most of the young male or bull calves would be castrated by cutting off their testicles, an intensely painful and stressful experience for the calf that caused them to lose weight and sometimes led to serious infections. Despite these risks, ranchers preferred having steers (castrated bulls) because their lower levels of testosterone made them less aggressive and easier to control. As ranchers later became more focused on controlled breeding, castrating most of the males also allowed them to select what they considered to be the best bulls to breed. When the open range began to close, ranchers also began to make heavy use of barbed wire to control the movement of their cows, counting on the pain inflicted by sharp barbs on sensitive skin to force the animals to stay within prescribed boundaries.[41] The historian of animals Susan Nance is surely correct that, at least in terms of such violent coercion and their ultimate slaughter, "animals did not willingly participate in this human-animal interaction and we are all complicit in this history."[42]

All of this, of course, was designed to maximize the efficiency and profit of getting high-protein meat onto the tables and into the bodies of human beings. No one should make the mistake of viewing the open-range cattle industry as some sort of harmonious Eden where the interests of humans and cows smoothly meshed. As Netz rightly argues, this was an extractive industry in which humans obtained a massive supply of caloric energy by dominating cows through violence or its threat. But in recognizing that humans often acted brutally, we should also take care not to avoid suggesting that humans were entirely in control, a mistake that simply contributes to an already-inflated sense of human hubris. To frame the open-range cattle industry solely as a case of human domination and exploitation is to risk losing sight of the equally important insight that much of the intelligence and skill that made open-range ranching and its associated human power possible came from the cows themselves, not from humans.

INTELLIGENCE, ENTROPY, AND POWER

Just how much social power the Longhorns and other breeds in the Deer Lodge Valley created for humans is difficult to precisely delineate. Nick

---

[40] Netz, *Barbed Wire*, 19.   [41] Netz, *Barbed Wire*, 31.
[42] Susan Nance, "Animal History: The Final Frontier?" *The American Historian* 6 (November 2015): 28–32, quote on 32.

Bielenberg, another of Kohrs's half-brothers, estimated that by the early twentieth century he had raised more than 100,000 head of cows.[43] Kohrs himself reported he had raised some 200,000 head since he arrived in the valley in 1864, and he eventually came to own nearly a million acres of land scattered around four states and two Canadian provinces. Enjoying a tremendous first-mover advantage, Kohrs and John Bielenberg were able to extract huge profits from the energy stored in the plants of the Deer Lodge Valley and other ranges. In 1882, for example, they shipped a herd of 1,100 steers to the Chicago meat-packing plants for which they earned some $93,500. Another big sale the next year brought in $94,000. Even accounting for shipping and labor costs, Kohrs and Beilenberg were making excellent returns.[44] Wisely, the two half-brothers refused to participate in the emerging "feeder-cattle" system favored by the railroads, where young, underweight cows were shipped off to feedlots in the east to be fattened on corn before then being sent to the Union Stockyard slaughterhouses in Chicago. The partners preferred to fatten the cows on the Montana range so they could sell them as three or four year olds at higher prices.[45] Both men became very wealthy. Bielenberg chose to remain in the Deer Lodge Valley actively running his ranching operations, but Kohrs invested his ranching wealth in other businesses and used it to pursue a successful political career.[46] Kohrs was among the original "Cattle Kings" who dominated the early politics of many western plains states. He became a territorial and later a state senator, was a delegate to the Montana constitutional convention, and served as the president of the Montana Stockgrowers Association.[47] However, in contrast to Wyoming, where the Cheyenne ranching interests dominated the state for a time, in Montana Kohrs and other ranchers had to compete for political power with timber, farming, and especially mining interests.[48]

Obviously, the social power of Kohrs and other successful ranchers was a product of the wealth generated from their cows. In 1899, when Kohrs and his wife Augusta built a fine new mansion in Helena, the Montana

---

[43] "Mr. Bielenberg Discusses Smoke," *Anaconda Standard*, March 3, 1906.
[44] Rosenberg, "Hard Winter Endurance," 20.
[45] Rosenberg, "Hard Winter Endurance," 57.
[46] "Washoe and Anaconda Are Good Customers," *Anaconda Standard*, February 18, 1906.
[47] *Progressive Men of the State of Montana* (Chicago: A. W. Bowen., 1903); McGrew, "Conrad Kohrs," 1–10; Conrad Kohrs, *Conrad Kohrs: An Autobiography* (Helena, MT: C. K. Warren, [1913] 1977); and Lewis Atherton, *The Cattle Kings* (Lincoln: University of Nebraska Press, 1972), 183.
[48] Atherton, *The Cattle Kings*, 67.

state capital, it might seem irrelevant whether the dollars that paid for it came from cattle raising, mining, or even betting on horse races. One of the defining characteristics of capitalism is its ability to reduce everything to the same unit of measurement, an abstract price that tends to obscure the original source of value. However, as William Cronon rightly argued some years ago, the true source of value for a commodity like beef, corn, or lumber has its origins in the energy from the sun that they store and concentrate: "This was the wealth of nature, and no human labor could create the value it contained. Although people might use it, redefine it, or even build a city from it, they did not produce it."[49] Such a materialist energy flow analysis should remind us that Kohrs's mansion was, in part, a reformulation of the energy first captured in the bunch grass of the Deer Lodge Valley and subsequently concentrated into the muscles of Longhorn cows. When we look at Kohrs's mansion, we should see sunshine, bunch grass, and Longhorns, as much as we see the granite and marble that builders cobbled together based on whatever the latest architectural style of the day happened to be. As Edmund Russell and his colleagues rightly suggest, the ability of some humans to control and direct the planet's finite flows of energy provides the essential material basis for their ability to exert control over other humans. "All power, social as well as physical," they argue, "derives from energy." Moreover, once built, Kohrs's mansion became part of a new material niche that generated further social power for Kohrs by helping to shape how other human beings thought and acted. Kohrs's mansion was not just a *symbol* of his power. Rather, it literally *constituted* his power, even long after he was dead. As humans grew up and lived in the material niche Kohrs had helped to create, their own ways of thinking and acting would henceforth be shaped by his mansion. The same can be said of the two-story brick addition Kohrs had earlier added to his home ranch in 1890. At a time when Montana was still widely seen as a primitive frontier, Kohrs's new home had central heating, indoor plumbing, and a carbide gas generator that provided light for the entire house. As Kohrs himself noted, the new addition, which included a room for his half-brother John Bielenberg, "proved a great comfort" and the "furnace, water-works and gas plant gave us all the conveniences of the city" while lightening the "burdens of the housekeeper perceptibly."[50] When neighboring farmers and ranchers

---

[49] William Cronon, *Nature's Metropolis: Chicago and the Great West* (New York: Norton, 1991), 149–50.
[50] Quoted in Rosenberg, "Hard Winter Endurance," 48.

passed by at night, the sight of Kohrs's ranch house ablaze with gas light in the midst of the otherwise almost-endless expanse of dark countryside surely shaped their ideas about the nature of human power in radically new ways. Here the flesh of cows and bulls defied even the dark and perhaps even promised a new era of enlightenment – a topic I will return to in Chapter 6.

As I have suggested, however, the energy content of Longhorn meat constituted only part of the material power of cows. Equally important was their ability to survive largely on their own, yet also cooperate with humans when asked. While the analogy is not entirely precise, this type of material power can be usefully thought of in terms of another closely related concept borrowed from physics: entropy. In physics, entropy is typically understood as a measure of the disorder in a moving or energy-using system. In a steam engine, for example, fuel is burned to generate heat that creates high-energy pressurized steam that is initially concentrated in a compressed cylinder, resulting in a relatively high-order (and low-entropy) state. When the steam expands and thus does useful work in moving the cylinder, the system loses order and entropy goes up as the useful organized energy of the steam is dissipated through a loss of pressure and heat. Hence, as the entropy or disorder of a system increases, it contains less usable energy available for doing real work.[51]

According to the second law of thermodynamics, all closed systems will either remain stable or increase in entropy; like the steam engine, once all the coal or other energy source in the system is used up, it simply stops working. However, the input of new energy from outside the system (as when we add coal to the steam engine, or the sun adds energy to the earth) can again increase order and decrease entropy. Likewise, humans and other animals can use their bodily energy and cognitive abilities to increase the order of a system. For example, humans might gather coal dispersed over a large mine into one concentrated area where its chemical energy content could be used to continually fuel a steam engine.

Viewed in this way, the behavioral abilities of Longhorns and their related hybrid species helped ranchers like Kohrs in some sense to decrease the entropy of the Deer Lodge Valley. First, by grazing widely using their own intelligence and skills, the cows concentrated the solar energy dispersed over a wide area into their relatively compact and portable bodies. Second, thanks to their long coevolutionary history with humans,

---

[51] An accessible explanation is Morton Mott-Smith, *The Concept of Energy Simply Explained* (New York: Dover, [1934] 1964), 173–91.

the Longhorns had brains and instincts that allowed ranchers and their cowboys to gather them efficiently in one spot during a roundup. Entropy thus decreased as dispersed cows concentrated in one area, such as a corral or feedlot, simultaneously increasing their potential to do further useful work for humans as a ready source of the caloric energy we call food.

In contrast to a tightly closed physical system like a steam engine, where entropy can be precisely measured, the Deer Lodge Valley ecosystem was far more complex and open to many inputs and variables. Nonetheless, the concept of entropy provides a useful way to understand how the intelligence of Kohrs's Longhorns helped to decrease the chaotic disorder of his ranch and thus increase its potential usefulness and value. At base, the social power of Deer Lodge Valley ranchers like Kohrs derived from a surprisingly complex system for energy conversion and concentration that depended on the unique physical and behavioral powers of the Longhorns themselves. In this sense, what is typically seen as solely the human intelligence behind successful open-range cows ranching is better understood as a type of distributed intelligence, one in which human and animal abilities merge almost seamlessly.[52] Order emerged from relative disorder, and usable energy replaced a sort of chaotic entropy. Ultimately, the energy that had been so efficiently concentrated in the muscles of the cows would feed thousands of humans, most of them well beyond the boundaries of the Deer Lodge Valley.

Likewise, much of what we consider to be the exclusively human-made culture of ranching – cowboys, roundups, the supposed freedom of the open range – were really behavioral by-products both enabled and dictated by the animals themselves. The cowboy is well named, as it was the particular behaviors and needs of the cow (and the horse as well – a topic for another time) that largely shaped the nature of the cowboy's daily patterns of work and rest, manner of dress, and even ways of thinking. Yet despite the dynamic and indispensable role that these animals played, historians typically credit only humans with having "domesticated" cows and "invented" the open-range stock industry. Most of the agency, and surely all of the culture and intelligence, are reserved for humans alone. Americans like to celebrate the western cowboy as the epitome of individual male freedom, when perhaps he is better understood as a human whose culture and ways of thinking were to a large

---

[52] Andy Clark, "Where Brain, Body and World Collide," in *Material Agency: Towards a Non-Anthropocentric Approach*, ed. Carl Knappett and Lambros Malafouris (New York: Springer, 2008), 1–18.

degree shaped by the need to cooperate closely with another social animal. The cows constructed the cowboy. Indeed, to the degree that Frederick Jackson Turner was correct that a culture of western independence shaped the American republic, surely some credit must go to the spirited independence and intelligence of the neglected Longhorn that permitted some humans to make their living on the vast wide-open spaces of the Great Plains.

That Longhorn and other cows evolved genetically as a result is undoubted. Kohrs and other ranchers increasingly bred their cows with the deliberate goals of producing desirable characteristics, such as faster growth rates and increased production of desired types of meat. Significantly, though, much of this "breeding" was again left to the ample abilities of the cows and bulls to make their own choices. In the 1890s Kohrs's herds of purebred Hereford and Shorthorns had grown so large that he did not have the space to keep what he referred to as the "different families" from mixing as they would. Never overly concerned about meticulous pedigree records, Kohrs was content simply to benefit from – and profit from – the hybrid vigor that emerged from the animals' own actions. However, the niches the cows had helped to create also influenced the animals. In the early decades of open-range ranching, even the tough and intelligent Longhorns suffered high mortality rates during severe winters. This was especially apparent during the "Great Die Up" of the winter of 1886–87. During the decade before 1886, ranchers eager to maximize profits, both for themselves and international investors who had rushed into the lucrative cattle industry, overran the range, crowding in far too many cows and steers. Combined with a relatively dry summer that limited the growth of range grasses, overgrazing meant that the range was already in poor shape as winter approached. Still, winters had been relatively mild for much of this time, creating an over-confidence that most of the animals could survive without supplementary feed. In late November, a powerful blizzard brought deep snow and temperatures as low as 30 degrees below zero Fahrenheit (-34 degrees Celsius). In earlier winters, cold weather had produced a fine powdery snow that the cows could easily dig through to feed on the grasses beneath. But this time a hard layer of ice formed on top of the snow, which was exacerbated when a short-lived warm wind that Montanans called a Chinook brought a brief thaw before a sharp drop in temperature created an impenetrable layer of thick ice. While many commentators bemoaned the human fortunes and lives lost, it was also difficult to ignore the immense suffering of the steers and cows themselves. As the animals tried to dig down to the sparse grass, the sharp-edged ice cut their hooves and legs until they were a mass of clotted and frozen blood. Desperate to find water, the cows would venture out on thin river ice and break through. Here their social herding instincts turned against them, and "the ones behind would push the front ones in."[53] If they were not trapped under the ice and drowned, they soon after died from hypothermia as the cold wind froze their wet fur. Many retreated into ravines that offered some protection from the biting wind, yet this is also where the snow would pile and drift most deeply. A newspaper reported that the dead cows were seen "buried in the snow standing up, and nothing but the horns visible." One wretched animal "was seen fully exposed standing against a rock, frozen stiff."[54] The greatest toll was often on the weakest: one ranch reported that of the 700 calves that had been alive the previous fall, only 15 survived until spring.

The soon-to-be-famous Montana artist Charles M. Russell was working on the Bar-R ranch in the Judith Basin in central Montana that winter. In the early spring he made a quick watercolor sketch that graphically captured the result. An emaciated steer stumbles through a cold gray field of snow, his ribs protruding, abdomen sunken, and his once-powerful hind legs scarcely more than bones. In the distance two hungry wolves, or perhaps coyotes, await an easy if lean meal. Russell captioned the illustration "Waiting for a Chinook" (when he painted a later oil version Russell added the phrase, "The Last of the Five Thousand") and the grisly image became a powerful symbol of human greed, the harshness of Montana winters, and the suffering experienced by thousands of Montana cows and steers.[55]

When a thaw finally began in March of 1887, the ghastly death toll gradually became apparent. As one newspaper reported, "It is an indisputable fact that almost every bull on the range has perished, and many more cows and young cows than was at first supposed."[56] While precise numbers are impossible to determine, a reasonable estimate from the time

---

[53] E. C. Abbott and Helena Huntington Smith, *We Pointed Them North: Recollections of a Cowpuncher* (Norman: University of Oklahoma Press),206–7.

[54] "The Condition of Stock All Over the Territory," *The River Press* (Fort Benton, MT), February 23, 1887, 8. Quoted in Kyle Tusler, "The Blizzard and Winter of 1886–1887: How It Devastated the Ranching Industry in Eastern Montana" (unpublished MA professional paper, Montana State University, Spring 2015).

[55] "Stock Notes," *The River Press* (Fort Benton, MT), February 23, 1887.

[56] "Items of Interest from Both Sides of the Divide," *The Philipsburg Mail* (Philipsburg, MT), June 2, 1887, 1.

FIGURE 4.3 The Montana cowboy turned artist Charles M. Russell captured the horrific carnage of the harsh winter of 1886–87 with this watercolor sketch called "Waiting for a Chinook." When he painted later versions of the image, Russell added the haunting phrase, "Last of the Five Thousand." Courtesy of the Montana Stockgrowers Association, Helena, Montana.

was that some 360,000 cows, bulls, steers, and calves died on the Montana range that winter, slightly more than half the total herd.[57] The percentage lost at individual ranches could be much higher. The D-S ranch in Fergus County had been running 22,000 head in the fall of 1886, but cowboys found only 240 cows alive in the spring. Kohrs also had a large herd in the same area, and he lost approximately two-thirds of his animals.[58] Not surprisingly, Kohrs's cows in the sheltered Deer Lodge Valley fared much better. Estimated deaths in the western valleys like Deer Lodge and the Beaverhead were about 8 percent versus the 30–50 percent of the eastern Plains. In addition to better weather conditions, Kohrs had already begun providing winterfeed to his Deer Lodge stock that year.[59]

Just how deeply the ranchers of Montana felt this tremendous carnage of the social animals that had made their lives and fortunes possible is hard to judge. Some, like the well-known Montana pioneer Granville Stuart in an oft-quoted passage said that "a business that had been fascinating to me before suddenly became distasteful. I wanted no more of it. I have never wanted to own again an animal that I could not feed or shelter." But whether Stuart's remorse stemmed primarily from his pity for the animals

---

[57] Rosenberg, 31.   [58] Rosenberg, "Hard Winter Endurance," 31.
[59] Horstman, "Historical Events Associated with the Upper Clark Fork Drainage," 31.

whose mass deaths weighed on his shoulders or for his sizable financial losses is not entirely evident. One student of Kohrs's experience notes that his concerns seemed to have been financial. If he did feel any sense of tragedy for the dead, his sentiments were never reported.[60]

Such severe environmental conditions surely selected for cows that were better able to survive cold weather. There is fragmentary evidence that the Longhorns, whose bodies were better suited to warmer climates, could become acclimatized to cold winters over several years in the north, both through biological and behavioral changes. Ranchers reported that some cows that survived earlier winters learned to dig through crusted layers of snow to reach forage – a behavior that older cows might have modeled for subsequent generations. Likewise, ranchers frequently spoke of the need to "acclimatize" the recently arrived Longhorns to the unique environmental conditions of the northern plains. After the Great Die-Off, the general wisdom was that the majority of the cows who had died were "non-native" animals who had only recently been brought in from the southern ranges.[61] Some even saw the harsh selection created by the winter as an opportunity. A French rancher named Pierre Wibaux reasoned that only the strongest cows had survived. Rather than bring in new cows from the south, Wibaux bought up these survivors at bargain prices and bred his new herd from this tough stock. These now "native" cows were perhaps better adapted, both biologically and behaviorally, to the severe northern plains winters that were sure to come again. In any event, Wibaux's ranch prospered.[62]

On the human side of the biological equation, as already noted, some populations have evolved on a genetic level through their long association with cows, most obviously through the ability of many Euro-Americans to drink milk into adulthood. There may well be other genetic aspects of the human-cows coevolution that have yet to be recognized. However, on a shorter timescale, historical change might also be found in nongenetic biological interactions. When humans consumed the meat of Longhorns as a source of bodily energy, these animals in effect became part of the human ecological niche. The alteration of vast swaths of western North America to niches more suitable to large-scale ranching greatly increased

[60] Paul C. Phillips, ed., *Forty Years on the Frontier as Seen in the Journals and Reminiscences of Granville Stuart* (Cleveland: Arthur H. Clark, 1925), 237–8.

[61] Tusler, "The Blizzard and Winter," 17; "Stock Notes," *The River Press* (Fort Benton, MT), February 23, 1887, 8.

[62] Donald H. Welsh, "Cosmopolitan Cattle King: Pierre Wibaux and the W Bar Ranch," *Montana: The Magazine of Western History* 5, no. 2 (Spring 1955): 2–15, here 9–10.

the supply of cows in the late nineteenth century. Combined with improvements in transportation, mass production techniques in slaughterhouses, refrigeration, and other technologies, the costs of beef declined and consumption soared. North Americans who had previously eaten mostly grains began to consume far more meat protein. Some historians have credited the increased consumption of beef with improvements in health and average height, while others have emphasized its adverse effects, as for example on cardiac health.[63] Recent insights into the importance of the human microbiome and its effects on bodily health, mood, and cognition also raise intriguing questions about the possible historical effects of this massive increase in the consumption of beef and protein.[64] If, as the director of the National Institute of Mental Health recently said, "we are more microbial than human," then perhaps we need to think of ourselves as being to some degree the products of the microbial niche construction resulting from the wide availability of cheap beef.[65]

In his classic 1968 work *The Cattle Towns*, the western historian Robert Dykstra provides a detailed and compelling history of Dodge City, Abilene, and other famous animal-buying and -shipping centers that have at times loomed so large in the imagination of Americans and many other peoples around the globe. Dykstra does much to dispel the mythos surrounding these towns, extracting them from the western dime-novel stories of dueling cowboys and swing-door saloons to portray them as the centers of business and corporate connections that they were. A self-proclaimed social history, Dykstra's book focuses on the humans who sought to rationalize and profit from the cows driven up from Texas and thereafter shipped by rail for slaughter in the north and east. Tellingly, however, Dykstra makes hardly any mention of the cows themselves in all of this. He has little to say about the types of cows that were driven north to create small-town fortunes, and nothing at all about the behaviors of these animals and their relationships to human beings. Although Dykstra provides a gallery of interesting historic photos, only one of these shows any cows, and

---

[63] David Cantor, Christian Bonah, and Matthias Dörries, eds., *Meat, Medicine, and Human Health in the Twentieth Century* (New York: Routledge, 2015), 3–6.
[64] Timothy G. Dinan, Catherine Stanton, and John F. Cryan, "Psychobiotics: A Novel Class of Psychotropics," *Biological Psychiatry* 74 (2013): 720–6.
[65] Peter Andrey Smith, "Can the Bacteria in Your Gut Explain Your Mood?" *New York Times*, June 23, 2015.

then only from such a distance that it is difficult to discern much about the animals themselves. Yet Dykstra includes dozens of photos of cattle entrepreneurs, railroads, solid-looking brick hotels and houses, and of course, the obligatory cowboys and even a Dodge City prostitute who at least sports the intriguingly animalistic name of "Squirrel Tooth Alice."[66]

Social history, in Dykstra's view, is unquestionably human history. Cattle towns were the creations of people, and despite having been named for cattle, the animals themselves appear to be almost entirely irrelevant. Of course, it is unfair to be overly critical of a book that is nearly half a century old and that appeared at least a decade before the field of environmental history had begun to emerge, and perhaps three decades before the even more recent rise of neo-materialist theory and animal history. Nonetheless, I would argue that Dykstra's framing of his history by and large remains the default approach among many historians today: cows and other animals and things are oddly absent from the many different types of "cattle towns" we choose to research and write about. But as I hope the previous points make clear, a social history of cattle towns or cattle ranching or even cattle slaughter and eating is badly flawed insofar as it fails to recognize that the "social" phenomena being studied cannot be separated from the social nature of cows. Human intelligence and culture emerged *with* the cows and depended to a very large degree on the fact that cows, too, are social animals. To pay attention to these animals is not to ignore the colorful variety of human experiences that emerged from them, but is rather to recognize where a good deal of that color originated, while also adding some vibrant new tints and shades to our historical palette.

Cows and other biological organisms, however, are not the only material entities that create history and culture. Even seemingly static and passive inanimate things can play a surprisingly powerful role as well. To mine and process the copper ores extracted from the mines of Butte that were next door to the Deer Lodge Valley, humans had no efficient and cooperative organisms that could consume the copper for them, concentrate it in their own bodies, and efficiently carry it to a central location for processing and use. To the contrary, in mining the energetic and entropic patterns of ranching were largely reversed. Instead of tapping into

---

[66] Robert R. Dykstra, *The Cattle Towns: A Social History of the Kansas Cows Trading Centers Abilene, Ellsworth, Wichita, Dodge City, and Caldwell, 1867–1885* (New York: Atheneum, 1968).

a system that *increased* order and energy, human miners *used* energy to power mechanical and chemical technologies that dispersed everything in the ore except the small amounts of copper over hundreds of square miles. Critically, if the power of ranching derived from increasing the systemic order of the Deer Lodge Valley, the power of copper mining derived in part from its sharp reduction. The human sociocultural systems emerging from these very different systems for organizing and channeling energy were inevitably also very different, and perhaps even fundamentally incompatible.

THE COPPER CITY

The copper mined in the town of Butte occurred mainly in two forms: chalcocite, an ore made up of two atoms of copper bonded with one atom of sulfur (Cu_2S), and enargite, which has three atoms of copper, four of sulfur, and one of arsenic (Cu_3AsS_4). As a result, humans who wanted Butte's copper would also have to deal with its less desirable colleagues. An Irish-born mining entrepreneur named Marcus Daly discovered the rich copper deposits under the town of Butte in 1882 while mining for silver in the Anaconda shaft. Daly was able to convince his old friend George Hearst and several others to invest heavily in developing the large-scale copper mining and smelting business that became the Anaconda Copper Mining Company. Mining eventually revealed an immense area of copper mineralization between 300 and 1,000 feet beneath the earth, one of the largest such deposits in the world. Daly and his partners invested in the latest mining technologies to remove the valuable ore. Deep underground mining was an energy-hungry enterprise, so the Anaconda operated its own coal mines elsewhere in the region to fuel the steam engines that drove the ore lifts, compressors, rock drills, and other mining machinery.[67]

In 1883, Daly and the Anaconda built a new smelter some 26 miles to the west of Butte in the Deer Lodge Valley. The smelter was nestled in the narrow ravine of Warm Springs Creek, which limited the spread of the resulting smoke to the wider valley. The company transported the ore from Butte via a dedicated steam (and later electric) rail line. By 1900, however, ore production from the mines had greatly increased and Daly determined the company needed an even bigger smelter. The new operation, called the Washoe, was constructed on a slope that faced directly out

---

[67] LeCain, *Mass Destruction*, 41–2.

onto the wide Deer Lodge Valley. When the workers smelted the first charge of copper ore in early 1902, the clouds of smoke and mist could now easily sweep down onto the ranches and farms of the valley.

Even the richest ore in Butte was only 4 or 5 percent copper. The remaining quartz, iron, silica, and other less valuable material had to be removed by crushing, concentrating, and smelting. In essence, the Washoe smelter operated by reversing some of the geochemical processes that had created the Butte copper ore deposits in the first place, though the source of heat was now wood and coal instead of geothermal energy. Relatively low temperature roasting of the concentrated copper ore provided enough energy to drive much of the sulfur off and into the atmosphere. This roasted ore was subsequently super-heated to around 2,700 degrees Fahrenheit, which pushed more sulfur and arsenic into the air and permitted the now relatively pure copper to be separated from any remaining iron, silica, and other substances, which were poured off as waste slag.[68]

Once released into the sky, the liberated atoms of sulfur and arsenic became powerful historical actors in their own right. The sulfur immediately bonded with atmospheric oxygen to form sulfur dioxide, which in turn could interact with water in the atmosphere to form a highly corrosive sulfuric acid. The arsenic also bonded with oxygen to form arsenic di- and tri-oxides of arsenic, both of which can be highly toxic to animal life. By the autumn of 1902, the smoke began to cause devastating crop and livestock losses for big ranchers like Kohrs and Bielenberg, as well as many other smaller ranchers and farmers. Bielenberg alone lost more than 1,000 head of cows, 800 sheep, and 20 horses in the course of just a few weeks.[69]

Ranching in the valley had relied on the ability of cows to intelligently concentrate solar energy and effectively reduce the entropic disorder of the valley. In contrast, copper smelting depended on the large-scale *application* of energy, mostly from hydrocarbons, which had the effect of increasing the overall disorder and entropy of the system. The Anaconda first used energy to break up the highly stable geological structure of the underground copper deposit, to transport it for smelting, to crush and concentrate the ore, and finally to smelt it. In every stage, the industrial

[68] James E. Fells, *Ores to Metals: The Rocky Mountain Smelting Industry* (Lincoln: University of Nebraska Press, 1979), 27–30, 273–4; Donald M. Levy, *Modern Copper Smelting* (London: Charles Griffin, 1912).
[69] Donald MacMillan, "A History of the Struggle to Abate Air Pollution from Copper Smelters of the Far West, 1885–1933" (PhD diss., University of Montana, 1973), 111.

system used large amounts of energy to concentrate and purify the copper. But this decrease in entropy gained from isolating the small amount of copper from the massive amounts of waste simultaneously resulted in a large increase in disorder for the system as whole. One result was that the molecules of sulfur and arsenic that had previously been concentrated in a small area of stable subsurface rock were now broken up and randomly dispersed into the atmosphere. Indeed, had the Anaconda been unable to disperse the smoke pollution from the immediate area around the smelter, the levels of arsenic and sulfur would have quickly become deadly to humans.

The Anaconda's success and its attendant social power thus derived from at least three material sources. First, the copper itself had unique material properties that permitted humans to develop electrical and heat transfer technologies – properties I will discuss in more detail in Chapter 6. Second, the stored solar energy extracted from the company coal mines and lumber operations was critical to powering the smelter. And, third, the ability of the surrounding environment to absorb the entropic pollution created by the application of this energy in mining and smelting was needed in order to prevent deadly concentrations of arsenical and sulfur compounds.

The extent of the resulting social power was apparent. By 1909, the Anaconda had produced 590 million pounds of copper, which supplied about 10 percent of the entire world demand and as much as 20 percent of the US demand.[70] The Anaconda paid about 30 percent of the total tax revenues of the city of Butte. Over just the previous seven years, it had also spent more than seven million dollars for labor, four million for coal, four million for coke, and more than a million for machinery.[71] Indeed, the Anaconda exercised so much economic might that in 1899 the Rockefellers' infamous Standard Oil trust purchased it in an ultimately unsuccessful attempt to establish monopoly control over the world copper industry.[72] Although Daly and most of the other executives who ran the company did not personally seek political office, there was also little need for them to do so, as the Anaconda kept a tight "copper collar" on the state of Montana. The company was by far the state's biggest single

---

[70] Montana Historical Society Archives, "Anaconda Copper Mining Company Records," Collection 169 [hereafter "MHS"], *Bliss v. Washoe*, Box 21, "Brief of Appellees," 333, 345.

[71] *Bliss v. Washoe*, MHS, Box 22, Folder 1, "Opinion" (January 25, 1909), 212–3.

[72] Charles K. Hyde, *Copper for America* (Tucson: University of Arizona Press, 1998), 94–100.

employer and economic presence, and it also controlled most of the major newspapers, giving it considerable power to pick cooperative candidates for state and federal offices.[73]

As with the power of Kohrs, Bielenberg, and other ranchers in the Deer Lodge Valley, the power of the Anaconda can all too easily be reduced to the abstraction of money or capital. Yet we should make a conscious effort to recognize that the company's economic influence and social power also ultimately derived from the material power of copper, the energy of coal, and the ability of the environment to absorb the entropic disorder of air pollutants. Most importantly, when the entropy-generating system of mining and smelting collided with the entropy-reducing system of ranching, both human power and material power clashed.

LONGHORNS VERSUS COPPER

In 1905, a front-page article in the *Butte Inter Mountain* celebrated Anaconda's three-year-old Washoe smelter with the headline "It Is the Largest in the World."[74] Just a month later, the *Anaconda Standard* reported on the "Monster Beef Cattle" from a neighboring valley that were on their way to Chicago via the Anaconda Stockyards: "There are 450 head in the herd and some of the largest will weigh more than 1,700 pounds, while there is one monster that is estimated at close to 2,000 pounds."[75] These two articles suggest the material and political nature of the escalating conflict in the Deer Lodge Valley. Both the Anaconda and the ranchers were using energy and other forms of biotic and abiotic material power to maximize the size of their output, but they were doing so in fundamentally incompatible ways.

By 1905, the Washoe smelter was generating about 2 billion cubic feet of smoke every day that carried some 48,100 pounds of arsenic and immense volumes of sulfur gas.[76] Nick Bielenberg estimated that the poisonous smoke subsequently spread over an area approximately 30 miles long and 12 to 14 miles wide.[77] Residents described it as

[73] K. Ross Toole, *Montana: An Uncommon Land* (Norman: University of Oklahoma Press, [1959] 1984); John McNay, "Breaking the Copper Collar: Press Freedom, Professionalization, and the History of Montana Journalism," *American Journalism* 25, no. 1 (2008): 99–123.

[74] "It Is the Largest in the World," *Butte Inter Mountain*, March 19, 1905.

[75] "Monster Beef Cows," *Anaconda Standard*, April 19, 1905.

[76] *Bliss v. Washoe*, MHS, vol. IV, 1218–9.   [77] *Bliss v. Washoe*, MHS, vol. I, 114.

a "white mist" or "a bluish color."[78] Some days, the smoke settled in low-lying areas and shifted with the surface winds. As the rancher Angus D. Smith noted, some mornings the cloud of smoke would be so thick on his property that he could not see more than two or three hundred feet.[79] But the ranchers and farmers noticed that the behavior of the smoke varied depending on atmospheric conditions. William T. Stephens reported, "Sometimes it comes in a stream across, and other times it settles and spreads out more, and sometimes it goes clear over head."[80] Regardless of their personal experience, many of the ranchers and farmers agreed that "the smoke from the stack is charged with large quantities of sulfur dioxide, arsenic, antimony, copper and other noxious and poisonous substances, which are deposited upon the farms of the valley, burning and dwarfing the crops, poisoning the soil and causing large numbers of horses, sheep, cows and other livestock to sicken and die."[81]

The sulfur and arsenic in the smoke stream attacked the material basis of the ranchers' power in at least three fundamental ways, each with its own dynamics. First, the sulfur dioxide and sulfuric acid undermined the energetic basis of ranching by killing or limiting the growth of the valley grasses – both the wild bunchgrasses and cultivated grasses like hay, oats, alfalfa, and other feed crops. Sulfur compounds were once a significant part of earth's atmosphere, and volcanic activity can still occasionally discharge large amounts of sulfur into the air. But sulfur is highly reactive and easily bonds with many other elements, including iron and copper. Over millions of years, much of the previous atmospheric load of sulfur was bound up in rocks in the lithosphere or absorbed by the oceans.[82] During the ages when most of the chlorophyll-based plant life of today evolved, atmospheric levels of sulfur compounds were low. When the Anaconda smelted the Butte sulfide ores, it reversed this primordial bio-geochemical cycle and shifted lithospheric sulfur back into the atmosphere at levels that harm most modern plants.

Sulfur dioxide damages grasses and other plants by directly interfering first with their ability to generate and then to store and use energy from sunshine. The sulfur dioxide dispersed by the Washoe smelter entered plants through the small holes, or stomata, that penetrate the protective

[78] *Bliss v. Washoe*, MHS, vol. IX, 3232.   [79] *Bliss v. Washoe*, MHS, vol. II, 646.
[80] *Bliss v. Washoe*, MHS, vol. IX, 3232.
[81] "Farmers Bring Action," *Anaconda Standard*, May 21, 1905.
[82] Pham, M. et al., "A 3D Study of the Global Sulphur Cycle: Contributions of Anthropogenic and Biogenic Sources," *Atmospheric Environment* 30(1996): 1815–22.

waxy cuticle of leaves and can open and close in response to environmental conditions.[83] Once sulfur dioxide gas enters the stomata, it spreads through the intercellular spaces in the leaf where most of it dissolves in water to form sulfuric acid and sulfite ions. These sulfur compounds attack the plant's chlorophyll-filled chloroplasts, destroying their ability to transform solar energy into the sugars that can be consumed for energy. The sulfite also interferes with the plant's mitochondria, the cellular structures that subsequently consume these sugars and generates adenosine triphosphate (ATP), the molecule that provides usable energy to cells in both plant and animal life.[84]

High concentrations of sulfur dioxide cause almost-immediate death of plant leaves, and lower concentrations can slow growth and reduce yields.[85] While any terrestrial plant can be harmed or killed by sulfur dioxide gas, sensitivity varies. Effects within a region are also highly variable depending on topography, soil conditions, wind directions, and other factors. For example, trees and other plants on mountainsides might be damaged at a greater distance from the pollution source than flat areas closer to the source.[86]

The farmers and ranchers observed all these effects. Several noticed that the smoke was particularly harmful to the quaking aspen trees that grew wild in moist areas of the valley.[87] One farmer reported that the smoke only sporadically affected plants in his kitchen garden: "Some things will stand a pretty good siege, while other garden truck will not recover from its effects." Bielenberg recalled how the smoke "once cut a path right through my grain crop, leaving about 200 yards [on each side] it did not touch."[88] The very complexity of the interactions between the sulfur and the plants made it extremely difficult to prove definitively that the Washoe smelter was responsible. The company-owned *Anaconda Standard* argued that since some ranches seemed to be untouched by smoke damage, ranchers like Bielenberg who complained must have been "unthrifty" farmers who failed to properly care for their land.[89]

[83] "Effects of Sulfur Dioxide on Vegetation: Critical Levels," in *WHO Air Quality Guidelines* (Copenhagen, 2000), 6.
[84] Wilhelm Knabe, "Effects of Sulfur Dioxide on Terrestrial Vegetation," *Ambio* 5/6 (1976): 213–8, 213.
[85] Knabe, "Effects of Sulfur Dioxide," 1.   [86] Knabe, "Effects of Sulfur Dioxide," 215.
[87] *Bliss v. Washoe*, MHS, vol. IX, 3223.
[88] "Nick Bielenberg and His Alfalfa," *Anaconda Standard*, March 6, 1906.
[89] "Green Fields and Fat Herds Down Deer Lodge Valley," *Anaconda Standard*, June 4, 1905.

By killing or reducing the nutrient value of wild grasses and cultivated crops, the sulfur smoke reduced the supply of energy available to the valley's ranching industry. Prior to the Washoe, hay yields were typically around a ton per acre.[90] Chronic low-level smoke exposure appears to have cut yields by at least two-thirds.[91] Acute exposure could kill an entire crop in just the course of a few days or even hours.[92] What hay and other feed crops did survive might still be "smoked," a consequence of arsenic and other poisons deposited on their surface. Even if hay from some areas of the valley may have actually been arsenic free, many potential buyers believed it to be poisonous, driving down prices or making it impossible to sell at all.[93]

The second way the smoke attacked the material basis of the ranchers' power occurred when arsenical compounds undermined the ability of the Longhorns and other cows to efficiently transform plant energy into meat, milk, and calves. Released by the Washoe as a gas or mist, when cooled, the arsenic trioxide (As_2O_3) molecules formed a fine white powder that settled unevenly over the valley. Ranchers and farmers quickly recognized that the white powder was toxic to humans. Many reported that it caused blisters on the mouth and nose. One woman noted, "I would become so dizzy that I could not walk across the room without staggering. My daughter was worse than myself, very much worse."[94] The rancher Nicholas A. Liffring recalled being poisoned, noting that "there was a white dust on the straw, and, while baling it made me sick; I broke out in boils around the hat band and sores upon the body."[95]

To some degree, ranchers and farmers could limit their internal exposure to arsenic dust through careful cleaning of garden crops and staying away from the smoke stream as much as possible. But avoiding the dust was more difficult for cows and other stock animals in the valley that consumed the wild and cultivated grasses. Longhorns possessed formidable defensive skills, but they were ill prepared to deal with a danger like arsenic. The Anaconda's power emerged in part from the ability of the surrounding environment to dilute and absorb the Washoe arsenic, but the cows' energetic and entropic basis drove them to do just the opposite. Because wild grasses are relatively low in caloric content, cows must spend most of their waking hours grazing over a wide area just to consume enough to stay alive. Typically, each day a steer or cow must eat about

[90] *Bliss v. Washoe*, MHS, vol. I, 53.   [91] *Bliss v. Washoe*, MHS, vol. II, 741.
[92] *Bliss v. Washoe*, MHS, vol. IX, 3295.   [93] *Bliss v. Washoe*, MHS, vol. I, 202–4.
[94] *Bliss v. Washoe*, MHS, vol. IV, 1196–7.   [95] *Bliss v. Washoe*, MHS, vol. IX, 3290.

two percent of its body weight in grass (excluding the water content), which for a large animal might be as much as 70 pounds of actual forage. What had previously been the valuable ability of cows to concentrate the dispersed solar energy of the valley's grass into muscle now had the damaging effect of reconcentrating the dispersed arsenic to poisonous levels. Further, since the sulfur dioxide was simultaneously reducing the size and caloric content of the valley grass, the cows had to eat more grass over an even wider area, further increasing their uptake of poisonous arsenic.

When consumed in relatively small doses, arsenic trioxide can actually be a mild stimulant. One sheepherder even reported that his animals deliberately ate each other's arsenic-contaminated wool – he believed the sheep were addicted to its effects.[96] But in higher amounts, arsenic trioxide is devastating to the basic biological functions of most animals. The biochemical toxicity of arsenic oxides comes in part from their molecular structure, which is very similar to that of phosphate (a phosphorous atom bonded with four oxygen atoms, PO_4), an essential cellular building block of all currently known life. Indeed, arsenic is immediately beneath phosphorous on the periodic table of elements, and it can easily bond with oxygen to form arsenate (AsO_4), a molecule that is structurally very similar to phosphate. In a normally functioning cell, phosphate is used in the mitochondria, the cellular "power plants" where the caloric energy of sugars from food is broken down to make the ATP to power cellular metabolism – a topic I will return to in the final chapter. Because of arsenate's structural (though not functional) similarity to phosphate, some of the cell's mitochondria bind with it instead, destroying their ability to generate ATP. Literally starved of energy, the cell begins to die, which in turn causes internal lesions and bleeding, organ failure, coma, and death. Cows, horses, sheep, and humans all shared this biochemical vulnerability to the energy-robbing effects of arsenic.[97]

Though they could not have known the complex biochemical causes, ranchers clearly observed the acute and chronic effects of arsenic in their cows and other animals. Morgan Evans, a 72-year-old rancher whose property was about two and a half miles from the Washoe stack, noted that the smoke "turned my place into a graveyard. I lost from 75 to 80 head of cattle in 90 days." As mentioned earlier, big ranchers like Kohrs

[96] "Abstract of Testimony of Lay Witnesses," MHS, 84.
[97] Brett Walker, *The Toxic Archipelago: A History of Industrial Disease in Japan* (Seattle: University of Washington Press, 2010), 96.

and Bielenberg lost thousands of head of cattle, horses, and sheep. Postmortem autopsies revealed the internal signs of arsenic poisoning: "lesions affecting the stomach, intestines, liver, kidneys, spleen, heart, respiratory organs, and membranes of the brain."[98] The death rate was so high that the Anaconda dug mass graves to quietly bury the thousands of dead animals that, in an implicit recognition of their responsibility, managers initially agreed to buy from ranchers.[99]

However, the effect of chronic but non-fatal arsenic exposure on the overall vitality and energetic capacity of stock animals could be harder to prove, though the anecdotal evidence seemed clear. Morgan Evans, for example, reported, "The horses have sore noses now and seem to be weak. They cannot stand the work they formerly stood." Another small rancher, George Parrott, said, "[The horses] are not nearly so good as they used to be, and they are soft, and sweat easy if you go to driving them, and they don't seem to have strength and cannot stand work like they used to."[100] Since the biological muscle power of these draft horses was as critical to successful ranching as the chemical power of coal was to mining and smelting, the Anaconda's arsenic was sharply reducing the energy available to ranchers for transporting supplies, hay, and other materials.

Even more critically, the arsenic interfered with the beef cattle's key task: to transform low-energy forage into high-energy meat and milk. Jerry Ryan, a small-holder rancher, noted, "I have 40 head of cattle and all they do is stand up and eat without seeming to derive any benefit from it. They are sickly and weak." George Parrott observed that his cattle "seem to eat hearty enough and a good deal of it, but it did not seem to do them any good."[101] Though Ryan and Parrott did not know that the arsenic was interfering with ATP production in their cows' mitochondria, they did recognize that the poison was somehow robbing the animals of the essential life-giving energy that made profitable meat. What meat cows did manage to put on often had little fat, and the slaughtered animals looked suspicious to local butchers. Ryan noted he tried to conceal the effects of the smoke on one beef cow: "Took him up and sold him to Mr. Wegner; and had to take some fat off his stomach and put it over his kidney to make it look respectable."[102]

The arsenic also affected the valley's dairy cows, reducing or eliminating their ability to give milk. Acute arsenic poisoning in the dairy cows

[98] *Bliss v. Washoe*, MHS, "Opinion," 202.   [99] *Bliss v. Washoe*, MHS, vol. IX, 3403.
[100] *Bliss v. Washoe*, MHS, vol. IX, 3179.   [101] *Bliss v. Washoe*, MHS, vol. IX, 3172.
[102] *Bliss v. Washoe*, MHS, vol. I, 85.

typically began with loose bowels followed by constipation. The cows then stopped eating, and as dairy farmer Angus D. Smith testified, "the hair turned on them and they would not lick themselves, and their noses got dry, which is unnatural for a healthy cow ... [and] it would take two or three months and sometimes weeks and then they would die."[103] As with smoked hay, former customers in the valley were suspicious of milk that came from smoked cows. Indeed, valley residents were wise to be concerned, as it is now widely recognized that dairy cows can concentrate arsenic in their milk.[104] Some dairy farmers reported that the milk from smoked cattle had a strong "garlicky" smell, which is characteristic of arsenic content.[105] As Kenneth Smith noted, the drop in consumer demand for milk was matched by a drop in supply, as his dairy cows soon stopped giving milk and he was forced to abandon his milk wagon business.[106]

Much of the material power of ranching derived from the cow's (particularly the independent Longhorn's) ability to reproduce without assistance, thus transforming the energy of plants not only into more meat but also into more cows. But as the rancher Eli Dehourdi noted, the smoke pollution also interfered with calving. Dehourdi had previously found that some 75–80 percent of his heifers would bear a live calf each year. After the Washoe opened, the rate dropped to 50 percent, either because the cows were unable to conceive or they miscarried their fetuses.[107] Kenneth D. Smith testified as to the tragic effects for the animals themselves. "We noticed the cows began to slink [miscarry] their calves, and as soon as a cow would get rid of her calf, she would kind of draw up, and we would find her behind a bush, behind a clump of willows, somewhere, leaning up against a clump of willows all drawed up and the hair all turned, it seemed as though the wrong way." After that, the cows could never again become pregnant.[108] George Parrott had previously kept a purebred (probably Shorthorn) bull to breed with his cows, but he had since castrated the animal. "In the winter time," Parrott noted, "the cows were throwing

[103] *Bliss v. Washoe*, MHS, vol. II, 648.
[104] B. K. Datta et al., "Chronic Arsenicosis in Cows with Special Reference to Its Metabolism in Arsenic Endemic Village of Nadia District West Bengal India," *Science of the Total Environment* 409 (2010): 284–8.
[105] "Jerry Ryan of Smoke Association Goes into Details of the Case," *Anaconda Standard*, February 28, 1906.
[106] *Bliss v. Washoe*, MHS, vol. II, 774.
[107] *Bliss v. Washoe*, MHS, vol. I, 44–6; vol. IX, 3170, 3222..
[108] *Bliss v. Washoe*, vol. II, 773.

[miscarrying] so many dead calves that I saw it was no use in trying to breed."[109] Others found that as many as 40 percent of mares miscarried their foals.[110] Clearly the arsenic and other heavy metals were limiting fertility and causing increased miscarriages, either because of a general weakening of the mothers or because the chemicals were directly harming fetal growth, or perhaps a combination of the two. William T. Stephens testified that even if calves did survive to term, they "are weak and puny when they come [and] some of them die, and some of them never do well afterwards, a great many of them."[111] Just as it could poison children, the arsenic-contaminated milk could also poison calves, since the poisonous dose of arsenic is much lower for both small cows and small humans.[112]

The third and final way in which the smoke damaged the material basis of the ranchers' power came from the way the sulfur and arsenic undermined the unique coevolutionary bonds between humans and cows that had made the previously lucrative "open range" possible. Prior to the opening of the Washoe smelter, many big ranchers in the valley like Bielenberg and Kohrs still provided little or no hay or other feed crops to many of their cows, and when they did, typically only during the winter. They depended instead on the ability of their Longhorns and hybrid breeds to graze widely over vast areas of range largely on their own.[113] But the pollutants from the Washoe made such free-ranging behavior nearly impossible. In 1905 the Montana state veterinarian advised the Deer Lodge Valley ranchers to stop allowing their cows or horses to range on open pastures and to instead corral them in smaller pens where they would need to be fed uncontaminated hay or other fodder daily.[114] William Stephens, who had previously let his cows run in the pastures, was now "keeping them shut up in corrals and barns and feeding some of them bran and hay and oats."[115] In the Deer Lodge Valley, the era of the open range declined not just because of farmers with barbed wire fences or harsh winters but because of copper minerals shot through with deadly arsenic.

CONCLUSION

In 1970 Conrad Kohrs's grandson, Conrad Kohrs Warren, agreed to sell his grandfather's ranch to the National Park Service with the proviso that

---

[109] *Bliss v. Washoe*, MHS, vol. IX, 3170.   [110] *Bliss v. Washoe*, MHS, vol. I, 114.
[111] *Bliss v. Washoe*, MHS, vol. IX, 3222.   [112] Datta, "Chronic Arsenicosis," 284–8.
[113] *Bliss v. Washoe*, MHS, vol. I, 114.   [114] *Bliss v. Washoe*, MHS, vol. VI, 2126.
[115] *Bliss v. Washoe*, MHS, vol. IX, 3228.

it continue to be operated as a living-history ranch. Two years later it was officially opened to the public as the Grant-Kohrs Ranch National Historic Site. If you visit today, you can tour Conrad Kohrs's original ranch house with its grand two-story brick addition that he had built in 1890. Mounted over a door not far from the elegant main dining room you will see a pair of impressively twisted black-tipped horns with a leather band in the middle marked with the brand "CK." A friend of Kohrs gave him this mounted monument to the Texas Longhorn as a token of thanks for his role in forming the Montana Stockgrowers Association.[116] Kohrs spent much of his career as a rancher raising more docile and profitable breeds. But when he displayed a symbol of the first source of his own abundant success and social power, the animal he celebrated was the Longhorn. In this he was perhaps not so different than the long-passed inhabitants of the Neolithic village of Çatalhöyük, in modern-day Turkey, who mounted the skulls of aurochs in their homes and appear to have worshipped the beasts in their temples. The villagers of Çatalhöyük knew real power when they saw it – perhaps Kohrs did too.[117]

Material powers come in many forms, both living and not. The Anaconda sulfur and arsenic attacked the practice of open-range grazing in the valley, and hence the cowboys and roundups that were even then becoming the mythic stuff of the American popular imagination. The advantage of the open range lay not only in the rancher's ability

FIGURE 4.4 For years Conrad Kohrs displayed these impressive horns from a Texas Longhorn in his Deer Lodge Valley home – perhaps an implicit tribute to the extraordinary animals that had helped create his fortune and career. Photograph by author.

[116] Email exchange with Chance Reynolds, Education Technician, at the Grant-Kohrs National Historical Site, February 2016, 29, author's possession.
[117] Katheryn C. Twiss and Nerissa Russell, "Taking the Bull by the Horns: Ideology, Masculinity, and Cattle Horns at Çatalhöyük (Turkey)," *Paléorient* 35 (2009): 19–32.

to extract free energy from range plants but also in the unfenced spaces that allowed the cows to maximize their own growth as they made constant decisions about the richest and safest places to graze. The knowledge of the individual cows, bulls, and steers was at least as important as human knowledge. But by forcing ranchers to confine and feed even their hardy Longhorns and hybrid Shorthorns, the arsenic undermined the material power ranchers had previously derived from the ancient evolutionary bonds between humans and cows. The Longhorns' ability to survive on their own, to find the best forage, to fend off predators, could no longer contribute to the power of the rancher. What the cows had once done for themselves, the Deer Lodge Valley ranchers were now forced to do for them.

Can a copper deposit make history? Not on its own, perhaps. But the same might well be said of the humans who have developed so many novel ways of *using* the material world to survive and create their variegated cultures. To emphasize the centrality of nonhuman matter in the history of the Deer Lodge Valley ranching and the subsequent battle over smoke is not to assert some sort of primitive environmental determinism. Rather, it is an attempt to resist the powerful human tendency to see the world solely as a reflection of ourselves, to suggest instead that we do not use matter so much as cooperate with it in ways that form and define us. Copper, Longhorns, sulfur, and arsenic did not dictate the course of events in the Deer Lodge Valley, but neither did humans, precisely because these "things" were much more than mere natural resources that could be bent freely to human will. The matter contained a type of power, a materiality that could be both beneficial and dangerous but was a fundamental basis for human social power. This material power took many forms, some of them identifiable with physical concepts like energy and entropy, others more subtle, like the distributed intelligence created by the interactions between clever Longhorns and ranchers. But when the material power of copper collided with that of cows, the humans whose social power derived from them also inevitably became entwined in the conflict. The humans involved could, of course, have handled the resulting political and legal conflicts in any number of fascinating ways, all of them well worth the attention of historians. Yet in our inevitable fascination with ourselves, we should also take care to remember we are not so far removed from the world of matter as we like to think. Matter makes us as much as we make it.

As I will argue in the next two chapters, just how free humans were to ignore the immense power provided by copper is also debatable.

If Americans, Japanese, or the peoples of any other nation wanted what modernity offered – national wealth, bright lights, instant communications, and military prowess, to name but a few benefits – abundant copper may not have been the sole path to it, but it was surely among the most accessible, proven, and effective. Given this, we should not be surprised that some Japanese would end up sacrificing their silkworms in almost exactly the same way as some Americans sacrificed their Longhorns and all the attendant human ways of life that went with them. For all their manifest worth, these living creatures could not compete with the sheer material power of a dead yet nonetheless transformative red metal.

5

The Silkworm

The Innovative Insects behind Japanese Modernization

The Panjiayuan Market in the southeast quarter of Beijing is a gigantic open-air bazaar filled with such a huge variety of things that it might well be seen as a material microcosm of this vast and diverse city of more than 20 million people. In the name of (supposedly) good order and oversight, in recent years the Chinese government shut down many of the once-ubiquitous informal street bazaars in Beijing and required vendors to move to officially sanctioned markets like Panjiayuan, which if nothing else at least has the advantage of offering some protection from the weather under a vast expanse of a metal roof supported by sturdy red columns. Here Beijingers and tourists alike can find everything from dignified statues of Chairman Mao to mah-jongg sets and purportedly ancient Ming relics. But locals know that Panjiayuan is no place to find true rarities and antiquities. Even a clueless American begins to harbor doubts after encountering the third identical version of a curious little mechanical bird clock that the two previous sellers both had insisted was very old and very unique. But then, prices are also entirely open to discussion, and if the vendors start off asking a tourist for 10 or 20 times what they would ask of a local, most seem to welcome a good bout of haggling. After some theatrical protestations on both sides, the 600 yuan bird clock changes hands for 60 yuan (about US$ 10) and all involved seem happy with the deal.

Deep in the heart of these seemingly endless rows of all things Mao and Ming, the persistent shopper will find several that are devoted to nothing but silk – one of the first of China's many gifts to the world. Here the floors and shelves are a rainbow of colors and patterns, iridescent indigos, reds like lacquered Chinese wood, and golds that have all the alluring shine of the metal itself. As potential customers kneel and bend close, without fail they stretch out their fingertips to caress the silky surface or drape the fabric over their hands to observe its cascading fall. As enticing as the colors and patterns are to the eye, the most fundamental appeal seems to be to the human sense of touch. Halfway down one long row, the burnished sheen of an embroidered silk wall hanging catches my eye. A small woman with a serene smile quickly spreads it out, encouraging me to handle the piece. I, too, run my fingertips across the smooth golden silk threads of the background, which shimmers almost like sunlight itself. The image is of two white cranes with red-capped heads and black-tipped wings perched in a pine tree. In the upper left are four black calligraphic characters, their meaning mysterious to me. Smitten nonetheless, my bargaining is half-hearted, and the woman's amused grin suggests she knows it. Later, I learn from friends that the Chinese characters offer a wish for a long and wise life – literally, "long life, like pines and cranes" – and that the birds are red-crowned cranes (*Grus japonensis*). For millennia these once-ubiquitous birds have been a symbol of longevity, luck, and scholarship in East Asia. But habitat loss, through the conversion of coastal wetlands to rice paddies, has reduced the entire global population to less than 3,000, making them the most threatened crane species on the planet. Whatever their symbolic meaning to some humans, luck and longevity are in short supply for the cranes themselves, as well as a lot of other creatures these days. Who knows if some wise scholarship might yet offer them a bit of hope.[1]

The two red-crowned cranes now perch peacefully in the entryway of our home in Montana, a souvenir of a memorable afternoon in Beijing and a hopefully effectual talisman for greater luck, longevity, and scholarly diligence. But whatever the promises of the Chinese characters, the vibrant sheen of the gold, green, and red silk fabric itself serves to remind me of the importance of also looking beyond images and symbols to consider the material things that convey them. Little remembered these days, the philosopher Marshall McLuhan was practically a household name in the 1970s, famed for his oft-quoted and oft-misunderstood assertion that the "medium is the message." He meant, in essence, that the informational or discursive content conveyed by diverse technologies like

---

[1] Hou Shen of Renmin University, Beijing, and Margaret Greene of Montana State University provided translations and analysis. On the red-crowned crane habitat destruction, see Mingchang Cao et al., "A Multi-scale Approach to Investigating the Red-Crowned Crane," *PLoS One* 10 (2015): e0129833.

newspaper, radio, or television was in many ways less important than the nature of the medium through which it was conveyed. McLuhan argued that the physical and mental experience of interacting with a specific material means of communication – a newspaper, a radio, a television – shaped our thinking and societies at least as profoundly as whatever messages or ideas they might carry. A newspaper and an electronic radio might convey precisely the same set of words or information, yet our embodied experience of engaging with these things would be very different, and perhaps more consequential from a long-term perspective. McLuhan died in 1980, but his ideas are if anything even more relevant in the present era of ubiquitous cell phones. The experience of 24/7 connectivity may well shape us more than the actual content of cute cat videos and disgruntled bird games that reportedly crowd much of the bandwidth.

Not surprisingly, McLuhan's once-influential theories fell out of fashion after the postmodern turn with its focus on the linguistic, semiotic, and cultural. This is not the place to resurrect them for our own post-postmodern (post²-modern?) age, as worthwhile a task as that might be. Rather, somewhat like McLuhan, I want to look beyond the characters and images on my silk wall hanging and focus more on the materiality of the silk itself, to ask how the human interface with this protein fiber and the insects who synthesize it have helped to make us who we are. To obtain just 200 grams (about half a pound) of silk thread, humans must spend weeks raising more than a thousand silkworms and feeding them 36 kilograms (80 pounds) of leaves from the mulberry tree before beginning the process of unwrapping the delicate silken strands from the cocoons to make thread.[2] For millennia, some humans essentially enslaved themselves – willingly or not – to the constant care of these white worms to obtain a ridiculously small amount of their silken thread.

Such was the case with the Japanese farmers and their families who raised silkworms and mulberry trees on the Shimotsuke Plain, about 100 kilometers north of Tokyo. For centuries, farmers supplemented their income from growing rice and other food crops by raising silkworms, creating a vibrant sericulture industry that also included silk spinning, dyeing, and weaving. Ultimately, the immense creative potential of silkworms and their silken threads contributed to the breakneck pace of industrialization that catapulted Japan to the status of a great world

---

[2] Penny Le Couteur and Jay Burreson, *Napoleon's Buttons: Seventeen Molecules That Changed History* (New York: Penguin, 2004), 106.

power. But the Shimotsuke silkworms were not well rewarded for their role in making Japan modern. When pollution from the newly industrialized Ashio copper mines in the mountains just to the north began to kill the silkworms and mulberry trees, the farmers discovered that their silk was no match for the tremendous potential of copper, the alluring metal of modern economic growth, electrification, and national power. When the Ashio copper pollution killed the Shimotsuke silkworms, it undermined not just an abstract economic enterprise but an ancient way of life – one that had sprung from an entirely serendipitous affinity between an unusually acute human sense of touch and a unique long chain of protein molecules.

THE POWER OF SILK

Why do humans like silk? Some may be suspicious of such a universalizing question. Obviously there are individuals past and present who have not cared for silk fabric, and the material has not found equal favor in every society and culture where it has been developed or introduced. Some past cultures have minimized the importance of the sense of touch and bodily comfort altogether, diminishing the interest in soft fabrics like silk. Likewise, while we can identify shared species-wide physiological aspects of our senses – most humans can see the color red, for example, but none can see infrared light – there is considerable diversity in how individuals and cultures have responded to such physiological factors.[3] Given what we are now learning about the plasticity of the human brain, these culturally rooted responses might even feed back to alter the brain itself and hence our bodily physiological responses.[4] These caveats noted, silk has nonetheless been treasured in an astonishingly wide variety of global cultures, from China and Japan to the Roman and Byzantine Empires, and onward to France, England, and other global trading empires that carried its allure far beyond Eurasia. It is a material whose basic appeal comes close to being universally human, a fabric equivalent to sweet fruits like grapes and apples or sparkling gemstones like diamonds and rubies. Despite being fiendishly difficult to obtain, or perhaps in part because of

---

[3] Mark M. Smith, "Making Sense of US History," *The American Historian* (February 2016): 18–23.

[4] Nancy Langston notes research suggesting that the actions of an organism can alter bodily hormone levels, which in turn affect brain structures: Nancy Langston, *Toxic Bodies* (New Haven, CT: Yale University Press, 2010), xx.

it, humans living in diverse cultures from around the world have been fascinated by silk nearly everywhere it has been introduced.[5]

As the historian Peter Frankopan suggests in his recent book on the storied Silk Road, this human bond with silk even gave rise to what was for many centuries "the world's central nervous system." Its name was coined by the German geologist Ferdinand von Richthofen (his nephew achieved fiery fame as the Red Baron during World War I), who christened the ancient network of informal trade routes the *Seidenstrassen*, or "silk roads."[6] While the caravans on the Silk Road carried many other things, the name was fitting, as silken threads bound together such distant and disparate cities as Peking (Beijing) and Byzantium (Istanbul). At first the Chinese had traded their silk closer to home. They used the fabric to pacify the Xiongnu, a fierce nomadic people who dominated the grasslands to the north of Beijing. The Chinese emperor sent many precious things to the Xiongnu, including rice and wine, but silk was by far the most important. The nomads treasured silk for its smooth texture and lightness and used it for making bedding and clothing – the things that touched human skin. Just as in Beijing, the leaders of the nomads wore thick layers of silk clothing not only to demonstrate but also to create and maintain their power. Buying the peaceful behavior of the nomads was not cheap: in the year 1 BCE alone, the Chinese gave 30,000 rolls of silk cloth to the Xiongnu and 370 items of Chinese-made silk clothes. During the Han dynasty (206 BCE–220 CE), Chinese rulers eventually wearied of both the high cost and the implied deference of paying tribute, and they waged a successful war to push the Xiongnu farther to the north. The retreat of the northern nomads also placed the Gansu corridor, which led westward to the still-mysterious lands of the Indus Valley, Persia, and central Asia, under Chinese control for the first time in centuries. Just as the necessity of buying off barbarous nomads with silk ended, the possibility opened up for trading China's most precious product on a much-wider and grander scale than ever before.[7]

Transporting silk to the far West was no easy task, however. The silk merchants of East Asia had to travel six thousand arduous miles to reach west Asia, braving harsh deserts, passing from oasis to oasis, depending on

---

[5] Shelagh Vainker, *Chinese Silk: A Cultural History* (New Brunswick, NJ: Rutgers University Press, 2004), 6–7; Yuji Yasukochi, Hiroshi Fujii, and Marian R. Goldsmith, "Silkworm," in *Genome Mapping and Genomics in Arthropods*, ed., W. Hunter and C. Kole (Berlin: Springer-Verlag, 2008), 43–57.

[6] Peter Frankopan, *The Silk Roads: A New History of the World*, xvi.

[7] Frankopan, *The Silk Roads*, 12.

their hardy Bactrian camels (the two-humped species) both to carry their wares and to warn them of approaching sandstorms.[8] Few merchants made the entire trip themselves, yet the profits to be gained by carrying the silk over just a fraction of the long passage could be immense. In the many areas where precious metals like copper, silver, and gold were scarce, silk was used as a type of currency: the value of silk was just as self-evident as gold, and its portability and permanence was greater than that of grains or other more obvious forms of payment. Still, when those caravans of silk arrived on the shores of Bosporus, the merchants sold not just a currency or a symbol of luxury and status. Rather, they sold a physical experience that was rare in the ancient world: the look and feel of soft shimmering fabric. The people of Rome, newly enriched by the conquest of the rich farming lands of Egypt, indulged themselves in this most marvelous of new materials. Strolling the public streets or wide squares of the Roman Forum, men and women alike luxuriated in its unparalleled ability to drape gently over the human form – a quality that sometimes brought the stormy moral condemnation of their less sybaritic neighbors. Seneca grumbled that silk clothing was barely clothing at all, as it hugged every bodily curve and swell, leaving nothing to the imagination. To the Romans, silk's soft embrace was not just sensual – it was downright sexual. Daring silk-wearing Romans could in effect parade about nearly naked in public. Because of its almost-universal sensual appeal, silk became the driver for the globalization of trade on the central east-west axis of Eurasia some 2,000 years before our own era. Even less prudish Romans worried about the huge amounts of Roman treasure that the camels carried back to the teeming metropoles of trade in Persia, not to mention the even stranger lands farther to the east where the sensual fabric had its still-mysterious origins. For centuries, the Romans and other Westerners had no idea how the silken fabrics they so admired were created, an occult Far Eastern secret that made the material even more exotic.[9]

Besides being a means of displaying wealth or sexuality, silk also gave humans around the globe new ways to think about and understand their environment. The names for many birds, fish, and insects around the world include the word "silk" or "silky" as a means to convey their smooth brilliant sheen. In China, where sericulture was first perfected, some 230 Mandarin characters (of about 20,000 in wide usage) include the symbol for silk. The Romans borrowed the Chinese word for silk, $s\bar{\imath}$ (which is also the root for the modern English word sericulture), to name

---

[8] Frankopan, *The Silk Roads*, 12.   [9] Frankopan, *The Silk Roads*, 19–20.

the entire eastern region of the world from whence it came: *Serica*. When the Romans thought of the Far East, they thought in no insignificant part through the look and feel of their silk fabrics, sheer material pieces of a distant world transported into their own.

As I pointed out in Chapter 3, cognitive linguists like Benjamin Bergen now argue that the human brain derives some of the meaning of words from prelinguistic brain structures dedicated to processing the input of our physical bodily senses. Brain scans reveal that even higher-level abstract thought processes often work through parts of the brain that evolved to provide reasonably accurate ways of perceiving and manipulating the material environment. As the cognitive linguist George Lakoff concludes, "The way our mind works, from the nature of our thoughts to the way we understand meaning in language, is inextricably tied to our bodies – how we perceive and act in the world." Far from being a cold, abstract, reasoning Cartesian machine, Bergen, Lakoff and others argue that even the most seemingly abstract aspects of human thought and philosophy – moral systems, political ideologies, mathematics – emerge from our embodied actions in a material world.[10] The archaeologist Bjørnar Olsen captures a similar idea when he argues that meaning often derives from our physical experience of the material properties of things: "'soft as steel' is *not* a metaphor we live by."[11] To the contrary, common English metaphors like "strong as steel" or "steely eyed" emerge from our physical sensory experience with the real material stuff that we call steel. Consider, for example, the 2,500-year-old words of the Greek playwright Sophocles, who, when trying to think about and understand (in his play *Antigone*) what it means for a human to be stubborn or willful turns to the most cognitively powerful metal of his day: "These rigid spirits are the first to fall. The strongest iron, hardened in the fire, most often ends in scraps and shatterings." Because humans had experienced real iron through their physical senses, they could think about the stubborn rigidity of Antigone in a way that had not previously been possible. The metaphor was not just a means of expressing a preexisting thought but rather was to some degree the basis of the thought itself and the feelings it engendered.

In other words, as humans first began to harvest, use, and experience the nature of silk, it became possible for them to think about their world in

[10] George Lakoff, "Foreword," x, in Benjamin Bergen, *Louder Than Words: The New Science of How the Mind Makes Meaning* (New York: Basic Books, 2012).
[11] Bjørnar Olsen, *In Defense of Things: Archaeology and the Ontology of Objects* (Lanham, MD: AltaMira, 2010), 156–7.

novel ways. In developing a conceptual rubric that encompasses things that are thin, soft, shiny, and elastic, silk is a material that not only captures that meaning but helps to create the meaning. Once a sizable number of humans had experienced silk fabrics, they would come to understand the world and themselves differently. The historian of the sense of touch Constance Classen suggests this dynamic when she notes:

The coarse, scratchy wool of a peasant's tunic was a tactile sign of the hardships peasants could expect to encounter in life as well as of their low social status and supposedly coarse natures. The smooth silk that caressed the bodies of the rich and noble, by contrast, signaled the life of ease to which they were entitled, as well as their supposedly more refined and delicate natures.[12]

Most of us would have no trouble admitting that coarse wool and smooth silk could become *symbols* of class division and status, and obviously they were. However, the more interesting and important phenomenon is the way in which these materials – in concert with thousands of other material things – help to *create* the very idea and practice of class distinctions and related patterns of thought. In noting that the difference between silk and nylon is not just symbolic or a marker for preexisting social distinctions between highbrow and lowbrow, Bruno Latour argues that the chemical and manufacturing differences between the two materials help to give rise to a specific type of class difference: "*Without* the many indefinite material nuances between the feel, the touch, the color, the sparkling of silk and nylon, *this* social difference might not exist at all."[13] Or consider the anthropologist Nicole Boivin's example of the transformative power of mud-brick walls in early Neolithic society in the eastern Mediterranean. When humans began to build their dwellings with mud bricks, Boivin argues, they were for the first time able to create malleable yet physically solid spatial divisions that assisted in both creating and reinforcing social divisions. Further, since the investment of time and energy needed to build a clay dwelling is not easily abandoned, its transformative effects on the humans who lived there could endure for many years. Even if some mud-brick dwellers might have preferred to tear down the conceptual walls between social groups, the persistence of physical walls would continue to act as a significant force favoring the survival of social distinctions. "The course of human history is therefore

[12] Constance Classen, *The Deepest Sense: A Cultural History of Touch* (Chicago: University of Illinois Press, 2012), 9.
[13] Bruno Latour, *Reassembling the Social: An Introduction to Actor-Network-Theory* (New York: Oxford University Press, 2005), 40.

a process not only of human decisions, choices, and ideas," Boivin concludes, "but also of the material force with which humans are surrounded, and with which they engage."[14]

Silk was not the only soft material available to premodern peoples. Alpaca wool or even just plain cotton, to name only two, could make for a soft fabric. Yet none of these other materials possessed precisely the same array of properties as silk. Humans liked silk because they just happened to have the sensory abilities needed to like silk – sensory abilities that evolved for largely unrelated reasons. To be sure, as I already noted, part of the ancient historical appeal of silk has been a result of its rarity and the relative ease with which it could be transported. Silk was a useful commodity of exchange or even a protocurrency. Yet it would be a mistake to think of silk solely as a signifier of economic value or elite status. Before silk could become a powerful economic or cultural symbol, biological humans first had to appreciate its essential biological properties. It seems unlikely that there is any genetically rooted human affinity *specifically* for silk – the material does not appear to offer much of an evolutionary advantage to humans. Yet to doubt the existence of a *genetic* basis for liking silk is not to say that there could not be a significant *biological* basis, one based in the physical nature of the human species.

Until recent decades, many historians tended to consider bodily biological phenomena like touch, taste, or other senses as largely outside their purview. The historical theorist R. G. Collingwood, you will recall from Chapter 1, suggested that true history only began when humans left their biological selves behind to become thinking creatures, who created cultures and societies that reflected abstract ideas. Assuming that human bodily "impulses and appetites" were largely fixed and enduring – outside of the realm of history, along with the rest of the nonhuman material world – Collingwood could safely talk about an abstract, almost-immaterial human "mind" as the essential driver of history, rather akin to Hegel's *Geist*. At least in Collingwood's view, history and the broader idea of humanism was built on a thoroughgoing belief in human exceptionalism.[15] While perhaps not the case with Collingwood, in an earlier age this marginalization of the bodily nature of humans could sometimes carry more than a whiff of racist Western exceptionalism.

---

[14] Nicole Boivin, *Material Cultures, Material Minds* (Cambridge, UK: Cambridge University Press, 2008), 136–8.
[15] R. G. Collingwood, *The Idea of History* (Mansfield Center, CT: Martino, [1946] 2014), 210–17.

As Classen notes, historians writing in the nineteenth century had often seen the sense of touch as a primitive means of understanding the world, one that dominated among the supposedly uncivilized peoples. The German natural historian Lorenz Oken, for example, asserted a hierarchy of senses in which the visually centered European "eye-man" was superior to the more tactile African "skin-man." The path to progress, whether for societies or historians, lay in escaping the base nature of our biological bodies to embrace the more abstract and thus purer realm of "high culture" that Oken associated with vision and an abstract, disembodied model of the human intellect.[16]

Not all historians accepted Collingwood's rejection of the body as suitable topic of study. Again, the inventive scholars of the Annales school were among the first to chart a more materialist course. Marc Bloch explored the corporeal nature of medieval senses in his 1973 book *The Royal Touch*, and as early as 1947 Lucien Febvre even hinted at the embodied nature of cognition in suggesting that "a series of fascinating studies could be done on the sensory underpinnings of thought in different periods."[17] The 1990s saw an efflorescence of studies devoted to the history of the senses, focusing particularly on sight and hearing.[18] Work on the supposedly "lower" senses like smell, taste, and touch was slower to develop, in part because of the many methodological challenges it presented. But scholars like Classen have now begun to bring even the sense of touch into history. Reflecting the enduring influence of the cultural turn, however, many scholars avoid discussing the actual bodily nature of touch and other human senses, fearing that to do so is to court a crude reductionist universalism. One scholar, for example, condemns those histories of touch that only "return over and over again to the physiological 'realities' for their understanding of the history or culture of touch."[19] Rather than viewing the physiological understanding of the senses as a useful tool for understanding the role of senses in creating culture, many scholars followed the path blazed by the French historian Alain Corbin whose studies of smell and sound emphasized that cultural context trumped any species-wide physiological factors.[20] As one recent

---

[16] Classen, *The Deepest Sense*, xii-xii.   [17] Quoted in Classen, *The Deepest Sense*, xv.

[18] See, for example, Robert Jütte, *A History of the Senses: From Antiquity to Cyberspace*, trans. James Lynn (London: Polity, 2004), and Mark M. Smith, *Sensing the Past: Seeing, Hearing, Smelling, Tasting, and Touching in History* (New York: University of Columbia Press, 2008).

[19] Quoted in Classen, *The Deepest Sense*, xv.

[20] Alain Corbin, *The Foul and the Fragrant: Odor and the French Social Imagination*, trans. Miriam Kochan, Roy Porter, and Christopher Pendergast (Cambridge, MA: Harvard

overview notes, historians of the senses stress not physiology but rather how the human senses have "changed over time and functioned according to the economic, cultural, and political imperatives of particular societies."[21]

How can we explain this almost-willful rejection of even a carefully measured use of the sciences to help us understand the history of human senses that are, after all, clearly biological and physical phenomena rooted in the specific, albeit mutable, nature of the human organism? Classen likely speaks for many scholars when she concludes that to use the physiological sciences to understand human perception is to "both disregard the ways in which science itself is a cultural construct and to detract from the significance of culturally specific models of sensation."[22] In other words, scientific insights cannot be trusted, but even if the science was valid, it would distract scholars from what should be their true focus: the sphere of human culture, which is presumed to be largely or entirely independent of the embodied existence of actual biological human beings. Classen, of course, is correct that science, like all forms of human thought and insight, has been shaped and sometimes warped by the biases of its time. Yet as I argued earlier, to therefore abandon contemporary scientific insights is a perversely self-destructive stance, and – since science offers the most effective means currently available to understand the nonhuman world – one that in essence concedes to the perpetuation of a long-standing and misleading anthropocentrism. Likewise, Classen is undeniably correct that different cultures and times might value the feel of things differently, yet this does not mean that the physiological means by which they literally *felt* that world were necessarily different. Or, if they were physiologically different – perhaps because of environmental shaping of the brain and body – surely it should be of great scholarly interest to know this and investigate its historical consequences. Even more problematically, such a postmodernist view assumes that cultural phenomena stand in opposition to biologically rooted ones, as if cultural diversity and creativity exist independently from human biological and material existence. Here again we see the common postmodernist assumption that to introduce a scientifically based understanding of biologically mediated

University Press, 1986), and, Corbin, *Village Bells: Sound and Meaning in the Nineteenth-Century French Countryside*, trans. Martin Thom (New York: Columbia University Press, 1998).
[21] Smith, "Making Sense of US History," 21.
[22] Quoted in Classen, *The Deepest Sense*, xv.

phenomena like touch is an attempt to reduce it to an entirely fixed and ahistorical scientific status. While this may have been the case with some earlier scientific and materialist theories, it is no longer. As I will discuss later in the chapter, contemporary scientific thinking points us toward not a fixed and deterministic material world but rather one that is a seething cauldron of constant innovation and growth. Culture does not emerge in distinction from a creative material world but in concert with a lively environment that both shapes and constitutes our bodies and brains.

Return again to those shoppers at Beijing's Panjiayuan Market, fingers splayed to judge the appropriately named "hand" or feel of the material. Recent research has shown that the human hand can perceive extraordinarily small irregularities on a surface, as little as 13 nanometers (.0000005 of an inch) in height when a finger is dragged across the material. This is roughly the size of a large molecule. To put the dimension into perspective, it would mean that if you had a finger the size of the Earth it could feel a ridge as small as an automobile.[23] Our sense of touch is far more powerful than our rather feeble sense of sight (raptors can see two to six times as well), and we can feel a bump roughly a hundred times smaller than we can see. Touch is also among the most basic of all our bodily senses, as it is with many other organisms. Even single-celled organisms that are unable to detect light or sound vibrations can feel something touch them and respond by pulling away – a very useful way of avoiding becoming another organism's lunch. In contrast to sight, sound, and scent, which we can effectively "turn off" by closing our eyes or plugging our ears and noses, our sense of touch is always with us. "Touch is so central to what we are, to the feeling of being ourselves," notes the Dutch neuropsychologist Chris Dijkerman, "that we almost cannot imagine ourselves without it."[24]

We cannot really imagine lacking a sense of touch because it is the very means through which we begin to imagine who we are as individuals and as a species. Writing on the recent efflorescence of scientific and humanistic research on touch, the writer Adam Gopnik observes that "what we see we long for; what we hear we interpret; what we touch we are." As a newborn, touch is the first of our senses to come online.

[23] Lisa Skedung et al., "Feeling Small: Exploring the Tactile Perception of Limits," *Scientific Reports* 3 (March 4, 2013). A popular account is Phillip Ross, "How Sensitive Is Human Touch? New Research Suggests Our Fingers Can Detect Nano-wrinkles on Near-Smooth Surfaces," *Science News* (September 17, 2013).
[24] Quoted in Natalie Angier, "Primal, Acute, and Easily Duped: Our Sense of Touch," *New York Times*, December 9, 2008.

The skin-to-skin contact of baby and parent is the sensory medium through which we first bond with another living creature, and it will continue to serve a similarly pivotal social role throughout our lives. As the Berkeley-based research psychologist Dacher Keltner puts it, touch is "the root moral precept of our sense of common humanity." Who we are as conscious beings emerges not from some abstracted sense of self that resides solely in the brain, but through our bodily sensory engagement with our environment and other humans and organisms. While modern peoples tend to think of themselves above all else as seeing and hearing creatures, in many ways the sense of touch embedded in our skin is the brain's most intimate interface with the world. Humans can rationalize the inputs of our eyes and ears, recognizing that they are imperfect reflections of a more complicated world, but it is much more difficult to think of our sense of touch as an abstraction.[25] We are, in significant part, the creatures whose brains and minds know the world through highly sensitive skin.

Our sense of touch is a complicated physiological phenomenon, a combination of a variety of neurological sensors that can distinguish hot from cold, a pleasant pressure from crushing pain, and a soothing caress from a maddening scratchiness. Given that our acute sense of touch is even today both helpful and harmful, we might well ask why it evolved to such an extreme level of sophistication. The answer depends on the type of "touch" being discussed. The unparalleled human ability to sense minute differences of pressure most likely coevolved with the hominin use of tools. Once early human ancestors developed the ability to walk upright, their hands were freed to do all sorts of other things, like throwing sticks and stones, and some 2.5 million years ago they began to deliberately reshape them into useful tools. Success in making tools depended on the ability to accurately feel and manipulate the stone material, kicking off a positive coevolutionary feedback loop in which tools spurred the development of finely tuned nerves and muscles in the palms and fingers, which in turn led to better tools. The more refined the sense of touch, the more refined the tool, and the more successful it could be in helping humans to survive.[26]

Another key aspect of touch is our ability to sense when something is "itchy," a sensation that everyone can instantly imagine but that is almost

[25] Adam Gopnik, "Feel Me: What the New Science of Touch Says about Ourselves," *The New Yorker*, May 16, 2016.
[26] Yuval Noah Harari, *Sapiens: A Brief History of Humankind* (New York: Vintage, 2011), 10.

impossible to describe. It was once assumed that an itch was just a subdued form of pain. But recently the Johns Hopkins neuroscientist Zinzhong Dong has demonstrated that mammals have a dedicated set of sensory nerve cells that are designed solely to detect the feeling that we call an itch. Evolutionary biologists suggest that such an elaborate system most likely evolved so that our ancestors could detect the unique feeling of parasitic insects like lice crawling on our skin, a feeling that is distinct from both pressure and pain. Early humans who could scratch such an itch, the argument goes, were better able to avoid parasites and the diseases they often carried.[27]

The reason we find the feel of scratchy fabrics like coarse wool so maddening and smooth fabrics like silk so soothing is thus in significant part because we long ago evolved a sophisticated sensory system for avoiding dangerous parasites. Yet there is at least one other obvious aspect to the story. Humans are unusually well suited to appreciate the smoothness of silk because most of our skin is not covered with a thick layer of hair or fur, as is the case with the vast majority of other mammals. Our closest living primate relatives are mostly covered with fur, which provides them with protection from sun, rain, cold, scrapes, and bruises. Precisely why it is that humans, along with a handful of other mammals like naked mole rats and elephants, lost this very useful layer of fur is a matter of some debate. The best current theory is that humans started to lose their body hair as a way to keep cool during the strenuous walking and running that became increasingly central to a way of life built around hunting and gathering. Sweat produced on naked skin evaporates quickly, acting like a sort of swamp cooler for the body. Tellingly, this superior cooling ability of bare skin became even more important as the size of human brains began to increase. As I will discuss in more detail in the last chapter, our brains consume a tremendous amount of our bodily energy, which in turn generates a great deal of bodily heat. Human brains are also highly sensitive to overheating, as we discover anew each summer with a sharp increase in incidences of heat exhaustion and strokes. While there were other factors that explain the evolution of large brains, the superior cooling power of our naked skin was pivotal. As one anthropologist puts it: "Shedding our body hair was surely a critical step in becoming brainy."[28]

---

[27] Liang Han et al., "A Subpopulation of Nociceptors Specifically Linked to Itch," *Nature Neuroscience* 16 (2013): 174–82; Gopnik, "Feel Me."

[28] Nina G. Jablonski, "The Naked Truth: Our Nearly Hairless Skin Was a Key Factor in the Emergence of Other Human Traits," *Scientific American* 22, no. 1 (Winter 2013): 22–9, quote on 29.

If humans had not coevolved with their tools to have such a sophisticated sense of touch, how many of them would later have gone to the difficulty of developing silk reeling, spinning, and weaving? Likewise, if their skin could not really sense much difference between rough wool and smooth silk, or was simply covered with fur, surely they would have been far less interested in trying to develop cloths and clothing that were soft. In sum, absolutely nothing about the human sense of touch evolved so that humans could appreciate silk per se. But much about the human sense of touch was nonetheless very well suited to appreciate silk. Genetic evolution gave humans a hyper-refined sense of touch, dedicated neurological sensors for detecting itchiness, and largely hairless bodies. But once these nearly universal human traits had evolved for wholly other reasons, all humans were in a very concrete material sense inclined to appreciate silk in a way no other animal on the planet could. They were not genetically predisposed to like silk, but the bodies that their genes and environment made certainly were.

It is in this physiological context that we can gain a richer appreciation of the rich variety of human cultural responses to silk. Consider, for example, the sensual words in the famous *Pillow Book* of the Japanese lady of the court during the Heian era (794–1185), Sei Shōnagon: "I love to slide a silk robe over my face and take a nap, breathing through the filmy scent of sweat."[29] Throughout her book she makes constant reference to the texture and color of silk and its symbolic centrality to life in the Heian court. She describes the magic of dancers entertaining the court: "the glossy sheen of their softened-silk robes, the way their long formal trains weave and twine about each other as they dance this way and that."[30] Even the "attractively intimate" sound of the silk robes of elegant gentlewomen enchants: "You hear the silk rustle of people as they leave or enter and, though it's only a soft sound, you can guess who each one would be."[31] For Lady Sei, much like the Romans and many others from cultures around the world, the pleasures of silk were intimately bound up with her bodily experience of its unique material properties. From this fusion of the human and the material, she crafted a portrait of silk that reflected the hyper-refined cultural sensibilities of the Heian court and her own unique position within it. The materiality of her experience of silk

[29] David Greer, "The Lists of a Lady-in-Waiting," *Kyoto Journal* 45 (October 31, 2000).
[30] Sei Shōnagon, *The Pillow Book*, trans. Meredith McKinney (New York: Penguin, 2007), 141–2.
[31] Shōnagon, *The Pillow Book*, 182

was not distinct from this cultural world – rather, it offered a uniquely powerful way of both creating and capturing the essence of this culture.

This silk obsession could also be self-destructive. For example, the Japanese conquest of the indigenous Ainu people of the northern island of Hokkaido was an often-violent and exploitive process. Yet the Ainu played a significant role in undermining their own means of local subsistence in part because they increasingly came to prize Japanese trade items, and most especially silk. In artist Kakizaki Hakyō's (1764–1826) late eighteenth-century paintings of famous Ainu chiefs from eastern Hokkaido, they all sport Qing (1644–1911) dynastic silk clothing favored by Chinese elites, which strengthened their status in Hokkaido as well as within the broader reach of the Chinese tributary order.[32] Along with swords, iron pots, rice, and sake, silk became a powerful means for the Ainu elites both to create and display their status, just as it did in countless other nations and cultures around the globe.[33]

There were other reasons humans might have developed silk beyond its utility in making soft itch-free robes and other clothing. As I will explain shortly, silk's chemical structure also makes it unusually easy to dye: perhaps some humans were initially attracted to silk cloth because it was useful for creating evocative banners, drapes, and wrappings – visual tools for both creating and marking status or power. Indeed, the earliest yet discovered remnant of silk fabric was not an item of clothing but rather a funeral shroud buried with a small child in China. But if the fiber's ability to absorb dyes might have played an early role, the eventual worldwide spread of silk was clearly driven by the fact that to the human sense of touch it feels unusually smooth and soft. Various cultures or subcultures have been known to develop an active antipathy for silky softness. The adherents of some ascetic Christian traditions thought they derived spiritual benefit from wearing rough and scratchy hair shirts or sackcloth – using the skin's ability to detect parasites as a means of torturing themselves.[34] Silk clothing might also be dismissed by a culture of a Spartan persuasion as too indulgent or effeminate, or be scorned by the more prudish members of a society

---

[32] Brett Walker, *The Conquest of the Ainu Lands: Ecology and Culture in Japanese Expansion, 1590–1800* (Berkeley: University of California Press, 2001), 111–12.

[33] Brett Walker, *A Concise History of Japan* (Cambridge, UK: University of Cambridge Press, 2015), 138–9.

[34] Classen, *The Deepest Sense*, 8. Intriguingly, the archaeologist Ian Hodder has found much earlier evidence for this practice in his excavation of the Neolithic settlement of Çatalhöyük in modern-day Turkey: Ian Hodder, *The Leopard's Tale: Revealing the Mysteries of Çatalhöyük* (London: Thames and Hudson, 2011).

FIGURE 5.1 When the Ainu chief Ikotoi posed for the samurai artist Kakizaki Hakyō in the late eighteenth century, he wore a silk robe embroidered with dragons in the style of Chinese elites of the time. Courtesy of Hakodate Central Library, Hokkaido.

as nothing more than a device for sexual display. Yet to some degree these contrary examples simply confirm the point. Whether silk is treasured or reviled for its soft smoothness, humans first understood it only through their biological bodies and their acute sense of touch. While various cultural approaches might spring from this embodied encounter with silk, at their base these were neither arbitrary nor solely cultural constructs but rather the products of a powerful synergy between the material properties of human beings and those of silk. Indeed, given this material-biological nexus, it is not too much to say that silk exerted an inherent biological attraction on humans, a sort of material gravitational pull. Human cultures and societies could resist that pull, even deny it altogether, yet it remained as a force to be reckoned with.

THE CHEMISTRY OF SMOOTH

But if the human body happens to be especially well equipped to appreciate the smoothness of silk, why is it that the silk itself is so smooth in the first place? To understand the answer demands a brief foray into organic chemistry, the fascinating science of molecular compounds that are built around the element carbon. Here, too, we will delve into a key theme of this book, which is the surprising creativity of a biochemical world that researchers have only recently begun to reveal. Humans often like to think they are the sole source of genuine creativity on the planet, yet a good case can be made that human technologies pale in comparison to, or in many cases heavily depend upon, the nonhuman inventions of organic chemistry.

At the beating heart of organic chemistry lies the seemingly humble element carbon, the very same stuff from which both messy black coal and sparkling diamonds are made. While there are some exceptions, *in*organic chemistry deals with all the molecules that do *not* have carbon in them. Given that carbon is only one of 97 other elements that occur naturally on Earth, you would be forgiven for assuming that the majority of compounds on the planet are therefore inorganic. But you would be wrong. There are actually vastly more organic (i.e., carbon-based) compounds on Earth than there are inorganic compounds. This is entirely because of the immense creative potential of the element carbon, which chemists assign the straightforward chemical abbreviation of "C." Carbon is a relatively light atom that has six electrons surrounding a nucleus of six protons and six neutrons, giving it the atomic number 6 (based on its six protons) and the atomic weight or mass of 12 (based on its six protons and six neutrons). Because of the way its six electrons are arranged, carbon is the most gregarious of elements: it can form bonds with more of its fellow elements than any other. A carbon atom also has the rare ability to form strong single bonds with another carbon atom that are resistant to chemical attacks. Carbon not only likes other elements but also is happy to pair up with its own kind. This sturdy self-bonding ability is important because it means carbon atoms can link up into durable long chains and rings that provide the basic structure and backbone for many parts of living cells and immense macromolecules like DNA.[35] On Earth, it was the versatile carbon atom that became the basic building block of life. It is possible, however, that life might be able to evolve using a different keystone element, such as silicon (Si), which not at all coincidentally is immediately beneath carbon in the periodic table of elements.

It has taken chemists about two hundred years to begin to understand the power of carbon. The Swedish chemist Jöns Jakob Berzelius first proposed the term "organic" in 1807 to designate chemical compounds that came from living things. Berzelius and other chemists were advocates of that broader form of anthropocentrism that we can recognize today as biocentrism: they believed that there was something fundamentally different about organic compounds, that they carried a mysterious essence called vital energy. Embracing this concept of vitalism, many chemists modestly assumed that while they could synthesize *inorganic* compounds in a laboratory, mere human beings could never create *organic* compounds, as these were the very stuff of life. However, in 1828 one of Berzelius' own students, Friedrich Wöhler, did just that when he made the organic compound urea by combining ammonia and cyanic acid. The resulting urea crystals were chemically indistinguishable from the urea derived from animal urine. Many other organic chemicals were soon synthesized in laboratories, and these very real compounds gradually undermined the vitalist faith that there was some fundamental essence that distinguished organic and inorganic matter. Thanks to the existence of these new synthetic carbon-based molecules, it increasingly seemed possible, perhaps even probable, that life itself somehow sprung from mere lifeless matter rather than through a process of divine creation.[36]

Yet if the idea of vitalism ultimately proved less than vital, chemists eventually discovered that the carbon atom offered a less mystical though no less extraordinary explanation for the nature of life. Carbon can indeed do great things. It is worth bearing in mind, for conceptual if not practical purposes, that humans and all of their history and cultures ultimately have derived from our carbon-based bodies and brains and their interactions with other organic and inorganic creatures and things in our environment.

---

[35] John Emsley, *Nature's Building Blocks: An A-Z Guide to the Elements* (Oxford, UK: Oxford University Press, 2001), 93–4.

[36] See the beautifully clear explanation of these topics by two organic chemists with an interest in history in Couteur and Burreson, *Napoleon's Buttons*, 8–9.

Our bodies are mostly water. But if you eliminate the hydrogen and oxygen that mostly occurs in the form of water (H_2O), it becomes evident that on an elemental level we are otherwise really walking and talking carbon: an average of 67 percent of our bodily tissue is carbon by dry weight.[37] How carbon atoms managed to give rise to life, and eventually living and thinking human beings, is far too big a question to deal with here. However, some recent scientific advances can provide insights into the simpler and not entirely unrelated question of how carbon-based molecules might have given rise to useful materials like silk.

To really understand silk and the role it has played in human history, we must first recognize that it is a protein, as are hooves, wool, and our own hair and nails. Proteins are key to life on Earth, and the word itself comes from the Greek *proteios*, meaning "of first or primary importance." These complex molecules are the basic building blocks of muscles, tendons, brains, and skin; and, in a somewhat different form, proteins play a pivotal role in carrying out cell reproduction, immune responses, digestion, and almost all other metabolic processes. All of the many millions of proteins that perform these diverse life functions are made from stringing together patterns of just 20 different basic chemical compounds – what chemists call the standard, or alpha, amino acids. The basic skeleton of these amino acids is the versatile carbon atom with its ability to strongly bond to itself in order to create chains and rings. Importantly, though, the unique properties of each of these 20 alpha amino acids, and hence the properties of the proteins from which they are formed, is determined by their *side group* – a molecule that sticks out from the side of each amino acid. So, when these amino acids with their side groups are linked together in long chains to become proteins, the properties of those proteins derive from the line of accompanying side groups that are called side chain.[38]

Think of a protein as somewhat like a bead necklace. Each of the beads is an amino acid whose properties are determined by its side group. Now the very simplest of these side molecules is nothing more than a lone hydrogen atom (H), and the resulting amino acid is called glycine. Slightly more complicated but still exceedingly modest side groups create the amino acids alanine (side group CH_3) and serine (side group CH_2OH). Other side groups can get *much* larger, but for silk 85 percent of its protein chain is made up of these three diminutive amino acids – a repeating sequence of glycine-serine-glycine-alanine-glycine-alanine. In an actual

[37] Emsley, *Nature's Building Blocks*, 93.   [38] Couteur, *Napoleon's Buttons*, 108–14.

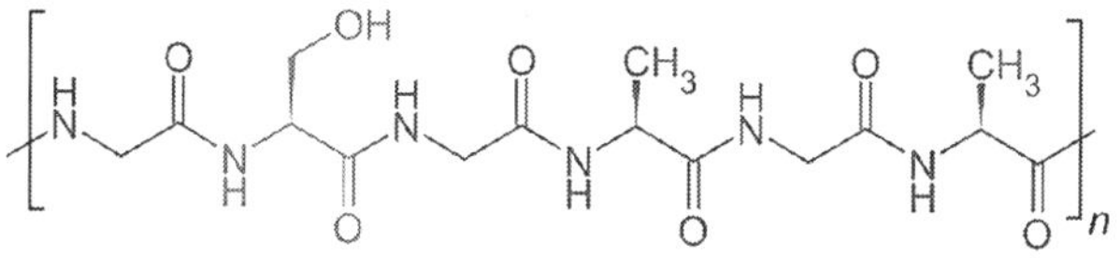

Gly   Ser   Gly   Ala   Gly   Ala

FIGURE 5.2 A highly simplified graphical representation (for greater clarity the structural backbone of carbon atom bonds are indicated only by the zigzag line) of the amino acids and their side groups that make up the silk protein: a repeating chain of glycine-serine-glycine-alanine-glycine-alanine. The relatively small size of these three amino acids is partly why silk feels so smooth to the human touch.

thread of silk, there are billions of these "necklaces," or chains, that are all lined up parallel to each other, forming a sort of pleated sheet that can expand and contract, which helps to explain why silk is strong but elastic. This structure also means that the side group molecules physically stick out and above the pleated sheet of foundational molecules below. The structural nature of the silk protein explains why it feels smooth to the human touch and why peoples as diverse as Roman elites, Chinese nomads, and Heian courtiers like Sei Shōnagon valued the graceful touch of silk on their skin. Since the three main amino acids in the silk protein – glycine, alanine, and serine – also have the three smallest side groups, these stick up far less than would be the case with some of the larger side group molecules. Simply put, they are less rough and itchy. When silk thread is woven together into a fabric, these small and relatively uniform side group molecules are a big part of what we feel when we touch the fabric. Even the acutely sensitive human finger, with its ability to sense irregularities as small as 13 microns, cannot feel these small irregularities, so to the human hand silk feels unusually smooth.[39]

Oddly, two other prized attributes of silk – its iridescent sheen and the ease with which it takes and holds vibrantly colored dyes – are actually a result of what small irregularities *do* remain on its otherwise relatively smooth surface. First, slight variations in the silk's protein side chains reflect the light at random angles, refracting it to create a rainbow of scintillating color. Second, the remaining 15 percent of amino acid side groups that are not among the smallest also just happen to be among the very best at chemically bonding with the first dyes humans were able to

[39] Couteur, *Napoleon's Buttons*, 108–14.

develop.[40] Why, we might well ask, should humans have even cared that silk could take and hold brightly colored dyes like the symbolically rich reds treasured by the Chinese? Here, too, we see an entirely serendipitous convergence between the biological evolution of a specific human protein and the properties of the silk protein. Humans have evolved three kinds of specialized complex proteins called opsins that reside in the back of our eyes, each of which is able to absorb one of the different wavelengths of light that we term blue, red, and green. Most mammals have only two opsins – the ones able to detect the wavelengths of red and blue – and they are unable to see green. But humans also evolved an opsin protein that can see green. Evolutionary biologists are not entirely sure why humans, as well as our close contemporary relatives like chimpanzees, evolved this ability. However, it may be because brightly colored red, blue, and yellow fruits then stood out much more clearly against the dominant background of green foliage, giving our hungry omnivorous ancestors an evolutionary edge.[41]

When Eve was in the Garden of Eden, she could not have helped but to remark and perhaps be tempted by the apple (the supposed identity of the forbidden fruit), as its bright red color jumped out at her from the green leaves of the tree in a way it simply could not for a wolf or a deer. (Though humans should not be overly boastful on this score – some moths and butterflies have as many as 15 different photoreceptors and can see ultraviolet and even polarized light – flowers that look dull to the human eye may be a riot of bright colors and patterns to a moth.) Just as that third protein opsin in Eve's eyes helped the apple to seduce her, so, too, have countless other human eyes been seduced by the lustrous sheen and color of dyed silk. Before the modern era, brightly colored clothing and fabrics were relatively rare. Dyeing was a labor-intensive technological process that was often too expensive or time consuming for the average person to enjoy. For a people accustomed to the somber natural grays and browns of wool, to see an iridescent scarlet red silk robe or wall hanging would have been a startling and even emotionally moving sight.[42] The authority of religious and secular leaders and institutions might rest in no small part on their ability to monopolize the display of

---

[40] Couteur, *Napoleon's Buttons*, 108–14.

[41] Andreas Wagner, *Arrival of the Fittest: How Nature Innovates* (New York: Current, 2014), 112–13. Of course, the bright colors of fruits may well have coevolved to attract humans in the first place. See Michael Pollan, *The Botany of Desire: A Plant's-Eye View of the World* (New York: Random House, 2002).

[42] Classen, *The Deepest Sense*, 127–8.

bright colors that had the power to inspire such strong human reactions and feelings. Even in our own era when bright colors are common, the flash of red on a gold background attracted me to that silk wall hanging in Beijing's Panjiayuan Market. However, keep in mind that silk cloth lent itself so well to such colorful and manipulative displays solely because it happened to have just enough bulky amino acid side groups to absorb the common dyes that appealed to the human eye, yet not so many as to make an otherwise smooth protein chain feel rough to the human hand. Human social and political power was thus generated from an exquisite balance between our bodily senses and the extraordinary material properties of the silk protein.

INNOVATIVE MATTER

Humans often like to claim that their ancestors "invented" sericulture, and obviously they deserve some credit. No other creature currently on the planet has even come close to figuring out how to unreel the threads of insect cocoons and weave them into fabrics, nor would any of them necessarily care to do so if they did. Yet to focus only on the creativity of humans is to risk losing sight of what is arguably an even more profound and powerful creativity at work in the wider material world, a creativity that has driven much of human history. That a substance like silk exists at all is a credit not to humans, or even just to the insects and spiders that I will turn to shortly, but rather to the surprising innovative powers of the biochemical environment. Modern humans certainly learned how to use silk, which was, so far as we are aware, a unique and highly significant accomplishment. But where did the novel organic chemical compound we call silk come from to begin with?

Darwin, of course, demonstrated that organisms like silkworms and spiders evolved through a process of natural selection, revealing that what had long appeared to be a fixed and enduring environment was actually in a constant state of creative flux. Yet at the time he formulated it, Darwin's theory had several gaping holes. First, Darwin had no mechanism to explain how parents could pass on traits to their offspring; but based on careful observation he made the reasonable assumption that it did happen and the mechanism would eventually be found. The subsequent rediscovery of Gregor Mendel's pioneering work on heredity through what are now termed genes helped to describe the biochemical means through which Darwinian natural selection could function, leading to the powerful

Darwinian synthesis combining evolutionary and genetic theories.[43] The second hole in Darwinian theory, however, proved even more challenging. Evolutionary science posited that natural selection operated on small variations among individuals within populations of organisms, selecting for those whose traits best suited them to survive and reproduce in a particular environment (or, more accurately, selecting *against* the organisms that were less well suited, as they would be less successful in passing on their genes through reproduction). But here was the big hole in the theory: what exactly was the biological mechanism through which these variations among individuals in a population were created? Darwin had seen such variations in domesticated animals like pigeons, so he knew they occurred. But he could only make educated guesses about how and why. As the developmental biologist Andreas Wagner suggests in the title of his recent book *The Arrival of the Fittest*, Darwin's idea of natural selection could explain the survival of the fittest, but it could not yet explain the arrival of the fittest. What was the mechanism through which biology *innovates* in the first place?

It was no fault of Darwin's that he did not know. The scientific tools needed to understand what Wagner terms nature's "innovability" have been gradually developing over the past century. After the Darwinian synthesis, most evolutionary biologists assumed that truly novel traits simply resulted from random genetic mutations in an organism's DNA. The majority of these mutations reduced an individual organism's ability to survive and were quickly weeded out by natural selection. But a very few mutations actually helped an organism to thrive and thus be slightly more effective in passing on the new gene to its offspring. However, as Wagner notes, to say that innovation comes from random genetic mutations is to say very little: "It sweeps our ignorance under the rug by giving it a different name."[44] To understand where and how these mutations occur and express themselves in organisms also demanded that biologists investigate the unimaginably complex biological process by which an organism's genetic code – its DNA – is translated into the development and continued maintenance of an actual living thing. Over the past few decades, biologists like Wagner and many others have developed the new discipline of evolutionary developmental biology, or "evo-devo" for short, to do just that. Evo-devo uses evolutionary and genetic theory to understand developmental biology – the process by which any living thing develops from an

---

[43] Wagner, *Arrival of the Fittest*, 15.   [44] Wagner, *Arrival of the Fittest*, 33.

embryo to become a fully grown organism.[45] Evo-devo is thus part of the broader shift toward the extended evolutionary synthesis (discussed in Chapter 3), which broadens the focus of evolutionary biology to better incorporate the many ways in which the environment influences development.

It is now becoming clear that innovations can occur in this developmental process in many ways and at many levels. Consider, for example, the death-defying abilities of the Artic cod, *Boreogadus saida*. Arctic cod are able to survive in and exploit an ecological niche that few other fish can. They live near the North Pole and thrive at depths of 900 meters below the surface, where the temperature of the high-pressure salt water frequently drops well below freezing. Most other fish would soon be frozen fish sticks at those temperatures. However, Arctic cod have somehow evolved the ability to synthesize a highly specialized protein that permeates their bodily fluids to keep them from freezing, somewhat like antifreeze in automobile coolant fluid. This could not be just the result of a random mixing of already-existing traits within the population. Rather, it was something truly new under the sea. Where, Wagner asks, did this useful antifreeze protein come from?[46]

Evolutionary developmental biology suggests that the answer lies in the immense innovative ability of the living material world itself, and particularly those carbon-based organic molecules that give rise to proteins and the various forms of RNA molecules involved in protein synthesis. Even after the Darwinian revolution, many modern thinkers still tend to think of the natural world around them as a relatively static and stable system, one which, if left untouched by humans, changes only through the geologically slow process of evolution. Yet at the molecular level, down where genes and proteins ultimately give rise to real living creatures, there is a complex system of nearly infinite innovative potential for change. Indeed, this is the very same inherent material creativity that produced life itself and ultimately helped to create the big-brained humans who

---

[45] In addition to Wagner's *Arrival of the Fittest*, there have been a number of recent accessible treatments relating to the revolution in evolutionary developmental biology and how nature innovates. See Sean B. Carroll, *Endless Forms Most Beautiful: The New Science of Evo Devo* (New York: Norton, 2005); Carroll, *The Making of the Fittest: DNA and the Ultimate Forensic Record of Evolution* (New York: Norton, 2007); Nick Lane, *Life Ascending: The Ten Greatest Inventions of Evolution* (New York: Norton, 2010); and Peter L. Hoffman, *Life's Ratchet: How Molecular Machines Extract Order from Chaos* (New York: Basic Books, 2012).

[46] Wagner, *Arrival of the Fittest*, 111–14.

would be just smart enough to overestimate their own crude creativity while largely dismissing the creativity of the world that had made them in the first place. Much of this creativity emerges at the metabolic level, where genes interact with the complex machinery of life to create innovative proteins like the Arctic cod's blood antifreeze. But the Arctic cod's specific antifreeze protein is only one of a nearly infinite number of potential proteins that can be synthesized, only a few of which might actually help an organism survive. Remember that all proteins are made up of a combination of 20 different amino acids. Even a relatively short chain of just three of these amino acids can be arranged in 8,000 different ways, and each of these arrangements can have unique biochemical properties. Yet most proteins are made up of much-longer chains of amino acids, vastly increasing the different ways in which they can be arranged. The number of possible arrangements of a chain of 100 amino acids is expressed by the numeral one followed by 130 zeroes! In practice, many proteins have thousands or even tens of thousands of amino acids. In sum, the number of ways in which these 20 amino acids can be arranged in a chain of thousands is not just astronomical, it is *hyper*astronomical, greater than all of the hydrogen atoms estimated to exist in the entire universe.[47]

Wagner suggests we might think of this gigantic collection of potential proteins as an immense biological library that the earth's living things are slowly wandering through. At this point, researchers have only identified an infinitesimally small part of this unimaginably vast library of possible proteins. Even more extraordinary is the fact that *life itself* has only just begun the task. "Even after 3.8 billion years of evolution," Wagner notes, "life has explored only a tiny fraction of the library." There are more potential proteins residing in this "library" than the total number of organisms that have ever existed in the entire history of the planet.[48] Proteins like the Arctic cod antifreeze, he argues, are "prototypical examples of nature's innovative powers." Make a small change in the process by which a particular protein is synthesized and "presto, huge areas of the earth's oceans become livable."[49]

---

[47] Wagner, *Arrival of the Fittest*, 32. The philosopher of science Stuart Kauffman makes a similar point: Stuart Kauffman, "Why Science Needs to Break the Spell of Reductive Materialism," *Aeon* (May 20, 2016), and Kauffman, *Humanity in a Creative Universe* (Oxford, UK: Oxford University Press, 2016).
[48] Wagner, *Arrival of the Fittest*, 92–3.   [49] Wagner, *Arrival of the Fittest*, 104.

However, the sheer vastness of this library of potential proteins raises the obvious question of how any organism could possibly have evolved just the right new protein needed to improve its fitness for the particular environment it happened to be living in at that time. Even over the course of millions of years, the mathematical odds of finding many usefully adaptive proteins in such an immense array of possible combinations would appear to be vanishingly small. However, by combining laboratory studies with computational modeling, Wagner and other researchers have demonstrated that life overcomes this limitation because there are literally millions of ways in which a protein can achieve the same biological end. In other words, there are many different arrangements for amino acids that can perform exactly the same task in an actual organism, such as serving as an antifreeze for a polar fish or as a protein fiber for making cocoons or webs. In this robust flexibility, Wagner points toward another critical insight into the innovative power of the material world: life can develop millions of different solutions to the same problem because there is a delicate balance between order and disorder. Wagner notes that evolution "must be simultaneously conservative and progressive," passing on proteins and other biological functions that work while also constantly searching for and trying out potentially risky innovations. Because the organic chemistry of life has not just one but millions of ways to make an antifreeze protein – because the system is robust – it can afford to act randomly and make small changes that otherwise might prove disastrous. Many of these small changes will be neutral, neither harming nor helping the organism. But even these neutral changes pave the way to innovation, permitting the organism to survive to reproduce so that its descendants can explore further changes, one of which might eventually prove beneficial. The result is to increase the rate of successful innovation far beyond what would be expected or possible with the earlier scientific model of random mutations in which there was only one solution to any problem and the vast majority of changes were likely to be harmful rather than neutral. Making an analogy to the popular science fiction series *Star Trek*, Wagner argues that nature has a sort of "warp drive" that greatly increases the speed at which organisms can innovate new proteins and other biological processes. Absent this creative warp drive, "life would never have crawled out of the primordial soup."[50]

All this does not mean that the DNA of complex organisms like humans evolves more rapidly than previously understood. (Although, as discussed

---

[50] Wagner, *Arrival of the Fittest*, 182.

earlier, epigenetics now has revealed other much-speedier mechanisms through which humans may adapt to their environments in "real time.") These new theories provide a clearer explanation of how nature innovates through the nearly infinite possible combinations of organic molecules like amino acids, yet by the standards of human historical time, the Darwinian process of natural selection and evolution often still moves at glacial pace. This is particularly the case with humans themselves, with their slow reproductive cycles and relatively small number of offspring. Yet evolutionary change can and does occur much more quickly in many of the simpler organisms with which humans have formed strong material partnerships. At historic time scales the creative power of the organic world may most directly affect humans through their interactions with legions of these more rapidly evolving organisms, like the bacteria that reside in our guts, the insects that eat our crops, and the worms that make our silk. Bacteria, for example, reproduce so quickly and have such efficient means of trading genetic information that they can evolve new traits over the course of a few days or even hours.[51] Or consider one recently discovered single-celled organism that has the ability to reengineer its own proteins to quickly adapt to the environment, a process researchers term guided mutation.[52] In this sense, humans are surrounded by other simpler but arguably more biologically innovative creatures, the speedy architects of a sort of "alien technology" whose benefits we often mistakenly attribute solely to our own creativity. Among these are the innovative silkworms that would engineer another of these alien technologies that humans would eventually learn to use, sparking a cascade of materially driven creativity that would change history.

THE MULBERRY WORM

The first known historical reference to sericulture, or deliberate silkworm raising by humans, comes from China in 1600 BCE, though the Chinese and possibly other peoples very likely harvested wild silkworm cocoons long before the worms were domesticated.[53] One problem with gathering wild cocoons is that the moths may emerge before humans have a chance

[51] Carl Zimmer, *A Planet of Viruses* (Chicago: University of Chicago Press, 2012).

[52] National Science Foundation, "The 'Intraterrestrials': New Viruses Discovered in Ocean Depths," NSF Press Release 15–024, March 23, 2015.

[53] E. J. W. Barber, *Prehistoric Textiles: The Development of Cloth in the Neolithic and Bronze Ages with Special Reference to the Aegean* (Princeton, NJ: Princeton University Press, 1992), 30–1; Yuji Yasukochi, Hiroshi Fujii, and Marian R. Goldsmith,

to harvest them. To escape their cocoon, the moths secrete an acid that breaks up what had previously been a single filament of silk, leaving only shorter fibers that are much harder for humans to twist together to make silk thread. Domestication may have begun simply as a means to keep the silkworms nearby so the cocoons could be harvested before the moths emerged.[54] The domestic silkworm – or, to be teleological about it, the silk moth, as the worm or caterpillar is the larval stage of the moth – appears to be descended from the ancestors of a wild silk moth that is common to this day in much of China, as well as Korea and Japan. The Chinese called the silkworm *cán* (the earliest Chinese character from oracular bones used in temples looked just like a worm), but when they were added to the western Linnaean classificatory system, they were given the Latin name *Bombyx mandarina*, the "Mandarin (or Chinese) silkworm." Recognizing the moth's close connection to its cocoon in the human imagination, *Bombyx* appears to derive from an Ancient Greek (possibly borrowed from Persian) word meaning silk or cotton. The contemporary English words "bombast" and "bombastic" share the same root, as a bombastic person is one unjustifiably full of themselves as if stuffed with cotton or silk padding – literally a "stuffed shirt."

Perhaps as long as 5,000 years ago, domesticated silkworms began to part genetic ways with their wild ancestors. Over the millennia, they would become so distinct that modern taxonomists granted them their own species name: *Bombyx mori*. The domesticated and wild moths can still interbreed even today, however, so some taxonomists suggest that the two are perhaps best thought of as variants of one species.[55] The *mori* in *Bombyx mori* refers to the Latin word for the mulberry tree, *Moro*. These "Mulberry silkworms" are aptly named because their domestication was closely tied to the domestication of their preferred food source, the green leaves of the white mulberry tree, *Morus alba*. In a pinch, silkworms will eat other species, but the white mulberry is by far their favorite. This taste for mulberry trees is more than a little strange, as the trees have evolved

---

"Silkworm," in *Genome Mapping and Genomics in Arthropods*, ed., W. Hunter and C. Kole (Berlin: Springer-Verlag, 2008), 44.

[54] On the general history of sericulture and silk production, see W. English, "The Textile Industry: Silk Production and Manufacture, 1750–1900," in *The Industrial Revolution, 1750–1850*, vol. 4 of *A History of Technology*, ed. C. Singer et al. (Oxford, UK: Oxford University Press, 1958), 308.

[55] Edmund Russell, "Spinning a World Wide Web: Silk Worms, Mulberries, and Manufacturing Landscapes," unpublished keynote address, Conference on Manufacturing Landscapes, Renmin University, Beijing, China, May 2015.

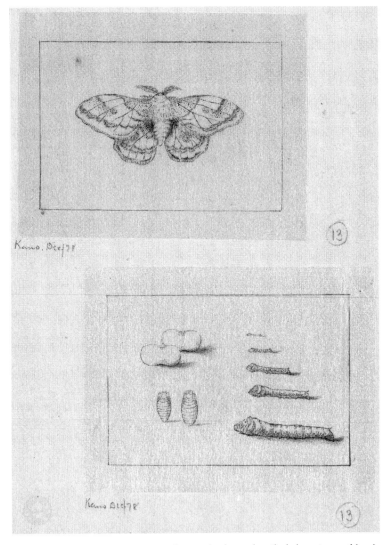

FIGURE 5.3 In 1876 a Japanese artist made these detailed drawings of both the moth and the rapidly growing larval forms of *Bombyx mori*, an insect whose genetic inventiveness would help to make Japan into a world power. The David Murray Collection, Library of Congress Prints and Photographs Division, image number LC-DIG-jpd-01050.

toxic chemical protectants in their leaves like latex that interfere with enzymes (yet another type of protein) that allow insects to digest sugars – an essential source of bodily energy. Most other moths and butterflies scrupulously avoid mulberry trees. Yet *Bombyx mori* caterpillars managed to develop a unique set of enzymes that lets them extract energy from mulberry leaf sugars even when exposed to the plant's nasty chemical defenses. Just as the Arctic cod's protein-based antifreeze allows it to exploit an environmental niche that would kill most other fish, so too does the silkworm's innovative protein enzyme give it access to the abundant mulberry tree leaves that most other worms cannot exploit. It is a bit as if humans evolved the ability to eat arsenic.[56]

As this ongoing biochemical arms race suggests, silkworms had a long coevolutionary history with mulberry trees that began hundreds of thousands of years before humans became interested in either of them. The historian Edmund Russell points out that it could well be that humans domesticated mulberry trees *before* silkworms, as the trees bear a tartly sweet fruit similar to a blackberry. Mulberry trees might have attracted the interest of humans with these tasty fruits, and humans repaid the favor by spreading the trees' seeds, which survive unscathed after a trip through their digestive system. Of course, birds, deer, and other animals could serve the same purpose, but humans were, so far as we are aware, the only ones who at some point began to deliberately plant the mulberry seeds and care for the trees. Besides being tasty, mulberry fruit contains many chemical compounds that some evidence suggests can encourage good health in humans and perhaps other animals. Russell speculates that the mulberry may have even evolved these chemicals because they fostered the robust health, and thus greater numbers and vigor, of useful animal seed spreaders like humans. Absent some such coevolutionary mechanism, it does seem odd that the trees should synthesize chemical compounds that just happened to be healthful to the humans who eat their fruit.[57] There may be other explanations, but as Michael Pollan has explained, over just the past few thousand years, many other plants besides mulberry trees have developed chemicals and compounds desirable to humans that have helped both the plants and their human partners to flourish.[58] Regardless, if the cultivation of mulberry trees did indeed come first, once the trees became a part of everyday human life so, too, did the *Bombyx mandarini* moths who would have continued to seek out the trees to lay their eggs. Since silk caterpillars do not usually cause severe damage to the mulberry

---

[56] Russell, "Spinning," 4; Chikara Hirayama et al., "Differential Effects of Sugar-Mimic Alkaloids in Mulberry Latex on Sugar Metabolism and Disaccharidases of Eri and Domesticated Silkworms," *Insect Biochemistry and Molecular Biology* 37 (2007): 1347–58.
[57] Russell, "Spinning," 7.   [58] Pollan, *Botany of Desire*.

trees they colonize, and they do not eat the fruit at all, early cultivators were probably not overly concerned by their presence. But living in such intimate proximity, people could have quite unintentionally learned a great deal about the silkworms and their mysterious white cocoons. Many would have at some point surely grasped that the white caterpillars transformed themselves into winged moths inside those silk cocoons.

But just how humans first realized that they could make thread and cloth from the silkworm cocoon is more difficult to know. Compared to ceramic potsherds or calcareous bones, the silk protein chain is relatively fragile and does not easily survive in the archaeological record. Yet the evidence that has survived suggests that the practice of silk making is very ancient. About 5,600 years ago in what is today Henan province in east central China's Yellow River Valley, a Neolithic people known as the Yangshao buried a small child wrapped in silk cloth. These tattered remains of what must have been an unimaginably precious fabric are the oldest evidence of silk cloth making yet discovered. The Yangshao people also made cloth from hemp plants, a process that was much easier than making silk but also produced a coarser fabric. It seems likely that only the elites among the Yangshao had the chance to personally experience the lustrous softness of silk. Certainly by the time of the Shang dynasty (1500–1050 BCE) some four millennia later, silk had become closely associated with royalty, as prominent rulers were routinely interred with at least some items of elaborately woven and dyed silk cloth. Within another thousand years, Chinese royalty would often go to their graves dressed entirely in silk.[59]

Given such evidence, archaeologists and historians generally credit these ancient Chinese peoples with being the first to develop the use of silk for cloth (versus just making silk thread or string). To this day, the Chinese are still the largest producers of silk in the world, devoting some 626,000 hectares (6,260 square kilometers) to mulberry tree cultivation.[60] But it is very likely that countless others also experimented with silk thread and yarns. Many peoples around the globe appear to have independently arrived at the basic idea of twirling plant or animal fibers together to make string or yarn. To date, the earliest evidence of deliberate human use of such fibers comes from the 34,000-year-old remains of flax

---

[59] Mary Schoeser, *Silk* (New Haven, CT: Yale University Press, 2007) 17–19.
[60] Manuel D. Sánchez, "World Distribution and Utilization of Mulberry, Potential for Animal Feeding," Food and Agriculture Organization, United Nations, Electronic Conference on Mulberry for Animal Production, 3.

threads discovered in a cave in the Republic of Georgia.[61] To groups of hunter-gatherers accustomed to spinning yarn from relatively common plants like flax or hemp, trying the same techniques with the silken threads of a cocoon would have required no great leap of the imagination, though certainly a great deal of patience and perseverance. The biggest initial technical challenge likely lay in figuring out how to unravel the sticky threads from each other by heating them in hot water. In Chinese myth, the ancient Chinese Empress Xilingshi discovered this when she accidentally dropped a cocoon in her hot tea. A simpler if less elegant explanation might be that early humans tried boiling the cocoons not to get silk but rather to get at the insect meal inside. Regardless, if many may have experimented on a smaller scale, the peoples living in what is now eastern China were the first to develop a fully realized system of sericulture and silk making. The archaeological record suggests the Chinese may have had some early form of sericulture and mulberry tree horticulture as long as 4,000 years ago. But the first clear evidence of cultivation of the trees on a large scale, as well as pruning to keep them short enough to conveniently harvest the leaves and fruit, is from the Western Zhou dynasty that flourished from 1050 to 771 BCE.[62]

For centuries, the Chinese managed to maintain a virtual monopoly on silk production in the ancient world by carefully keeping the secret to themselves. As a lucrative Eurasian silk trade (over the Silk Road discussed earlier) began to flourish during the Han dynasty, various Chinese rulers issued dire threats to execute anyone who attempted to smuggle silkworms, eggs, or mulberry seeds out of the kingdom. These draconian measures seem to have succeeded for a surprisingly long time, but by the sixth century CE the secret clearly had escaped. According to legend, two Christian monks carried silkworm eggs and mulberry seeds to Constantinople (modern Istanbul) in their hollowed out canes. Regardless, by the fourteenth century sericulture and silk making had spread throughout the Mediterranean world, first flourishing most exuberantly in the northern Italian merchant cities of Venice and Florence. The immense profits the silk trade brought to these city-states provided a sizable part of the funds that underwrote the Italian Renaissance and its efflorescence of humanist thinking.[63] Ironically, to the degree that an increasingly anthropocentric humanism derived from this earlier Italian

---

[61] Eliso Kvavadze et al., "30,000-Year-Old Wild Flax Fibers," *Science* 325 (2009): 1359.
[62] J. M. Suttie, "*Morus Alba L.*," FAO Report.
[63] Couteur, *Napoleon's Buttons*, 107–8.

Renaissance, humanism itself might be said to have it roots in the nonhuman power and creativity of the lowly silkworm.

THE SILK MAKERS

While the Chinese were the first to develop sericulture and a lucrative
transcontinental trade in silk, in many ways the real, if often unacknow-
ledged, stars of this vast historical pageant were the little alchemical
wizards who could turn mulberry leaves into silk. I previously explained
how the inherent innovative power of complex biochemical systems could
invent the chain of amino acids that gives us the silk protein. Yet another
material mystery remains: why should any organism go to all the bodily
expense of producing silk? This is not a trivial question, given that an
extraordinarily large number of invertebrate animals (not a single verte-
brate is similarly gifted, unless we count the American comic book hero
Spiderman) are able to make some type of silken thread, including moths
and butterflies, but also spiders, grasshoppers and crickets, silverfish, and
thrips. These insects create a wide variety of different silk fibers, and they
use the silk for an even wider variety of purposes, from making webs to
creating nests and burrows, and, of course, for the spinning of cocoons.
We use the term "silk" to refer to all of these fibers, but all have substantially different properties. This immense variation within silk fibers is in
part a product of the creative potential inherent in the many subtly
different ways the chain of proteins that make up silk can be synthesized.
Entomologists note that silk production is a "hot spot" of evolutionary
creativity, as the amino acids in silk can be arranged in a greater variety of
combinations than any other type of structural protein.[64] Variations in the
protein chains occur frequently, and, when one proved helpful to a spider
or silkworm, it was preserved by natural selection and passed down.
In fact, variations in silk production and use appear to be one of the
most important factors in giving rise to the immense diversification of
species among insects. New species of insects emerged because there were
so many different ways to use so many different types of silk to establish
unique niches.[65] Such diversity suggests that the innovative power of
organic chemistry and natural selection might have created not just one

---

[64] T. D. Sutherland et al., "Insect Silk: One Name, Many Materials," *Annual Review of Entomology* 55 (2010): 171.
[65] Catherin L. Craig, *Spiderwebs and Silk: Tracing Evolution from Molecules to Genes to Phenotypes* (Oxford, UK: Oxford University Press, 2003), 193–9.

distant silk-making ancestor from which all others have descended. Rather, the ability to synthesize silk might well have evolved several times among distinctly different branches of the insect world.[66]

All silk-making organisms manufacture the chemical precursor to silk in their bodies, storing it as a gel-like substance in an internal sac until needed. They then secrete the gel through a variety of different glands, a process of protrusion rather than extrusion, as there is no pressure pushing the silk out. Rather, the insects or spiders must pull the thin thread out by using their legs, bodies, or gravity. With silkworms the silk is produced by salivary glands in their jaws – in a very loose way, it might be thought of as a sort of silkworm "spit." This might strike some as distasteful, yet perhaps they would prefer it to the many other animals whose silk glands are located near their anus, such as spiders. However, the spider's spinneret – which unlike the one-trick silkworms can produce a variety of different special-purpose silks – has nothing at all to do with its excretory functions.[67] Regardless, when the silk gel leaves the animal's body, it rapidly reacts with the air to harden into a tough crystalline chain of proteins that becomes the silk fiber. Many may have heard the slightly misleading claim that on a per-weight basis the tensile strength of some spider silks is several times greater than that of steel. This is true, but partly because silk also stretches much more than steel, which is not always a desirable property. An elastic web is an advantage for orb weaver spiders, but most humans would prefer not to have bridges and car bodies that bounce and bend.

Evolutionary biologists estimate that the ability to make silk in the ancestors to Lepidoptera – the order of insects that includes more than 180,000 different species of butterflies and moths – first evolved some 250 million years ago.[68] For the caterpillars of silkworms and other moths and butterflies, silk became a tool for undergoing the extraordinary process of metamorphosis. The worms weave silk cocoons as a sort of second egg inside of which they essentially consume their previous body in order to grow a new winged one. The cocoon is both a receptacle for this complex biochemical process and a means of protecting the defenseless insect from the environment and predators while it is metamorphosing. The silk fibers,

---

[66] František Sehnal and Tara Sutherland, "Silks Produced by Insect Labial Glands," *Prion* 2 (2008): 145–53. See also Russell, "Spinning," 2–3.

[67] Catherine L. Craig, "Evolution of Arthropod Silks," *Annual Review of Entomology* 42 (1997): 231–2.

[68] Sehnal and Sutherland, "Silks Produced by Insect Labial Glands," 2–3.

held together and made rigid by a coating of yet another clever protein, the glue-like sericin, render the cocoon less palatable while also making it more difficult for would-be predators to get at the tasty protein-rich prize inside. Nonetheless, many animals are still happy to eat the vulnerable worms during metamorphosis, raising the question of why any organism would have evolved such a risky behavior in the first place. It seems counter-adaptive if not downright suicidal. Evolutionary biologists are not entirely sure, though since some 45–60 percent of all the animals on the planet (80–90 percent of which are insects) undergo metamorphosis, it must confer some useful advantage. The strongest current theory suggests that metamorphosis permits insects to more fully utilize available food sources in their niche while avoiding intragenerational competition. In the case of silkworms, the larval caterpillars grow rapidly by eating the leaves of mulberry trees, but the adult moth form feeds solely on the nectar of flowers. This permits any given environmental niche to support both more worms and moths, conferring an evolutionary advantage.[69] Metamorphosis also allows the wingless larval form to burrow into plants, fungi, and meat, which would likely harm the delicate wings of the subsequent adults. Since their larvae are such efficient feeding machines (recall Eric Carle's famous children's book *The Very Hungry Caterpillar*), some adult insects even have enough stored energy that they do not have to eat at all during their short life spans, freeing them to concentrate all their energies on the more important tasks of mating and egg laying.[70]

It is equally fortuitous that at least some silkworms are even capable of coevolving with humans in a way that led to the animal partnership that we call domestication. As Edmund Russell notes, the term itself is something of a misnomer, as it implies humans are capable of domesticating passive and pliable organisms however they wish. But as discussed in the previous chapter, domestication is always a two-way street in which another species must have the inherent capacity to tolerate and cooperate with humans. Silkworms' ability to tolerate domestication becomes evident if we compare them to spiders. Spiders actually produce a superior silken fiber, yet modern attempts at domesticating spiders have largely failed because they are very territorial creatures and will often engage in cannibalism if forced to live in

---

[69] James W. Truman and Lynn M. Riddiford, "The Origins of Insect Metamorphosis," *Nature* 401 (1999): 447–52; Ferris Jabr, "How Did Insect Metamorphosis Evolve?" *Scientific American* (August 10, 2012).

[70] Scott Richard Shaw, *Planet of the Bugs: Evolution and the Rise of Insects* (Chicago: University of Chicago Press, 2014), 104.

close proximity.[71] Indeed, the spider's need to make silk as adults – rather than just during a larval stage as with silkworms – may explain why they do not play well with others. As is the case with mammals like wolves and humans, in many insects social behaviors are linked to juvenile hormones that make them more cooperative than aggressive. However, in spiders these juvenile hormones just happen to interfere with the biochemical synthesis of silk. So for spiders to enjoy the many adaptive advantages that come from a lifetime of silk making, it appears they had to give up the many potential benefits of social cooperation.[72] In any event, there is also another obvious problem with domesticating spiders: unlike harmless silkworms, spiders can literally bite the hand that feeds them. As we will see, in Japan families often maximized silk production by sharing their homes with thousands of silkworms. Even to gain something as precious as silk, would the Japanese or anyone else have been willing to live side-by-side with thousands of cranky cannibalistic spiders?

CREATING A JAPANESE SILK

The best available evidence suggests that the domesticated silkworm and sericulture came to Japan mostly via the Korean peninsula in the fourth to eighth centuries CE, a few centuries after the Chinese had initiated the vast Eurasian trading networks of the Silk Road. The practice spread steadily through the archipelago, eventually becoming as deeply embedded in Japanese culture as was the cultivation of essential food grains like rice and wheat. By the year 712 the Japanese "Record of Ancient Matters" (*Kojiki*) recorded that silkworms had grown from the eyes of an ancient Japanese food deity, suggesting that over the course of just a few centuries the Japanese had come to think of silk as being nearly as significant as food.[73] This equation is all the more striking given that some 70 percent of the Japanese archipelago is covered with steep-sided mountains, leaving comparatively little arable land for raising food to feed hungry people. Nonetheless, in some areas the profits to be made from raising mulberry trees and silkworms pushed Japanese peasants to devote ever more of their land and labor to feeding insect larva instead of humans.

[71] Thomas Scheibel, "Spider Silks: Recombinant Synthesis, Assembly, Spinning, and Engineering of Synthetic Proteins," *Microbial Cell Factories* 3 (November 16, 2004): 14.
[72] Craig, *Spiderwebs and Silk*, xvii.
[73] Brett L. Walker, *Toxic Archipelago: A History of Industrial Disease in Japan* (Seattle: University of Washington Press, 2011), 30.

As was the case in China, Rome, and many other places, in Japan the pleasures of soft and colorful silk fabrics were long reserved solely for elites. However, unlike the Romans who sometimes wore silk in order to wear almost nothing at all, in Japan silk robes were often worn in multiple layers, particularly during the colder seasons. During the Heian period (794–1185), a single elaborate kimono called a *jūnihitoe*, or "twelve-layer robe," could contain as much as 35 kilos (about 80 pounds) of silk. Here the goal was often not so much to display one's bodily form as to demonstrate one's superior wealth, taste, and cultivation.[74] One silk kimono of this sort required about 160,000 cocoons – the entire annual output of roughly eight Japanese households. During the Tokugawa period (1603–1867) brisk economic growth gave a growing number of successful farmers, artisans, and merchants the wealth needed to purchase silk. The deeply status-conscious Tokugawa shoguns tried to combat the spread of the most noble of fabrics to lesser folks with harsh if unevenly enforced sumptuary laws.[75] Japanese elites were particularly offended when lowly merchants dared to wear silk. According to the neo-Confucian philosophy that dominated during the early modern period, merchants were at the bottom of the social scale, little better than pestilent parasites. Merchants produced nothing of any real material value, like rice or copper, yet somehow managed to siphon off much of the wealth that should have gone to more useful classes like warriors, farmers, and even artisans. The shogun Tokugawa Tsunayoshi passed some of the first sumptuary laws in 1683 to keep merchants from causing disorder and jealousy through public displays of their wealth.[76] Though kimonos were made with other fabrics like cotton or linen, the Japanese considered silk to be the ideal. What better way to show off one's nouveau riche status than with the colorful shimmer of a material that easily stood out in a sea of lesser fabrics? Still, much of Japan's silk production was not for the domestic market. Instead, it was traded around the world, and especially with neighboring China, making silk (along with tea) one of the nation's most important export items and a vital source of foreign currency.[77]

---

[74] Walker, *Toxic Archipelago*, 29.

[75] Tessa Morris-Suzuki, *The Technological Transformation of Japan: From the Seventeenth to the Twenty-First Century* (Cambridge, UK: Cambridge University Press, 1994), 42, and Brett L. Walker, *A Concise History of Japan* (Cambridge, UK: University of Cambridge Press, 2015), 127.

[76] Walker, *A Concise History of Japan*, 129–30.

[77] Lisa Onaga, "Toyama Kametaro and Vernon Kellogg: Silkworm Inheritance Experiments in Japan, Siam, and the United States, 1900–1912," *Journal of the History of Biology* 43 (2010): 216–64, see especially 216–20.

FIGURE 5.4 During her 1926 coronation the Japanese Empress Kōjun (wife of Emperor Hirohito) wore a silk kimono called a *jūnihitoe*, an elaborate "twelve-layer robe" first worn by the elite ladies of the Heian-era court in the tenth century. Such a robe demanded as much as 35 kilos (80 pounds) of silk, roughly the total yearly output of eight Japanese households. Source: The Japanese Imperial Household Agency.

The most sophisticated Japanese silk production had initially centered around the ancient imperial city of Kyoto, some four hundred miles to the west of modern-day Tokyo. However, during the Tokugawa era the military rulers known as the shoguns shifted the center of power to Tokyo, which was then still a modest fishing village called Edo. (The city would be renamed Tokyo in 1868.) As the city thrived under the aegis of the Tokugawa shoguns, Edo also became one of the most important markets for silk producers. Peasant farmers in the regions to the north of the city that now roughly coincide with the prefectures of Nagano, Gunma, Tochigi, and Fukushima, devoted increasingly large swaths of land to growing mulberry trees to feed worms. Often, planting the mulberry trees came at the expense of raising food crops. However, the Japanese also learned to grow the hardy mulberry trees in more arid and mountainous lands where the cultivation of rice and other grains was difficult or impossible, making sericulture an ideal supplement to conventional farming.[78] Unfortunately, this geographic shift of Japanese sericulture brought some of these trees and worms into close proximity with the copper mines of Ashio, a topic I will return to shortly.

The expansion of Japanese sericulture into less hospitable mountainous terrain had a further pivotal though largely unintended effect: it provided a spur to the innovative powers of the silkworms that eventually proved very beneficial to their human partners. Japan's long sinuous coastline and isolated mountain valleys offered an extraordinarily wide variety of microclimates in a relatively compact area. As the Japanese tried to expand sericulture into these diverse niches, the worms themselves became the crucial players, as they responded by quickly evolving new traits. Recall that the three key amino acids that make up the silk protein can be arranged in a vast number of ways, making silkworms and their processes of silk synthesis a genetic "hot spot" for biological innovation. Likewise, the silkworm's rapid rate of reproduction and large number of offspring permitted the insects to evolve in response to environmental changes far more rapidly than their human caregivers ever could. Driven by their desire for silk, the Japanese pushed sericulture into ever more diverse ecological niches, resulting in the rapid coevolution of local "breeds" or "brands" of silkworms that synthesized silk of differing colors and textures. In essence, the silkworm's biological creativity provided a sort of technological power that the Japanese depended upon to *genetically* adapt to novel environmental niches, though the genes were their worms' rather than their own. The combination of the inherent genetic creativity of silkworms, the diversity of the mountainous central Honshu topography, and the Japanese desire for silk (with its own roots in the biology of human senses, as discussed earlier) thus conspired to become a powerful force for material innovation. Building on these chance genetic gifts, some silkworm farmers in the Fukushima area subsequently pioneered deliberate efforts to breed worms that produced the

---

[78] Onaga, "Toyama Kametaro and Vernon Kellogg," 216–20.

desired quality of silk in larger quantities. A few began to specialize solely in breeding silkworms and selling their eggs to other farmers. The successful sericulturalist and merchant Satō Tomonobu, for example, meticulously maintained several different varieties of silk moths that he would breed with local moths. The resulting hybrid worms were capable of synthesizing silk that both shaped and best fit Japanese fashion.[79]

Some Japanese sericulturalists eventually realized that only hybrid silkworms born from breeding two distinct strains could produce the desired quality and quantity of silk – a phenomenon that is today termed heterosis, or hybrid vigor. Sometime around the 1790s two key silkworm strains emerged – called Ogusa and Hakuryu – which grew faster and produced more high-quality silk than their less genetically refined cousins.[80] Though it would take a century before true hybrids from pure lines of Ogusa and Hakuryu and other strains would become widely used, by the early 1800s the silk industry was already becoming increasingly centralized and rationalized in order to benefit from the innovative potential of their silkworm partners.[81] As the historian of Japanese sericulture Lisa Onaga notes, the Tokugawa government created and enforced regulations to prevent careless breeding that could undo decades of painstaking efforts.[82] The results were remarkable. In 1702 a Japanese sericulture manual had listed five varieties of silkworms. But by the 1860s there were roughly 200. Some of these were no doubt duplications, yet they nonetheless suggest an extraordinary efflorescence of genetic diversity among domesticated silkworms.[83] While simultaneous improvements in the care and feeding of the silkworms also played a role, selective breeding helped to nearly double the amount of silk each worm produced, increasing from about 130 milligrams to nearly 250

---

[79] Morris-Suzuki, *Technological Transformation of Japan*, 39.

[80] Yuji Yasukochi, Hiroshi Fujii, and Marian R. Goldsmith, "Silkworm," in *Genome Mapping and Genomics in Arthropods*, ed., W. Hunter and C. Kowle (Berlin: Springer-Verlag, 2008), 44.

[81] Rather than these later true hybrids, which were always bred each time from two carefully maintained pure lines, these early worms were actually "hybrid strains": the first silkworms in the lineage were the product of a hybrid mating between two distinct strains, but thereafter the new strain was maintained simply by controlled inbreeding within the strain. My thanks to Lisa Onaga for clarifying this point for me.

[82] Onaga, "Toyama Kametaro and Vernon Kellogg," 216–17. See also Lisa Onaga, "More Than Metamorphosis: The Silkworm Experiments of Toyama Kametarō and His Cultivation of Genetic Thought in Japan's Sericultural Practices, 1894–1918," *New Perspectives on the History of Life Sciences and Agriculture* 40 (2015): 415–37.

[83] Morris-Suzuki, *Technological Transformation of Japan*, 39. See also Tessa Morris-Suzuki, "Sericulture and the Origins of Japanese Industrialization," *Technology & Culture* 33 (1992): 101–21, here 114.

milligrams. These efforts also reduced by two full weeks the interval between the time the silkworm larvae hatched and the time it began spinning its cocoon.[84] The effect was to greatly increase what the economic historian Alfred Chandler terms "throughput": the speed with which a productive system is able to produce a given amount of manufactured goods. Increased throughput, Chandler demonstrates, is critical to lowering the cost of production and the mass production of inexpensive consumer goods.[85] Chandler had in mind factories producing steel and cars, but in this case the factory responsible for the crucial first stage of production was entirely inside the silkworm's body.

The immense value of Japan's creative little silkworms became even more apparent in the mid-nineteenth century when a severe outbreak of a silkworm larvae disease called pébrine began to devastate the European industry.[86] After considerable difficulty and investigation, the famous French biologist Louis Pasteur began to realize that pébrine was caused by a single-celled fungus that easily spread its spores among European silkworm larvae. The damage done to the European silk industry, along with instability in Chinese silk production caused by the Taiping Rebellion, provided the Japanese with a critical window of opportunity to expand its silk imports to Europe and other areas of the world.[87] Eventually Pasteur found that pébrine disease was also present in Japan, but it appeared that Japanese sericulture techniques had kept it from becoming pandemic.[88] Given this, one French study in the 1860s criticized European sericulture techniques and argued Europeans should learn from

[84] Morris-Suzuki, "Sericulture and the Origins of Japanese Industrialization," 110.

[85] Alfred Chandler, *The Visible Hand: The Managerial Revolution in American Business* (Cambridge, MA: Belknap, 1993).

[86] Yukiko Kawahara, "Silk Culture and Silk Reeling in Western Japan in the Late Nineteenth and Early Twentieth Centuries, *Journal of Asian History* 35 (2001): 124; Morris-Suzuki, *Technological Transformation of Japan*, 41. For a general history of the Japanese silk industry during this period, see Stephen William McCallion, "Silk Reeling in Meiji Japan: The Limits to Change" (PhD diss., The Ohio State University, 1983). On the modernization of the silk industry itself, see David G. Wittner, "Mechanization of the Silk Industry and the Quest for Progress and Civilization, 1870–1880," in *Building a Modern Japan: Science, Technology, and Medicine in the Meiji Era and Beyond*, ed., Morris Law (New York: Palgrave Macmillan 2005), 135–60; on the devastation of the European industry, see Claudio Zanier, "Japan and the 'Pébrine' Crisis of European Sericulture during the 1860s," *Bonner Zeitschrift für Japonologie* 8 (1986): 51–63.

[87] Morris-Suzuki, "Sericulture and the Origins of Japanese Industrialization," 101.

[88] For an excellent analysis of the complex history of *pébrine* in Europe and Japan, see Lisa Onaga, "Bombyx and Bugs in Meiji Japan: Toward a Multispecies History," *Scholar and Feminist Online* (Summer 2013).

the Japanese who had developed a more "natural" method of sericulture. "The real teacher is not Japan but nature," one European expert scolded, since "Japan has had the wisdom to follow nature, while we have made the mistake of trying to force it."[89] To be sure, the Japanese sericulture techniques might well have more effectively limited the spread of pébrine spores as the author suggests. However, this characterization of the Japanese as more "in tune" with nature than the modern West was more reflective of European orientalist stereotypes than reality.[90] Further, modern genetic studies suggest an important contributing factor to the pébrine epidemic was the excessive inbreeding among the European silkworm stock that had sharply decreased genetic diversity and even eliminated some genes entirely. If so, then the Japanese sericulture industry was, at least in part, spared the scourge of pébrine thanks to the biological inventiveness of the silkworms themselves.[91] Given how critical the sericulture industry was to the rapid economic growth and industrialization of the nation in the second half of the nineteenth century, it is perhaps not too much to say that Japan's rapid technological modernization and related rise to global power was built in no small part by the biological innovations of their humble silkworms.

As the historian of technology W. Brian Arthur notes, "Technology builds itself organically from itself," as "it is a fluid thing, dynamic, alive, highly configurable, and highly changeable over time."[92] In this Arthur means to suggest a deep parallel between mechanical technologies and organic life – a theme I will discuss in more detail in the next chapter. Yet when the technology in question literally *is* organic, the power of Arthur's observation is all the more apt. As I noted earlier, simple organisms that generate frequent mutations and breed rapidly can evolve in response to their environments much more quickly than humans. Yet as scientific and

---

[89] Quoted in Morris-Suzuki, *Technological Transformation of Japan*, 42. The original is L. de Rosny, *Traité de l'Éducation des Vers à Soie au Japon par Sirakawa* (Paris: Maisonneuve et Cie, 1868), 118.

[90] Robert Stolz, *Bad Water: Nature, Pollution, and Politics in Japan, 1870–1950* (Durham, NC: Duke University Press, 2014), 23. On Japanese ideas about nature and technology, see Tessa Morris-Suzuki, "Concepts of Nature and Technology in Pre-industrial Japan," *East Asian History* 1 (1991): 81–96.

[91] Kee-Wook Sohn, "Conservation Status of Sericulture Germplasm Resources in the World, Section 2.2: Sericulture Is Depending on the Rich Silkworm Gene Pool" (Rome: Food and Agricultural Organization of the United Nations, 2003).

[92] W. Brian Arthur, *The Nature of Technology: What It Is and How It Evolves* (New York: Free Press, 2011), 24, 88.

humanistic research increasingly reveals how deeply entangled humans are with multitudes of other organisms that both surround us and are in some cases literally within us, it becomes apparent that humans may not always need to evolve quickly on their own. Rather, we are constantly coevolving with other material partners, many of which are far more genetically versatile and speedy than we are. In this churning environment of alien technologies, human innovation is inseparable from what Andreas Wagner terms the "innovability" of the organic world.

This is precisely what happened when the Japanese coevolved with their creative silkworm partners. The Japanese did not deliberately set out to breed new varieties of silkworms when they first sought to expand sericulture into the diverse niches of their mountainous nation. Rather, the silkworms began to engineer innovative responses to these challenging new environments entirely on their own. To be sure, the Japanese then took advantage of this biological creativity, yet even when they began to consciously breed the worms for their own ends, they depended entirely on a genetic ingenuity that they did not create nor really understand. Increasingly, the silkworms came to respond to and reflect human desires and environments: they grew bigger and produced substantially more silk much more quickly than their wild cousins. Ultimately the insects became entirely dependent on their human caretakers, unable to fly, find food, or even reproduce on their own. Given such immense changes, humans have understandably been tempted to see silkworms, cows, dogs, and other domesticated animals as social constructs, further evidence of the seemingly god-like human ability to shape the world to their own ends. Yet before we congratulate (or condemn) ourselves for being so mighty, we might do well to pause and reflect that humans in no sense created or invented the ability of animals like silkworms to engineer new protein structures, metabolic processes, or any other significant biological innovations. Silkworms had been creating innovations that helped them to better fit a constantly changing environment for millions of years before humans came to take any interest in them. Humans needed to exercise some cultural creativity to turn this process to their own ends, but a far more fundamental creativity lay within the silkworms themselves.

It might strike some as untoward to compare biological creativity with cultural creativity. We typically understand biological creativity, if we even deign to call it such, as a largely fixed and mechanical process, the result of nothing more than random molecular variations and the predictable operation of immutable laws of biochemistry and natural selection. By contrast, we tend to see human cultural creativity as the infinitely fertile product of an abstract human mind whose potential is unbounded by the laws of a mere material world. Such a view is not entirely wrongheaded. Human beings can imagine all manner of things that do not exist in reality – recall my discussion of flying pigs in Chapter 2 – or that are perhaps inherently abstract, such as the concept of justice or liberty. However, as I discuss in more detail in the next two chapters, these seemingly abstract ideas often emerge at least in part from our engagement with the material world, not in contrast to it. Further, cultural creativity achieves its greatest historical effect only after it moves from the realm of abstract thought to material execution, whether that involves the careful breeding of two specific strains of silkworms or creating texts and laws that encourage or require other humans to do so. As Edmund Russell rightly notes, human social power might emerge first from abstractions like ideas and knowledge, but "nothing happens without some physical action, at minimum by human bodies."[93] Once this engagement with the real material world begins, abstract human ideas may or may not achieve the outcome imagined and expected. In this sense, cultural innovations are not so different from biological innovations: they both emerge at least in part from the substrate of matter that exists at any particular point in time, and the degree to which they subsequently affect historical events depends heavily on interactions with that world that are often unpredictable or even random.

Based on such contemporary ideas, it seems reasonable to acknowledge that the innovative ability of the silkworms themselves deserves a fair amount of credit for driving the development of the modern silk industry. However, in the eighteenth and nineteenth centuries neither Japanese nor Western sericulturalists knew anything about the biological intricacies of silkworm and human coevolution. To the contrary, they were understandably tempted to reach the opposite conclusion: that humans had achieved a new level of control over the material world around them. As the historian of Japanese technology Tessa Morris-Suzuki argues, the Japanese success in shaping and controlling their silkworms may have helped them to think about the natural world in bold and potentially dangerous new ways.[94] The conventional historical explanations for the success of Japan's rapid industrialization in the second half of the nineteenth century emphasize the spread of Western cultural influences and

[93] Edmund Russell, "AHR Roundtable: Coevolutionary History," *Journal of American History* 119 (2014): 1512–28, quote on 1523.
[94] Morris-Suzuki, "Concepts of Nature and Technology," 81–96.

the role of aggressive governmental efforts to modernize following the Meiji Restoration of 1868. Morris-Suzuki acknowledges that these factors were certainly important, yet she argues they neglect the equally important role of earlier Japanese steps toward modernity, particularly in sericulture. From the earlier Japanese success with sericulture, Morris-Suzuki suggests, a new "intellectual framework" emerged through which silk farmers and other Japanese "came to appreciate the importance of the deliberate improvement of techniques and developed a practical, empirical approach toward technological experimentation."[95] In Europe and the West, a similar intellectual and cultural evolution may have been driven by human interactions with a different set of domesticable animals, like cows or sheep. But as the environmental historian Brett Walker notes, since the Japanese had relatively few large stock animals in the nineteenth century, the care and breeding of silkworms constituted one of the nation's most important forms of animal husbandry.[96] For many Japanese, their silkworms might well have provided the most powerful and immediately palpable evidence of the human ability to reshape the natural world at even its most fundamental level. For better or worse, the mutable and cooperative silkworm helped to teach the Japanese that they could derive considerable personal and national power by trying to aggressively shape the world to their own ends.

The lesson of the silkworms came none too soon, as it turned out. The arrival of the American naval commander Commodore Matthew C. Perry in Edo (soon to be Tokyo) Bay in 1853 with a flotilla of heavily armed ships sent shockwaves through Japan. In the wake of the subsequent Meiji Restoration of 1868, the further modernization and industrialization of silk became a central goal of the new government. Along with tea – and increasingly copper, as discussed in the next chapter – silk exports provided a critical source of the foreign capital needed to fuel many other industrial modernization projects. Organic silk would provide Japan with the profits needed to fuel other more inorganic and mechanical industries, including the mining of copper.[97] Unfortunately, one of Japan's biggest and richest deposits of copper happened to be located on the edge of the Shimotsuke Plain north of Tokyo that had over the course of more than a thousand years become one of Japan's most important centers of sericulture. Both silkworms and copper were essential to the modernization and industrialization of Japan, yet just as had been the case

---

[95] Morris-Suzuki, *The Technological Transformation of Japan*, 5.
[96] Walker, *Toxic Archipelago*, 31.   [97] Walker, *A Concise History of Japan*, 173–4.

for Longhorns and copper in Montana, the one did not easily coexist in close proximity to the other.

THE SILKWORMS OF THE SHIMOTSUKE

The Shimotsuke Plain is the northern section of the larger Kantō Plain, the biggest relatively flat area in this mountainous nation and one of its richest agricultural regions. At the heart of the plain is the Watarase River, a powerful stream that has its headwaters near the ancient copper mines of Ashio, high in the rugged mountains to the north. After cutting its way down the steep mountainsides, the Watarase flowed through several narrow valleys where farming of any sort was possible only near the banks. Where the river emerged from the mountains, it passed through the centers of silk production in Kiryū and Ashikaga before joining the Tone River that flows through Tokyo and out to the Pacific.[98] To the south of Ashikaga, the lands were low and marshy, and they were frequently flooded by the often-unruly Watarase. In the very lowest areas, the river had to be controlled with earthen dikes, and the farmers built their houses on elevated mounds. But these periodic floods were also a blessing, since they brought rich volcanic soil down from the mountains to periodically rejuvenate exhausted fields. Even in the late nineteenth century, some farmers claimed that they did not need to fertilize their fields to maintain productivity. Because the land was so fertile, life on the Shimotsuke Plain was easier than in many other areas of Japan. The people enjoyed periodic breaks from their labor during so-called spring and autumn visits, which could last for several days. For those who did not have land to farm, the Watarase also abounded in fish, yielding as much as 45 kilos (100 pounds) in a single night of net fishing. By the middle of the nineteenth century some four thousand fishermen were at work along the Watarase and its tributary streams, often selling much of their catch in Tokyo. Transportation downstream was easy, as boats sailed daily with the river currents, carrying cargos of silk, rice, fish, and huge mountain bamboo poles to markets in the bustling capital.[99]

References to raw silk production in the region occur as early as 713 CE, and temple records in what is now the Tochigi prefecture show that

---

[98] Alan Stone, "The Vanishing Village: The Ashio Copper Mine Pollution Case, 1890–1907" (PhD diss., University of Washington, 1974).

[99] Kenneth Strong, *Ox against the Storm: A Biography of Tanaka Shozo – Japan's Conservationist Pioneer* (Kent, UK: Japan Library, [1977] 1995), 1.

farmers in the tenth century often paid their taxes in silk cloth rather than in rice.[100] However, sericulture remained a relatively small-scale enterprise until Tokugawa shoguns began to shift the center of power from Kyoto to Edo (later Tokyo) in the seventeenth century. With a burgeoning new market just down river, many households along the Watarase found that sericulture increasingly offered a vital second income. Men could continue to care for their fields, now supplemented with mulberry trees, while women and younger children cared for the worms at home.[101] By the early 1880s the neighboring prefectures of Nagano and Gunma accounted for 37 percent of Japanese raw silk production.[102] In Tochigi prefecture, sericulture was most common in the upper reaches of the Watarase, where the industry had taken root in the second half of eighteenth century in the many small villages centered around the commercial center of Ashikaga.[103] As noted earlier, peasants found sericulture attractive because the hardy mulberry trees could grow in the more arid mountain regions where rice cultivation was difficult or impossible. The purity of the mountain water in the Watarase River also made it well suited for the delicate tasks of boiling the cocoons, unreeling the threads, and dyeing the raw silk.[104]

As the production of hybrid silkworms became more centralized in the nineteenth century, many of the Japanese living in Shimotsuke obtained their silkworm eggs from specialized agents in the late spring and early fall. While women did much of the work of tending the silkworms in most households, everyone in the family would pitch in during the busiest stages of the process. The women began the process by spreading out as many as 20,000 tiny white eggs over wooden trays. After the eggs hatched, they would transfer the larvae to larger rearing trays where they were fed chopped leaves from the family's white mulberry trees. After three to four days, the larvae ceased eating, hibernated, and shed their skin to emerge as caterpillars. As the caterpillars grew, their human caretakers had to transfer them to ever more trays, where they consumed an extraordinary amount of mulberry leaves: about 590 kilograms (1,300 pounds) for a typical household population of worms. Eventually, the worms grow to be almost 10,000 times larger than the tiny eggs from which they hatched.[105] To get some sense of just how extraordinary this growth rate is, consider that even

[100] Stone, "Vanishing Village," 17.   [101] Stone, "Vanishing Village," 15, 17.
[102] Kawahara, "Silk Culture and Silk Reeling in Western Japan," 126.
[103] Morris-Suzuki, "Sericulture and the Origins of Japanese Industrialization," 107.
[104] Strong, *Ox Against the Storm*, 1.   [105] Walker, *Toxic Archipelago*, 31–3.

FIGURE 5.5 A woodblock print from around 1800 showing Japanese women spreading mulberry leaves over a tray of silkworms. Women typically bore all the responsibility for the care of a household's worms, which included the around-the-clock feeding of about 590 kilos (1,300 pounds) of leaves as they grow nearly 10,000 times in size. Library of Congress Prints and Photographs Division, image number LC-DIG-jpd-02712.

a modern-day hypertrophic chicken is at most about a thousand times larger than a newborn baby chick. To measure up to silkworms, our hens and roosters would end up as ten-foot-tall monsters.

Finally, after weeks of meticulous care, the silkworms began to spin their cocoons in a figure-eight pattern of one continuous thread made from protein filaments synthesized by specialized salivary glands in their mouths. To keep the thousands of cocoons from touching each other, which would destroy the continuity of the long filaments, the women transferred them to special frames from which the worms would suspend their cocoons. During this critical stage when the worms spin their cocoons, environmental conditions had to be carefully controlled. Any loud noises could startle the worms and cause them to stop spinning.[106] Even if they subsequently resumed, any pause could result in breaks or weak spots in the silken thread. The women also did their best to keep the temperature at a constant 23–30 degrees Celsius and 60–90 percent humidity.[107] One Japanese farmer built screens around silkworm trays and required everyone in the family to sleep there during chilly periods, using human body heat to keep the worms comfortable.[108] When the cocoons were completed, but before the caterpillars could destroy them by emerging as moths, the farmers rushed them to the silk agents for payment. The cocoons were then boiled to dissolve the sticky sericin protein bonds, so the fine filaments could be carefully pulled out and reeled together in skeins of "raw silk." A single silkworm cocoon could yield as much as half a mile of thread, which may seem like a lot. However, the thread is so fine that it still took 2,000–3,000 cocoons to weave just half a kilo (one pound) of Japanese silk fabric.[109] A typical harvest of 20,000 cocoons by a Shimotsuke household would thus only be enough to weave about five kilos (10 pounds) of silk fabric, which in turn was about one-eighth the silk needed to make a really elaborate multi-layered silk kimono. But consider as well that to feed 20,000 silkworms required some 1,300 pounds of mulberry leaves. Japanese silk farmers had to devote considerable time and land to growing and harvesting mulberry trees rather than to the rice, millet, wheat, and vegetables needed to feed

[106] Morris-Suzuki, *Technological Transformation of Japan*, 39.
[107] Jetki Prihatin et al., "The Effect of Exposure of Mulberry to Acid Rain on the Defects Cocoon of *Bombyxmori L*," *Proceedia Environmental Sciences* 23 (2014): 186–91, here 190.
[108] Morris-Suzuki, "Sericulture and the Origins of Japanese Industrialization," 110.
[109] Walker, *Toxic Archipelago*, 32–3.

themselves. But the resulting silk could be so profitable that many farmers concluded it made sense to feed the hungry worms and use the proceeds to buy their own food from elsewhere.

In all this, a distinct sociocultural system emerged from the intimate relationship between the Japanese and their silkworms, one in which humans changed through their encounters with silkworms. How was the "culture" of this seri*culture* system created? Certainly not by humans alone. Instead, somewhat like the culture of western open-range ranching in the Deer Lodge Valley was the product of a long coevolutionary relationship with another intelligent social species, so too was the sericulture of the Shimotsuke the product of a more recent yet still-ancient human-animal bond. After many centuries of coexistence with humans, the silkworm's wild instincts for self-protection had diminished to the point where it could thrive even inside the odd environment of a Japanese home. Likewise, the worm had evolved through both accidental and deliberate breeding to grow much larger and produce far more silk than its wild cousin, though at the price of losing its ability to survive and reproduce without the intimate assistance of human caregivers. Surely if there had been a way for humans to maximize their access to silk fibers without having to become silkworm nursemaids and "mothers," they would have likely done so. However, the biological and coevolutionary properties of a silkworm demanded that humans conform to the worm's needs every bit as much as the worm had been shaped to conform to human needs. Likewise, the Japanese had no knowledge of how their silkworms were able to synthesize the lustrous protein chains called silk, knowing only that they must care for their worms in certain specific ways, learned through long trial and error, in order for the worms to weave cocoons. As already noted, the particular quality or quantity of silk produced by the hybrid silkworms was also as much the product of biological creativity as human creativity. True, the ultimate end of all these materially rooted processes might be an elaborate kimono, the style and decoration of which would be shaped by decorative tastes that were largely human inventions. Yet even here we should keep in mind that the power of silk as a symbolic representation derived in some degree from its rare status as a soft, shimmering material that easily absorbed bright, intensely colored dyes. Remember, too, that when considering an elaborate silk kimono, we are really looking at the product of more than 10,000 pounds of mulberry leaves as transmuted through the bodies of some 20,000 silkworms.

Given all this, it seems clear that the culture of sericulture resided not just in human brains or disembodied, abstract ideas but rather had emerged from a long and dynamic history of bodily and material interactions between humans and another creative creature existing in a richly variable environment. A separate *a priori* human culture did not shape or construct the silkworm – rather, human culture literally *was* the silkworm, as it could not in any logical sense exist independently of the very material thing that had brought it into existence. In this sense, the material is fundamentally cultural, not because a distinct and abstract human culture has imprinted itself on the material world but rather because that culture could only have emerged in the first place through the interactions between embodied humans and a creative material world. To suggest a parallel to the concept in cognitive science of an extended mind, discussed in Chapter 3, we might well refer to the relationship between the Japanese and their silkworms as a type of extended culture, a culture that leaked out of its conventional analytical isolation in the human skull and into the materiality of the silkworm. This extensive culture leaked into other areas as well, reshaping the material landscape from rice paddies to mulberry plantations and changing the sociocultural landscape with new lending practices, increased child labor, and perhaps most strikingly living arrangements where humans shared their homes with thousands of voracious insects.[110] In the end, Japanese humans and Japanese silkworms had become so "entangled" over the centuries that the sociocultural was the material and vice versa.[111]

Finally, bear in mind that Japanese farmers were willing to make radical changes in their traditional agrarian practices and culture because of the social power they gained from silkworms. In this they were essentially no different from the Deer Lodge Valley ranchers like Conrad Kohrs who derived social power from their Longhorns. However, in contrast to the mostly caloric energy that Longhorns created in their flesh, silkworms generated a different form of material power, one oddly more akin to

[110] Walker, *Toxic Archipelago*, 32–33. Similar though regionally specific patterns can be found among the many other peoples who have embraced sericulture. A good account of the role of women in Chinese sericulture is Francesca Bray, *Technology and Gender: Fabrics of Power in Late Imperial China* (Berkeley: University of California Press, 1997). Sericulture was also pursued aggressively by Americans prior to the Civil War, often using largely women's labor. See Ben Marsh "The Republic's New Clothes: Making Silk in the Antebellum United States," *Agricultural History* 86 (2012): 206–324.
[111] Ian Hodder, *Entangled: An Archaeology of the Relationship between Humans and Things* (Malden, MA: Wiley-Blackwell, 2012).

minerals like copper than to meat or milk from cattle. To be sure, the Japanese did not waste the concentrated caloric energy of the silkworms – after boiling and removing the thread, they would eat the plump worms or feed them to their fish – but the silkworms were obviously only a means to an end.[112] The ability of the worms to transform the caloric energy and organic compounds contained in mulberry trees into uniquely useful and beautiful silk fibers was the real source of the silk farmer's increased social power, as well as the ability of the international silk traders to bring crucial foreign currency back to Japan. Unfortunately, just as the material nature of cattle raising in the Deer Lodge Valley clashed with the copper industry of Anaconda, so, too, did the tightly entangled materiality of Japanese silkworm raising on the Shimotsuke Plain clash with the copper industry of Ashio. The red metal exacted its own demands from those who sought its powers.

THE YEAR WITHOUT INSECTS

The troubles began in the late 1870s. Farmers noticed that the Watarase River, upon whose waters they were so dependent, had at times begun to turn a strange bluish-white color. Fishermen reported that the once-abundant fish suddenly disappeared. Children told their parents how they had waded into the river to easily scoop up dazed eels. Later, their legs broke out in festering red sores where the skin had touched the oddly colored Watarase water. By the mid-1890s even the tough willow and bamboo groves along the river began to die. Some residents took to calling the once life-giving Watarase "the river of death."[113] Even miles away from the banks of the rivers, residents remarked other ominous portents. The abundant insects and birds that had once filled the summer air with chattering trills vanished, leaving behind only an eerie silence. "Peasants could remember no previous time," one historian writes, "when earth-worms, spiders, crickets, and even ants died, or when the birds totally disappeared."[114] This mysterious disappearance of wild insects did not bode well for silkworm farmers, and soon the governor began to receive reports that silkworms fed mulberry leaves from the polluted region shriveled and died.[115]

---

[112] Walker, *Toxic Archipelago*, 33.   [113] Stolz, *Bad Water*, 33.
[114] F. G. Notehelfer, "Japan's First Pollution Incident," *Journal of Japanese Studies* 1 (1975): 351–83, quote on 367–68.
[115] Stone, "Vanishing Village," 29.

What was happening? The answer lay far upstream near the headwaters of the Watarase where a soon-to-be-famous industrialist named
Furukawa Ichibei had begun to resurrect the ancient copper mines of
Ashio. As I will discuss in more detail in the next chapter, the Japanese
had mined the Ashio copper deposits for centuries, particularly during the
lively Tokugawa period. By the early 1800s, however, the most easily
accessed deposits had been mined out and operations stagnated for more
than half a century. Responding to the national push to modernize after
the Meiji Restoration, in 1877 Furukawa began to shock the long dor-
mant corpse of the Ashio mines back to life with a powerful charge of
modern technology. When he first arrived at Ashio, Furukawa found
collapsing tunnels and mining technologies that had changed little from
the century before. Entering the warren of twisting underground mining
tunnels and shafts, he later recounted, was "like entering a haunted
house." Furukawa said he could only induce his workers to go into the
mines by leading them in personally, though whether the workers feared
ghosts or the all-too-real danger that a crumbling mine tunnel could
collapse on their heads is debatable.[116] Initially, Furukawa's investment
in Ashio seemed ill advised, as he lost money on the mine for four years.
But in 1881 his miners happened by chance to intersect a promising new
vein of ore that had not previously been identified or expected. Three years
later they discovered a second and even richer vein of chalcopyrite copper
ore, a find that would fuel Ashio's rapid growth over the next two decades.
Soon the Ashio mines would be producing more than a quarter of Japan's
copper.[117]

Both fittingly and ironically, Furukawa's first experience with technological modernization and industrialization had come with the silk industry.
During his early twenties he worked with an uncle in the northern city of
Morioka dealing in raw silk, and he helped to set up one of the first modern
silk-reeling mills in Japan.[118] But if Furukawa was the face of Japanese
modernization in both silk and copper, by 1884 copper increasingly took
precedence. As Furukawa rapidly ramped up copper mining at Ashio, he
also increased the scale and efficiency of ore processing, grinding the hard
rock deposits into a fine dust to separate the small amount of valuable
copper from the worthless waste rock and sending the resulting concentrate
to enlarged smelters. Heedless of his downstream neighbors, Furukawa
dumped the remaining waste, called tailings, into the Watarase River. Like

[116] Stone, "Vanishing Village," 4.   [117] Walker, *A Concise History of Japan*, 195.
[118] Stone, "Vanishing Village," 3.

finely ground glacial till, the tailings gave the water the strange bluish-white tinge observed by the downstream farmers and fishermen. Just as at Anaconda, Ashio's copper ores were heavy in sulfur, constituting some 30–40 percent of their content by weight. Ashio ore, like Anaconda ore, also contained significant amounts of arsenic, cadmium, and lead, all of which ended up in the tailings. Subsequent investigations showed that the Watarase water was polluted with large amounts of copper sulfate, chlorine, arsenic, sulfur, and mercury. When the river flooded the low-lying agricultural fields, these poisons settled out into the soil. Rice paddies with their standing pools of water were particularly prone to contamination. Where the river had once brought rich new volcanic soil full of nutrients, now it brought mine tailings that killed the rice, barley, and other crops, as well as the mulberry trees whose leaves were fed to silkworms. As one of the first-ever Japanese scientific pollution studies conclusively demonstrated in 1892, the Ashio tailings essentially rendered the soil infertile.[119]

The Ashio pollutants wreaked havoc in other ways. A vibrant indigo silk-dyeing industry had grown up in the region to take advantage of the previously pure Watarase River water. Yet the copper and other metals in the water now reacted with the dyes in such a way that the deep indigo color failed to form.[120] One owner of a silk-weaving and -dyeing factory just south of Kiryū had previously built a canal to bring in clear Watarase River water. After the Ashio pollution began, he was forced to abandon the canal and dig a well instead.[121] The Watarase was also a key source of drinking water for many inhabitants, either directly or through closely linked shallow ground water flows. Even as late as the 1990s, tests found that during periods of heavy rainfall the amount of arsenic in Watarase River water reached levels toxic to humans, suggesting the levels a century earlier must have been even more deadly. Many decades after the worst pollution problems had been minimized, farmers continued to report health problems from eating rice raised in the soil. Today, it is well understood that rice plants absorb and concentrate heavy metals like arsenic and cadmium in their seeds. While inevitably somewhat imprecise, these measures all indicate that the mine pollution was causing severe health problems for both human and animal life.[122]

[119] Y. Kozai, "Research on the Infertility of Soils Caused by the Refuse Water from Ashio Copper Mine," *Journal of Scientific Agriculture Society* 16 (1892): 55–96.
[120] Stolz, *Bad Water*, 34–5.   [121] Stone, "Vanishing Village," 28.
[122] Kichiro Shoji and Masuro Sugai, "The Ashio Copper Mine Pollution Case: The Origins of Environmental Destruction," in *Industrial Pollution in Japan*, ed., Jun Ui (Tokyo: United Nations University Press, 1992), 44–5.

The disappearance of much of the insect life in the area was perhaps even more worrisome, as not all could have been harmed by the pollutants carried in the Watarase River. In this case, Furukawa's rapidly growing copper-smelting operation was the likely culprit. Making no effort to capture any of the sulfur and arsenic gases and dust driven off by the smelting process, Furukawa simply released these and other pollutants into the atmosphere. The air pollution caused the most obvious damage in the immediate area around the smelters, where it quickly killed the broad-leaf trees and other plant life, leaving behind a denuded moonscape that soon became scarred with deep gullies as rains washed away the unprotected soil. The winds, however, could easily carry the pollutants farther to the south where some of the air-borne poisons likely settled out over the Shimotsuke Plain. The nearest silkworm farmers were less than 20 miles downwind from the smelters, and some of the lighter arsenical dust might well have travelled that far before settling out over their homes and fields, directly poisoning the silkworms that ate the contaminated leaves. As was the case with the Anaconda smelter, there were also reports that horses and other livestock south of Ashio were harmed.[123] However, this never became a major issue in the Ashio case, perhaps in part because the Japanese had far fewer stock animals than was the case in the Deer Lodge Valley. Further, what horses and cattle the Japanese did have would not have grazed widely over an open range, thus protecting them from bioaccumulating the dispersed arsenical poisons in their bodies.

Smelting the sulfur-laden Ashio copper ore also produced huge volumes of sulfur dioxide, which today is well known to damage mulberry leaves and trees, either directly or by reacting with moisture in the air to create sulfuric acid and acid rain. (See my discussion of the effects of sulfur dioxide on plants in the previous chapter.) Such acid rain deposition, however, would have been doubly damaging to the silkworm farmers. First, it reduced the productivity of their mulberry trees or killed them outright. Second, it either killed or reduced the productivity of silkworm larvae, which proved to be highly sensitive to industrial air pollution and the resulting sulfur deposition on the leaves they consumed in such large quantities.[124] As one later manual on silkworm diseases explains, after ingesting mulberry leaves contaminated with sulfur dioxide and other exhaust gases, the growth of mature silkworms greatly slows. Many form dark brown lesions that burst easily and exude a yellowish fluid.

[123] Shoji and Sugai, "Ashio Copper Mine Pollution Case," 40–1.
[124] Walker, *Toxic Archipelago*, 30, 94–5.

If younger worms are contaminated, "the whole body atrophies, the thorax swells, and the tail shrinks." Depending on the severity of the contamination and other environmental factors, some percentage of the worms die, their corpses becoming a dark brown shell that was so dried out it would not even rot.[125] It seems likely that the Ashio air pollutants were having a similar effect on many of the other wild insects, as well as the birds and countless other animals who ate them. For the human inhabitants of the Shimotsuke Plain, the result was an experience few could have imagined was even possible just a year or two before: the ghostly stillness of what Rachel Carson would later call a "silent spring."

CONCLUSION

The English words "creature" and "creativity" have the same root: the Latin verb *creare* – to create. If you were a speaker of Latin, whenever you called something a *creatura*, or a creature, you were essentially implying that someone had created it, just as today we refer to a sculpture or painting as an artist's creation. Perhaps it is no coincidence that the word *creatura* came into wide use at roughly the same time that Christianity rose to dominance during the later centuries of the Roman Empire. In the English King James translation of the Christian Bible, Genesis 1:25 notes: "And God made the beasts of the earth after their kinds, and cattle after their kinds, and every thing that creeps upon the earth after its kind: and God saw that it was good." In the earlier Latin version of this passage the authors used the verb *fecit* for "made" rather than *creavit* for "created." But if you go back to the very beginning of Genesis, the creative creator of creatures is clear: "In principio creavit Deus cælum, et terram."

The more secular among us today no longer tend to think that a supernatural being literally created the fellow creatures with which we share the planet. The scientifically inclined give the credit to evolution, or perhaps a divine creator acting through evolution. Nonetheless, I suspect that even this supposedly scientific view has yet to fully eclipse some aspects of the older idea that creatures are *created* rather than themselves being *creators*. Just as a secularized version of the soul endures today in the persistent faith that humans possess a largely immaterial and abstract mind – what I earlier termed a Soul 2.0 – so,

---

[125] Lu Yup-Lian, *Silkworm Diseases* (Food and Agriculture Organization of the United Nations, Bulletin 73/4, 1991), 70–1.

too, do we persist in thinking that humans and their cultures are the sole source of the truly novel, that humans alone have a spark of a quasi-divine creativity. Now scarcely a month goes by without the release of yet more scientific evidence that other animals formulate creative solutions to problems and even invent new techniques and fashion simple technologies. Yet, in considering the silkworm, I hope to have convinced you that even seemingly simple creatures like insects play a powerful role in inventing humans and their cultures. Humans are not the sole or even primary creators on the planet. To the contrary, many aspects of the culture and history that we regard as most uniquely human are also best understood as the creations of other organisms. Indeed, humans might well be the ultimate *creatura* precisely because we are so adept at making alliances with so many other organisms and are so able and willing to conform to their demands.

The protean power of silkworms to shape human culture and history had its fundamental origins in the convergence of two entirely material and biological phenomena: the extraordinary sensitivity of the human sense of touch and the unusual smoothness of silk. There was nothing "natural" in the human attraction to silk, at least not in the sense that humans were instinctually or hardwired specifically to like silk. But there was everything natural in that our most fundamental sensory abilities happened to be well suited to appreciate silk, even if our refined sense of touch and lack of body hair had evolved for entirely different reasons. If we fail to recognize the nature of this and other material attractions and incorporate them into our models of historical causality, our understanding of the past will be fundamentally flawed. Likewise, the Japanese relationship with their creative silkworms did not in any simplistic sense *determine* that the nation would successfully embark on a course of rapid industrialization. Yet by providing some Japanese with new ways of understanding and manipulating their material environment, the humble silkworm played a central historical role that deserves at least as much attention as that of its human caretakers. Indeed, which was the greater achievement: the invention of a wholly new protein of extraordinary strength and the closely related evolution of insects who spun silk cocoons for metamorphosis, or the human discovery that the threads in these cocoons could be unraveled in a pot of hot water and woven into a soft fabric? Humans tend to believe that the real inventing only begins when they take a hand in it, though the organisms they depended upon had been inventing and reinventing themselves and their environments for millions of years.

Referring to the central role of the human coevolution with a useful species of New World cotton plant in sparking the European industrial revolution, the historian Edmund Russell writes: "English inventors did not mechanize the cotton industry purely because of their own ingenuity. They used their ingenuity to respond to an opportunity created for them by coevolution between cotton populations and human populations elsewhere."[126] In a similar way, the Japanese coevolution with their creative silkworms helped to spark a unique path to industrialization, one in which increased human ingenuity and power derived from an intimate relationship with a highly sensitive and often-fragile fellow living creature. As one Japanese manual put it, during critical stages the female "guardians" or "mothers" of the silkworms should not leave their small charges untended for a single moment.[127] Humans became the nursemaids of silkworms. Yet if this nurturing and even maternal relationship with living silkworms provided a critical early foundation to Japanese industrialization, the nation was also developing less subtle ways of extracting power from the inanimate things around it. In the end, the power to be gained by the brute-force mining of copper would often overwhelm the more delicate ways of coaxing power from fragile insects, no matter how creative these small creatures might be.

[126] Russell, "Coevolutionary History," 1526.
[127] Morris-Suzuki, *Technological Transformation of Japan*, 41.

6

The Copper Atom

Conductivity and the Great Convergence of Japan and the West

Occasionally even a simple bit of household maintenance can remind us of the power of material things to shape history. Shortly after my wife and I moved into our new house in Montana, we noticed that the builder had not bothered to install any gutters, so we hired "Gus the Gutterman" to install his seamless aluminum wares along several eaves. Rather than use conventional enclosed downspouts, we opted for three sets of shiny copper rain chains, tulip-shaped bowls with holes in the base designed to let the water gently cascade down. The tulips hang one from the other by copper wires a bit thicker than a coat hanger, and they worked fine all summer. But when winter came heavy columns of ice began to build up on the chains. The connecting copper wires bent under the weight and pulled through their holes, and all three of the chains collapsed and spent the rest of the winter buried under the snow. When spring came, I bent the wires back into their proper shape and rehung the chains. The next winter they promptly fell again, and come spring I again bent and rehung. This went on for a number of years. Until finally about two years ago the chains stopped falling. As I write this in early January after a long cold snap, the rain chains are encased in a heavy layer of ice, yet they are still holding strong. Not one of the copper wire hangers has bent enough to fail. What happened?

If you buy a length of moderately thick copper wire at a hardware store, you can discover the answer for yourself. Take four or five inches and bend the wire at a right angle in the middle. Initially, it will bend fairly easily. You will also be able to straighten it back out without too much trouble. But keep bending and straightening your copper wire, and after four or five cycles the resistance will begin to increase, to the point that you might not be able to bend it at all with your bare hands. If you keep going, perhaps with the aid of a pair of pliers, the wire will eventually break rather than bend. Although I only vaguely understood this at the start of my almost decade-long battle of the rain chains, it turns out that my copper tulips were still hanging in there that winter because copper metal has a seemingly magical ability to become stronger just by bending or hammering it, a material phenomenon called work hardening.

Think about this for a moment: What other material do you know of that will actually become stiffer and harder when you bend it? Certainly not most of the other common stuff you will find in a household today. Wood, paper, and some plastics may bend, but they do not become stronger just for having *been* bent. To the contrary, they become weaker. Now, to be fair, copper is not the only material that can pull off this trick. Other common household metals like iron and aluminum can also be work hardened. Nonetheless, it would be copper that first taught humans about the potential power of work hardening, mostly because it is relatively easy to smelt pure copper metal from raw copper ore. Iron, by contrast, demands a hotter furnace, while humans only figured out how to make aluminum from bauxite ore thousands of years later in the mid-nineteenth century. So it would be copper's ability to be work hardened – by hammering rather than bending – that proved so essential to the rise of increasingly complex human civilizations. As I will explain in more detail later in the chapter, copper's strange ability to be both soft and hard gave humans the critical metal tools that would help push them out of the Stone Age. While my copper rain chains have yet to help me build a civilization or expand an empire, they are still hanging today because of the very same material properties that helped create the Copper and Bronze Ages (bronze is copper alloyed with tin).

American and Japanese mining companies did not extract and smelt the copper at Anaconda and Ashio primarily because it could be work hardened. In the then-dawning new age of electricity, humans treasured copper more for its conductivity, though its malleability still proved useful. Copper and other metals conduct electricity because their atomic structures happen to have one or more loosely bonded electrons that can be put to work transporting electrical charge. All those footloose copper electrons would play a key role in pushing Anaconda and Ashio and their neighboring regions toward striking similar fates. Until the closing decades of the nineteenth century, Anaconda with its open-range Longhorns and Ashio with its home-raised silkworms could scarcely have seemed more different. But within just a few years after the start of large-scale copper mining and smelting, the human and nonhuman diversity at both sites had converged toward radically simplified states. There were new material and human cultures to be found, ones associated with complex sulfide copper ores and the demands they made on humans who wished to enjoy their benefits. Yet these were symptoms not of regional and national differences but rather of a broader global phenomenon that several historians of Japan have recently termed the "great convergence."

As the historians Brett Walker and Julia Adeney Thomas argue, this great convergence between Western and Japanese societies in the late nineteenth century was not just the result of Japanese imitation of Europe or the United States. Rather, it stemmed from the convergent development of what Thomas terms a "particular orientation toward 'nature' as a material, social, and ideological resource."[1] Walker takes this convergence even deeper, drawing on Daniel Lord Smail's work in neurohistory to suggest that it might have its roots in the structural properties of the brain that are common to all humans and persist even among the most seemingly disparate of cultures.[2] As Thomas and Walker both suggest, to understand the convergence of Japan and the West, we must set aside the old analytical divisions that posited a clear separation between culture and nature, mind and matter, body and environment. Humans and their diverse cultures did not stand above and apart from the material world but rather emerge from and with the other organisms and material things they partnered with. As I argued in the previous two chapters, wily Longhorns and inventive silkworms are the co-creators of human intelligence, creativity, and culture, not just passive and malleable social constructs. In this chapter, I turn squarely to the red elephant that has thus far sat more or less politely in a corner of the room: the copper whose potential powers were so great that they justified the destruction of those Longhorns and silkworms, as well as just about anything else that got in the way. It is obviously much easier to identify the creative powers of living creatures – the essence of life itself is novel creation. Yet to focus

[1] Julia Adeney Thomas, "Reclaiming Ground: Japan's Great Convergence," *Japanese Studies* 34 (2014): 253–63, quote on 260.
[2] Walker first proposed the term the "great convergence" in a conference paper that was later published in Japanese: Brett L. Walker, "Idai naru shūren: Nihon ni okeru shizen kankyô no hakken [The great divergence: Japan and the discovery of the natural environment]" in vol. 4 of *Nihon no shisō: shizen no jin'i*, ed. Karube Tadashi, Makoto Kurozumi, Hiroo Satō, and Fumihiko Sueki (Tokyo: Iwanami Koza, 2013). See also Brett Walker, *A Concise History of Japan* (Cambridge, UK: Cambridge University Press, 2015), 124.

solely on the biotic world is to concede to yet another form of anthropocentrism, one that ignores an abiotic world of chemical and physical processes that are also always pregnant with possibilities. Copper, of course, had no intelligence of its own like Longhorn cows, nor could it evolve new properties like mulberry silkworms. Yet we should not take this to mean the metal was a mere cipher, an empty "signifier" waiting mutely for humans to assign it meaning and significance. To the contrary, when copper and its complex geological properties intersected with humans, Longhorns, and silkworms, its sheer material power shaped everything it touched in ways that were both intended and not. Here, too, was a type of creativity, a material power and wildness that humans sometimes judged beneficial, sometimes harmful, but that was almost always far greater than their own self-aggrandizing understanding of the world recognized.

In the previous two chapters, we saw how both the Japanese and the Americans had begun to embrace the material potential of copper. Both engaged in copper mining, milling, and smelting operations that spread sulfur and arsenic toxins over hundreds of square kilometers. Both depended on the ability of the surrounding geological, chemical, and biological systems to absorb these wastes so that they remained below levels acutely toxic to human life in the area immediately around the smelters even as chronic exposure caused serious health problems over a much-wider area. Both discovered that neighboring animals and biological systems were often more vulnerable to these pollutants than were humans. Ultimately, both Japanese and American farmers fought to stop industrial copper mining and smelting or to at least minimize the release of harmful pollutants. Yet as we will see, despite making some progress in mitigating the worst pollution, farmers in both nations failed to halt or even significantly slow the rapid growth of copper mining and smelting and its damaging effects on their animals, crops, and health. In both Japan and the United States, the abiotic power of copper ultimately triumphed, and silkworm people and Longhorn people converged toward something much more like copper people.

RESISTANCE

The farmers of the Deer Lodge Valley and of the Shimotsuke Plain did not accede to the destruction of their plants, animals, and ways of life without a fight. To the contrary, both groups of farmers waged long and determined battles against the copper mining companies that produced such

huge amounts of toxic pollutants and the governments that often supported them. Reflecting the growing dominance of a global capitalist
market and its associated legal and political structures, both the
American and Japanese farmers stressed the economic importance of
their activities to the nation and their legal rights to be protected from
damaging pollution. However, the resistance to copper mining in the two
regions also differed in telling ways. At least some of the Ashio farmers
and their defenders raised much-deeper questions about the course of
Japanese industrialization and modernization than did their Anaconda
counterparts. While the Americans limited themselves largely to legal and
economic arguments, the Japanese also emphasized the dignity and value
of the farmer and the importance of a life lived within the rhythms of
nature. No Deer Lodge Valley farmer, rancher, or politician would even
come close to the scorching condemnation of modern technological
society developed by the fierce defender of the Watarase River basin,
Tanaka Shōzō.

In part, these differences stemmed from the different avenues for effective protest available in each nation and their previous histories of success
or failure. In Japan, Ashio was the first nationally recognized case of large-
scale industrial pollution, and it became a forum for a much-broader
debate about the wisdom of Japan's breakneck race to modernize.
The Japanese farmers also had to work within the constraints of the
newly adopted Imperial Constitution (1889) under which individual
rights were sharply limited in deference to the power of the Emperor.
Accustomed to a hierarchical neo-Confucian societal order in which elite
power carried with it the responsibility to protect the interests of com-
moners, many of the Ashio farmers hoped and expected that the new
Imperial Diet or even the Meiji emperor himself would come to their aid.
When they failed to do so quickly or forcefully enough, the farmers turned
to the ancient practice of "peasant uprisings," or *ikki*, to express their
anger and frustration.[3] By contrast, in the United States the Anaconda

---

[3] Kichiro Shoji and Masuro Sugai, "The Ashio Copper Mine Pollution Case: The Origins of
Environmental Destruction," in *Industrial Pollution in Japan*, ed., Jun Ui (Tokyo: United
Nations University Press, 1992), 23–4, and F. G. Notehelfer, "Japan's First Pollution
Incident," *Journal of Japanese Studies*, 380–2. The turn to peasant uprisings in a similar
case of smelter pollution at the Besshi mine is discussed in Takehiro Watanabe, "Talking
Sulfur Dioxide: Air Pollution and the Politics of Science in Late Meiji Japan," in *Japan
At Nature's Edge: The Environmental Context of a Global Power*, ed. Ian Jared Miller,
Julia Adeney Thomas, and Brett L. Walker (Honolulu: University of Hawaii Press, 2013),
73–89, here 75.

pollution problems were just the most recent in a long line of similar cases stemming from the rapid growth of American industrial mining in the second half of the nineteenth century. The Deer Lodge Valley farmers were well aware that legal actions against copper-smelter pollution had already proved successful in other states. It seemed wise to approach the problem not so much as a moral issue or an occasion for mass protests but rather as an economic and legal matter that might very well have effective technological and technocratic solutions.[4]

There were other more subtle differences as well. By the late nineteenth century, Americans had already been shaped by at least a century of technological development and enthusiasm. Direct heirs and major suppliers to the British industrial revolution, the Americans had increasingly built their own national economy on technological ventures like the textile mills of Lowell, the gun-making factories of Springfield, the steel mills of Homestead, and even the high-pressure steamboats that brought their slave-grown cotton to the world, much of it back to Britain.[5] Already proud of their self-proclaimed "Yankee ingenuity," in the years following the Civil War many Americans worshipped unashamedly at an altar of technological progress, casting men like the former telegraph operator Thomas Edison as an industrial wizard whose magical light bulb had transformed the world and turned night into day. To be sure, many others still held tightly to the older national ideal of the yeoman farmer and an Agrarian Republic of "free labor," which is to say independent non-wage-earning labor. Much like today, however, even the most nominally conservative of Americans frequently remained willing to embrace and celebrate new technologies in the name of economic growth and national progress. Americans excelled in that peculiarly modern delusion that their cultural ideals could be kept distinct from the material world, that they could make immense material changes without fear that these would necessarily change the essential character of their society. As a result, they overestimated the human ability to turn the course of industrialization to their own ends and too often failed to recognize how corrosive it could be to the traditional ideals that they professed to most treasure. Even many farmers and ranchers, the supposed backbone of a traditional agrarian economy, increasingly embraced the same faith in

---

[4] Timothy J. LeCain, *Mass Destruction: The Men and Giant Mines That Wired America and Scarred the Planet* (New Brunswick: Rutgers University Press, 2009), 74–7.
[5] Walter Johnson, *River of Dark Dreams* (Cambridge, MA: Harvard University Press, 2013).

technology, efficiency, and rapid growth that characterized the new industrial sector.[6]

Such was the case for many of the ranchers and farmers of the Deer
Lodge Valley, who from the moment of their arrival had been introduced
to and shaped by the specific set of industrial technologies associated with
mining. The first alluvial gold deposits in the valley were discovered in
1852, and by the 1860s a small community of miners had settled along the
banks of what they called Gold Creek. The valley literally ran rich with
precious metals, as nearly every stream and gulch in the mountains had at
least some showings of gold, silver, lead, and copper.[7] These alluvial
mineral deposits attracted the first significant population of Euro-
Americans to the valley: miners who were metaphorically hungry for
gold but literally hungry for food. Some who quickly tired of the backbreaking work and fickle luck of mining realized that there were often
better and more reliable profits to be had in "mining the miners." Decades
before the Anaconda built its first big smelter there, Conrad Kohrs and
other ranchers came to the Deer Lodge Valley to supply the neighboring
miners who were hungry for the beef they had to sell. In the valley of the
Deer Lodge, the industries of ranching and mining were deeply entangled
from the start.

Given that the region was first settled by miners looking to make quick
profits rather than farmers searching for the traditional yeoman life, it is
perhaps no surprise that by the late nineteenth century the residents of the
valley seemed quite modern in their views. Local newspapers and other
sources suggest that many, for example, were coming to accept the modernist idea that germs alone were the principal cause of ill health – not an
insalubrious environment tainted with smelter smoke. In one 1900 article
in a Butte newspaper, the author insisted that smelter smoke actually
helped to *sanitize* the environment. Exposed to the "tons of sulphur,
liberally adulterated with arsenic, vomited forth each day from our
capacious smoke stacks," one author concluded the "marauding bacteria
fell helplessly by the wayside."[8] Similar claims were made for heavy-
metal-contaminated water.[9] Such accounts have to be read with a rather
large grain of salt, as smelter owners and their backers used newspapers to

[6] Deborah Fitzgerald, *Every Farm a Factory: The Industrial Ideal in American Agriculture*
    (New Haven, CT: Yale University Press, 2010).
[7] Virginia Lee Speck, "The History of the Deer Lodge Valley to 1870" (MA thesis, Montana
    State University, 1946), 47.
[8] "Bacteria and Smoke," *Butte Miner*, May 9, 1900, 4.
[9] "General Health of Butte Is Good," *Daily Intermountain*, October 15, 1904.

convince residents that mine pollutants were beneficial rather than harmful. Nonetheless, these articles suggest that the modern idea of the clearly bounded, rather than porous, human body had gained at least some purchase, even if big business exploited the idea for its own interests. Much the same could be said for the associated belief that humans could effectively remediate environmental damages through technology. Just as was the case in the Watarase River in Japan, the Deer Lodge Valley's Clark Fork River, Silver Bow Creek, and other streams saw a precipitous drop in fish populations due to mining pollutants. Some were essentially sterile wastelands by the late nineteenth century. However, the Anaconda cooperated with local residents to provide a seeming technological fix, loaning some $9,000 to create a fish hatchery in the Deer Lodge Valley and providing all the materials, water, and electricity for its operation. In 1905, the hatchery released 37,500 fry into creeks in the valley, which were transported around the area by specially equipped automobiles and railcars.[10] While the hatcheries also supplied fry to streams that had not been damaged by mining, such elaborate techno-fixes nonetheless were clearly meant to suggest that whatever problems the Anaconda pollution caused could be alleviated through modern technology.

In sum, by the turn of the century, the rapid course of national industrialization, the acceptance of the modern germ theory of disease, the associated idea of a clearly bounded human body, and the promise of painless techno-fixes had already taught many of the Deer Lodge Valley farmers to think in the efficient instrumental terms of the modern industrial economy. To be sure, their personal experiences of the complex and insidious ways in which smelter pollution harmed their crops and livestock suggested a very different understanding of the world. Nonetheless, most of the farmers and ranchers viewed their struggle with the Anaconda Company not as a contest between traditional agrarianism and modern industry but rather as a legal conflict between two equally modern and economically important industries. One of the key leaders of the movement to stop the Anaconda smelter was not some modest Jeffersonian yeoman farmer – if any such creature still existed – but rather one of the biggest and wealthiest ranchers in the valley: Conrad Kohrs. As I discussed in Chapter 3, Kohrs had made a fortune by running his Longhorns, Shorthorns, Herefords, and other breeds on the open ranges of western

---

[10] Bill Alvord, "The History of Montana's Fisheries Division, 1890–1985," Montana Department of Fish, Wildlife and Parks, Helena, MT, typewritten ms., Vertical Files – Fish Hatcheries, Montana Historical Society.

and eastern Montana, benefiting from having been one of the first to bring these powerful animals into the territory. However, Kohrs was not in any sense philosophically or ethically opposed to mining or the environmental damage it caused. To the contrary, he invested some of the capital he earned from raising cattle into the Montana mining industry, and Kohrs even owned a highly destructive but profitable hydraulic gold-mining operation in the valley.[11] On a more personal level, he had no qualms about selling a pair of purebred trotting horses to the manager and part owner of the Anaconda, Marcus Daly, whose smelter was responsible for the smoke that was killing his animals.[12] Aside from their regrettable conflicts over poisonous smelter smoke, one suspects the two men saw each other more as comrades in modern capitalism and industry rather than as natural enemies.

In 1905, after the Anaconda's latest effort to fix the Washoe smoke pollution problems with a taller smokestack had largely failed, Kohrs joined with his half-brother Nick Bielenberg and a number of smaller ranchers and farmers to form the Deer Lodge Valley Farmers' Association. The association sued the Anaconda, asking for more than a million dollars in damages and an injunction against any further smelting at the Washoe. In the ensuing trial, which became one of the longest and most technically complex in the nation up to that time, the Anaconda and the farmers brought in scientific experts to spar over how much arsenic, sulfur dioxide, and other pollutants were being released by the smelter and how much harm they were doing to the farmers' livestock and the land. Predictably, the Anaconda's experts minimized the guilt of the smelter while the farmers' experts maximized it. Tellingly, however, the farmers did not raise any serious questions about the importance of copper mining and the broader course of national industrialization. The competing parties sharply disagreed about whether the smelter smoke was damaging the crops and livestock of the valley, but they were largely in agreement that industrialization and electrification were both good and essential. Unfortunately for the farmers, the judge also saw electricity as the future. He ruled in favor of the Anaconda, largely on the basis that the mining company's copper was central to the economy of the nation, the state, and the valley, including the farmers themselves. The judge reasoned that the

---

[11] *Mining Reporter* (Denver), March 17, 1904, 266.
[12] Anna Fay Rosenberg, "Hard Winter Endurance: Conrad Kohrs' Cattle Raising Operation, 1887–1900" (MA thesis, University of Montana, 1996), 51.

farmers and ranchers depended on the Anaconda mine and smelter workers to provide a local market for their goods.[13]

After losing in court, the tactics of the ranchers and farmers took
a course somewhat more similar to those in Japan. Just as the
Shimotsuke farmers hoped that the emperor might intervene on their
behalf, the Deer Lodge Valley farmers concluded their last best hope
was to make a direct appeal to the president of the United States,
Theodore Roosevelt. As a younger man, Roosevelt had operated a sort
of gentleman's ranch in the western Dakotas, where he had become good
friends with Conrad Kohrs, who ran some of his Longhorns and other
breeds nearby. The ranchers in particular hoped that this personal relationship with Kohrs, combined with Roosevelt's long-standing affection
for Montana and western ranching, would convince the president to
threaten the Anaconda with legal action on the grounds that the smelter
smoke was damaging the neighboring Deer Lodge National Forest. In two
letters to Roosevelt, they argued that the federal government must come to
their aid because the Anaconda dominated the Montana state government. Further, they had already spent "more than the best farm in the
Valley" was worth in lawyers fee and other costs in pursuing a legal
solution. Yet even as they made this last-ditch plea, the ranchers and
farmers did not raise any deeper questions about the destructive course
of modern American industrialization. The most profound ethical argument offered was an appeal to Roosevelt's affection for a romanticized
ideal of the western frontier: the ranchers and farmers deserved consideration, they argued, because many of them had been the "pioneers" who had
first tamed the Deer Lodge Valley through their own courage and hard
work.[14] (Tellingly, the Longhorns received no mention.) Kohrs and the
farmers, however, apparently knew best: their appeal worked and
Roosevelt agreed to intervene on behalf of the farmers, though as we
will see, even the efforts of the federal Department of Justice would not
ultimately solve the problem.

In contrast to the decidedly legalistic, economic, and instrumentalist
approach pursued by the Deer Lodge Valley farmers, at least some of the
Japanese critics of the Ashio pollution raised much-deeper questions
about industrialization and its destructive consequences for both human
beings and nature. In part this was surely because the Japanese farmers

[13] LeCain, *Mass Destruction*, 73.
[14] Quoted in Donald MacMillan, *Smoke Wars: Anaconda Copper, Montana Air Pollution,
and the Courts, 1890–1924* (Helena: Montana Historical Society, 2000), 142.

and their supporters had yet to be as deeply shaped by the modernist promise as the Americans. When the Watarase River first turned milk-blue from the Ashio tailings, the crash program of Japanese industrialization was still only a few decades old. While overly simplistic, it is still not unreasonable to date the beginnings of rapid Japanese industrialization and modernization to the seismic shifts that began with the Meiji Restoration of 1868. Fearing domination by the expanding European and American powers, Japanese reformers raced to break through the limits imposed by what some historians have termed the biological Old Regime, the earlier era when agriculture and nonhydrocarbon power sources had long been dominant. As Julia Adeney Thomas notes, many Japanese believed they had no choice but to embrace industrialization and modernization if their nation was to "withstand the gunboats, unequal treaties, and racial disdain of Europe and the United States."[15] Indeed, at mid-century the material circumstances of Japan and the West were still radically different. Consider that in 1869, a year after the Meiji Restoration, the United States celebrated the completion of its first transcontinental railroad line – a 1,907-mile connection to the west that emerged like a thin tendril from the already-vast tangle of existing railroads in the eastern half of the continent. By contrast, the Japanese would not complete their first railroad until 1872, and it would span only the seventeen miles between Tokyo and Yokohama. The Japanese railroads and other technological accomplishments would come to match and often surpass those of the United States with breathtaking speed, yet in the final decades of the century industrial practice and thinking were still taking root in Japan.

Which is not to say that Japanese industrialization rose from nothing in 1868 or was simply a case of "copying" the West. As a number of historians have argued, Japan began to develop early forms of capitalism, science, technology, and other modernist practices well before the Meiji Restoration. As the historian David Howell suggested some two decades ago, it was a case of "capitalism from within."[16] These laid the essential groundwork for, and help to explain, the rapidity of the nation's later industrial ascent.[17] In an insightful study of the material conditions of late

---

[15] Thomas, "Reclaiming Ground," 3.
[16] David L. Howell, *Capitalism from Within: Economy, Society, and the State in a Japanese Fishery* (Berkeley: University of California Press, 1995). For the importance of Japanese agriculture in spurring these developments, see Thomas C. Smith, *Agrarian Origins of Modern Japan* (Palo Alto, CA: Stanford University Press, 1959).
[17] Walker, *A Concise History of Japan*, 124.

Tokugawa-era Japan, historian Susan Hanley notes that the industrialization after 1868 was only possible because the nation had already achieved high agricultural productivity, nationwide commercial networks, a sophisticated monetary system, and bank-like means of monetary exchange. Moreover, Hanley argues that the Japanese people themselves had been prepared for the demands of industrialization, as they had already developed the physical and mental stamina needed to build, operate, and manage factories, transport systems, and other critical pieces of a modern industrial economy. "Examples do not exist," Hanley notes, "of a population eking out a subsistence living in agriculture suddenly and directly establishing a modern industrial economy." Hanley makes a convincing case that the standard of living in Japan at the time of the Meiji Restoration was roughly similar to that of England when it had begun to industrialize a century earlier. Contrary to the common understanding that the expansion of industrial techniques typically precedes increased agricultural production, Hanley argues that increased agricultural production provided the essential energetic and material preconditions for industrialization.[18]

Most importantly for the Ashio story, Japan also had a history of pre-industrial yet large-scale mining that stretched back many centuries. Today Japan is often thought of as a resource-poor nation. Yet when Marco Polo brought news of the land of *Jipang* back to the West in the thirteenth century, he referred to the archipelago as the "Golden Land." The Japanese had been mining and smelting the nation's many rich ore deposits since at least the sixth century, though silver and copper were far more common than gold. By the late medieval period, Europeans already thought of Japan as one of the richest mining areas in the world.[19] As one European observer put it: "There are mines everywhere and the metal is of high quality; the gold ore is so rich that they obtain ten taels [about 40 grams] of gold from every spadeful" and " there is a great deal of copper and iron which they extract very easily."[20] Given the indispensable role of geothermal forces and tectonic uplift in creating concentrated mineral deposits that are accessible to humans, it should not surprise us that a nation dominated by volcanic mountains might have many rich and

[18] Susan B. Hanley, *Everyday Things in Premodern Japan: The Hidden Legacy of Material Culture* (Berkeley: University of California Press, 1997), 2–3, 13.

[19] Kazuo Nimura, Andrew Gordon, ed., *The Ashio Riot of 1907: A Social History of Mining in Japan*, trans. Terry Boardman (Durham, NC: Duke University Press, 1997), 12–14.

[20] Michael Cooper, *They Came to Japan: An Anthology of European Reports on Japan, 1543–1640* (Berkeley, CA: University of California Press, 1965), 10.

relatively accessible ore deposits. The mineral deposits of the American west like those at Butte may have been geologically older, but they had been formed by many of the same tectonic forces. Mount Bizendate, home to most of the principal Ashio copper deposits, is today riddled with narrow *tanuki-bori*, or "raccoon dog holes," that date from as early as 1610. The name is fitting. For centuries, husband and wife teams used just pick and hammer to laboriously gouge out the hard rock. To minimize such backbreaking labor, they dug only the bare minimum of space needed for a slender human body to squeeze between the worthless country rock and reach the valuable copper ore. While perhaps somewhat bigger than raccoon dog holes, the resulting nightmarish maze of twisting narrow tunnels can nonetheless inspire claustrophobia even just in the imagining. During the long and prosperous Tokugawa period (1603–1867), the Japanese developed increasingly sophisticated methods for surveying and digging deep underground mines, including ventilation tunnels and "wind funnels" (designed to channel winds down into a mine), hand-cranked water pumps, ore hoists, and other technologies that strongly resembled those developed in Europe. Given these similarities, historians have not unreasonably speculated that at least some of this technology may have been European imports to China that later made their way to Japan.[21] In 1621 a Jesuit missionary had brought to China the original Latin version of the seminal text on late medieval mining technology, Agricola's *De Re Metallica*. Quickly recognizing its value, Emperor Ch'ung-chen ordered that the book be translated into Chinese and serve as guide for mining throughout the empire.[22] Still, at least some of the similarities between European and Japanese mining techniques might also have resulted from convergent technological evolution, as humans facing similar material challenges not infrequently arrive at similar technical solutions – a point I will return to later in this chapter.

Regardless, Japan was certainly no stranger to hard-rock mining. Yet by the nineteenth century Japanese progress in mining technology had clearly stagnated. In 1850, many mining techniques were little different from those used a century, or in some cases, even two or three centuries before. Nowhere was this more apparent than at the Ashio mines, where ore production began to decline sharply in the late eighteenth century. Even as late as 1883 the mines were still using what was largely

[21] Walker, *Toxic Archipelago*, 77–83.
[22] Pan Jixing, "The Spread of Georgius Agricola's *De Re Metallica* in Late Ming China," *T'oung Pao* 77 (1991): 108–18.

Tokugawa-era technology, eking out a mere 647 metric tons of copper in a year.[23] Such modest production obviously presented relatively little threat to the neighboring silkworm and rice farmers to the south. Yet the Shimotsuke farmers did not escape the material and cultural steamroller of industrialization for much longer. As the Meiji government in Tokyo aggressively pursued a new modern industrial age, it increasingly turned its back on the farmers who had once been seen as so central to the survival of an island nation with precious little arable land. In the earlier neo-Confucian system of tightly fixed social hierarchies, the "honourable peasants" who produced the grains that fed the nation had ranked second only to the mighty samurai in prestige. But as part of its efforts to modernize, the Meiji government began to gradually sweep aside traditional social orders, going so far as to elevate the once-lowly "merchants" – now recast as leaders of industry and business – to new positions of respect. Farmers discovered that they were no longer automatically accorded the reverence they had once enjoyed. At precisely the same time, the farmers were often faced with declining crop prices, adding economic insult to social injury. Nor were they sharing in the benefits that were supposed to come from modernization. While people in the cities increasingly enjoyed the latest modern conveniences, many farmers still lived in conditions that were little changed from a century before. The historian Mikiso Hane refers to this as the "underside of Japan," noting that even as late as the 1930s many Japanese peasants still faced a life of unremitting hard labor. Even famine had yet to be fully eliminated in some regions.[24] As all these pressures simultaneously bore down on the farmers in the early Meiji period, uprisings and violent riots in the countryside became increasingly common.[25]

In sum, industrial modernity had yet to either shape or benefit the farmers of Shimotsuke as deeply as it had the farmers in the Deer Lodge Valley. Still comparatively free from both the illusions and benefits of modernist techno-scientific hubris, the Japanese farmers and their supporters were perhaps better prepared to wonder whether modernity was an unalloyed good and to question whether a nation could truly become stronger even as it permitted industry to destroy some of its richest agricultural lands. When the farmers who lived downstream along the Watarase River petitioned the

[23] Walker, *Toxic Archipelago*, 89.
[24] Mikiso Hane, *Peasants, Rebels, Women, and Outcastes: The Underside of Japan* (Oxford, UK: Rowman and Littlefield, [1982] 2003), 4, 30.
[25] Walker, *A Concise History of Japan*, 180–5.

Meiji government for relief from the Ashio pollution, they went well beyond a narrow instrumental focus on competing economic interests and their own financial losses. They pointed instead to the grievous harm done to the land itself, to the creatures both wild and domestic, and to their own health. Farmers were the "national backbone," they asserted, and the blessings they brought to the nation came from the land itself. It was a basic universal law of nature, some argued, that the foundations of all societies lay with the food, clothing, and shelter provided by agriculture.[26] Another noted that "the productivity of the land is eternal and without limit, while the profit from the mine is transient and limited."[27] In a passage that evokes the ideas popularized by the American environmentalist Rachel Carson some sixty years later, the farmers warned that Ashio was destroying not just the land, but nature itself: "There are few birds and insects and we seldom hear their songs ... Spring comes but there is no spring."[28] To be sure, many farmers also understood the issue in the same utilitarian terms that the farmers in the Deer Lodge Valley did. In his examination of a similar pollution case at the Besshi mines to the south, the historian Takehiro Watanabe argues that most farmers there saw the conflict as a matter of damage to property rights, not in terms of a need to preserve nature.[29] Nonetheless, in sharp contrast to the Deer Lodge farmers, some of the Ashio farmers articulated critiques that suggested a much-deeper defense of the value of farming and a pre-industrial human relationship with the material environment.

The contrast between the Anaconda and Ashio protests is especially evident in terms of the most prominent leaders of the two movements. If the best-known critic of the Anaconda smelter pollution was the capitalist "cattle king" Conrad Kohrs, the most profound critic of the Ashio mines, and of Japanese industrialization more broadly, was the radical proto-environmental thinker Tanaka Shōzō (1841–1913). The child of a moderately prosperous farmer and local leader, Tanaka grew up in the small village of Konaka about five miles from the banks of the Watarase River. There some 200 households of small farmers tended their rice paddies and other fields, and many raised mulberry trees and silkworms. Quick to anger and often stubborn, Tanaka was also hardworking and charming. As a young man he had planted the family's first mulberry trees with his own hands, hoping that sericulture would add to the modest

[26] Alan Stone, "The Vanishing Village: The Ashio Copper Mine Pollution Case, 1890–1907" (PhD diss., University of Washington, 1974), 39.
[27] Stone, "Vanishing Village," 53.   [28] Quoted in Stone, "Vanishing Village," 203.
[29] Watanabe, "Talking Sulfur Dioxide," 85.

翁 造 正 中 田

FIGURE 6.1 Tanaka Shōzō (1841–1913) developed a prescient ecological philosophy and ethic through his intimate experience of the once-vibrant Watarase River human and nonhuman community and its subsequent devastation by pollution from the upstream Ashio copper mines. Source: National Diet Library.

household income. Perhaps at least in part because of these silkworms, the family did prosper, and Tanaka eventually took his father's place as village leader.[30]

Tanaka had a deeply physical experience of the life of the Shimotsuke farmer: the feel of the young rice seedlings in the hand, the tart blackness of the mulberry fruit, and the strange rain-like whisper of thousands of feeding silkworm caterpillars were all as familiar to him as his own breath.

---

[30] Kenneth Strong, *Ox against the Storm: A Biography of Tanaka Shozo – Japan's Conservationist Pioneer* (Kent, UK: Japan Library, [1977] 1995),6–7.

In December of 1891, at the age of fifty, he was elected to Japan's newly created National Diet, and it was not long before he emerged as a vocal critic of the devastation caused by the growing Ashio mine pollution. Although his rhetorical attacks were often merciless, initially Tanaka's goals were relatively moderate, as he sought only reasonable controls on the Ashio pollution and fair compensation to farmers whose lands had been damaged. However, as the promise of a series of technological fixes repeatedly proved deceptive (just as in the Deer Lodge Valley), Tanaka began to develop a more radical critique of Japan's new industrial society, even going so far as to suggest the Ashio mines should be entirely shut down, regardless of the cost to Japanese economic and national power.[31]

Recalling the traditional neo-Confucian argument that the true "treasure of the people" lay with rice, wheat, and other agricultural products, Tanaka attacked both the Ashio mine and the Meiji government that permitted its owner, Furukawa Ichibei, to "ravage the fields that gave the nation its very life."[32] The farmers had spent years building their fields and paddies, and these were a truly inexhaustible source of wealth so long as they were properly nurtured. Yet now the very people who tended the true sources of Japanese wealth were being poisoned by the Ashio pollutants: "Over 130,000 victims eat and drink poison," he warned, and "in their poverty they lack food and clothing." The mine, he argued, was really just a form of plunder, whereas true wealth came from more proper means.[33] Brett Walker, one of his most passionate biographers and admirers, argues that Tanaka gradually began to develop a deep environmental ethic, one that consciously rejected the modernist distinction between the human and material world that was rapidly becoming so influential in Meiji Japan. Drawing on both Buddhist and Shinto holism and animism, he arrived at his own unique understanding of the human being as an extension of nature rather than its master. "To care for mountains, your heart must be as the mountains," he wrote, "to care for rivers, your heart must be as the rivers."[34] As Walker notes, such ideas anticipate by several decades the "thinking like a mountain" ecological holism of the influential American conservationist Aldo Leopold. If the mountains and river died, Tanaka believed, he too would die.[35]

Where did such extraordinary ideas come from? While significant, the influence of existing Buddhist and Shinto traditions cannot tell the whole

---

[31] Stone, "Vanishing Village," 51.   [32] Walker, *A Concise History of Japan*, 198.
[33] Stone, "Vanishing Village," 70.   [34] Walker, *A Concise History of Japan*, 198–9.
[35] Walker, *A Concise History of Japan*, 199.

story. Instead, Walker explains Tanaka's insights not just as a product of personal courage or brilliance, though the man certainly had plenty of both, nor solely as an outgrowth of earlier Japanese cultural ideas and beliefs. Instead, Walker argues that Tanaka's ideas were *themselves* products of his close relationship to the material world of Meiji-era industrialization, a sort of "social system accident" that emerged as the "heavy metals and sulfuric acid saturated the land of his birth." Tanaka was able to think in new ways because a changing environment gave him the material tools needed to do so. In some very concrete sense, Tanaka was thinking through the world around him in a way akin to the concept of the extended mind developed by the contemporary cognitive scientists and philosophers. Absent the poisons of the Ashio mines, Walker concludes, "he might never have dreamed of the myriad ways in which people are connected to the physical environment." Ironically, the powerful Ashio toxins themselves showed Tanaka "the interconnected nature of all things."[36]

The work of another of Tanaka's recent biographers, the historian Robert Stolz, suggests that his ideas even prefigured one of the key arguments of this book: that all human social power is really a form of material or "thing" power. Stolz notes that Tanaka came to believe that nature itself possessed a type of animate power, a *nagare*, or "flow," that existed independently of humans. If humans understood this flow and managed its power wisely, it could bring them great benefit – the result would be what Tanaka evocatively called a "civilization of rivers." Yet if humans continued to see themselves as the masters of a passive material world, the result would be a steady increase in *doku*, or "poison," that would destroy both nature and human society.[37] Again, Tanaka appears to have arrived at these startling ideas at least in part through his close personal experience of the material environment itself. Stolz estimates that Tanaka had explored, by foot or boat, nearly the entire course of the Watarase River and its major tributaries, a journey of over 1,900 kilometers.[38] Bearing in mind these years of intimate engagement with a polluted but still-vibrant landscape, it is perhaps really not too much to say that the Watarase River spoke through Tanaka Shōzō.

[36] Walker, *Toxic Archipelago*, 106–7.
[37] Robert Stolz, *Bad Water: Nature, Pollution, and Politics in Japan, 1870–1950* (Durham, NC: Duke University Press, 2014), 91–2.
[38] Stolz, *Bad Water*, 85–6.

As I discussed in Chapter 3, a number of prominent cognitive theorists now argue that we do not think *about* the material world around us through an abstract set of concepts that reside in a disembodied mind; rather, we think *through* that material world as we experience its smell and taste, its feel and form. We feel and see the world through an embodied or even extensive mind whose capacities emerge in no small part from the material environment itself. The more abstracted cultural ideas of Tanaka's own day obviously played an important role in his thought. Yet what was really *new* at that moment, what gave Tanaka the sheer cognitive power necessary to push his thinking in radical directions, was the real material world of physical things: the feel of tender rice seedlings in the hand and the hushed roar of a thousand hungry silkworms on the ear; and later, as the arsenic and sulfuric acid began their insidious seep into the arteries of Watarase life, the crisp snap of yellowed stems turned brittle, the white bodies oozing brown lesions, and the haunting silence of tens of thousands of dead insects.

The protests of the Ashio and Anaconda farmers and ranchers were not without effect. But despite some significant differences in the tactics used by the two groups, the end results were strikingly similar in the modesty of their success. In Japan, the Meiji government was reluctant to saddle Furukawa with any additional costs that would make the nation's copper less competitive in a global market dominated by powerful high-tech western mining companies like Anaconda, Calumet-Hecla, and Rio Tinto.[39] Yet the Ashio pollution was so blatant and so severe that the government finally issued an order in 1897 that required the Furukawa *zaibatsu* – the term for a new generation of powerful business conglomerates – to adopt significant pollution controls or face a possible shutdown. The industrialist responded quickly with a crash program to capture air- and water-borne toxins, hiring as many as 7,000 workers and ultimately spending more than 1,000,000 yen on the projects.[40] Furukawa's engineers invented a novel (though not very effective) type of smokestack scrubber designed to remove sulfur dioxide; constructed tailings ponds, where heavy metals could settle out before the water went back into the Watarase; and adopted several other pollution-control technologies.[41] The Japanese government itself took an active role in the

[39] Notehelfer, "Japan's First Pollution Incident," 365–6.
[40] Stone, "Vanishing Village," 85.
[41] Notehelfer, "Japan's First Pollution Incident," 375.

FIGURE 6.2 Despite the early efforts of the Furukawa *zaibatsu* to control the release of sulfur dioxide pollution with a novel scrubber technology on its main smokestack (seen here in 2008), the Ashio smelter would continue to emit large amounts of sulfur and other destructive pollutants well into the 1950s. Photograph by author.

effort, sponsoring an ambitious program to replant trees on the denuded mountainsides in an effort to control erosion. However, most of the newly planted seedlings quickly died – the meager soil that remained was apparently too impregnated with toxins to support little other than the most hardy of weeds.

In Montana the Anaconda also improved its tailings ponds and built a 350-foot-tall smokestack designed both to dilute the pollutants over a wider area and to support a much-larger chimney flue where heavy-metals dusts could settle out of the smoke stream. The farmers' efforts to enlist the help of the American president also paid off, albeit only long after Roosevelt had left office. Under pressure from the federal Department of Justice, in 1919 – nearly two decades after the pollution problems had begun – the Anaconda finally invested in a powerful new smoke pollution-control technology called an electrostatic precipitator that proved quite effective. The company also built an even taller smoke-stack, which at 585 feet was the largest freestanding masonry structure in the world. In both Japan and the United States, these technological mea-sures significantly reduced pollutants released into the water and air, permitting some semblance of productive agricultural activity to resume. However, in both cases these measures also fell well short of eliminating the pollution altogether. The Ashio's sulfur-control technology was only a modest success – by the company's own likely optimistic estimate, the process removed less than half of the sulfur dioxide.[42] The Ashio smelters would not have a reasonably effective sulfur pollution-control system until 1955.[43] Likewise, while the Anaconda's electrostatic precipitator captured as much as two-thirds of the arsenic, this meant that some twenty-five tons of arsenic were still released into the atmosphere every day. Despite this, the Anaconda engineers and managers confidently insisted that the remaining arsenic was no longer of any "nuisance to the outside surrounding community."[44] Just as at Ashio, the Anaconda did not begin to capture significant amounts of its sulfur dioxide until after World War II, even though a practical technology for doing so had been available since the early twentieth century. The two towering smokestacks at Ashio and Anaconda thus became fitting symbols for the convergence of the two sites, as their illusory promise of an effective technological fix to the smelter-pollution problems seemed to constantly retreat into a never quite realized future.

Perhaps most importantly, at both Ashio and Anaconda the benefits of new pollution-control technologies were offset by subsequent increases in overall ore production and smelting: even if a larger percentage of the toxins was being captured, the aggregate amount released could still go up

[42] Stone, "Vanishing Village," 88–9.
[43] Shoji and Sugai, "Ashio Copper Mine Pollution Case," 46.
[44] LeCain, *Mass Destruction*, 101.

FIGURE 6.3 While its 585-feet-tall smokestack and electrostatic precipitators significantly reduced pollution, the Anaconda smelter continued to release large amounts of arsenic, sulfur dioxide, and other pollutants well into the postwar period. Source: *The Anaconda Reduction Works* (Anaconda, MT, 1920).

as overall production increased.[45] In both cases, the technological fixes did not eliminate the pollution problems so much as reduce them to levels that were deemed tolerable enough to permit copper mining and smelting to continue. Ultimately both companies found that the most effective and lasting "solution" was to pay the farmers and ranchers for the permission to pollute their lands, or to simply buy their properties outright.[46] In Montana, the Anaconda even managed to engineer a trade with the federal government that gave the company control over all the national forest lands near the smelter, effectively eliminating the threat of future federal suits. The Furukawa *zaibatsu* also paid for smoke pollution rights and bought up agricultural lands so it could pollute with impunity.[47]

[45] Toyoaki Morishita, "The Watarase River Basin: Contamination of the Environment with Copper Discharged from Ashio Mine," in *Heavy Metal Pollution in Soils of Japan*, ed. Kakuzo Kitagishi and Ichiro Yamane (Tokyo: Japan Scientific Societies Press, 1981), 165–79, especially 165.

[46] Notehelfer, "Japan's First Pollution Incident," 365–6.

[47] A similar practice occurred at the Japanese Besshi copper mines, where by 1902 the Sumitomo *zaibatsu* had purchased 12.7 percent of the agricultural land surrounding their smelter. See Watanabe, "Talking Sulfur Dioxide," 78.

Take, for example, the case of Matsugi, a small village a few miles north of the smelter, where the toxic smoke was so thickly oppressive that for years the inhabitants had been forced to keep their windows shut during the daytime hours when the smelter operated. At its peak, the village had been home to 267 souls. But while the Ashio smoke-damage payments perhaps offered some solace, many found living near the smelter physically unbearable. The population steadily dwindled to just 74, and in 1903 the company simply bought the entire town and evicted those who still remained. A village that had been continuously occupied for more than six centuries became a ghost town, emptied of all human and most other forms of life.[48]

Having mitigated the most heinous pollution and conceded to or actively collaborated in the removal of farmers and townspeople from the most severely damaged areas, both the Japanese and American governments considered the pollution problems solved. In the end, the Japanese government decided that the copper mined at Ashio was more important than the damage done to farmers and silkworms, much like the American government decided that the copper mined at Anaconda was more important than the damage done to ranchers and cattle. As they moved into the first decades of what would prove to be an extraordinarily violent and turbulent century, both governments recognized what was in many ways a harsh but simple material reality: the national power to be gained by extracting, selling, and using copper could not be matched by that offered by silkworms and mulberry trees, cows and bulls, wheat and rice. All these things could, in any event, be grown and raised in other places, but rich deposits of copper ore were far more rare. In this light, Tanaka Shōzō's hard-earned insights into the interconnectedness of humans and the material world no doubt appeared to many as the deluded ravings of a feeble-minded old man whose time had clearly passed. Modernists, both American and Japanese, believed copper mining was the source not of national decline and death but of a transcendent power that was already ushering in a bright new society in which humans would be liberated from the very mundane materiality that Tanaka had so prized. In this, the Japanese and American modernists were not entirely wrong: copper did indeed hold immense potential power. Their error lay in an unquestioning faith that this power could lift humans out of the material world, when in fact it would sink them ever more deeply and

---

[48] Stone, "Vanishing Village," 92–3.

inextricably into a dynamic nature that could be far more surprising and dangerous than they could imagine.

THE POWER OF COPPER

In contrast to the meat and milk of the Deer Lodge Valley Longhorns, the material power of copper has relatively little to do with its chemical energy content – the metal does not readily oxidize or burn, either in human digestive tracts or furnaces. Instead, copper is in some ways more like silk, in that it derives its power from its unique molecular structure. Like gold and silver, with which it shares a column on the periodic table of elements, copper has an atomic structure in which its outermost orbit is occupied by only one electron that is very weakly bonded to the nucleus. When electrical current or heat is applied to a wire made up of copper atoms, this single outer electron is easily stripped away. Thanks to these relatively rootless electrons, copper can easily conduct both electricity and heat, making it the human metal of choice for electrical applications, as well as for use in pans, radiators, air conditioners, and other heat-transfer technologies.[49] The peculiar way in which atoms of copper pack together at room temperature is also critical to its material potential. You'll remember the rain chains I discussed at the start of the chapter: copper deforms easily at first but then becomes harder when hammered or bent. As a result, deposits of pure (or "native") copper metal can easily be shaped by humans for jewelry or decorations, but it can also be substantially hardened simply by pounding it with a rock or a hammer to make sharp copper knives or deadly arrowheads.[50] Copper is also one of only three metals on the planet that is not a silvery gray color. Like colorful silks, the lustrous red of copper stood out to the human eye, making the metal attractive for crafting statues, jewelry, and other decorations. That copper tastes like human blood and also has a hint of its red color surely made it all the more evocative. The only other colorful metals on earth are yellow-hued gold, which is vastly more rare, and the silvery yellow cesium, which in its pure state will explode if it comes into contact with human skin – a less than ideal property for jewelry.[51]

---

[49] LeCain, *Mass Destruction*, 30–1.
[50] C. R. Hammond, "The Elements," in *The Handbook of Chemistry and Physics*, 81st ed. (Boca Raton, FL: CRC Press, 2000).
[51] Theodore Gray, *The Elements: A Visual Exploration of Every Known Atom in the Universe* (New York: Black Dog and Leventhal, 2009), 77.

For millennia humans had no idea how one in the same material could, depending on how it was handled, be either soft and malleable or hard and stiff. It would not be until the twentieth century that material science had developed adequately to explain copper's extraordinary properties. Like all metals, in its solid state the atoms of copper form into regular geometric shapes called a crystalline lattice. This is a result of the same type of natural self-organization that creates diamonds and quartz crystals, and in some sense is a very simple example of the self-organizing atomic and molecular processes that gave rise to life and the amino acids and proteins that continue to make it function. Because of its particular atomic structure, each individual unit in a crystalline lattice of copper atoms takes the shape of a "face-centered cube," with eight of the atoms at each corner of the cube but also six others in the center of each face. Each of the eight corner atoms is shared with the neighboring cells, binding the whole lattice together. Since each unit is made up entirely of triangles, this crystalline lattice of atoms *should* be extremely strong and resistant to deformation – far too strong for early humans to have been able to bend or hammer it into new shapes. However, a bit like imperfections and mistakes in proteins and other organic compounds permit useful variations to emerge (recall the versatility of the silk protein), so, too, do small variations in the lattice of copper crystals make the metal far more malleable than it otherwise would be. This random or material "wildness" of copper had already proved extraordinarily useful to humans for millennia before the state of material science had reached a point where it could be coherently explained. It would not be until the 1930s that material scientists discovered that copper's seemingly uniform crystalline structure is actually riddled with imperfections called dislocations – areas where the lattice pattern of copper crystals is not precisely aligned and connected. The presence of millions of these small dislocations allow what would otherwise be perfectly rigid cubes to slide past each other, making it possible for humans to hammer copper metal into the shape of a plow, a knife, or countless other useful things.[52]

But if the surprising malleability of copper is wonderful for shaping the material, it might not prove so wonderful for using it: a copper plow that continued to be easily bent would be worse than a wooden one. Luckily for humans, copper has yet another trick up its sleeve: those crystalline dislocations that make it malleable will only slide so far before they begin

---

[52] Stephen L. Sass, *The Substance of Civilization: Materials and Human History from the Stone Age to the Age of Silicon* (New York: Arcade, 1998), 44–5.

to collide with each other and stick together, rather like an atomic-level logjam. As a result, coppersmiths have a brief window during which the metal can be easily beaten into a specific shape, but as they continue to hammer, it becomes increasingly stiff and brittle – the work hardening mentioned earlier. The trick was to hammer the copper into the desired shape just at the point where the copper also began to become hard enough to make for a useful tool, but not so hard as to be overly brittle and easy to break. Now this would have been a very difficult art indeed, were it not that copper has yet another surprising ability: if the smith heats a hammered copper object up to about 600 degrees Fahrenheit (315 degrees Celsius) – a temperature humans first began to achieve in simple furnaces about 2000 BCE – the hammered shape will remain but the log-jam of dislocations will disappear as the copper atoms pop back into their previous crystalline order. Amazingly, the copper does not have to be melted again to regain its crystalline structure, as one might expect – just heated. In English this nearly miraculous process is called annealing, and its importance to the advent of modern metal-based civilizations is difficult to overestimate. Because copper could be both work hardened and annealed, smiths could subject the metal to repeated cycles of hammering and heating, allowing them both to shape the metal into the desired object and exercise considerable control over how hard and stiff its various parts became.[53] The cutting edge of a plow or sword, for example, could be hammered to maximize its hardness while leaving the structural metal more flexible and less prone to breaking. To better grasp just how extraordinary these metallic properties must have been to the Neolithic humans who first stumbled upon them, compare copper to the properties of another critically important early material, pottery. Ceramic pottery made from clay was even more malleable than copper, able to take on a nearly infinite array of shapes. However, in contrast to copper, once a ceramic object is fired its shape is permanently fixed – it cannot be softened and reworked by reheating. Try to work harden or anneal a clay pot and you will end up with nothing more than a dusty pile of charred shards.

Because it is so absurdly easy to work with, humans began to make jewelry and other objects from rare surface deposits of pure native copper as long ago as the seventh millennium BCE. But if copper's first appeal was to the human aesthetic senses, it soon came to serve more utilitarian purposes. Along with cattle and silkworms, copper eventually became

[53] Sass, *The Substance of Civilization*, 45–8.

one of the most influential material things with which humans have formed close sociocultural bonds. A good case could be made for referring to a Cow Age or Silkworm Age, and that we do not probably stems at least in part from the modern tendency to think that domesticated animals are not genuine technologies like metal plows and swords. Regardless, copper is the only one of the three material stars of this book that inspired Western scholars to name an entire historic period in its honor: the Bronze Age (3300–600 BCE, depending on the region). Bronze is copper with a small amount of tin, which serves both to lower the melting point of the copper, making it easier to smelt and cast, and to increase the strength of the resulting metal. Bronze was initially just a lucky accident, as many copper ores happened to occur in association with tin that ended up in the copper mix during smelting. Metalsmiths only learned to deliberately add tin much later.[54]

The Bronze Age is in many ways aptly named, as this alloy of copper and tin deeply shaped human history. Surely among the most significant of these shaping forces was the human use of copper to make plows. The earliest plows were likely made of wood, which obviously broke and wore down quickly. In comparison, bronze was not only more durable but could be shaped and sharpened to more effectively cut the earth's skin. Once the bronze plow was harnessed to oxen – the not-so-distant descendants of the fearsome aurochs discussed earlier – agricultural productivity began to accelerate rapidly, providing enough food to sustain growing urban settlements. Copper also increased the human ability to control oxen and other draft animals, as bronze mouth bits were far more durable and effective than the earlier leather versions that draft animals quickly chewed to shreds. While it may sound like hyperbole, it really is not too much to say that this human partnership with copper and cattle was among the most important material foundations of the modern world.[55]

Given such an immense material potential, the earth's supply of copper exerted an increasingly obvious allure to intelligent urban-dwelling humans, much like coal and oil would many centuries later. Copper is actually relatively rare compared to many of the other metallic elements that occur on the planet. The earth's crust is about 5.8 percent iron and 8.0 percent aluminum, but only 0.0058 percent copper. Less than 1 in 1,000 parts of the extreme outer crust of the planet that has historically been accessible to human beings is copper. Why then was copper the first

---

[54] Sass, *The Substance of Civilization*, 61–2.   [55] Sass, *The Substance of Civilization*, 66.

widely developed metal rather than iron or aluminum? Simply because copper was more easily refined from its common mineral forms, where it is bound to other elements like oxygen, sulfur, and iron. Pure copper is found only rarely, but there were sizable and easily accessible deposits of more complex copper minerals in the lands in and around the Mediterranean Sea, most famously on the island of Cyprus, which became the origin for the Latin word for copper, "cuprum."[56] People living in what is today Iran – not at all coincidentally near the supposed Garden of Eden discussed earlier – appear to have been the first to develop the technology of smelting in which they used high heat to drive off impurities and melt down complex mineral ores to remove the purified copper. Archaeologists speculate that copper smelting might well have been an accidental consequence of pottery making. A simple campfire is not hot enough to smelt any copper ore, but an early pottery kiln could reach the necessary 650 degrees Celsius (1,200 degrees Fahrenheit). A pottery maker might have accidentally dropped a piece of colorful copper ore like malachite into a kiln, or perhaps have embedded it into the ceramic clay for decoration. Regardless, it would have taken no great insight to realize that the heat had somehow transformed the pretty but useless copper ore into nodules of pure and useful copper, though the process must have seemed almost magical. As with so many technological developments, once humans had reached a material state where kilns came into proximity with copper deposits, they were likely to stumble across the basic principles of copper smelting. Obviously humans did not in any logical sense of the word "invent" the process. Yet once the basic process was understood, it launched humans on an incremental course of technological improvements in smelting and metal working. Subsequent copper smelters typically used wood and charcoal as a heat source, just as with pottery kilns, so making copper also often contributed to local shortages of timber. In England the smelting of copper, iron, and other metals ultimately helped to wipe out the island's forests, though the British were able to turn to another carbon source thanks to the island's abundant deposits of coal.[57]

Fundamentally, these early copper smelters were no different from those used centuries later at Anaconda and Ashio: they used heat to melt the ore so the copper could be separated from the waste rock, or "slag." However, increasingly sophisticated smelting techniques were needed to process the complex copper ores (often referred to as refractory or difficult) that were the most abundant and easily mined. The copper mined

[56] Sass, *The Substance of Civilization*, 52.   [57] Sass, *The Substance of Civilization*, 53–4.

under the city of Butte and processed at the Anaconda smelter was mostly of two types: chalcocite, an ore made up of two atoms of copper bonded with one atom of sulfur (Cu_2S), and enargite, which had three atoms of copper, four of sulfur, and one of arsenic (Cu_3AsS_4). The dominant copper mineral at Ashio was a common iron sulfide ore called chalcopyrite, with an atom of iron and two of sulfur joined with its single copper molecule ($CuFeS_2$). But the Ashio chalcopyrite also often appeared in close association with a deadlier mineral, the nasty arsenopyrite that paired a harmless iron molecule with a molecule each of arsenic and sulfur ($FeAsS$).[58] Ironically, the very same solitary outer electron that makes the copper atom so useful in conducting heat and electricity also allows copper to easily bond with other atoms like sulfur and arsenic. Humans lured by the potential power of copper at Butte and Ashio had no choice but to deal with its less desirable elements.

The chemical nature of the Anaconda and Ashio copper all but guaranteed that they would become difficult and demanding partners. If the Americans and Japanese wanted the benefits of face-centered cubes, crystalline dislocations, and loose electrons, they had to become intimately acquainted with arsenic, sulfur, and others of copper's less attractive colleagues. During the Bronze Age the partnership with copper had helped to push some humans into a new era of agricultural abundance, urbanization, and social complexity. Now copper promised to transform humanity again, this time by underwriting the development of a new era of electric light, power, and communication. For most American and Japanese citizens, copper's alluring promise seemed worth whatever costs that partnership might demand. Indeed, as they tied their fates ever more closely to copper, it became increasingly difficult for them to even imagine a world without it. They did not use copper so much as they thought, acted, and understood the world through that copper and the technologies it enabled. They became – in a very real material, bodily, and cognitive sense – "copper people."

COPPER PEOPLE

When environmental historians have studied the many ways in which the material environment interacts with porous human bodies, they have

[58] Takeshi Nakamura, "Tin Mineralization at the Ashio Copper Mine, Japan," *Journal of Geosciences* 2 (1954): 35–47; Takaaki Kusanagi, "The Mineral Zoning at the Ashio Mine," *Kozan chishitsu* 13 (1963): 95–100.

often focused on how toxins like DDT or radioactive particles caused adverse health effects. Indeed, the toxicity of the arsenic and sulfur at Ashio and Anaconda is also central to this book's story. Nonetheless, this unilateral emphasis on the toxicity of things also tends to obscure or marginalize the many ways in which the things that penetrate our porous bodies are beneficial. When environmental historians do consider the positive benefits of things, it is often in the rather instrumentalist terms of "ecosystem services" that provide clean air and water. Yet this seems far too narrow an understanding of the many ways in which humans emerge from and with their engagement with the material. How, for example, have powerful material things contributed not only to human health but also to human intelligence, creativity, and culture?

Absent this more positive understanding of the human engagement with things, it is difficult to truly understand the course of events at Ashio and Anaconda. Obviously, the Japanese and Americans were not attracted to copper because they wanted to release vast amounts of toxic arsenic and sulfur into the neighboring countryside. Rather, the siren song of the red metal lay with its power to fuel economic growth, electrify cities and nations, and create political and military power. Yet in our histories these (at least nominally) positive benefits are often framed as economic or political stories rather than environmental ones, leaving only the messes left behind by copper mining and smelting for what must now be the inevitably declensionist ministrations of the environmental historians. I would argue that this is a fundamental conceptual error, one that reflects the false modernist dichotomies between technology and nature, or more broadly, culture and matter. To avoid further propagating these mistaken polarities, all aspects of the human relationship with copper, from its initial extraction to its ultimate use, should be understood as coming under the purview of an environmental or material historical analysis. Further, these material realties were not just *restraints* on what clever human beings could do with copper and other things, as is frequently assumed, but were rather powerful *catalysts* for entirely new ways of thinking, acting, and existing, both good and bad. In discussing Japanese industrialization, Brett Walker provocatively asserts that "both people and the natural world became artifacts of modern and industrial life" – the Japanese people were also material beings whose manifold forms emerged from the machines, rhythms, and objects of industry.[59] Much the same can be said for the United States and any other

---

[59] Walker, *A Concise History of Japan*, 179.

industrialized nation, suggesting that similar material forces shape humans in similar ways. To be sure, not every nation followed precisely the same path to industrial modernity. Yet the nature of key industrial materials, technologies, and processes helped to push the humans who used them down similar, though never identical, paths. As the ever-perceptive historian of technology Langdon Winner notes, modern technological things remake who we are at our most vital core, restructuring "habits, perceptions, concepts of self, ideas of space and time, social relationships, and moral and political boundaries."[60] Even the toxic pollutants cast off by copper mining and smelting gave critics of modernity like Tanaka Shōzō the ability to think in ways that few, if any, before him had been able to think. Yet contemporary environmental historians should not repeat Tanaka's error in seeing only the destructive power of copper. Copper was, as are all material things, always richer than any merely human imagination might suppose. The creative possibilities enabled by the metal itself were equal to – perhaps even inextricable from – its destructive powers, permitting Japanese and Americans to feel and see, to think and act, in ways that would have literally been impossible only a generation before. Copper was no mere "raw material" that Japanese and Americans used to construct an abstract, *a priori* idea of modernity out in the real world – it was the very stuff from which those ideas were forged.

Nowhere was this creative material potential more apparent than in copper's intimate association with the transformative technologies of electric light, power, and communication, technologies that would hammer the American and Japanese into surprisingly similar molds. These convergences are all the more striking in that Japan's modern relationship with copper began very differently than it did in the United States, yet the powerful material pull of the metal nonetheless ultimately swung the two nations into similar orbits. After the Meiji Restoration, the Japanese government for a time continued to see the copper mined at Ashio mostly as a source of foreign currency, a role it had already been playing for centuries.[61] By the latter half of the nineteenth century the Japanese need for foreign capital had become all the more pressing, as the nation's relatively small stores of domestic capital were clearly inadequate to fund its costly dream of rapid industrialization. Western banks and

[60] Langdon Winner, "Technologies as Forms of Life," in *Readings in the Philosophy of Technology*, ed., David M. Kaplan (Oxford, UK: Rowman and Littlefield, 2004), 107.
[61] Watanabe, "Talking Sulfur Dioxide," 74.

investors would have happily offered funds, yet this raised the grave danger that foreign money would inundate the nation, seizing de facto control of its richest mines and other enterprises. Determined to avoid external economic domination, the Meiji government opted instead to follow the plan of rapid industrialization crafted by the powerful politician and later Prime Minister Matsukata Masayoshi. The government operated many mines on its own or in close cooperation with the major *zaibatsu* and other industrial concerns, investing heavily in foreign technologies and experts that would quickly make the mines into exemplars that private operators were to duplicate. Japan's new Industry Ministry, established in 1870, was in the words of one Meiji reformer, designed to "make good Japan's deficiencies by swiftly seizing upon the strengths of the Western industrial arts."[62] Japanese mines would serve not only as models of modernity but also as a critical source of the national wealth and foreign capital needed to purchase yet even more Western technology. Gold, silver, and copper were in demand around the globe – they could be easily and profitably sold to bring foreign cash to Japan. As Inoue Kaoru, one of the Meiji government's top financial officials, put it in 1873, copper, silver, and other minerals were the keystone to Japan's future: mining "ought to be considered the country's most important industry and ought to produce large profits."[63]

This government-directed modernization of mining was not always completely successful. The Meiji fetish for importing technologies that seemed modern and "Western" at times overwhelmed common sense and a reasonable sensitivity to local material and economic conditions. Government and private operators alike, for example, at times insisted on using seemingly more modern coal to fire steam engines and bricks to build factories, even when the abundant Japanese forests could have provided wood for both more cheaply. Nonetheless, Japanese mining modernized with astonishing speed. Once these model mines proved effective, the government gradually began to hand control over to the new class of industrial capitalists that it had helped to create. As profits boomed, these modernized mines became the foundation for the great industrial and financial *zaibatsu*, breeding vast economic empires that went far beyond mining.[64]

---

[62] Walker, *A Concise History of Japan*, 195.

[63] Fumio Yoshiki, *How Japan's Metal Mining Industries Modernized* (Tokyo: United Nations University, 1980), 12.

[64] Kazuo, *Ashio Riot of 1907*, 17.

As we have already seen, this is precisely what occurred at Ashio, where the efforts of Furukawa Ichibei quickly transformed the moribund mines into an economic powerhouse. In the course of little more than a decade, Ashio became the most important copper producer in Japan and the largest mining complex in all of Asia, a leading exemplar of Japan's drive to modernize and industrialize.[65] By 1890 the Ashio mines under Furukawa's direction were already producing almost 42 percent of Japan's national copper output, and the international sale of Ashio copper accounted for an astonishing 9.5 percent of Japan's total export earnings.[66] While he would be criticized for the Ashio pollution problems, Furukawa's success also transformed him into a model of Japanese modernization and the Japanese work ethic. In 1899 the readers of the magazine *Taiyō* voted him one of the nation's top industrialists, part of a select group referred to as the "twelve great men of Meiji."[67]

But while it would continue to be an important export commodity and source of foreign currency, the copper extracted from Ashio and other Japanese mines offered what was in some ways an even more alluring promise: the possibility of wide national electrification. The most spectacular of the many late nineteenth-century global inventions, electricity promised to make Japan into a shining beacon of modern economic and technological prowess. The Japanese began first with the rapid electrification of factories for lighting, but, soon after, the webs of electrical networks began to spread steadily outward to entangle the wider nation. Japan saw the founding of its first electric company, the Tokyo Light Company, in 1883, a mere three years after the founding of the pioneering Edison Illuminating Company in the United States. By 1895 the ore dug from the Ashio mines had already helped to create more than 4,000 miles of thick copper transmission wires. Fifteen years later, some houses in the ancient imperial city of Kyoto had electric lights, and by 1933 more than 90 percent of Japanese homes had electricity – this at a time when the figure for the United States was only 68 percent.[68] A literal industrial enlightenment, incandescent electric lights were 10 to 100 times as bright as earlier candle, kerosene, and gas lights and eliminated the problem of

---

[65] Alan Stone, "The Japanese Muckrakers," *The Journal of Japanese Studies* 1 (1975): 385–407, here 386.
[66] Stolz, *Bad Water*, 34.   [67] Stone, "Vanishing Village," 9–10.
[68] Quoted and translated in Ian Jared Miller, "Tokyo in the Age of Electricity: Energy and the Great Convergence," draft manuscript of a forthcoming book chapter. Miller's original source is Hashizume Shin'ya and Nishimura Kiyoshi, *Nippon denkashi* (Tokyo: Nihon Denki Kyokai Shinbunbu, 2005), 53.

dirty soot that plagued these earlier technologies.[69] In 1910 one Japanese woman recalled that electric lights had transformed her home so profoundly that she returned one night and it "was so bright that I felt as though I had walked into the wrong house."[70]

Homeowners in the United States were equally enthusiastic about electric light. As one Tennessee farmer proclaimed in the 1920s: "The greatest thing on earth is to have the love of God in your heart, and the next greatest thing is to have electricity in your house."[71] Starting in the 1880s, Thomas Edison, George Westinghouse, and other inventor-capitalists had engineered one of the world's first commercially viable systems of electric light and power. Compared even to England, France, and other European countries, Americans proved unusually eager to embrace electric lighting. As in Japan, the first wave was lights for factories and public streets. Americans living in towns big and small considered even just a few streets lined with electric lights as prima facie evidence that they were modern municipalities with "bright" futures.[72] Most Americans first witnessed electric lighting on a city street or in a department store, not in their private homes. Even as late as 1900, just three percent of American homes had electricity, and this would only increase to a still-modest 16 percent by 1912. In contrast to the more densely populated Japan, Americans were spread painfully thin in many areas – power companies balked at the cost of extending expensive copper trunk lines out to a mere handful of rural customers. By 1940 electric lights had reached nearly all Americans living in cities – 96 percent – yet only 31 percent of rural farmhouses had been electrified.[73]

As these differences suggest, the American and Japanese electric lighting and power systems did not develop in lockstep. Each had its own peculiarities that stemmed from different political, social, and material circumstances. Indeed, Americans often framed their achievements in electric lighting as further confirmation of the supposed superiority of the Anglo-Saxon race. The inferiority of dark-skinned peoples, they believed, was confirmed by the "darkness" stemming from their lack of artificial illumination. Electric lighting even offered Western racists

---

[69] Robert J. Gordon, *The Rise and Fall of American Growth: The US Standard of Living Since the Civil War* (Princeton, NJ: Princeton University Press, 2016), 118.
[70] Quoted in Walker, *A Concise History of Japan*, 174.
[71] Gordon, *Rise and Fall of American Growth*, 113.
[72] Ernest Freeberg, *The Age of Edison: Electric Light and the Invention of Modern America* (New York: Penguin, 2014), 58–9.
[73] Gordon, *Rise and Fall of American Growth*, 120.

a particularly tempting symbol of what I earlier identified as the idea of a Soul 2.0. As the historian Ernest Freeberg notes, many Europeans and Americans believed that "stronger lighting pushed back not only the physical darkness but also a spiritual one." Electricity was supposed to illuminate "the higher reaches of the soul," Freeberg observes, and the "quality of a culture's artificial lighting revealed its level of civilization."[74] The rapid adoption of electric lighting by the Japanese, however, presented something of a challenge to the simple equation of bright white lights with bright white people. Having long dismissed all Asian peoples as innately inferior, Americans were forced grudgingly to admit that the Japanese were quickly proving every bit as technologically capable as any westerners. Some preserved pride by dismissing the Japanese as little more than clever imitators – their evident success explained as the product of a derivative civilization skilled at nothing so much as parroting the true inventiveness of Anglo-Saxons. Only slightly more gracious, others admitted that the Japanese were indeed the "Yankees of Asia," but still found a racial explanation: as one US government report explained, Japanese technical prowess must stem from a trace of "Aryan" blood in their racial lineage. If the Japanese had white lights, their genes must also contain a "white strain."[75]

Of course, today we dismiss such explanations as the crudely racist claims that they were. Yet what often goes unnoticed is that such views were not only racist but anthropocentric. Inherent in these claims was an underlying faith that technological advances stemmed not from the creative potential of a constantly evolving material world, whose benefits might be unevenly distributed among different regions and peoples, but rather from some mysterious and even divine spark of inventive genius. Different peoples might possess a greater or lesser portion of creative energy, but in this view there was no question that human genius drove technological progress, while the material world was nothing more than a passive resource or tool. For Americans and Europeans to proclaim their racial superiority, they first had to assume a broader human superiority over nature. Westerners were superior because they most fully dominated nature. If the contrary were true – if technological progress was not a product of human genius but rather a largely unintended and unplanned outcome of the creative material conditions at any particular place and time in history – then the complex technologies that westerners took so much pride in would be as much the product of nature as of humans. Not

---

[74] Freeberg, *Age of Edison*, 223.   [75] Freeberg, *Age of Edison*, 226.

only had they not come from any Anglo-Saxon *racial* superiority, they did not really even come from any inherent *human* superiority but rather were the gifts of a richly creative material world – a theme I will return to later in the chapter.

A similar tendency to emphasize human inventiveness while ignoring the role of other organisms and things was also reflected in the way the Americans and Japanese understood the process of electrification. Both then and now, the tendency has been to identify electricity with its more obvious expressions in electric lights, and subsequently electric stoves, irons, refrigerators, and all sorts of other appliances. All of these technologies can most easily, though still erroneously, be reduced to expressions of solely human ideas and genius. The light bulb itself even became a popular symbol of pure, abstracted human thought: when we say a light bulb went off in our heads, we reinforce the belief that the key to invention is an abstract idea – not the material antecedents that typically gave rise to it, nor the subsequent material execution necessary to make it a reality. Yet none of these inventions for using electric power would have been possible absent the masses of copper that generated the electricity in dynamos, transported the resulting power over a network, and powered the electric motors with copper armatures. When formed into immense nets of wire stretched out over the landscape, copper became a geographical force of nature not dissimilar to rivers, a conduit that could be used in many ways yet whose creative potential was inherent in its material powers of flow, transmission, and connectivity. As the historian of technology Thomas Zeller points out, such an infrastructure constitutes a seamless melding of material extracted from nature and the technological input from human beings – what he terms an "envirotechnical system."[76] Given this seamless fusing of the material environment and human technology, we might usefully think of things like copper ores and metals as exerting a sort of gravitational pull on humans, whatever their nationalities, bending their history and culture to their own arc. Humans may extract copper to meet a clearly defined historical need and goal. Yet once the copper is embedded into the built environment, it shapes how people act and think in unexpected ways. These new human

---

[76] Thomas Zeller, "Aiming for Control, Haunted by Its Failure: Towards an Envirotechnical Understanding of Infrastructures," unpublished manuscript presented at the workshop "Manufacturing Landscapes – Nature and Technology in Environmental History," Renmin University, Beijing, China, May 2015, 28–31.

niches filled with immense rivers of copper became a fertile source of new ideas, technologies, and cultures, much as the niches created by Longhorns or silkworms had done in their own ways.

To better understand the power of copper wires, consider that for the vast majority of human history on the planet, energy was geographically bound to the places where it generated power. The kinetic energy of a river, for example, could be harnessed with a waterwheel to create power to grind grain or saw wood. This waterpower could be transported a modest distance through belts or other physical linkages, but the place where power was used was rarely far from the source of energy. To be sure, the chemical energy of coal or wood could be transported far from its site of extraction. As the historian Christopher F. Jones explains, in the nineteenth century the United States and other nations built increasingly sophisticated "routes of power" like canals and pipelines that vastly increased the speed and volume at which fuels could be moved.[77] Nonetheless, the transformation of that chemical energy into useful power typically occurred where the power was used. Furukawa might fuel his steam engines with coal from a mine far to the north in Hokkaido, but he would burn that coal near his copper-mining operations in Ashio. In this spatial relationship, the linkage between Ashio and the site of energy extraction remained entirely physical and material: a portion of one part of the world, the coal, was literally extracted and moved to a different part of the world. The connection could scarcely have been more concrete.

On one level, this was also true with copper. Once mined and purified of undesirable elements like sulfur and arsenic (with often-disastrous results for silkworms, cattle, humans, and other organisms, as we have seen), copper was transported to other sites, where it could be used to make pots and pans, tools, bells, and many other items. Copper from the Ashio mine was used in the nearby shrine and mausoleum of the shogun Tokugawa Ieyasu and for roof tiles on Edo Castle in what would later become Tokyo. When shaped into immensely long wires and connected to electrical power systems, however, copper's spatial dynamics became very different. Because of its excellence as an electrical conductor, copper wires could carry electric power far from where it had been initially generated, whether that was at a hydropower plant driven by a river or a steam engine driven by the heat of burning coal. In contrast to earlier means of

---

[77] Christopher F. Jones, *Routes of Power: Energy and Modern America* (Cambridge, MA: Harvard University Press, 2014).

transporting energy, nothing material is visibly moved when transmitting electric power over a copper wire, though invisible electrons are in some sense "flowing."

It was from this mysterious power of copper-transmitted electricity that a radically new and modern idea of physical space began to emerge. As the historian of technology David Nye notes, prior to Thomas Edison's development of a practical electric light bulb, it was assumed that to create light something must be burned.[78] With candles, gaslight, and fireplaces, the generation of light had been inseparable from the burning of wax, gas, and wood – material things that had been transported from their original sites of extraction.[79] With an electric light bulb, nothing material appeared to have been moved and no combustion took place. Even in the case where some material thing actually *was* burned, like coal, combustion might take place tens or even hundreds of miles away. Where moving water generated electric power, even combustion itself could be entirely eliminated.[80]

While few Americans or Japanese fully grasped these extraordinary physical realities, many did understand that the electricity flowing over copper wires had deeply changed the spatial nature of their world. The American historian and cultural critic Lewis Mumford argued in his 1934 classic *Technics and Civilization* that copper wires and hydropower would usher in a "neotechnic" age of civilization in which the dirt and grime of coal and gas would be eliminated by bringing the power of distant rivers to the cities. Likewise, the American mining engineer Henry Janin realized that traditional ideas of space, time, and distance would collapse, as copper wires take "the waterfall to the city; one instant tons of water drop; the next, tons of machinery hum."[81] Some Japanese thinkers also rushed to embrace this modern spatial order. The historian Ian Jared Miller points out that many Japanese also believed that electrification was indispensable to the nation's rapid modernization. Miller's preceptive investigation into the life and ideas of the prominent Japanese engineer, Motono Tōro, reveals a deeply held faith that electricity would link the immense untapped power of nature and bring it into the city, thus ushering Japan into a modern new age of advanced civilization.[82]

---

[78] David E. Nye, *American Technological Sublime* (New York: MIT Press, 1996), 176.

[79] The knowing reader might rightly object that gas light does not entirely fit this model, as the gas was generated from heating up coal, so it was one step removed from the initial site of coal extraction.

[80] Jones, *Routes of Power*, 162–3.   [81] LeCain, *Mass Destruction*, 29–30.

[82] Miller, "Tokyo in the Age of Electricity," 8.

When Americans or Japanese turned on their electric lights – and eventually their electric stoves, refrigerators, and countless other devices – they were interacting with a strange new material world which in and of itself created novel spatial relationships. Lewis Mumford, Motono Tōro, and other contemporary observers rightly noted that electricity allowed humans to use power far from the sites where it was generated, eliminating the need to burn coal, gas, wood, or other materials in the urban environment. Yet if the earlier transportation of coal or other combustible materials into the city for burning occasioned dangerous pollution, it also provided much more tangible bodily connections to the surrounding countryside that electrification largely eliminated. To burn coal or gas is to physically experience a material piece of a distant place, and to have a sense of its properties and dangers. Surely someone who has smelled the volatile scent of coal and felt its dusty grains as they shoveled it into a hot stove has a visceral understanding of the dangers of a coal-mine fire – a bodily understanding that an electric stove largely eliminates, even if its power was generated by a distant coal-fueled dynamo.

Likewise, the material nature of electricity made it easy for modern Japanese and Americans to ignore the actual wires of copper strung between and through their homes, businesses, and factories, surrounding them with a vast if often deliberately concealed copper net that in every second courses with billions of electrons. In reality, though, the ability to collapse space through the nearly instantaneous transmission of electric power was entirely dependent on immense amounts of highly material copper. As Christopher F. Jones rightly notes, the ephemeral nature of electricity means that its existence requires the construction and maintenance of an elaborate and expensive network of transmission wires.[83] The distant hydropower plant was not connected to an urban factory or home by *electricity* but rather by *copper*: whatever the distance, a continuous strand of copper or other conductor literally *connected* them. Even the smallest gap in this line of copper – a short circuit – would bring the flow of electricity to an abrupt halt.

In an earlier age, sites of extraction provided coal that was physically moved to the city to be burned. Now different sites of extraction, like those at Ashio and Anaconda, provided copper that was physically moved to the city to provide conduits of power so that coal could instead be burned near the mine – only its purified power was to be carried to the city on the swarming backs of countless copper atoms. As the historian of

---

[83] Jones, *Routes of Power*, 162.

Japan, Julia Adeney Thomas, notes, the concepts of modernity and frictionless global markets depended on maintaining the illusion of a modern new separation between the city and the country, the human and the material. Separation was "fundamental to ideas of 'market efficiency' which eliminate environmental and human costs" as well as to a new human faith in "culture's complete divorce from natural constraints."[84] In reality, the illusion of immaterial spaces of power was only created and maintained by the immense amounts of very real material copper from Ashio and Anaconda that had been permanently embedded into the infrastructure of Japanese and American society. Modern humans and their ways of thinking about space and time had actually become more connected to a powerful material world, not less.

Finally, the Americans and Japanese also shared a devotion to copper because it was critical to the more brutally obvious forms of power and societal change associated with military strength and violent imperial expansion. By the latter half of the nineteenth century, copper had become essential to modern warfare and the projection of national power at home and around the globe. Having largely completed its century-long conquest of the North American continent through a combination of outright war and settler colonialism, in the 1890s the United States began to pivot toward the building of an overseas empire. Great Britain and other European and Latin American nations had constructed increasingly formidable ocean-going "blue water" navies, sparking concerns about the ability of the United States to protect its growing global interests. The publication in 1890 of the American naval strategist Alfred Thayer Mahan's book *The Influence of Sea Power on History, 1660–1783* further suggested the nation was falling dangerously behind. A merely coastal navy could not protect American interests at home or abroad, Mahan argued. Successful national defense demanded an ocean-going navy capable of meeting threats anywhere around the globe and well before they reached American shores, he argued, thus justifying the creation of a powerful navy that could easily enough be turned to offensive purposes on the more palatable grounds of homeland defense.[85]

One result of this American shift in naval strategy was an armored steam-powered cruiser christened the USS *Maine*. Already technologically

[84] Thomas, "Reclaiming Ground," 2.
[85] Alfred Thayer Mahan, *The Influence of Sea Power on History, 1660–1783* (New York: Little, Brown, 1890).

outdated by the time it went into service in 1895, the *Maine* nonetheless represented the growing American commitment to building a modern global navy. Three years later when tensions rose with Spain over its harsh suppression of a rebellion in nearby Cuba, the Americans sent the *Maine* to Havana harbor, a none-too-subtle material manifestation of the nation's growing military reach. When the ship mysteriously exploded and sank, it provided the Americans with an excuse to declare war on Spain. Less than three months later, an American fleet under the command of Commodore George Dewey in the battle cruiser USS *Olympia* decimated an antiquated fleet of Spanish ships at Manila Bay in the Philippines. Dewey's deadly barrage sent all of the best Spanish ships to the bottom of the bay and killed 77 sailors. By contrast, Dewey lost not one of his ships and suffered only a single death when one his men collapsed from heat stroke in a boiler room. Reneging on promises, either explicit or implicit, that they would give the Philippines their independence in exchange for their help in defeating the Spanish, the Americans subsequently fought a bloody war of conquest to keep the archipelago as a permanent part of its new overseas empire.[86]

The lessons of Manila Bay and the American conquest of the Philippines were not lost on the Japanese, who were in any case already well on their way to buying or building their own deep-water navy. If anything, the Imperial Japanese Navy was even more obsessed with Mahan's "blue water" naval strategies than were the Americans.[87] The United States military had not yet even completed its harsh "pacification" of the remaining Filipino rebels when Japan went to war with Russia over control of Manchuria and the Korean peninsula. In late May of 1905, the Japanese and Russian navies met in the famous battle of the Tsushima Strait, a relatively narrow passage between Korea and the Japanese main island of Honshu. The subsequent victory of the Japanese fleet under Admiral Tōgō Heihachirō was as lopsided as that of Dewey's at Manila Bay. The Japanese sank six of Russia's eight battleships and killed more than 4,300 of its sailors while losing only a handful of minor ships and suffering just over 100 deaths. For the first time an Asian nation had decisively defeated the naval forces of one of the great European powers.

[86] A good short account of the conflict is David J. Silbey, *A War of Frontier and Empire: The Philippine-American War, 1899–1902* (New York: Hill and Wang, 2008).
[87] David Evans and Mark R. Peattie, *Kaigun: Strategy, Tactics, and Technology in the Imperial Japanese Navy, 1887–1941* (Annapolis, MD: Naval Institute Press, 2012), 514–16.

Theodore Roosevelt called the Russian defeat "the greatest phenomenon the world has ever seen," while the many victims of European colonialism in Asia and around the world looked with pride and hope at Japan's success.[88] To be fair, most of the major warships the Japanese used to defeat the Russians at Tsushima were not made in Japan. Even Admiral Tōgō's flagship, the *Mikasa*, was built for the Japanese by the British. But this would not be the case for much longer. The imperial navy launched its first domestically built battle cruiser, the *Satsuma*, in November of 1906, just a year after their spectacular victory over the Russians. The *Satsuma* still had many components imported from the West – the Germans forged the nine-inch-thick hardened-steel armor at their famous Krupp iron-works. Yet the Japanese built the ship at the Yokosuka Naval Arsenal at the mouth of Tokyo Bay, a shipyard that had been established just before the Meiji Restoration, and would later build several of Japan's most formidable World War II aircraft carriers.[89]

FIGURE 6.4 The semi-dreadnought *Satsuma* under construction at Japan's Yokosuka naval shipyard near Tokyo. When launched in 1906, it became the first domestically produced battleship in the Imperial Japanese Navy's increasingly formidable fleet. Photo by: Universal History Archive/UIG via Getty Images.

---

[88] Quoted in Walker, *A Concise History of Japan*, 223.
[89] J. Charles Schencking, *Making Waves: Politics, Propaganda, and the Emergence of the Imperial Japanese Navy, 1868–1922* (Stanford, CA: Stanford University Press, 2005), 19, 117–18. See also Tom Tompkins, *Yokosuka: Base of an Empire* (Novato, CA: Presidio Press, 1981).

The lesson, both then and now, is obvious: any nation that aspired to global power, or simply wanted to protect itself from other global powers, would need a modern navy. At a time when battles on land were still being fought with horses, rifles, and other technologies that had not fundamentally changed from the days of Napoleon, at sea the fate of nations depended on enormous floating fortresses equipped with many of the most advanced technologies of the day. In explaining the sheer death-dealing power of the turn-of-the-century battleships, or dreadnoughts as they were sometimes aptly called (the British navy had named one of its first modern battle ships the *Dreadnought*, meaning "fearing nothing"), most naval historians emphasize their hydrocarbon-powered engines, hardened-steel armor, and increasingly accurate battalions of guns using deadly new high explosives. Yet bear in mind that the emerging twentieth-century battleship was also another manifestation of the material power of copper. By World War I a typical battleship used about a million pounds of cast copper alloys, half a million pounds of sheet and tube copper, and a quarter of a million pounds of copper wires, cables, motor windings, switchboards, and the like. All told, an average World War I battleship required almost two million pounds of copper. As one 1916 engineering report put it: "A modern battleship is literally threaded with a maze of wires for telephone, telegraph, signal and electric lighting systems, and more than 75 miles of copper wires fed 3,000 electric lights."[90] Indeed, one of the most modern features of the USS *Olympia* that was Dewey's flagship at the battle of Manila Bay were the electric lights and power produced by steam-driven generators, making it the first ship in the US Navy to use electricity.

As the world entered the twentieth century, pivotal naval battles would be won or lost in incandescently lit rooms where captains and admirals were literally connected to their ships and sailors via filaments of copper wire; in boiler rooms where high-speed engines depended on the efficient exchange of heat through copper tubes; and in many other parts of the ship where a growing number of electric motors turned around copper armatures to move everything from torpedo doors to gun turrets. In short, copper was the stuff of modern technological destructive power. Later battleships and aircraft carriers used even more copper. During World War II the Japanese would build the massive *Yamato* which, along with her sister ship, *Musashi*, were the biggest battleships ever made and

---

[90] "Materials of Engineering Construction," *Transactions of the International Engineering Congress* (San Francisco: Neal, 1916), 533–4.

FIGURE 6.5 The protected cruiser USS *Olympia*, Commodore Dewey's flagship at the battle of Manila Bay during the Spanish-American War, was one of the first ships in the United States Navy to have electricity. Here the cruiser's portside electrical generator is illuminated by an incandescent light bulb. Library of Congress Prints and Photographs Division, image number HAER PA, 51-PHILA, 714–68.

appropriately classed as "super-dreadnoughts." At 263 meters in length and displacing some 73,000 tons, they weighed nearly twice as much as a typical World War I ship. Commissioned mere days after the Japanese attack on Pearl Harbor, the *Yamato* became the flagship of the Imperial Japanese Navy's Combined Fleet and a potent material expression of the nation's formidable military might.[91] Indeed, the Japanese imperial navy had long made effective use of elaborate public launchings of warships to win support for naval expansion. Though it was launched with little fanfare to preserve wartime secrecy, the *Yamato* – named for an ancient and highly nationalistic word for Japan – was one of the most powerfully symbolic ships in the fleet.[92] The very existence of such an immense ship

[91] Januz Skulski, *The Battleship Yamato (Anatomy of the Ship)* (Annapolis, MD: Naval Institute Press, 1988). On the symbolic meaning of the ship, see Yoshida Mitsuru, *Requiem for Battleship Yamato*, trans. Richard H. Minear (Annapolis, MD: Naval Institute Press, 1999).

[92] Schencking, *Making Waves*, 107–37.

surely played a significant role in convincing some Japanese that their nation just might be capable of defeating, or at least repulsing an attack from, even the mighty United States. As one naval historian puts it: "The *Yamato* became the mythical symbol not only of Japanese sea power, but of the entire nation."[93] When naval strategists, imperial leaders, and regular Japanese citizens thought about the world and their nation's future, they henceforth thought through and with the *Yamato* – at least until American carrier-based bombers sent the ship and more than 3,000 men and millions of pounds of Japanese copper to the bottom of the Pacific just south of Kyushu in April of 1945.[94] Ironically, the largest battleship ever built had been launched at the very moment when a new class of massive aircraft carriers (also strung with vast webs of copper) had made it largely obsolete.

The Japanese fully recognized the intimate connections between national military power and their domestic copper mines. As two historians of the Ashio pollution problems observe, the Ashio copper mine was seen as "the foundation upon which Japan's imperialism was built."[95] Not only copper but the government's imperfect copper-pollution controls that permitted mining and smelting to continue at Ashio were justified in part by the belief that Japan had little choice but to build a powerful deep-water navy if it wished to expand its own imperial reach and resist economic and military domination by the United States, England, and other Western powers.[96] With the cult of the Emperor-father allied with a distorted state-supported version of Shinto, it became increasingly common to view any further complaints about pollution caused by copper mining and smelting as disloyal threats to national security.[97] In the United States, the ties between the Anaconda pollution and the concurrent ascent of the nation as a global imperial power were not always as explicit, if for no other reason than the giant nation had many other sources of copper with the big mines of Utah and Arizona. But the connection was no less real. Ultimately, it mattered not at all whether one was American, Japanese, British, French, Russian, or any other nationality – the modern age of naval warfare demanded ductile conductive metals like copper. Copper did not just symbolize or enable global

[93] Mark E. Stille, *The Imperial Japanese Navy in the Pacific War* (Oxford, UK: Osprey Publishing, 2014), 132.

[94] Skulski, *The Battleship Yamato*, 1988.

[95] Shoji and Sugai, "Ashio Copper Mine Pollution Case," 25–6, 29.

[96] Shoji and Sugai, "Ashio Copper Mining Pollution Case," 38–9.

[97] Jun Ui, *Industrial Pollution in Japan* (Tokyo: United Nations University, 1992), 3–5.

power – it *was* global power, every bit as much as the coal and oil that fueled ship engines and the steel that protected them from shells and torpedoes.

There were, of course, substitutes for copper. But in the early twentieth century these were all more expensive, less effective, or both. As Mimi Sheller notes in her path-breaking book *Aluminum Dreams: The Making of Light Modernity*, a few decades later the centrality of copper and steel would be challenged by the rise of cheap mass-produced aluminum. Aluminum can be effectively used for electrical wiring, though its conductivity is about half that of copper. But the key material power of aluminum lay with its extraordinarily high strength-to-weight ratio, allowing engineers and designers to use it as a much-lighter replacement for copper, iron, and steel. Lightness made for faster cars, ships, and airplanes, greatly accelerating the pace of modern society and drawing far-flung regions of the globe into a rapidly tightening web of commercial relations and commodity flows. Much like copper before it, aluminum transformed the weapons and strategies of war. The American military provided much of the motive and funding for expanded use of aluminum during World War II, particularly for building a new generation of planes and ships. Increasingly, modern military strategy was linked to speed, and speed was in turn largely a product of lightness. "Physical lightness and the ever-greater capacity for movement and speed," Sheller convincingly argues, "were the defining qualities of twentieth-century transport and material culture more generally."[98]

If aluminum was the material of speedy light modernity, copper was the material that lit its way, carrying power and information at the speed of light. When millions of pounds of this copper were embedded in the Japanese and American infrastructure, it transformed the very nature of space, becoming a force of nature as powerful as geographic features like rivers and highways. As Japanese and Americans increasingly became "copper people," they began to think, feel, and act in ways that were impossible only a few decades before, creating a distinctly modern and, at times, dangerous belief that humans had somehow fully escaped the bonds of the mere material world. For Japan, copper was a critical source of the foreign capital it used to buy not only its first battleships but all manner of other Western technologies from German hydropower dynamos to American air-powered rock drills. As the Japanese surrounded themselves

---

[98] Mimi Sheller, *Aluminum Dreams: The Making of Light Modernity* (Boston: MIT Press, 2014), 258.

with these new technologies, they inevitably came to think with this imported material environment, pushing Japan toward a convergence with other modernizing nations like the United States.

CONVERGENT MATTERS

Given the vast range and extent of the powers created by copper at the turn of the century, is it really any surprise that silk and cows were often unable to compete? Silk might titillate the touch and beef fill the belly, but to many Japanese and Americans these no doubt seemed relatively modest losses in comparison to the indisputably transformative and supposedly liberating power of electricity, bright lights, and deadly battleships. Even critics of the industrialization, modernization, and militarization created by copper often saw little alternative to them. The Japanese psychologist and social Darwinist Okaasa Jirō warned that the effects of modern material "progress" were destroying Japanese society "like termites eating away at a temple." Yet he still concluded that Japan had no choice but to embrace modernity, lest both unruly natural forces and dangerous imperial rivals bring the nation to its knees.[99] Likewise, though he continued to believe the Japanese might still somehow change course, Tanaka Shōzō recognized that humans were often blind to the power of material things to shape their fate in ways that they did not always anticipate or desire. As Tanaka warned in his diary, the supposed "progress of material, artificial civilization casts society into darkness." Humans may create new technologies, but Tanaka suggested they do not fully control them. "Electricity is discovered," he wrote, "and the world is darkened."[100]

The degree to which Japan was truly free to chart its own course in the later nineteenth and early twentieth centuries can be debated. Perhaps the government might have found alternatives to the wealth and power offered by the Ashio copper. There were other deposits of copper like the rich Besshi mines in the south, though these, too, caused serious pollution problems.[101] Or Japan might have simply accepted a weaker economic and military role on the world stage. Regardless, once Japan set out to become a nation of copper, it began importing both mining technologies and mining experts from the West. As a result, Japan came to resemble the United States and other Western nations not just in the way it *used* copper but also in the way it extracted and processed copper.

---

[99] Quoted in Stone, "Vanishing Village," 205.   [100] Stone, "Vanishing Village," 203.
[101] See Watanabe, "Talking Sulfur Dioxide."

This wholesale importation of Western technologies further pushed the nation toward a convergence with the West, creating a material substrate at Ashio that was strikingly similar to that of Anaconda.

The Japanese government began to invite foreign mining experts to the nation as early as 1862. The first to accept were the 25-year-old Raphael Pumpelly, an American geologist and mining engineer, and William Phipps Blake, a geologist and mining consultant. Pumpelly and Blake spent much of their time conducting a geological survey of Hokkaido, the northernmost of Japan's large islands that the government hoped, correctly as it turned out, would become a major source of coal. The two also seem to have been among the first to introduce chemical explosives like black powder into Japanese mines.[102] The men opened a mining school in Hakodate where they taught the latest Western mining technologies and management techniques, importing Western mining tools and instruments as well as chemicals and books by the world's top geologists and mining experts.[103] On his way back home, Blake sent a note from Shanghai encouraging his sponsors to "send students to America in order that they might see my country's mining equipment and improved weaponry," and so he could "instruct them in all matters concerning my country's mines and ships."[104]

As noted earlier, after the Meiji Restoration of 1868, the push to modernize mining became much more aggressive. In the fifteen years between 1868 and 1883, the government employed 78 foreign mining and geological experts. Oddly, the largest number, 24, were from France, perhaps betraying a Japanese preference for the supposed theoretical sophistication of French engineers which seemed particularly modern and scientific. Of the others, 14 were from Germany, a nation famous for its mining technology and schools, and 13 were British, who brought a century of experience with waterlogged coal mines similar to many in Japan. Despite the pioneering role of Pumpelly and Blake, during this period only 2 were Americans.[105] At the same time, the Meiji government invested heavily in education in mining engineering, geology, and allied disciplines. In 1877 a department of mining and metallurgy was created at Tokyo University. In 1886 the Tokyo Imperial University followed suit, as

[102] Junnosuke Sasaki, *Modes of Traditional Mining Techniques* (Tokyo: United Nations University, 1980), 13.
[103] Yoshiki, *How Japan's Metal Mining Industries Modernized*, 5–7.
[104] Yoshiki, *How Japan's Metal Mining Industries Modernized*, 62n10.
[105] Yoshiki, *How Japan's Metal Mining Industries Modernized*, 13–15.

did Kyoto Imperial University in 1897. By the early years of the twentieth century there were no fewer than 14 Japanese institutions providing advanced training in mining and metallurgy.[106]

If they hired relatively few American experts, the Japanese nonetheless sent many young mining engineers to the United States to observe the mines and receive training. Several visited Butte, establishing a direct technological link between Anaconda and Ashio. A 1905 article with the headline "Young Jap from Tokio on Mission to Butte" described the visit of Motozi Shibasawa, a graduate of the engineering department of the University of Tokyo, who spent several weeks in Butte and Anaconda examining the mine works, smelters, and power plants. Shibasawa was reportedly impressed by the technical sophistication of the Anaconda operations, and the article noted that he would soon "be returning to Japan to put in practice the ideas gained on his travels."[107] Articles in the *Anaconda Standard* discussing similar visits from other Japanese often both revealed and flattered the American sense of technological superiority. In one, a visiting Japanese student was reported to have said that in Japan "all our textbooks were written by Americans" as these "are undoubtedly the most practical in the world." The paper could also demonstrate a sincere if grudging admiration for the rapidity of Japanese progress. As one article on the Japanese mining exhibit at the 1904 World's Fair in St. Louis observed, "The Japanese exhibit was a revelation to many" and "the ancient mines of Ashio and Besshi are now supplied with the latest appliances for mining and smelting the ores." A 1904 advertisement for a Japanese elixir in a Butte newspaper captured the essence of this self-congratulatory American view, proclaiming that "the Japs are the Yankees of the Orient."[108]

The rapid progress in Japanese mining was nowhere more evident than in the technical and managerial modernization of the Ashio mines. Furukawa was adept at identifying and importing the world's best new mining and smelting technologies. He also sent his own technical experts

[106] Yoshiki, *How Japan's Metal Mining Industries Modernized*, 54–5. On the development of Japanese science, and engineering more broadly, see Fumiko Fujita, *American Pioneers and the Japanese Frontier: American Experts in Nineteenth-Century Japan* (Westport, CT: Greenwood, 1994); Hiromi Mizuno, *Science for the Empire: Scientific Nationalism in Modern Japan* (Stanford, CA: Stanford University Press, 2009); and Aaron S. Moore, *Constructing East Asia: Technology, Ideology, and Empire in Japan's Wartime Era, 1931–1945* (Stanford, CA: Stanford University Press, 2013).
[107] "Young Jap from Tokio on Mission to Butte," *Anaconda Standard*, December 13, 1905.
[108] "A Japanese Drug Store," advertisement, *Daily Intermountain*, October 1, 1904.

to view the Anaconda mines and smelters in Montana, recognizing that these were among the most technologically advanced in the world.[109] Drawing on the advice of foreign experts, Furukawa reorganized the Ashio mine for more efficient production and introduced horizontal (adit) mining techniques.[110] Prior to 1887 Ashio had 48 separate refining operations. Furukawa shut most of these down and replaced them with a large-scale modern concentrator and three smelters.[111] Mine operations were increasingly fueled by coal, which was used as a source of both heat and power in the Ashio smelters and refineries. The Furukawa *zaibatsu* was not just a copper company but an energy company, producing some 196,000 tons of coal and 16,000 tons of coke in 1897 alone. In this Ashio again represented a broader national transformation. As the Japanese used modern technologies to mine the rich coalfields in northern Kyushu and Hokkaido, coal production soared. In 1874 the nation's total coal production had been a modest 208,000 tons, but by 1919 the amount had reached 31 million tons.[112]

Nor did Furukawa ignore the transformative potential of electric light and power. In 1890 he bought a 400-horsepower hydroelectric turbine generator from the German Siemens Corporation and constructed the nation's first hydroelectric plant on the Watarase River. The hydropower operated an imported water pump, a powerful ore lift, and an underground electric lighting system. Furukawa also built the first electric railroad in the entire nation, using it to transport copper ore to the newly centralized concentrators – a plan that was very similar to Anaconda's electric rail between the Butte mines and the Anaconda concentrators and smelter. Furukawa also imported the new Bessemer furnaces which had been perfected for use with copper at the Anaconda, and he adopted electrolytic refining – an effective but energy-intensive technology that could only have made economic sense thanks to his hydropower dam on the Watarase. All these efforts slashed the time needed to process the Ashio ore from 32 days to only 2, increasing production while lowering costs.[113] The results were dramatic: in just the four years from 1887 to 1891, production from the Ashio mines more than doubled, increasing from 6,638,619 to 16,770,118 pounds of copper. Even more striking, the

[109] Stone, "Vanishing Village," 5.
[110] Shoji and Sugai, "Ashio Copper Mine Pollution Case," 19.
[111] Shoji and Sugai, "Ashio Copper Mine Pollution Case," 21.
[112] Walker, *A Concise History of Japan*, 191–3.
[113] Stone, "Vanishing Village," 5; Shoji and Sugai, "Ashio Copper Mine Pollution Case," 21.

16 million pounds of copper production in 1891 was *165 times* greater than the production had been in 1877. The Ashio mines were now responsible for producing fully 40 percent of Japan's copper.[114]

How did such a massive importation of Western technologies shape the Japanese nation and people? As discussed in Chapter 2, in recent decades historians of technology have tended to emphasize the many ways in which societies and social groups shape technology, often giving less consideration to the ways in which technology shaped society. This social constructivist approach brought many valuable insights, yet it also tended to frame human culture as clearly distinct from, rather than embedded in, the technological environment, which in turn tended to exaggerate the degree to which humans could understand, control, and shape this environment. Likewise, while some social constructivists had a commendable desire to discover a useful history that challenged a fatalistic determinism and encouraged people and governments to take greater control over their technological destinies, this drive to empower humans could come at the price of neglecting or underestimating the power of technology to shape the course of events. In the social constructivist model, humans were often the primary or even sole architects of historical change – not the merely material things that those humans used, made, or lived with. As a resurgent materialism has emerged in more recent years, however, historians are developing a new understanding of the many surprising ways in which technology is a powerful driver of historical change, while still avoiding a simplistic determinism. Here I want to make the case that we do not invent and control technologies so much as we emerge from and with them. Hence, when societies like Japan and the United States adopt very similar technological environments, these often push them to think and act in similar ways.

Particularly in its more popular guises, historical accounts have often celebrated the lone genius as the source of brilliant technological innovations that solved some vexing human problem. Edison "invents" the light bulb, the Wright brothers the airplane, Nikolaus Otto the internal combustion engine. Historians of technology have convincingly debunked the still-common idea that "necessity is the mother of invention." Certainly clean electric lights might prove to be an improvement over sooty gaslights, speedy airplanes might one day outpace slow passenger

---

[114] Notehelfer, "Japan's First Pollution Incident," 360–1.

ships, and automobiles might eventually replace horse-drawn wagons. In retrospect, these transitions did all happen and they look like progress. But at the time it was not at all clear that anyone really needed these inventions or that they would even prove to be successful. Just to offer one example, it would take almost half a century before gasoline-powered cars and trucks fully supplanted horses in most American cities. Horse-drawn wagons had both advantages (they could be compact and maneuverable) and disadvantages (limited speed and a power source prone to disease, injury, and the unpredictable release of large amounts of noxious horse manure) compared to trucks.[115] At base, for most people of the past the world they lived in at any moment in time works reasonably well, at least in part because they have never experienced anything else. The "need" only emerges after a technology has become widely adopted, at which point people find it difficult to imagine living without it. Yet, of course, people had lived without all sorts of seemingly essential technologies for millennia, never realizing how badly deprived they were.

There are obviously exceptions. Once people understood how germs spread disease, for example, inventing and improving urban sewage and water technologies became a pressing need. Likewise, implementing a new technology often generates genuine needs. To build electric light and power networks, Edison and others had to invent countless sub-technologies to reliably and safely deliver electricity to homes and businesses. Mass automobility created a pressing need for traffic lights and safer cars, just as widespread air travel created a need for air-traffic-control systems and navigation systems. However, for every invention that helped solve a clearly identifiable problem, there were countless others for which there was no pressing need whatsoever. But if necessity is not the mother of invention, what *does* drive technological change?

There has been considerable debate on this score.[116] Yet from a neo-materialist perspective that takes the power of things seriously, technological innovation is best understood as a quasi-organic or self-catalyzing process that constantly builds upon itself. Consider again the coal-fired

---

[115] See especially Ann Norton Greene, *Horses at Work: Harnessing Power in Industrial America* (Cambridge, MA: Harvard University Press, 2008), and Clay McShane and Joel A. Tarr, *The Horse in the City: Living Machines in the Nineteenth Century* (Baltimore, MD: Johns Hopkins University Press, 2011).

[116] A good overview of the question viewed through the related topic of technological determinism is offered in Merritt Roe Smith and Leo Marx, eds., *Does Technology Drive History? The Dilemma of Technological Determinism* (Cambridge, MA: MIT Press, 1994).

steam engine. The basic material phenomenon at the heart of Thomas Newcomen's pivotal 1712 steam engine – that a vacuum could be created in an enclosed space by condensing hot steam – had been known for many years before his "invention." Newcomen was probably aware that 14 years earlier Thomas Savery had used the same basic principle to pull water up a pipe, creating a simple steam-powered pump. Newcomen's contribution was to instead create the vacuum in a moving cylinder attached to a pivoting beam, which greatly increased the engine's water-pumping capacity. Some 57 years later, James Watt, who is often misleadingly credited with single-handedly inventing the steam engine, was repairing a working model of a Newcomen engine when he had a critical insight: constantly heating and cooling the same cylinder was inefficient and wasted coal. Watt realized he could keep the cylinder hot and save coal by cooling the steam in a separate "condenser." Eventually Watt's insight would result in the steam engine of choice for powering mine pumps, mills, railroads, warships, and all sorts of other machines.[117] Yet the Watt engine emerged as a logical extension of the existing collection of material artifacts of his day – most especially Newcomen's engine – not just from Watt's mind. The Oxford-based philosopher of science and technology, Nick Bostrom, has termed the possibility that technological systems work themselves out to their logical extent the "technological completion conjecture": "If scientific and technological development efforts do not effectively cease," he conjectures that, given adequate time, "all important basic capabilities that could be obtained through some possible technology will be obtained."[118]

Today some advocates of the Anthropocene concept – the idea that the earth has entered a new geological "age of humans" – would suggest that their proposed new epoch had a clear beginning with Watt's "invention" of the steam engine. Yet the actual history of this technology not only challenges Watt's centrality but also the anthropocentric assumptions inherent in the Anthropocene concept. A more nuanced understanding of the steam engine suggests that technological change is largely a cumulative process, one in which creative humans are pushed along by the possibilities inherent in the material state of technology at any point in history. Once the material phenomenon of creating a vacuum by

---

[117] Jared Diamond, *Guns, Germs, and Steel: The Fate of Human Societies* (New York: Norton, 1999), 233–5.

[118] Nick Bostrom, *Superintelligence: Paths, Dangers, Strategies* (Oxford, UK: Oxford University Press, 2014), 229.

condensing steam was recognized, many inventors would try their hand at harnessing this power to do useful work, often building incrementally on earlier developments. As the economist and student of technological change W. Brian Arthur notes, technological innovation is often a matter of combining the existing technologies available at any particular place and time in a novel way. "The overall collection of technologies bootstraps itself upward from the few to the many and from the simple to the complex," Arthur observes. Given this, it is not unreasonable to conclude that, in some sense, "technology creates itself out of itself."[119] Of course, Arthur does not mean to suggest that technology is autonomous – the human is still the keystone species in this creative material system. Yet Arthur rightly notes that the humans in, say, early industrial England had already been shaped and formed by the technologies around them: before humans socially construct technologies, they have been constructed by earlier technologies. The heroic-inventor idea emphasizes the breakthroughs of individual human beings like Watt. Yet Watt had only been able to *think* in new ways because of his intimate personal experience of working with the existing technologies of the day. Watt was an instrument maker at the University of Glasgow, so he was already mentally and materially prepared to make his conceptual breakthrough while repairing the university's Newcomen engine. In effect, Watt had been taught to think in certain ways by his material environment and its associated social and cultural dynamics. Moreover, had Watt not come up with the idea of a separate steam condenser, it seems exceedingly likely that the ongoing evolution of the technologies of the day would have eventually led others to arrive at a very similar if not identical concept.

Now, if it is really the cumulative material state of technologies at any particular point in history that "creates" innovation, rather than individual human genius, then we would expect that many people would often arrive at similar technologies at roughly the same time. This is precisely the case with the widely noted phenomenon of simultaneous independent invention. History is replete with instances of multiple inventors who arrived at similar if not nearly identical ideas, sometimes in complete isolation from each other. Americans like to attribute the invention of the incandescent light bulb to Thomas Edison in 1879. But while Edison's particular design eventually won out in the United States, there were dozens of others who invented similar devices, many well before Edison. The Cincinnati inventor J. W. Starr developed an incandescent bulb in the

---

[119] W. Brian Arthur, *The Nature of Technology* (New York: Free Press, 2009), 21

early 1840s, and the German immigrant Heinrich Goebel had a workable bulb by the 1850s. These earlier attempts were stymied in part by the need to use expensive chemical batteries as the source of electricity. To be a practical technology, electric light needed the dynamo, an electromechanical device for generating electricity that was not perfected until the 1870s. Once the dynamo became part of the material environment in the United States, Great Britain, and other countries, it was arguably only a matter of time before someone developed a workable incandescent light bulb. As a heated series of legal battles subsequently made clear, the British inventor Joseph Swan demonstrated and patented a working light bulb in Britain almost a year before Edison independently arrived at a very similar design. Another Englishman with the wonderfully British name of St. George Lane Fox exhibited his own version of an incandescent bulb in 1881. Hiram Maxim installed a small electric-power and incandescent lighting system in New York City not long after Edison demonstrated his own system in Menlo Park, New Jersey, and before he had built his famous Pearl Street Station.[120]

What all this technological convergence clearly suggests is that by the late 1870s the collection of available materials, techniques, and knowledge had, at least in a few regions of the world, reached a state where the incandescent light bulb was not only possible, but almost inevitable. Again, the inspiration and perspiration of human beings were obviously needed to bring the material possibilities together into a working technology, as were the political and economic systems necessary to make it both desirable and a reality. Yet in the end, it did not matter very much *which* humans did so. If Thomas Edison had never been born, Swan, Fox, Maxim or some other inventor would have presided over the birth of an incandescent light bulb and the related electric-power-generation and -distribution system. In any society, some percentage of the population must necessarily have mastered the current state of a particular technological system – otherwise, the existing technologies would soon fail and disappear. As these technical experts think with and through the multitude of ways in which the existing body of technologies might be recombined, improved, or extended, they will arrive at many of the same basic, novel ideas. Does the novelty then spring solely from the human mind, or is it also a product of the creative possibilities of a specific material environment at a specific moment in time?

---

[120] Freeberg, *The Age of Edison*, 38–40.

The answer, of course, is both. Yet in our infatuation with ourselves and a misleadingly abstract idea of cognition and creativity, we often overemphasize the human role while largely denying the material. This neglect of the material impetus is partly deliberate. Many historians of technology have not unreasonably feared that a less anthropocentric understanding of technological development can result in an overly simplistic determinism. Indeed, more than a few scholars have concluded that technology is autonomous and largely beyond human control. The German philosopher Martin Heidegger argued that "technology is in no sense an instrument of man's making or in his control" but is rather "centrally determining of all Western history." In a somewhat similar vein, the French sociologist Jacques Ellul concluded that technology had become an autonomous thing ruling all human life, "an 'organism' tending toward closure and self-determination; it is an end in itself."[121] Yet the idea that technology is literally autonomous and deterministic is just as flawed as the idea that it is entirely a social construct, as both positions still embrace the modern anthropocentric view in which humans are clearly distinct from the material world around them, whether we categorize that world as "natural" or "technological." Because we assume that all the invention and creation takes place solely within an isolated human brain, we are constantly surprised to discover that our technologies continue to evolve in entirely unexpected ways, and we misidentify what is really the inherently rich *creativity* of the interactions between humans and material things – natural and technological – as autonomy.

Given the quasi-organic way in which technology changes over time, a number of historians have suggested that a useful parallel might be made with the biological process of evolution. Indeed, if we include animals like cows and silkworms in our definition of technology, these creatures literally do coevolve with humans. This is precisely the point suggested by Jared Diamond's ambitious macrohistory *Guns, Germs, and Steel*. Why did the West come to dominate so much of the world during the past 500 years? Not because of any inherent superiority of mind or body rooted in the racial makeup of Europeans, Diamond argues, but rather because of the rich natural gifts offered by the Eurasian continent: a diverse collection of easily domesticated grains and animals that was nearly unmatched by any other region in the world. Yet Diamond's analysis not only undercuts Western claims of racial superiority, it also undermines conventional anthropocentric claims to human greatness.

---

[121] Quoted in Arthur, *The Nature of Technology*, 214.

Eurasians did not knowingly "invent" agriculture, Diamond argues, nor did they consciously set out to domesticate cows, sheep, and other animals. Rather, these technological developments that were so critical to the rise of complex human societies were, at least in their critical early stages, largely accidental and depended heavily on the inherent potential of certain plants and animals to *become* domesticated.[122] As the historian John McNeill notes, Diamond's argument has some weaknesses, most notably in its failure to adequately explain the narrower question of why western Europe rather than some other area of Eurasia (such as China) ultimately rose to world dominance. McNeill suspects ideological factors might have played a bigger role than Diamond's materially rooted geographical model suggests. Nonetheless, McNeill finds Diamond's central point about the pivotal importance of Eurasia's many domesticable species convincing.[123] As discussed in Chapter 3, the historian of technology and environment Edmund Russell has further highlighted the historical importance of other organisms with his powerful idea of coevolutionary history. It seems highly unlikely, Russell points out, that any human deliberately set out to domesticate wolves: how could they have even imagined that such a fierce animal might one day become a gentle companion who could be trusted to guard their flocks of sheep rather than eat them? Instead, Russell argues that domestication was largely an unintended process of coevolution in which both species played a role. In this sense, wolves domesticated humans as much as humans domesticated them.[124] As I argued in Chapter 4, the same might well have been the case with the dangerous aurochs who coevolved with human to become the modern species of cows.

   Yet if we have clearly coevolved with living technologies like wheat and cows, does something similar occur with nonliving technologies? Certainly there are some very intriguing parallels. As the archaeologist Ian Hodder suggests, we domesticate technologies much like we domesticate other living creatures, because the things we use also domesticate us. Likewise, the historian of technology George Basalla argues that the unique synergies between humans and their material technologies tend to generate a creative efflorescence of new devices, somewhat like

[122] Diamond, *Guns, Germs, and Steel.*
[123] John McNeill, "The World according to Jared Diamond," *The History Teacher* 34 (2001): 165–74.
[124] Edmund P. Russell, *Evolutionary History: Uniting History and Biology to Understand Life on Earth* (Cambridge, UK: Cambridge University Press, 2011), see especially ch. 6.

biological systems constantly generate novel traits. Just as only a small number of novel biological traits prove adaptive and are preserved by natural selection, only a small number of novel technologies are widely adopted and preserved by human selection.[125] There is, in other words, a sort of random wildness at work in technological environments, one in which humans continually churn through a large number of novel technological combinations, somewhat akin to the way evolution explores the much-vaster number of novel variations in amino acid chains and proteins. Arthur makes the metaphor specific: "Technology builds itself organically from itself," he observes, "it is a fluid thing, dynamic, alive, highly configurable, and highly changeable over time."[126] The philosopher of technology Langdon Winner makes a similar point, arguing that we should understand technologies as "forms of life." Human existence emerges from human engagements with the material means of subsistence available at any point in time, including both raw materials and technologies, which unite to create what Winner terms a distinct "mode of life" in which humans and technologies merge seamlessly. Echoing Marx, Winner argues that as humans change the shape of the material things around them, they also inevitably change themselves.[127] In this model of technology as an evolving and almost-organic phenomenon, humans are not the sole or perhaps even the primary creative force behind the process of technological change. Rather, creativity emerges from the many ways in which the novel things around us can be put together. As the Cambridge anthropologist Nicole Boivin concludes, the course of history is shaped not just by humans, or even just by our interactions with other living things, but also by our engagement with the very real forces exerted by nonliving matter. "If material is alive only because humans interact with it," Boivin observes, "it is also true that humans are alive only because they have material to engage with."[128]

If this evolutionary understanding of technology is correct, then it seems evident that the importation of a foreign technology into a society necessarily imports its associated possibilities for being combined with

---

[125] George Basalla, *The Evolution of Technology* (Cambridge, UK: Cambridge University Press, 1989).

[126] Arthur, *Nature of Technology*, 24, 88. A similar and even broader argument is offered in Kevin Kelly, *What Technology Wants* (New York: Penguin, 2011).

[127] Winner, "Technologies as Forms of Life," 110.

[128] Nicole Boivin, *Material Cultures, Material Minds: The Impact of Things on Human Thought, Society, and Evolution* (Cambridge, UK: Cambridge University Press, 2010), 136–8.

existing indigenous technologies and for sparking new ways of thinking and acting. In this light, the Japanese adoption, adaptation, and extension of foreign technologies makes for an intriguing test case. Even if they were pressured to do so by global events partly beyond their control, the Japanese deliberately and consciously chose to import new technologies to the archipelago with the very clear aim of creating a modern industrial system and society. However, once these technologies were introduced, they interacted within the earlier technological, material, and cultural environment in Japan. Like a bird-eating snake arriving on a previously snake-free Pacific island, these technologies altered the material ecosystem of the Japanese archipelago in complex ways that were both expected and novel. They did not alone *determine* that Japan would in some ways come to resemble the West, but nor were they completely malleable place-holders that could be freely shaped by Japanese society and culture. When Furukawa and dozens of other industrialists imported the latest Western machines, processes, and even laboratory equipment and books, they created a technological and environmental substrate through which the Japanese would henceforth think about and understand their material world, as well as the fertile new ground in which their own innovations would take seed and flourish.

CONCLUSION

Whatever their differences, and there were many, the people of Ashio and Anaconda were also first and foremost simply human beings struggling to comprehend and control the complex material forces their efforts had often unwittingly unleashed. Their fates were in significant part driven by powerful material things like copper, arsenic, cattle, and silkworms that shaped both who they were and who they might become. As I noted at the start of this chapter, historians like Brett Walker, Julia Adeney Thomas, Ian Miller, and others have identified what they term a great convergence to describe the growing similarities between Japan and the West that reached an apogee in the twentieth century. Focusing particularly on the many similarities between Japan and Great Britain, Thomas writes that it is "a matter of jaw-dropping wonder that environmental, economic, political, and intellectual developments in the string of islands on the far eastern edge of the Eurasian continent resembled so closely those of the islands and protuberances on the other Eurasian edge."[129] In contrast to

---

[129] Thomas, "Reclaiming Ground," 9.

the claims of Marxist, world systems, and modernization theorists, Thomas argues these striking similarities were not just the result of Japanese imitation of the West. Rather, they arose from a shared drive to break with the Malthusian limits of a "biological Old Regime" by exploiting "peripheral lands, new energy sources, new modes of inquiry, and new understandings of society beginning in the late eighteenth century." Most importantly, the Japanese and British both made a profound shift toward an increasingly anthropocentric and instrumentalist understanding of the material world of "plants, animals, soil, minerals, climate, and the human body."[130] Nature was no longer seen as a force that shaped humans, but was instead reduced to the status of a mere storehouse of pliable raw materials that humans freely shaped to their desires. In reality, though, this material sphere of things could not be so easily cordoned off from the sphere of human culture and society, as it constantly oozed out and between the abstract conceptual boxes within which humans attempted to contain, channel, and limit its formidable powers. In this light, Thomas argues that the key failing of modernism (including the more recent commitment of some humanists to extreme versions of social constructivism) has been its efforts to assert and enforce the supposed independence of conceptual categories like environment, power, and knowledge that are in reality inextricably entangled.[131]

What makes the Ashio and Anaconda stories so intriguing is that in both cases the Japanese and Americans did not just use a pliable material and technological environment, but were rather constantly created and recreated by the things they professed to control in ways that were often strikingly similar. If, as Thomas, Walker, and others suggest, the material world also suffuses human knowledge, power, and culture, then we should not be surprised that even societies as different as the United States and Japan would converge as they created, both by design and by accident, increasingly similar material environments. To be sure, both nations in some sense chose the powers enabled by copper mining, even in the face of its manifest destructiveness to earlier organic technologies based in cows and silkworms. Regardless, as the Japanese surrounded themselves with thousands of kilometers and kilograms of copper wire, as they pushed back the night with incandescent street lights, as they collapsed time and space with instantaneous electric power transmission, their material environment increasingly came to resemble that of the United States, Great Britain, and other Western nations. At the same

---

[130] Thomas, "Reclaiming Ground," 3.   [131] Thomas, "Reclaiming Ground," 2.

time, industrialists like Furukawa were literally importing discrete material pieces of these nations in the form of generators, pumps, and motors, further deepening the similarities of their technological infrastructures. Since modern sulfide-copper-mining and -processing technologies harmed Longhorn cattle and coniferous forests in precisely the same way it harmed silkworms and broadleaf forests, the environments at Ashio and Anaconda soon after came to resemble countless other industrial mining wastelands around the globe.

Given such striking technological and environmental similarities, it would be a surprise if Japan did *not* converge toward the United States and other Western countries. Indeed, we only find this convergence astonishing because of the persistent modernist faith that humans are above all determined by a disembodied culture that somehow floats like a ghostly spirit over the mere base realities of the material world. Ironically, one of the most striking similarities between Ashio and Anaconda lay in their growing allegiance to precisely this modern idea. Both the Japanese and the Americans had to struggle mightily to *stay* modern, pushing back against the roiling tides released by material complexities and creativities, trying repeatedly to wall off the human body and culture from an unruly world that constantly undermined these distinctions. Convergence emerged not just in shared practices but perhaps even more powerfully in shared attempts to control the resulting messy realities.

The champions of human autonomy will insist that choices always remained, and they are correct. But we should not let pride or an excessive faith in human agency keep us from recognizing that even these choices were increasingly created and defined by earlier decisions, whose consequences were now embedded into the material nature of the two nations. As copper mining destroyed earlier ways of life like sericulture and ranching, they also destroyed the creativity, intelligence, and other cultural phenomena that emerged from and with them. These fragile human-animal cultures, which could never again be created in precisely the same way, were consigned forever to the past. Instead, more and more humans would come to understand the world through copper wires, bright electric lights, and massive battleships, fewer and fewer through hay fields, mulberry trees, silkworms, and cows. Whether they were Japanese or American, they were henceforth different for it. Though they badly underestimated the power of nonhuman things, the nineteenth-century materialists Marx and Engels were correct in this: who we are as human beings emerges first and most profoundly from the diverse ways in which we coax our bodily existence out of the things around us. As we change the things we work and live with, we change ourselves.[132] Convinced that our souls reside in abstract minds or in transcendent heavens, the modern age was characterized by a systematic denial of the very material things that had brought it into existence. In the end, perhaps Tanaka Shōzō came closest to the truth: when our mountains, silkworms, and cows die, some essential part of who we are as human beings dies with them.

---

[132] Winner, "Technologies as Forms of Life," 110.

7

The Matter of Humans

Beyond the Anthropocene and toward a New Humanism

The biggest machine I have ever seen up close and in operation was in the Khouribga phosphate fields of central Morocco, about 120 kilometers southeast of Casablanca. There a Marion walking dragline was systematically stripping the topsoil and rocks from the earth to expose the thick seams of phosphate beneath. The Marion dragline is roughly the size of a ten-story building – except it is a building that can rotate on its own axis and even pick itself up and walk, albeit slowly. The entire dragline weighs 3,600 tons and can dig up 60 cubic yards of material in one bite, which is a cube about 4 meters (13 feet) long on each edge. It would have no difficulty lifting a full-size American SUV.

Mining companies are usually reluctant to let visitors get too close to these massive pieces of technology, which could easily crush, electrocute, or bury the unwary. But I was at the Khouribga mine at the invitation of a team of scholars from the Federal Institute of Technology (or more accurately, Eidgenössische Technische Hochschule) in Zurich who had organized a tour. Our guides gave us a bit more latitude than normal, though they took care to frequently remind overeager visitors like myself not to get too close. Still, to stand just 10 meters from the Marion dragline was to experience one of the ultimate expressions of modern human technological might. Each time the giant shovel pivots to dump its load of dirt and rocks, the electric throb of its motors swells, the gears and bearings squealing like a flock of demonic birds under the immense pressure of its own weight. This, I thought, must be what it would be like to be near a clanking AT-AT, the enormous walking battle machines in the popular *Star Wars* science fiction saga.

To witness a machine like the Marion dragline at work is to easily understand why many of us conclude that humans and their technologies are the antithesis of the natural world. We seem to have become almost godlike in our powers, able to move mountains and radically reshape the planet. The Khouribga mines are a prime example of what I have elsewhere termed "mass destruction" technologies, or what the historian Paul Josephson calls a "brute force technology."[1] Humans use such amped-up hydrocarbon technologies to gouge minerals from the earth, often with devastating ecological results. While the state-owned Office Chérifien des Phosphates that operates Khouribga and other Moroccan phosphate mines (technically, the mines are the personal property of King Mohammed VI) does make efforts to reclaim this fragile semi-arid land, much of the area is currently a stark, lifeless moonscape of dusty-white waste rock piles and wide phosphate canyons that spreads over many square kilometers. But as I have argued throughout this book, it would nonetheless be a dangerous mistake to think of even the Marion dragline and the Khouribga phosphate mines as somehow fundamentally unnatural. Rather, even these machine-ravaged mines need to be understood as evidence not just of human power and creativity but rather of the power, both creative and destructive, of the material world around us. Obviously humans were critical to the creation of the Marion dragline. But this should not keep us from recognizing that much of its power comes from nonhuman things like steel, copper, and hydrocarbon fuels like coal and oil. Nearly 90 percent of Morocco's energy is generated by burning oil and coal. When I visited the Khouribga dragline, I had to take care not to trip over the fat electrical power lines, conduits of copper atoms that literally connect the machine to the distant power plants that continually feed its Herculean electric motors.

But Khouribga can defy our tendency to see technology and large-scale mining as entirely unnatural endeavors in an even more surprising way. As the stylish website of the Office Chérifien des Phosphates suggests – under a prominently placed picture of a tender sprouting plant – the phosphate they mine is a "key element of sustaining life." This is not just corporate green washing. The phosphorous extracted from the Khouribga phosphate ore is a vital essential element for all plants and

[1] Timothy J. LeCain, *Mass Destruction: The Men and Giant Mines That Wired America and Scarred the Planet* (New Brunswick, NJ: Rutgers University Press, 2009); Paul Josephson, *Industrialized Nature: Brute Force Technology and the Transformation of the Natural World* (New York: Island, 2002).

animals on the planet. I discussed the importance of phosphorous for mammalian life in Chapter 3, where I explained how the chemically similar arsenic poisoned the cattle of the Deer Lodge Valley. But the element is just as vital for plant life. Historically, a lack of phosphorous (in the form of phosphate) has frequently been one of the key limiting factors in the growth of crops. Once repeated cycles of intensive farming had depleted the soil's reservoirs of phosphate, crop yields plummeted, leading to many historic famines. For centuries, humans searched for ways to revitalize soil with manure, guano, bone meal, and other organic fertilizers.[2] But in the mid-1800s the technology to make fertilizer from deposits of phosphate rock was discovered, providing a seemingly almost infinite supply of the essential element. Along with nitrogen, phosphorus is today a critical ingredient in the chemical fertilizers that sustain the extraordinarily high modern levels of food production for an extraordinarily large population of humans and even larger population of domesticated animals. Roughly, it takes about one ton of phosphate to produce 130 tons of grain, a starkly simple correlation that explains why the world mines about 170 million tons of phosphate rock every year.[3] Unlike nitrogen, which can be extracted from a nearly unlimited atmospheric supply, most of the phosphorous for fertilizers today is mined from phosphate deposits.[4] As with so many other natural resources, humans once assumed that these phosphate deposits were essentially inexhaustible, and even after more than a century of intensive mining, the global reserves still remain immense. However, the earth's stores of accessible phosphate are not infinite, and in recent years some analysts have begun to suggest that the supplies may begin to run short, reaching a "peak phosphorous" point sometime in the next century rather like that for "peak oil."[5] Other analysts emphasize that the remaining major deposits are concentrated in only a handful of nations around the world, like Morocco and China, raising concerns about supply-chain disruptions and the specter of sharp and potentially devastating price increases.

[2] An excellent account of the importance of guano is Gregory Cushman, *Guano and the Opening of the Pacific World: A Global Ecological History* (Cambridge, UK: Cambridge University Press, 2014).
[3] Fred Pearce, "Phosphate: A Critical Resource Misused and Now Running Low," *Environment* 360 (July 7, 2011).
[4] For a superb account of the importance of nitrogen and its technologies, see Hugh S. Gorman, *The Story of N: A Social History of the Nitrogen Cycle and the Challenge of Sustainability* (New Brunswick, NJ: Rutgers University Press, 2013).
[5] James Elser and Stuart White, "Peak Phosphorous," *Foreign Policy*, April 20, 2010.

Here is a number every person on the planet should know: Morocco has about three-quarters – yes, a stunning 75 percent – of the known reserves of phosphate on the planet. Today, the nation supplies about a third of the world demand. Much of it goes to densely populated nations like India that had once struggled with famines but, thanks in part to phosphate-based fertilizers, are now able to feed their burgeoning populations.[6] When I visited Khouribga in 2012, phosphate prices were high, and some predicted that Morocco was on the verge of becoming the "Saudi Arabia of phosphate." Prices have since declined by almost half, and the fear of immediate global shortages declined accordingly. However, over the long term the prospects for Morocco's phosphate deposits are good. Unlike oil and many other critical natural resources, there is no known substitute for phosphorous – the element is simply indispensable to feeding the current global population of just over seven billion, much less the additional two billion people projected to be added to that number by 2050. As one team of academic analysts wrote in 2010, the threat of future shortages can likely be managed with more sustainable agricultural practices and careful capture and recycling of existing phosphorous supplies, much of which now ends up running off into lakes and oceans or buried in landfills filled with food that wealthy nations carelessly throw away. Yet if the globe fails to take aggressive action to conserve these precious phosphorous supplies, they warn "humanity faces a Malthusian trap of widespread famine on a scale that we have not experienced."[7]

In recent years, a growing number of scientists and humanists have suggested that human activities have pushed the globe out of the previous geological epoch, the Holocene, and into a new state that some propose to call the Anthropocene. The most obvious evidence for this shift is the human role in altering the global carbon cycle and the resulting destabilizing effects of planetary climate change. But another important indication of the growing human effects on the great planetary cycles can be measured in the rapid increase in phosphorous flows in the post–World War II period.[8]

---

[6] Pearce, "Phosphate." Although, as Mike Davis explains, the nineteenth-century famines in India and elsewhere were primarily the result of drought and brutal imperialist policies, not a lack of fertilizers. See Mike Davis, *Late Victorian Holocausts: El Niño Famines and the Making of the Third World* (London: Verso, 2001).

[7] Elser and White, "Peak Phosphorous."

[8] Will Steffen, Jacques Grinevald, Paul Crutzen, and John McNeill, "The Anthropocene: Conceptual and Historical Perspectives," *Philosophical Transactions of the Royal Society* 369 (2011): 842–867, here 854.

During this period, which some now aptly term the "great acceleration,"[9] the flows of phosphorous and nitrogen have shot up, radically altering one of the basic global biogeochemical cycles and leading to widespread eutrophication of lakes, streams, and oceans. In 2009, an international team of researchers under the leadership of the Swedish scientist Johan Rockström developed the concept of "planetary boundaries:" a set of nine measurable limits which, if exceeded, threatened to further push the planet out of the relatively stable Holocene epoch and into an unpredictable and potentially disastrous new state. In a 2015 update, the researchers noted that of these nine planetary boundaries, four of them had already been exceeded, including those set for the biogeochemical cycles of both phosphorous and nitrogen.[10] The widespread use and overuse of fertilizers has caused increases of phosphorous and nitrogen on the order of 200 to 300 percent over their Holocene levels, whereas the carbon implicated in global warming has increased by about 10 to 20 percent. As one of the lead scientists studying these effects puts it: "We've changed nitrogen and phosphorous cycles vastly more than any other element."[11]

When I recall the experience of standing by that Marion dragline as it gouged shovel after massive shovel full of soil from the Moroccan earth, it is easy to understand why some propose to name the modern era the Anthropocene – the epoch of humans. All the more so when I consider the millions of tons of phosphorous, from Morocco and elsewhere, that humans spread around the planet every year in their efforts to maintain a modern abundance of food that exceeds even the wildest cornucopian dreams of any earlier age.[12] Everywhere I look the evidence of human power and dominance seems inescapable, from the vast megacities of Tokyo and Mumbai, to the fertilizer-fueled algal blooms in the American Great Lakes, to the steady drumbeat of climatic data charting yet another record-high temperature caused by elevated atmospheric levels of carbon. Surely if ever the time were right to proclaim that the planet had entered a new Age of Humans, this would seem to be it. Yet for

---

[9] J. R. McNeill and Peter Engelke, *The Great Acceleration: An Environmental History of the Anthropocene Since 1945* (Cambridge, MA: Harvard University Press, 2016).

[10] Will Steffen et al., "Planetary Boundaries: Guiding Human Development on a Changing Planet," *Science* 347 (2015): 736–46.

[11] Adam Hinterthuer, "Humanity Has Exceeded 4 of 9 'Planetary Boundaries,' according to Researchers," *University of Wisconsin-Madison News*, January 15, 2015.

[12] On the concept of modern cornucopianism, see Fredrik Albritton Johnson, "The Origins of Cornucopianism: A Preliminary Genealogy," *Critical Historical Studies* 1 (Spring 2014): 151–68.

all the reasons I have discussed in the previous chapters of this book, I fear it would be a deeply regrettable error to name the modern era after human beings. If, as I have argued and tried to empirically demonstrate, human power is best understood as an extension of the power of a dynamic and creative material world; and if among the greatest errors we humans have made is to see ourselves as separate from nature; and if we have instead long deluded ourselves into believing that this materially rooted power was a product solely of our own ingenious efforts; then you will, I hope, forgive me if I just say no to naming this new global era after humans. In rejecting the term "Anthropocene," I in no way mean to question the reality of the global changes that inspired it, whether those caused by excessive carbon levels, phosphorous, or any of the multitude of other global cycles that have already or may soon exceed the safe Holocene boundaries. Rather, just as the Ashio pollution taught Tanaka Shōzō to conceive a new understanding of the place of humans in nature, I wish to argue that our modern epoch of global changes is already teaching us to think in new ways – perhaps even to at last abandon our long-standing anthropocentrism and instead develop a very different understanding of what it means to be a modestly intelligent species on a planet that is far more powerful, creative, and dangerous than we had previously understood or could have even imagined.

THE CASE FOR THE CARBOCENE

Whether you knew the source or not, you have almost certainly seen the now-iconic image of Earth taken by the crew of Apollo 17 in 1972. One of the few photographs to show the fully illuminated disk of the planet, it eventually came to be known as the *Blue Marble* for its swirls of white clouds floating above the vast blue of the oceans. Pinned up on countless dorm room walls in the 1970s, the photo became an enduring emblem of the emerging environmental movement. The image seemed to capture both the power and the fragility of the planet, a tiny blue-green island of life in the immense blackness of space. Though it was made possible by one of the greatest technological achievements of the day, the image itself offered little obvious evidence of the human presence on the planet. To the contrary, it seemed to suggest just how dependent humans were on "spaceship Earth."

Fast forward to our own era, however, and a surprising converse image has recently emerged: a composite of satellite photos showing Earth at night that some, perhaps ironically, call the *Black Marble*. As the environmental historian Daniel Zizzamia suggests, if the earlier *Blue Marble* conveyed the stark reality of the human dependence on the earth, the vast webs of bright electric lights captured in the *Black Marble* seem to offer a contrary message: that humans have all but conquered the planet, eliminating even the night itself, at least in the Global North.[13] Indeed, the very contrast between the bright lights of Europe and the still-remaining tracts of darkness in Africa seem to further highlight the accomplishments of the modern high-tech human societies. In this sense, if the *Blue Marble* was a symbol of the dawning era of ecological awareness in the seventies, today we might well be tempted to read the *Black Marble* as a symbol of the dawning era of the Anthropocene, the supposed Age of Humans when our machinations have grown so powerful that we have fundamentally changed the very nature of the planet.

This is an understandable conclusion. Yet there is a deeper and in some ways even more troubling way to understand the *Black Marble*. To be sure, the network of lights seems to brightly proclaim the growing magnitude of human power and dominance. But before we rush to either celebrate or bemoan this, we should consider that these lights are evidence not just of the power of humans but of the power of hydrocarbon fuel sources like coal and oil that have shaped the course of history over the past three centuries. Despite more recent progress in shifting toward new energy sources, lights around the globe are still kept on by burning coal and other hydrocarbons. As Zizzamia points out, in the giant Bakken oil fields of the north-central plains of the United States, even some part of the lights there are a direct product of thousands of intensely bright oil-well flares that burn escaping methane gases. The *Black Marble*, in other words, is a creation of black fuels. Given this, might the *Black Marble* be an apt symbol not of the "Anthropocene" but rather of a much less anthropocentric understanding of the world and its material history, what we might instead term the "Carbocene" – the Age of Coal and Oil?

Prior to the recent developments in neo-materialist theories discussed in this book, such a retreat from anthropocentrism in favor of granting a more central role to nonhuman things would have found few supporters, at least in academic circles. As I argued in Chapter 2, the final decades of the twentieth century were dominated by a postmodern cultural turn that emphasized the power of various human social groups to construct their

---

[13] Daniel Zizzamia, "Making the West Malleable: Coal, Geohistory, and Western Expansion, 1800–1920" (PhD diss., Montana State University, 2015).

world. Rather than succumb to the seemingly fatalistic belief that history is often shaped by powerful material forces beyond our control, postmodernism countered that humans choose their own destinies through their social, cultural, economic, and political decisions. This was an optimistic and empowering vision, and it may have had the good effect of encouraging people to take a greater role in political and policy matters. However, as I have argued throughout this book, a danger of this postmodern optimism was its tendency to underestimate both the creative and destructive powers of the material world and the deep human entanglements within these. Humans certainly construct their world, yet they do so as embodied material creatures who have already been deeply shaped by the very world they claim to construct. Once they threw their lot in with things like copper and coal, it would be no easy matter to wean themselves from the ways of thinking, acting, and feeling that these things helped to generate. Oily black hydrocarbons fueled human culture every bit as much as they fueled steam engines and power plants. If the Anthropocene emphasizes the human domination of the earth, the Carbocene would emphasize the earth's domination of us.

The term "Anthropocene" is derived from the Greek roots *anthropo-*, for "human," and *–cene*, for "recent" or "new." This "recent human" name is meant to suggest that anthropogenic changes to the planet have become so pronounced as to constitute a new geological epoch. Since first catching on in 2000, the Anthropocene has increasingly been embraced by humanistic, scientific, and popular audiences, offering a broadly useful intellectual space in which to discuss the many changes and challenges associated with global climate change, massive species extinction, and other contemporary environmental problems. Reflecting the growing acceptance of the term, in 2014 the Deutsches Museum in Munich, Germany, among the world's greatest museums of science and technology, opened a major new exhibit titled *Welcome to the Anthropocene: The Earth in Our Hands*. At least three scientific journals now use the word in their title, and the Amsterdam-based academic publisher Elsevier recently launched a new interdisciplinary humanistic journal called *Anthropocene*, dedicated to "addressing the nature, scale, and extent of the influence that people have on Earth."[14]

Clearly, a sizable and growing number of scientists, environmentalists, humanists, and others have found the Anthropocene name and concept to

---

[14] Ian Sample, "Anthropocene: Is This the New Epoch of Humans?" *The Guardian*, October 16, 2014.

be useful. This is understandable, as the immense environmental, social, and political changes caused by global climate change and other environmental shifts cry out for some sort of unifying term and concept. Nonetheless, I fear that the "Anthropocene" is a poor choice for that term and may actually be hindering human progress in combating climate change and other global environmental threats. While perhaps not the intent of its creators and advocates, the term itself is obviously anthropocentric. Indeed, part of its appeal is that it forcefully counters the contemporary climate-change deniers who misleadingly argue that global warming – if they acknowledge that it exists at all – is a result not of human actions but rather of "natural" processes. Yet in suggesting that humans alone were indeed powerful enough to cause such global ecological shifts, the Anthropocene concept also tends to encourage the modernist faith in the human ability to fix the resulting problems. Almost as soon as the term was coined, advocates of a so-called Good Anthropocene began to emerge, suggesting that humans will be able to create painless technological fixes through massive geoengineering projects.[15] Alarmed by the breathtaking hubris inherent in such proposals, critics have countered that these optimistic plans to reengineer the planet are a perverse misreading of the Anthropocene idea. While this is clearly true at some level, the eco-pragmatist arguments for a Good Anthropocene can also be understood as a logical extension of the essential anthropocentrism of the concept itself. As soon as we begin talking about "man as a geological agent" who is taking us into a new Age of Humans, we begin to overestimate human power and agency, tending toward a celebratory stance even when the intent is to be critical. Superman, one might observe, can use his superpowers for good or evil, but he is still super either way.

It is at this point where neo-materialist thinking sharply parts ways with the Anthropocene. As the human geographer Andrea Nightingale notes, we would do better to begin by understanding that "humans are nowhere near understanding the complexity of physical processes" and thus "we *cannot* make nature."[16] Rather than emphasizing human power and accomplishments, a neo-materialist view suggests that we are neither particularly powerful nor especially intelligent and creative – at least not

---

[15] Clive Hamilton, *Earth Masters: The Dawn of the Age of Climate Engineering* (New Haven, CT: Yale University Press, 2013).

[16] Andrea Nightingale, "Can Social Theory Adequately Address Nature-Society Issues?" *Institute of Geography Online Paper Series: GEO-027*, online paper archived by the Institute of Geography, School of Geosciences, University of Edinburgh, 2006.

on our own. As I have tried to explain in the previous chapters, a neo-materialist approach suggests that we humans derive much of what we like to think of as *our* power, intelligence, and creativity from material things like cattle, silkworms, and copper. Because we now realize that humans are much more deeply embedded in their environments than previously recognized, in many ways the countless material things and processes that surround and permeate us should be understood as constituting who we are. We don't just *use* organisms and things. Rather, like the microbiomes in our guts, these and countless other material fellow travelers are the very things that *make* us.

Humans have obviously become quite powerful – powerful enough to populate nearly every habitable niche on the planet and alter its fundamental biogeochemical cycles. But rather than crediting humans alone, neo-materialism suggests that they accomplished these things only at the price of throwing their lot in with a lot of other powerful things, like coal and oil, whose potentials they only vaguely understood and certainly did not really control. What did Conrad Kohrs know about the millennia-long coevolutionary history that made it possible for his cowboys and cows to cooperate? What did the silkworm breeders of Japan know about the ability of their small partners to synthesize useful new chains of silk proteins? What did the Americans and Japanese know about the ways in which copper wires could radically alter their sense of space and time? Yet once these partnerships were made, these and countless other material things began to shape humans and their cultures in all sorts of unexpected ways, many of them not necessarily for the better. In sum, neo-materialist theory pushes us to realize that the earth is not in human hands so much as humans are in the earth's hands – and that these hands are not necessarily benevolent.

The term "Anthropocene" seems to have first been coined in the 1980s by the ecologist Eugene Stoermer, who used it informally for many years. But the neologism only began to gain wide currency after the Nobel Prize–winning chemist and climate scientist Paul Crutzen began using it in 2000. Tellingly, Crutzen himself admits that he gave no great thought to the name. During a scientific meeting in Mexico, he grew increasingly frustrated by his colleagues' use of the accepted geological term for the modern age – the "Holocene," which began about 12,000 years ago – when discussing the anthropogenic changes to the planet's global cycles over the past few centuries. Trying to express how deeply humans were altering and damaging the planet, Crutzen seized on the term "Anthropocene," perhaps unconsciously recalling Stoermer's earlier use of the word, or adding a "po" to a similar neologism, the "Anthrocene," previously suggested by the science writer Andrew Revkin.[17] Regardless, while Crutzen's recognition of the planetary-scale changes he sought to give some label to was certainly well thought out in a scientific sense, it seems that his choice of a term for capturing this was more spontaneous than considered. He was simply trying to find an appropriate word to express the immense anthropogenic changes in global biogeochemical cycles of the past two hundred years. Precisely what neologism was used might well have seemed relatively trivial. What mattered was the pressing need to recognize that human activity was taking the planet out of the relatively stable climactic period of the Holocene and into a more volatile new geological epoch.

Yet words and names do matter, of course, especially when they move beyond a small circle of early adopters. Crutzen's somewhat impulsive choice of the term "Anthropocene" may have been less than ideal, and it has been criticized from a variety of different angles. If the starting point of the Anthropocene is identified as the advent of industrialization in Great Britain around 1800, as Crutzen and others suggest, some object that it is premature to designate a new geological epoch based on an event that by the geological scale of deep time happened mere nanoseconds ago. Likewise, while the cumulative atmospheric, terrestrial, and oceanic effects of human activity are today readily evident, it can be difficult to find a marker in the physical geological record of rock strata (the traditional scientific standard) that is adequately permanent and fine grained to identify a clear point of transition from the Holocene to an Anthropocene over such a brief period.[18] Others argue that measurable anthropogenic effects on the planet began well before the industrial era, perhaps as early as the advent of agriculture in the Neolithic era, the so-called Early Anthropocene thesis. Yet these events roughly coincide with the start of the already-accepted geological term for the modern age, the Holocene (meaning "entirely recent") epoch, which began about 12,000 years ago.[19]

---

[17] Steffen et al., 'The Anthropocene," 843.

[18] Jan Zalasiewicz et al., "Are We Now Living in the Anthropocene?" *GSA Today* 18 (2008), 5.

[19] The 'Early Anthropocene' thesis is most closely associated with the work of the University of Virginia paleoclimatologist William Ruddiman. See William F. Ruddiman, "The Anthropogenic Greenhouse Era Began Thousands of Years Ago," *Climatic Change* 61 (2003): 261–92.

Ultimately, it will fall to the International Commission on Stratigraphy (ICS) (a subcommittee of the International Union of Geological Sciences) to parse these technical debates. In August of 2016 a working group of international scholars that had been studying the topic for seven years announced that they had voted to recommend that the ICS formally recognize the Anthropocene as a geological epoch. Departing from Crutzen's earlier suggestion that it began with the British Industrial Revolution, the working group instead recommended that the Anthropocene began with the postwar boom of the late 1940s and early 1950s, what some now also term the "Great Acceleration." This shift to a later date was made at least in part for technical reasons: the postwar proliferation of nuclear isotopes, plastics, elemental aluminum, and fly ash from high-temperature combustion of coal and oil all might provide a clearer marker in the geological record – a so-called golden spike – than did the more gradual increase in coal burning that began with the Industrial Revolution. Likewise, as this list of markers suggests, the definition of what constitutes the Anthropocene has expanded far beyond Crutzen's earlier focus on climate change and atmospheric levels of carbon dioxide to include many other types of anthropogenic change. Regardless, the proposal to formally recognize a postwar Anthropocene remains controversial, and whether it will ultimately convince enough of the voting members of the ICS to win acceptance remains to be seen.[20] The decision may well turn not just on whether the proposed Anthropocene meets the stratigraphic standards for designating a geological epoch but also on whether the designation of an Anthropocene epoch might provide a tool for more effectively grappling with the growing crisis of climate change and other global environmental problems. Indeed, some ICS scientists object to the term for this very reason, seeing it more as a political than scientific idea.[21]

From a historical and broadly humanistic perspective, however, the Anthropocene name and concept raises other issues. As the Australian ethicist Clive Hamilton notes, "almost as soon as the idea of the Anthropocene took hold, people began revising its meaning and distorting its implications."[22] Hamilton notes that the so-called ecomodernists or eco-pragmatists, such as Michael Shellenberger and Ted Nordhaus of the

---

[20] Paul Voosen, "Anthropocene Pinned to Postwar Period," *Science* 353 (2016): 852–3.
[21] Voosen, "Anthropocene," 852.
[22] Clive Hamilton, 'The New Environmentalism Will Lead Us to Disaster,' *Scientific American Online* (June 19, 2014).

"neogreen" Breakthrough Institute, have begun to argue that humans can engineer a Good Anthropocene. Some advocates of this optimistic view – what Hamilton aptly calls the Promethean position – suggest that humans can manage the effects of global warming through immense and entirely unprecedented geoengineering projects. For example, it might be feasible to spray huge volumes of sulfate aerosol particles into the upper atmosphere, thus reflecting more of the sun's heat back into space. Another plan suggests that humans could remove more carbon dioxide and other global warming gases from the atmosphere by fertilizing the world's oceans to encourage the growth of carbon-absorbing plants.[23] Buoyed by such technical promises, one advocate of the Promethean approach concludes, "We must not see the Anthropocene as a crisis, but as the beginning of a new geological epoch ripe with human-directed opportunity."[24]

Hamilton observes that the promise of such a Good Anthropocene has broad appeal, as it "absolves us all of the need to change our ways." Yet he warns that by promising a painless technological fix, the eco-pragmatist arguments may help to delay or derail more aggressive international actions to cut the production of global warming gases. Further, the longer the world delays, the more likely it will be that humans will ultimately be left with no choice but to engage in such risky geoengineering projects, with potentially disastrous results. "We find ourselves in a situation where geoengineering is being proposed," Hamilton observes, "because of our penchant for deceiving ourselves and inflating our virtues."[25]

In all this, Hamilton's analysis seems apt. However, he is less convincing when he argues that the idea of the Good Anthropocene and its related faith in geoengineering are solely the products of a perverse misreading of the original Anthropocene concept. To be sure, Crutzen and many other advocates of the concept clearly view the arrival of the Anthropocene as a dangerous existential threat to humans and the planet at large, not as an opportunity. They no doubt hope that formal designation of the Anthropocene epoch, or even just the term's informal use, will encourage the world's nations to make serious reductions in carbon emissions – not put their hopes in risky geoengineering projects. But at a deeper level, the rapid emergence of these optimistic scenarios was in

---

[23] Hamilton, *Earthmasters*, 57–71, 25–35.

[24] Quoted in Hamilton, *Earthmasters*, 203. The original is Erle Ellis, "The Planet of No Return," *Breakthrough Journal* 2 (Fall 2011) 39–44.

[25] Hamilton, *Earthmasters*, 182.

many ways an entirely logical outgrowth of the Anthropocene term and concept. At base, both optimistic and pessimistic views of the Anthropocene often share the conventional modernist belief that powerful humans and their cultures are distinct from the natural material world. Crutzen and others may have wanted a term that would put the onus of responsibility on human beings, no doubt hoping to push back against the foolish climate-change deniers, or those who admit the reality of climate change but doubt that humans are the cause. Yet in trying to ward off one threat, the advocates of the Anthropocene may have unintentionally given support to another and perhaps more insidious challenge. As the overwhelming evidence of anthropogenic global climate change continues to accumulate, the unsubstantiated arguments made by the overt climate-change deniers may well fade into obscurity. Instead, the greater danger may increasingly come from the supposed eco-pragmatists who accept the reality of these global changes, but continue to largely embrace the modernist faith in a clear separation between human culture and nature. Indeed, arguments made by both the optimistic and pessimistic camps often depend on the idea that it is precisely this separation that gives humans their extraordinary power over the natural world. The two groups diverge only in the degree to which they believe humans can be trusted to use their power to effectively reengineer the planet's climate.

By proposing to name the planet's new geological epoch solely after humans, the advocates of the Anthropocene thus trap themselves in a dilemma. If humans are truly powerful enough to justify naming an entirely new geological period for them, then it is difficult to argue against the proposition that they might, at least in theory, be capable of using that same power to engineer a Good Anthropocene. Perhaps recognizing this contradiction, some advocates of the Anthropocene have tried to minimize the implicit hubris of the term. In a 2011 article Paul Crutzen and his coauthor, the environmental journalist Christian Schwägerl, freely embrace the idea that humans have become uniquely powerful, noting that they are "taking control of Nature's realm, from climate to DNA." But having implied that such human power justifies the term "Anthropocene," they then insist that it should not be understood as supporting a Promethean view of the human species. "Rather than representing yet another sign of human hubris," they argue, the Anthropocene "would stress the enormity of humanity's responsibility as stewards of the Earth" and "highlight the immense power of our intellect and our creativity, and the opportunities they offer for shaping the future." The authors' desire to limit human self-aggrandizement seems sincere here. Yet it is difficult to understand how highlighting "the immense power" of the human intellect and creativity is likely to be taken as anything *but* "another sign of human hubris." Elsewhere in the article, Crutzen and Schwägerl even begin to sound rather like eco-pragmatists themselves. "The awareness of living in the Age of Men," they argue, "could inject some desperately needed eco-optimism into our societies." Likewise, the authors give an odd twist to the modernist belief that humans have left the natural world, exhorting the reader: "Remember, in this new era, nature is us."[26] Humans, they seem to suggest, were unnatural in the past, or at most mere manipulators of their environments. Now, however, human technological abilities are so vast that they have *become* nature itself. Tellingly, the authors make no attempt to explain where these vast human powers came from in the first place.

A seemingly more radical solution to the dilemma of the Anthropocene is offered by Mike Ellis, a member of the ICS Working Group and the head of climate-change studies at the British Geological Survey. Ellis insists that the case for the Anthropocene term is simple: the "principal process of change on the planet is us, so the name of our epoch should reflect that." But perhaps in part to counter the human power and hubris implied by this, Ellis goes a step further to insist that, whatever their power, humans remain entirely a product of nature. The Anthropocene, he argues, "acknowledges that humans and the human process is as much a natural process as any other natural process that we are used to thinking about, such as volcanoes and earthquakes." Even more radically, Ellis strikes at the heart of modernist thinking by insisting that human cultures too are natural: "The things we do and the things we make; the rules and legislation we come up with to control the way we live, they are a natural process and it emerges out of this thing called the Earth."[27] This argument perhaps comes closest to that suggested by the neo-materialist ideas in this book. However, absent a compelling explanation of exactly how the earth plays a role in creating human cultures and power, Ellis's assertion seems to be a bit of whistling in the dark. Perhaps he recognizes that the Anthropocene runs the risk of exaggerating human power over nature, yet he is unsure how to fix the problem, other than by simply declaring everything humans do to be natural. (See my discussion of the problems with this approach in Chapter 1.) Further, if Ellis is indeed correct that the

---

[26] Paul J. Crutzen and Christian Schwägerl, "Toward a New Global Ethos," *Environment* 360 (January 24, 2011).
[27] Quoted in Sample, "Anthropocene."

earth helped to create human culture and power – the very things that made them the "principal process of change on the planet" – then it obviously begs the question of why the resulting geological epoch should be named for humans alone.

At their essence, these debates and contradictions reflect the faltering state of the modernist project, with its insistence that human power derives from abstract intellectual and cultural abilities that have lifted the species out of the natural material world to the position of managing and controlling it. Whether they view this unique human position as predominantly destructive or constructive, most advocates of the Anthropocene accept it as true, while the few who question it lack the tools to do so effectively. This is not surprising. Particularly in the Western-influenced civilizations whose technologies and practices have generated many of the global changes that the Anthropocene concept seeks to recognize, humans have long understood themselves as the divinely dominant species whose mission it was to subjugate and harness the earth. As I discussed at length in Chapter 2, the modern Western drive to master the material world and create a New Eden can be seen as a secularized version of the earlier Christian belief that humans were destined to regain the god-like powers they lost after they were banished from the original Eden. Perhaps this Anthropocene, this "New Human Age," has not yet turned out quite as well as hoped. But for the transcendentally inclined, this may be just a rough spot on the millenarian road to New Eden. Surely humans with their nearly miraculous intelligence and creativity will rise above it all to triumph in the end? As the American writer Stewart Brand, an unapologetic advocate of geoengineering, puts it: "We are as Gods and HAVE to get good at it."[28]

Simply to avoid even the appearance of giving aid and support to such an arrogant understanding of the human place on the planet would arguably be reason enough alone to reject a term like the "Anthropocene," although not the physical phenomena it seeks to describe. Yet this historic moment also offers a rare opportunity to embrace an understanding of, and a term for, the modern age that would support, rather than undermine, a more humble vision of the human place on the planet. By decentering the human to instead emphasize the many ways in which the material world both creates and entraps

[28] Steward Brand, *Whole Earth Discipline: Why Dense Cities, Nuclear Power, Transgenic Crops, Restored Wildlands, and Geoengineering Are Necessary* (New York: Penguin, 2010), quote on p. 1, emphasis in original.

humans, neo-materialist theory offers a possible alternative, one in which the present predicament is understood as resulting in part from the partnerships humans formed with other powerful material things whose potentialities often pushed them in directions they neither envisioned nor intended.

As the first hydrocarbon fuel to see intensive human use, coal offers a compelling example of such a material partner. Humans probably began to burn surface deposits of coal as a convenient source of heat not long after they mastered fire. But the earliest intensive use of coal came during the Song dynasty (960–1279) when the Chinese began to burn it to smelt iron, a process in which the coal contributes both the necessary heat and the carbon that helps to strengthen the resulting metal. On the other side of the Eurasian landmass, by the seventeenth century, inhabitants of the city of London were increasingly using coal as a heat source. The region had sizable and easily accessible deposits of coal that had a higher energy-to-weight density than the wood that was also becoming increasingly scarce. This thoroughgoing familiarity with burning coal for heat primed the British to see coal as the logical choice for fueling the new heat or steam engines developed in the early 1700s in order to power pumps that dewatered tin, copper, and of course, coal mines. When Thomas Newcomen built the first successful engine in 1712 to dewater the Conygree Coalworks just west of Birmingham, England, humans were able to transform the energy of coal into mechanical power that could do many types of useful work. Prior to this, they had primarily relied on wind and water, energy sources that were ultimately powered by the solar energy that heated the atmosphere and drove hydrological and atmospheric dynamics. Given the technologies of the time, water and wind power were inherently limited and tied to specific regions, presenting a bottleneck to human growth and power. However, once Newcomen and others developed a way to burn coal to create mechanical power, humans bypassed these limits because they could tap the solar energy of millions of years of plant growth that had been compressed into coal to do much more than just keep them warm. The resulting industrial societies were founded on intensive use of stored solar energy in fossilized biomass, increasing their energy consumption by three to four times that of earlier agrarian societies. Fundamentally, the growth of human numbers and inventiveness after this industrial revolution was fueled by coal.[29]

[29] Steffen et al., "Anthropocene," 846–8; Alfred Crosby, *Children of the Sun: A History of Humanity's Unappeasable Appetite for Energy* (New York: Norton, 2007).

In understanding the human affair with coal, the archaeological theorist Ian Hodder's concept of an entangling process of material domestication is useful. Humans like to believe that they choose to use essentially passive raw materials like coal for their own purposes, and in a limited sense this is true. Obviously coal deposits did not force humans to extract and burn them any more than wild wheat plants forced humans to select those with the biggest grain heads and carry them back to their settlements, thus sparking the development of agriculture. But to therefore conclude that humans alone were responsible for the course of events that resulted from burning coal or domesticating wheat is equally nonsensical, and can only be sustained by placing humans and their cultures firmly outside of the material realm. As Hodder suggests, humans initially "domesticated" material things like coal to meet very limited and immediate needs. Yet once they began to recognize the tremendous ability coal had to increase their own power, they became increasingly entangled in sustaining and maintaining the resulting relationship. Indeed, as I discussed in Chapter 3, Timothy Mitchell and others suggest that the material nature of coal even helped to create phenomena like democratic states – historic events that humans subsequently insisted were solely the product of their own abstract and immaterial cultures. Coal shaped the humans who used it far more than humans shaped coal for the simple reason that humans are so malleable. Once the partnership with coal was begun, those who domesticated it increasingly became "coal people," just as others would become cattle, silkworm, and copper people.

Recently some scholars have critiqued the Anthropocene concept from more of a social-justice or Marxist perspective, taking issue not with its anthropocentrism but rather with the term's tendency to place the blame on *all* human beings rather than the small minority who engineered and benefited from an exploitive system of global capitalism. Rather than blame the entirety of past and present humanity, they suggest a more apt term for the modern epoch might be the "Capitalocene."[30] Again, there is some logic to this – the immense material powers of coal and oil have often been monopolized by the minority, while billions who have received little benefit, or worse, have been saddled with much of the pollution, ecological destruction, and other negative consequences of maintaining the minority's luxurious and materially intensive ways of life. Yet in pointing the finger of blame primarily at a human-made socioeconomic system, some of these social-justice critics seem to suggest that there is *no* genuine

---

[30] Jason W. Moore, ed., *Anthropocene or Capitalocene? Nature, History, and the Crisis of Capitalism* (Oakland, CA: PM Press, 2016.)

material reason for why the world has become so dependent on hydro-carbons, as if modernity might just as easily have been built on a foundation of wood, wind, and water. The Swedish historian Andreas Malm, for example, suggests that British industrialists adopted coal not because it offered an immense reserve of easily extracted material power but because it permitted capitalists to more tightly control and exploit their workers. Malm makes a convincing case that the drive to extract more labor from workers helped propel the shift to coal, yet in the process he seems overly intent on dismissing the energetic potential of the coal itself. To Malm, there is little value in asking how the immense amounts of stored solar energy in coal provided the power necessary to fuel the explosion of productivity and material wealth of the Industrial Revolution.[31] To the contrary, he argues that to consider humans as a biological species or coal as a historical force has the effect of "dehistor-icizing, universalizing, eternalizing, and naturalizing a mode of produc-tion specific to a certain time and place," errors which he considers to be nothing more than strategies "of ideological legitimation."[32] In a manner oddly akin to that of the postmodernists, Malm suggests that social relations must explain everything. Such arguments thus leave little room to explore how those social relations *themselves* emerged from the embo-died human engagement with a dynamic and powerful material world. As Ian Hodder puts it, whatever the human social system at work, power itself is best understood as "the differential flow of matter, energy and information through entanglements."[33] The labor of human workers contributed a large part of the surplus value (and thus profitability) of manufactured products like textiles, yet so did the energy stored in the coal that fueled the textile factories. Capitalism may not be the wisest or fairest social arrangement for allocating the differential flows of power that benefit some and harm others, yet we are unlikely to arrive at a more just and equitable system unless we begin by taking the material and energetic foundations of human power and culture seriously.[34]

[31] Andreas Malm, *Fossil Capital: The Rise of Steam Power and the Roots of Global Warming* (New York: Verso, 2016).

[32] Andreas Malm, "The Anthropocene Myth: Blaming All of Humanity for Climate Change Lets Capitalism Off the Hook," *Jacobin* (March 30, 2015).

[33] Ian Hodder, *Entangled: An Archaeology of the Relationship between Humans and Things* (Oxford, UK: Wiley-Blackwell, 2012): 214.

[34] An insightful recent effort to incorporate a more ecologically grounded materialism with Marxist theory is Jason Moore, *Capitalism in the Web of Life: Ecology and the Accumulation of Capital* (London: Verso, 2015).

The Industrial Revolution was far from being solely a human creation in other ways as well. As already mentioned in Chapter 3, Edmund Russell points out that a critical component in this first industrial "take off" was the recent British access to the long-staple cotton from a plant that had coevolved with the native peoples of the New World for many centuries.[35] Further, there are good reasons to doubt that humans, whether capitalists or workers, really controlled the development of crucial industrial technologies in any conscious sense. In building his early "fire engines" to dewater coal mines, Newcomen had no idea that improved versions of his crude clanking machines would become the prime mover of industrialization, much less that they would be used by British industrialists to exploit their workers in factories. Technological developments are, as I discussed in the chapter on copper, often self-generated, autocatalytic, and even autopoietic, emerging from the possibilities inherent in the material matrix available at any particular historical moment. This is not to excuse the greed or cruelty of the human actors, but rather to also recognize that they acted within and were shaped by a material environment or niche that they did not fully understand or control.

In sum, a neo-materialist perspective pushes us to recognize that critical historical events like the British Industrial Revolution were the product not only of humans and their cultural and social relations but also of the material things they partnered with, like coal and cotton. The same might well be said for the postwar proliferation of other materials like plutonium, plastics, and elemental aluminum. Yet if other nonhuman material things played such an important role in creating an era of deep changes to our global environment, why would we wish to name the resulting epoch solely after ourselves? At least some of the advocates of the Anthropocene surely hope that the idea is useful in educating the public and inspiring more support for action on critical issues like global climate change. I doubt neither the sincerity of their efforts nor the urgency of achieving their goal. However, it seems fair to ask whether the name and concept of the Anthropocene is really an effective means of achieving these ends. For all the reasons suggested here, I suspect it is not. The concept does have the good effect of drawing our attention to the scale and rapidity of recent global changes. However, intentionally or not, it also tends to reinforce the very same set of modernist ideas that caused many of these problems in the first place: that humans and their cultures are distinct from their

---

[35] Edmund Russell, *Evolutionary History: Uniting History and Biology to Understand Life on Earth* (Cambridge, UK: Cambridge University Press, 2011).

material environment; that material things are essentially passive "natural resources" that humans bend, with more or less success, to their own will; and that humans largely chart their own course through history, unmoored from the "natural" world that encompasses everything but for themselves. A neo-materialist understanding suggests a different and perhaps in some ways older human understanding of the material environment, one in which nature is recognized as a powerful and at times even dangerous force for making humans. Contrary to our naïve and often religiously rooted beliefs, the earth may now be in the process of revealing itself to be deeply inhospitable to intelligent hominid life. Perhaps our planet is filled with deadly things that any species with a modest allotment of intelligence and an opposable thumb can all too easily use to harm and even destroy themselves. If this age has anything of value to teach us, it may well be that humans are not in control, that we do not create our world in any conscious sense but are swept along by powerful material things that we only dully comprehend. Humans may appear to be the dominant species of the moment, yet it is because the planet we pretend to dominate has made us so. As Naomi Klein rightly observes, humans evince a dangerous delusion when they believe that the earth is like a fragile pet that all-powerful humans must save. Rather, Klein argues the opposite is true: "It is we humans who are fragile and vulnerable and the earth that is hearty and powerful, and holds us in its hands. In pragmatic terms, our challenge is less to save the earth from ourselves and more to save ourselves from an earth that, if pushed too far, has ample power to rock, burn, and shake us off completely."[36]

Yet if the Anthropocene concept is fatally flawed, what might be some less anthropocentric terms for the modern age of massive global change? The biologist Edward O. Wilson argues that the extent of species extinction in the modern era will be so great as to mark not just an *epochal* change from the Holocene but rather the closing of the much-longer Cenozoic Era that began with the rise of mammals some 65 million years ago. He suggests this rapidly impending new era of species death might be termed the Eremozoic Era: the "Age of Loneliness."[37] Given everything I have said in this book about the essential role our fellow creative creatures like cows and silkworms have played in history, I think Wilson's name is a good one. Should humans survive into this Eremozoic

---

[36] Naomi Klein, *This Changes Everything: Capitalism vs. the Climate* (New York: Simon and Schuster, 2015), 285.

[37] E. O. Wilson, *Consilience: The Unity of Knowledge* (New York: Vintage, 1999), 321

Era, we will do so as a much diminished and weaker species, as we will have lost incalculable opportunities for creative and potentially transformative partnerships with countless creatures, many driven into extinction before humans had even identified them. Historians have long understood that one reason why the peoples of the New World found it difficult to resist the western Europeans was because the invaders brought the immense power and intelligence of their horses, cows, and other large domesticated animals with them – it was a conquest made not just by people but by countless other organisms. Yet Jared Diamond reminds us that the New World, too, had once been home to many large mammals that might potentially have been domesticated had they not all gone extinct after the first humans crossed over from Asia.[38] Although recent evidence confirms that a period of extreme warming also played a critical synergistic role, many scholars now believe that several thousand years after they first arrived in the Americas, human hunters helped drive the very creatures whose cooperation might eventually have won them so much power into extinction.[39] Who knows what similarly incalculable possibilities humans are squandering today as they blindly sail into the Age of Loneliness? Given the immensity of such potential costs, Wilson's audacious recent proposal that fully half the planet should be set aside to preserve biodiversity seems not only reasonable but essential.[40]

Yet if I second Wilson's proposal to name our new *era* the Eremozoic, we would still need a better name than the "Anthropocene" for our much-briefer modern epoch of rapid global change. Again, my preference would be the "Carbocene," the age of coal and other hydrocarbons. A more technically accurate term would be the "Hydrocarbocene," though whether the increased accuracy justifies the increased awkwardness is debatable. More importantly, the briefer Carbocene would offer an entirely fitting echo of the ancient Carboniferous Period, an era that geologists named for the thick strata of rich British coal deposits that, having sat more or less quietly for some 300 million years, rumbled back to life in the eighteenth century to fuel that nation's industrial revolution as well as most of the others that followed elsewhere around the planet. The etymological symmetry between the Carbocene and Carboniferous

[38] Jared Diamond, *Guns, Germs, and Steel: The Fates of Human Societies* (New York: Norton, 1997), 44–9.

[39] Alan Cooper et al., "Synergistic Roles of Climate Warming and Human Occupation in Patagonian Megafaunal Extinctions during the Last Deglaciation," *Science Advances* 2 no. 6 (June 2016): e1501682.

[40] Edward O. Wilson, *Half-Earth: Our Planet's Fight for Life* (New York: Liveright, 2016).

would serve as a useful reminder that the modern era was a product not just of humans but rather of the solar power accumulated over the course of 50 million years that clever humans managed to burn through in just a few centuries. It is no exaggeration to say that almost every other major change in global conditions associated with the modern era derives in significant part from the abundant energy generated by burning coal, oil, methane, and other hydrocarbons. The Khouribga mines in Morocco offer a good example, as coal and oil fueled both the extraction and processing of the phosphate which in turn fueled the growth of crops that then fueled the postwar explosion in human numbers – a mere 2.5 billion in 1950, about 7.2 billion in 2015 – with all of its obvious consequences for increased land and resource use, pollution, habitat destruction, and species extinction. The term would also capture the broader role of the many carbon-based medicines, dyes, and chemicals that have been and still are being synthesized from the rich soup of organic compounds found in coal tar, a byproduct of making coke and coal gas once thought to be worthless but that eventually helped to ignite the explosion of synthetic chemicals in the twentieth century. The same can be said of the immense flow of bags, containers, toys, and countless other plastic things derived from oil that will endure for hundreds of thousands of years and have already begun to be incorporated into the geological strata in the form of so-called plasti-glomerates. Finally, the Carbocene would offer a much-needed reminder that we "Anthropos" are, at our most basic level, creatures whose very existence depends on the innovative abilities of amino acids, proteins, enzymes, and other organic compounds, all of which are built around one of the most creative and useful elements on the planet. We humans are mostly carbon by dry weight: the "Anthropos" are really the "Carbos." Indeed, with humans, the most atomically gregarious of elements helped to create the most materially gregarious of organisms, as no other animal has come to depend so deeply on so many other things to sustain and define itself. Now, when a few centuries of human self-obsession and overconfidence have taken the planet into uncharted waters whose dangers are impossible to fully predict, is the organism whose success has depended most heavily on the power of other things really going to name an entire planetary epoch after itself?

THE MATTER OF A HUMAN

A few years ago my older brother died in an intensive care ward in Coeur d'Alene, Idaho. It was the day after Christmas. He had always been a big man, but from middle age onward he fought a losing battle with obesity and developed diabetes and other problems associated with the modern plague of metabolic syndrome. We all knew his health seemed to be slowly declining, but the suddenness of his passing was still a shock. The summer after his death, those in the family who could make the trip met in Montana's Glacier National Park, where he had worked several summer seasons driving tourists around the park in big red open-topped buses. It was a time in his life he counted among his happiest. We had planned to spread his ashes in the high-alpine meadows at the top of the Going-to-the -Sun-Road, but we did not count on the mobs of tourists eager to see an unspoiled slice of authentic capital-N "Nature." They all drove cars to get there, as did we. There was not a parking spot to be found. Instead, we drove back down the pass and hiked a few kilometers into a lower valley that until recently had been a thick forest. But a fire in 2005 had killed most of the trees and opened up the canopy to a spectacular view of the northern Rocky Mountain "Crown of the Continent," including the nearly 9,000-foot-high summit of Heaven's Peak, the tallest mountain in the range.

On the hike in, and later as we spread the ashes in that freshly minted meadow awash with the red and blue bloom of mid-summer alpine flowers, I thought again about a question that had been troubling me for months. I had been working on this book, and though it was mostly about how to develop a more materially grounded understanding of humans and their histories, it had an undeniable metaphysical or ethical element as well. I wanted to argue for a more humble view of the human place on the planet, one that gave more historical credit to a lively and intelligent material world of organic and inorganic things. Yet as I struggled to comprehend the life and premature death of this one individual human who had been my brother, I wondered what value such ideas might have in this. If we had never left Eden, if this imperfect and often-callous natural world of living and nonliving things was all that we have and ever will have, where was the consolation in that? Supernatural gods at least offered the promise of an immortal soul, that spark of the divine that could ease the existential terror of death. A later generation of humanists, historians among them, turned away from the heavens to focus their attention on more earthly explanations, finding truth less in revelation than in the careful study of human words and texts. Yet the humanists preserved an element of the divine as well, a transcendent human mind distinct from both body and matter. In the first half of the twentieth century, some thinkers like Vernadsky and de Chardin even proposed the existence of a "noösphere," a third realm of the collective human mind that they believed was even then lifting an immaterial human intellect out of the geosphere and biosphere from which it had evolved.[41] In our own era transhumanists like Kenneth Hayworth and Nick Bostrom hold out the possibility that, in some perhaps not-too-distant future, humans will achieve the "singularity" of digital immortality by uploading our brains to a vast network of computers.

This desire to avoid death may be among the most deep seated of all our human traits, and one we likely share with every other living thing on this planet. We humans, with our unmatched ability to imagine a future in which we no longer exist, may fear death most intensely of all, and not only our own, but also the death of those we love. In this we are perhaps not so far from early hominins like Mrs. Ples, trapped in the darkness of Sterkfontein Cave at the heart of that first human Eden, staring desperately upward from the cave that would be her tomb at the alluring light from the heavens that streamed down, a tantalizing promise of salvation from above. The Greek philosopher Plato, whose ideas inspired so many early humanists, preached that transcendence from the dark cave of human existence lay only through escaping the false illusions of this base material world in order to seek the true eternal forms that existed at a higher, purer realm of abstracted perfection. As I have argued in this book, I am convinced all such transcendent views are fatally flawed. Yet, by comparison, what salvation or transcendence lay in a materialist view in which there was no enduring soul or mind, no heavenly path of salvation, but only a fragile body and brain mired in a transient material world?

Just a few weeks after bidding farewell to my brother in Glacier, the *New York Times* published what would turn out to be the last essay written by the wonderful neurologist and writer Oliver Sacks, a man whose abundant humanism somehow never strayed too far from the material. Now, with the end of his own life imminent from advanced metastatic cancer – he died five weeks later – Sacks chose as the subject of his final essay not the great mysteries of the human mind that he had spent a lifetime elucidating, but a far more earthy subject: his life-long affection for the chemical elements. As a six-year-old boy in London, his parents sent him into a lonely exile at a boarding school to protect him from the London Blitz. Consigned to the care of a harsh headmaster, who had little

---

[41] A good introduction is David Pitt and Paul R. Samson, *The Biosphere and Noosphere Reader: Global Environment, Society, and Change* (New York: Routledge, 1999). I am indebted to Lisa H. Sideris for sharing her research and ideas on this topic.

appreciation for Sacks's incessantly roving mind, the boy escaped instead into the abstractions of mathematics. Later, after he returned to London, he developed a similar passion for the chemical elements and the periodic table, that visual chart that captures the beguiling patterns of elemental things. Now, a lifetime later and facing his own mortality, Sacks wrote, "I am again surrounding myself, as I did when a boy, with metals and minerals, little emblems of eternity." For each of his 83 years, Sacks had collected a sample of the element with the corresponding atomic number. A piece of machined beryllium – **Be**, atomic number 4 – reminded him of his childhood. In the months before his death a friend had already given him bismuth – **Bi** atomic number 83 – though he would not live to celebrate that birthday.[42]

Among Sacks's lifetime accumulation of the basic building blocks of the world he had, of course, phosphorous, an element whose mysterious ability to glow or phosphoresce had fascinated him since his teens when he had experimented with the substance in his basement laboratory. Phosphorous was the stuff of "fireflies and glowworms and phosphorescent seas; of will-o'-the-wisps," he later wrote, and the unearthly beauty of its cold luminescent light had nothing of the "comforting familiarity of fire and warm light."[43] In yet another example of the mercurial creativity of things, in its elemental form phosphorous is a deadly poison for many organisms. Humans also used the element in one of the more horrific weapons of a horrific war: the allied forces' incendiary bombs that turned Hamburg and Tokyo into literal hells on earth were made of a white phosphorous that stuck to buildings and human skin and burned at white-hot temperatures. Yet if phosphorous can kill, it is also indispensable to life. As I noted at the start of this chapter, it is an element without which no plant or animal on the earth today can survive. During times of stress, Sacks turned to the physical sciences as an escape, "a world where there is no life, but also no death." Yet as a doctor and scientist, Sacks also surely knew that when he surrounded himself with his periodic table of dead elements, he had within the reach of his own hands the stuff that made life.[44] If beryllium marked Sacks's childhood and bismuth an advanced old age he would never reach, then phosphorous (P) had the atomic number 15: perhaps a symbol of those difficult teenage years when

[42] Oliver Sacks, "My Periodic Table," *The New York Times*, July 24, 2015.
[43] Oliver Sacks, *Uncle Tungsten: Memories of a Chemical Boyhood* (New York: Knopf, 2001), 223.
[44] Sacks, "My Periodic Table."

Sacks, like my brother, struggled to find his place through the things and people around him.

The technical definition of cremation is the reduction by heat of a deceased organism until only its elemental and molecular chemical components are left. Aside from water, humans are mostly made of carbon: by dry weight, our bodies are on average 67 percent carbon. The chemical symbol is C, atomic number 6 – perhaps a kindergartner or first grader on Sacks's elemental calendar of life.[45] During cremation the hydrogen and oxygen in the form of water in the body are among the first elements to be volatilized and driven off. The carbon, in the form mostly of proteins and other organic molecules, is easily oxidized and burns not unlike coal and oil do. (Crematoriums are themselves typically fueled by oil or natural gas.) What is left after this purifying passage of fire is mostly the hard rock-like parts of our bodies, the bones and teeth. The crematorium pulverizes the remains down to a coarse powder.[46] These can fit into a modestly sized plastic box whose small size belies its dense mineral weight.

Until the late nineteenth century, crushed or ground bones from cows, horses, and other animals were often used as fertilizers. After the once-vast population of American bison was hunted to the verge of extinction – in part to open the West for colonization by Longhorns – human ghouls scavenged the prairies and plains for bison bones to sell to eastern fertilizer makers.[47] This works because bison, humans, and many other animals derive the flexible strength of their bones from the mineral hydroxyapatite, which is a form of phosphate combined with calcium. Not at all coincidentally, hydroxyapatite is also found in phosphorite, the principal mineral extracted at the Khouribga phosphate mines in Morocco. Why should mineral deposits in North Africa happen to have precisely the same mineral as is found in your own bones? Because deposits like those at Khouribga are themselves vast bone yards, the remains of millions of years of dead sea creatures, some of which had calcium-based skeletons a bit like our own. Just as coal is the concentrated legacy of eons of sunny days past, the hydroxyapatite in phosphate

---

[45] John Emsley, *Nature's Building Blocks: An A-Z Guide to the Elements* (Oxford, UK: Oxford University Press), 93.

[46] John J. Schultz et al., "Analysis of Human Cremains: Gross and Chemical Methods," in *The Analysis of Burned Human Remains*, ed. Christopher W. Schmidt and Steve A. Symes (Cambridge, MA: Academic Press, 2008), 76.

[47] Ruth DeFries, *The Big Ratchet: How Humanity Thrives in the Face of Natural Crisis* (New York: Basic Books, 2014), 113–18.

deposits are the remnants of countless organisms that bioconcentrated phosphorous in their own bodies during their brief lives and have now passed it on to us in their eternal deaths.

When bones are heated to a high temperature, part of their hydroxyapatite is converted into tricalcium phosphate, a molecule that further breaks down in the soil to release the phosphorous essential for plant growth. While not chemically identical to a human-made phosphorous fertilizer, it works in much the same way. Humans, cattle, silkworms, mulberry trees, and every other organism on the planet need phosphorous to grow – recall that it takes about one ton of phosphate to produce 130 tons of grain.[48] Likewise, the old saying that "kids grow like weeds" is not far from true. Compared to an adult, a growing human child needs nearly twice the level of phosphorous (in the form of phosphate) in their blood in order to fuel the body's breakneck pace of bone growth and the related cell metabolism necessary to support it. But regardless of age, the highest concentration of phosphate to be found in the human body when at rest is in the brain, the most energy hungry of all the major human organs.[49] If you are reading this book while sitting down, at this moment about 20 percent of your bodily energy is going to your brain to create the electric discharges of your neurons.[50] Every single one of those billions of sparks of thought depends utterly on phosphate in the form of the critical energy-transport molecule called ATP: adenosine triphosphate. The ATP molecule takes energy provided by the food you have recently eaten, stores that energy in its own chemical bonds, and then carries it to all of the complex protein nanomachines that make your cells do what they are supposed to do, including firing your neurons. You might think of ATP as millions of little chemical fireflies flitting about in the dark engine room of your brain cells, their bright lights flickering off and on as they pass their tiny payload of energy to the cellular nanomachinery. At this very second as you read this "word," trillions of ATP molecules are carrying the energy needed for the oversized collection of neurons in your head to translate the little black marks on this white page into a meaning: word.[51]

---

[48] Fred Pearce, "Phosphate: A Critical Resource Misused and Now Running Low," *Environment* 360 (July 7, 2011).

[49] Emsley, *Nature's Building Blocks*, 310.

[50] Fei Du Xiao-Hong Zhu et al., "Tightly Coupled Brain Activity and Cerebral ATP Metabolic Rate," *Proceedings of the National Academy of Sciences* 105 (2008): 6409–14.

[51] Nick Lane, *The Vital Question: Energy, Evolution, and the Origins of Complex Life* (New York: Norton, 2015), 63–75.

Once we understand the basic energetic basis of the human brain, we can appreciate the seemingly inhuman and unnatural Marion dragline stripping the Khouribga phosphate deposits in an entirely new way. The dragline is mining not just a raw "natural resource" but rather one of the essential elemental things that makes us human. Stone tools, controlled fire, settled agriculture, steam engines, copper, electricity, and now phosphate strip mines might all be understood as ways of creating and powering larger brains. Over the course of millions of years of evolution, perhaps the greatest accomplishment of the energy-hungry human brain has been to find ever more elaborate and effective ways of providing itself with energy – to keep itself alive. We are the product of what to this point has proven to be a nearly limitless positive feedback loop between our brains and the material world. Barring some unforeseen technological breakthrough, by 2050 the Khouribga phosphate mines will be indispensable to sustaining the life and thoughts of about 9.6 billion people. Every single one of them will need about 60 grams of phosphorous-rich ATP, or a total of 576 million kilos for the planet. Of this, 115 million kilos will go solely to the paramount task of fueling our brains.[52] If there is indeed a third noösphere constituting the abstract thought of a grand collective human mind, as de Chardin and others claim, it turns out it depends rather heavily on a lot of plain old material things like phosphate produced by the geosphere and biosphere and mined by big Marion steam shovels.

It goes without saying that we cannot reduce the thoughts of any human individual or group to the electrical charges in their brains, much less to the macromolecules that provide the necessary energy. My ability to think may depend on phosphorous, but what I think is not in any sense determined by the ATP that fuels my brain – other than perhaps the thought that I feel hungry that pops into my head unbidden every three or four hours. To the contrary, throughout this book I have tried to make a related but somewhat different point: that humans think through and

---

[52] These are very rough estimates based on the amount of ATP in an average human adult whose brain uses about 20 percent of this when at rest. There is an intriguing analogy here to the contemporary misunderstanding that the collective abstract information or "data" of the internet also exists in an entirely immaterial realm, when in truth the millions of computer servers that store and process this information constantly consume immense amounts of very real energy, much of it generated by burning hydrocarbons. In 2013, US data centers consumed an estimated 91-billion kilowatt-hours of electricity, roughly the output of 34 large 500-megawatt coal-fired power plants. See Pierre Delforge, "America's Data Centers Consuming and Wasting Growing Amounts of Energy," NRDC (February 6, 2015). A similar point about the materiality of the internet is made in Ian Bogost, "The Cathedral of Computation," *The Atlantic*, January 15, 2015.

with all sorts of other material things around and within them, from the intelligent cunning of Longhorn cows to the creative protein synthesis of silkworms to the space- and time-warping ability of copper and electricity. Still, it is worth stressing the deep geological, evolutionary, historical, and cultural linkages between our brains and the Khouribga phosphate mines because it drives home the two overarching claims of this book: first, that humans and their ideas and cultures are embedded in and derived from the material world; and, second, that this material world is a dynamic and innovative place that creates us even as we interact with and recreate it. Humans are the animals that excel at abstract thinking, yet even this central cognitive ability is also the expression of a highly material energetic system based in part on the element phosphorous. Indeed, we have expended a good deal of that phosphorous-fueled brain energy trying to think up ways to get more energy. At another level, we should also stand in slack-jawed awe that a universal biological battery like ATP exists at all. As the evolutionary developmental biologist Andreas Wagner puts it: "Every organism today can trace its descent from the inventor of life's most successful power storage innovation."[53] Humans may in some ways now invent themselves, but their ability to do so depends entirely on the sheer inventiveness of a nonhuman world whose breathtaking powers we have only just begun to appreciate.

Whatever the multitude of creative thoughts the 9.6 billion humans who may live on this planet a mere 35 years from now may have, I hope they will know better than to believe that their clever ideas somehow separate them from the material world around them. The abstract symbolic nature of the mind has long given human beings the ability to conceive of many things that are not true. But perhaps there was none so mistaken or destructive than the idea that, alone among all the other creatures on the planet, humans somehow left Eden behind to become the only unnatural animal, the only creature whose essence was of pure spirit and thought, offering the promise of either spiritual or secular immortality. Yet as foreign as they may seem today, there have always been humbler and less anthropocentric humanist traditions. More than 2,000 years ago, the Epicurean philosophers argued that to be human was to be a living, feeling body embedded in a material world of random swirling atoms. The Roman poet and philosopher Lucretius, whose book *De rerum natura* (*On the Nature of Things*) was only rescued from extinction

---

[53] Andreas Wagner, *Arrival of the Fittest: How Nature Innovates* (New York: Current, 2014), 65.

by the dogged efforts of a Renaissance bibliophile, saw reason for neither fatalism nor pessimism in such a material world. As his more recent champion Stephen Greenblatt writes, "Lucretius insisted that those things that seemed completely detached from the material world – thoughts, ideas, fantasies, souls themselves – were nonetheless inseparable from the atoms that constituted them."[54] Like motes of dust floating in a sunbeam, Lucretius argued that humans faced no predetermined fate, no inevitable chain of causalities, because there was always the possibility of the unforeseen interaction, that slight yet decisive swerve to the right or left that could never be predicted beforehand.

This was the very same wild material creativity that the idealist Greeks and later generations of modernists sought to wall off from their cities, from their civilizations, from their perfect forms in perfectly abstracted minds. In the pursuit of a transcendent immortality, they sought to deny the countless fellow travelers that had accompanied humans on their long historic journeys and that had provided that uniquely human spark of life and mind in the first place: the wild creativity of phosphorous and adenosine triphosphate, mulberry trees and copper, cattle and silkworms, embodied humans and thirsty dust, dry as bones.[55] Because they denied the essential creative power of these and all other things, they robbed themselves of the perhaps more modest, yet nonetheless intensely real, joy and solace that could be found in being a part of such a richly creative world. They were left with nothing more than the faith that there might, perhaps, be another.

"There is not anything which returns to nothing," Lucretius wrote, "but all things return dissolved into their elements." Perhaps that seems meager fare to a creature that, through a quirk of evolution, happened to develop the ability to imagine the possibility of its own immortality. But to echo Darwin, there is grandeur in such a view of life, a sense that the brief measure of any individual life is part of some greater earthly symphony. Moreover, it is a symphony whose source is neither occult nor supernatural, a beauty that can be most fully heard in all its grandeur when humanists and scientists come together to recognize the essential common nature of their enterprises. The task is begun, though much remains to be done.

As I write these words, winter has come to far-northern Montana and my brother's ashes lay buried under the silent, deep snows of the Glacier

---

[54] Stephen Greenblatt, *The Swerve: How the World Became Modern* (New York: Norton, 2012), 260.
[55] Greenblatt, *The Swerve*, 98, 191.

Park highlands. When spring comes, snowmelt will dissolve the tricalcium phosphate in his ashes, and some will find its way down to the roots of one of the young pine trees that grew up in the wake of the 2005 fire. With that extra phosphate, perhaps that tree and others nearby will grow a bit faster and a bit lusher than the rest. In 20 or 30 years, the trees will block out the spectacular view of the rugged crown of mountains that divide the North American continent – the very reason we had picked that spot. Yet as my brother's lifetime of accumulated phosphate slowly becomes the wood and needles of a towering green conifer, the tree will also obscure from view the soaring rocky summit of Heaven's Peak. When we return some-day, perhaps generations passed, we will know better than to look upward to find him. The trees themselves will teach us that everything that had made him special lies right there under our feet.

CONCLUSION

On the Fourth of July, 1994, just five years after the Velvet Revolution in Prague had finally rid the Czech people of that most idealist of materialist theories of human history, the writer, poet, and unorthodox revolutionary Vaclav Havel took aim at the failings of both postmodernist humanism and modern reductionist science in a speech at Philadelphia's Independence Hall. Havel argued that, as these two very similar strains of "modern anthropocentrism" had taken hold, scholars had largely abandoned the search for greater enduring truths. In its place came a rootless and atomizing humanism and a timid and cramped science that was reluctant to grapple with anything more profound than probing the "surface of things." Though humans today know far more about the nature of the universe and the planet than our ancestors did, Havel observed that "it increasingly seems they knew something more essential about it than we do, something that escapes us." Yet a return to the earlier transcendent faiths that had once gripped the human imagination offered no solution, as these had all too often become an excuse for narrow intolerance. Ironically, for all its manifest failings, it was the modernist faith that created the powerful idea of inalienable human rights, rights that stemmed from the "modern notion that man – as a being capable of knowing nature and the world – was the pinnacle of creation and lord of the world."

What then the path forward? Havel hoped that humans might yet escape the double trap of postmodernism and scientism through what he called the anthropic cosmological principle: the idea that the universe and this planet were the true creators of humans in all their dimensions. The best hope for the present and future, he suggested, "is probably a renewal of our certainty that we are rooted in the earth and, at the same time, in the cosmos," deriving our sense of higher goods like universal human rights from "the respect of the miracle of Being, the miracle of the universe, the miracle of nature, the miracle of our own existence." Peaceful coexistence in a multicultural world must be rooted in "self-transcendence" and the recognition of our commonality in "the human community, to all living creatures, to nature, to the universe." If humans continued instead to cling to their parochial cultural and national differences, Havel feared the species might well be doomed: "Transcendence is the only real alternative to extinction."[56]

At least within the Western tradition, many historians and other humanists long took it for granted that their principal subject of study was a creature apart, natural in some sharply limited sense, but ultimately the only animal on the planet that had transcended nature to create itself. This, too, was at the heart of the modernist spirit, with its alluring promise of infinite possibilities unbound from the mundane muck of a merely material world. Prometheus stole fire from the heavens – the lowly earth did not give it to him. Today, despite the steadily accumulating evidence that it is in many ways a dangerous chimera, we remain reluctant to abandon the modernist project – at least in part for entirely good reasons. Thanks to modern hydrocarbon energy use and modern innovations in technology and medicine, humans are in many ways far better off than even just half a century ago. Life spans are longer, malnutrition is lower, health care is better, and literacy rates are higher across the globe. By some measures the percentage of people living in poverty has decreased by more than half in just the past two decades.[57] These accomplishments have emerged from the human partnership with oil and other hydrocarbons and many other things like phosphate and copper, as well as the necessary political will to spread their benefits more widely. Despite this progress, though, much of the planet's population still remains mired in poverty. Given the evident success of modernist science and technology, we are understandably tempted to double down on further technological

[56] Vaclav Havel, "The Need for Transcendence in the Postmodern World," speech made in Independence Hall, July 4, 1994.
[57] Leif Wenar, "Is Humanity Getting Better?" *New York Times*, February 15, 2016, and Wenar, *Blood Oil: Tyrants, Violence, and the Rules That Run the World* (Oxford, UK: Oxford University Press, 2015).

solutions to global poverty, just as we will be tempted to use geoengineering to solve global climate change. I am convinced, however, that there remain other alternatives, although they are perhaps in some ways more challenging. To take Havel's call to recognize our common humanity seriously will demand a far more equitable distribution of the planet's creative things and attendant wealth. These are, after all, not truly the achievements or possessions of any one nation or group, much less individual, but rather gifts of a generous world that should be to all humans. Moreover, I suspect we have only just begun to explore the rich material affordances of the earth that might yet lead us in new directions. If we can recognize the many ways in which our technologies embed us ever more deeply into their material natures, it might yet be possible to shepherd a more humble and just material and technological infrastructure into existence, seeking partnerships with things that nurture the kind of human beings we wish to be. People of sun and wind will, I suspect, be very different from people of coal and copper.

From the beginning, the task of the humanist was to make sense of the human condition, including the painful brevity of the roughly four score years and change we are each typically allotted. Seeking wisdom, many sided with Plato and other idealists to offer the reassuring conceit that we are the creatures who create ourselves through the brilliant abstractions of immaterial minds. Today, some transhumanists foresee the day when those abstract minds might be united with computers to achieve digital immortality, at last freed from every sordid vestige of a material world understood as a realm of decay and corruption. As improbable as this may be, it is perhaps a no less reasonable matter of faith than believing in an immortal soul, and both provide a similar solace. Anyone who has stood by helplessly as a loved one is pulled into that black hole of mortality whose gravity seems to permit nothing of what they had once been to escape will understand the appeal of either.

Perhaps stretching all the way back to our *Australopithecine* ancestors, this is who we big-brained hominins have always been. It defines us. Yet just as Mrs. Ples's only realistic hope of salvation was to leave that comforting light from above behind to explore the dark cave around her, so, too, do I suspect that the best hope for myself, and perhaps others, lies not with idealist dreams but rather with the inescapable materiality of our existence on this planet. The "singularity" we need now is not the unity of abstract minds and digital codes but the unity of material minds and material cultures with the things of *this* world. That we live not in an Age of Humans, but rather an age of coal and steel, of oil, an age of cows and silkworms, cotton and copper, an age of corn and rice: we live in an age of sulfur, of arsenic and asbestos, an age of diethylstilbestrol and bisphenols; we live in an age of hard concretes and soft plastics and sharp, shiny aluminum, and an age of bright electric lights that erase the infinite stars from our eyes. This supposed Age of Humans is all of these *things* and many more, but never just human, because these are the very things that have made us human, the "quintessence of dust" from which we emerged only to quickly turn away to look upward to seek divinity beyond. To discover the true human animal and its history as a species on this planet, we must then tear our gaze away from ourselves and look instead at the countless things that have made us. Because, like a faint evening star that we see only out of the corner of our eye, we may see the human star most clearly only when we look away.

Index

Printed in Great Britain
by Amazon